Eating Well

Eating Well

A Guide to Foods of the Pacific Northwest

by John Doerper

Pacific Search Press

To Victoria,
for her patience and forbearance

Pacific Search Press, 222 Dexter Avenue North,
    Seattle, Washington 98109
©1984 by John Doerper. All rights reserved
Printed in the United States of America

Edited by Marlene Blessing
Designed by Judy Petry

Cover: *The author, enjoying an informal repast of northwest foods in Wildcat*
       Cove at Larrabee State Park, Bellingham, Washington. (Skiff courtesy of
       Jerry Fry and The Bellingham Bay Rowing and Chowder Society; Photo by
       Don Anderson)

Library of Congress Cataloging in Publication Data

Doerper, John.
    Eating well.

    Bibliography: p.
    Includes index.
    1. Cookery, American—Northwest, Pacific. 2. Food.
I. Title.
TX715.D656 1984   641.59795   84-3205
ISBN 0-914718-88-6

Contents

Acknowledgments

My special thanks go to Deborah Easter, who kindled my enthusiasm and got the project going; to Marlene Blessing of Pacific Search Press, who edited the book and kept it rolling; to Carolyn Threadgill and Jeanne Martin and the other members of the Pacific Search staff, who assisted with advice and kept me on track; to Warren Dimmick of Burlington, Washington, who explained the finer points of northwest lamb, beef, veal, and pork; to Sinclair Philip of Sooke, British Columbia, who was willing to discuss the nature of northwest foods at great length (and at odd times); and to my numerous dinner guests, who were brave enough to eat the sometimes surprising results of the recipes I tested.

Introduction

Outside the back door of our Bellingham apartment, on the far side of its well-manicured lawn, lies a wild field of white and red clover, melilotus, tansy, and ox-eye daisies intermingled with goldfinch thistles and hay-scented grasses. This small, unkempt meadow rises from the blackbird thickets of alder swamp and lakeshore sedge to a low ridge where it quickly loses itself in lupine, bramble, and broom.

I have watched this meadow grow for eight summers now. Only some dozen years ago, it held the woodpiles and saw shed of a lumber mill; it was a dry, gravelly expanse of shacks and rusty metal, crisscrossed by roadways and railroad tracks, colonized by only the most courageous mice, swallows, hawk's beards, lamb's-quarters, shot weeds, thistles, and black-berries. All of this changed overnight when the mill burned to the ground, destroying the works of man and nature alike. The organic and inorganic debris was simply bulldozed into the lake to make room for new construction. No new building has risen on the site, however, and grasses, trees, herbs, and a new generation of brambles have reclaimed the va-cant lot. Year after year, the vegetation has become lusher, as the roots of the colonizing plants pry the hardened soil apart, creating openings for rainwater to penetrate and for seeds to sprout. Each new season brings a yield of berries that grow plumper, tastier, and more plentiful than before.

Deer cross over from a nearby copse and feast on tender blackberry shoots or, some-times, on the fuchsia baskets hanging from our back porch; rabbits nibble on herbs and garden flowers; mallards waddle up from the lakeshore to prey on slugs and grubs and seeds. In winter, drab armies of coots teeter and cluck across the lawns, pulling up the grass by its roots, leaving squishy green pellets in their train.

I sometimes find it difficult to believe we do not live out in the country, but rather in the middle of a large town; that our meadow is surrounded by roads, houses, backyards, and fences. The deer, perhaps, might not be as tame outside the city, but the rabbits stay shy, though they have spread along embankments and fence rows clear across town. The mallards, well, mallards must be mallards and they are at home on lakeshore, ponds, and even puddles—wherever water and food may be found. They get underfoot, shamelessly beg for food, pursue each other lecherously through rhododendrons, brambles, air, and water, and lay their large, greenish eggs into flower beds, walkways, and berry thickets. These birds seem quite tame, but are wilder than the unwary suppose. Yet a good, tender Lake Whatcom mallard, fattened on bugs, grubs, corn, and bread is a gourmet's treat.

Breeding all along the shore of our lake, mallards are plentiful throughout the year, and in fall and winter, when their numbers swell with the wild, migrating northern birds, you can't help stumbling over them. We have eaten lots of mallards—supplied by a hunting neighbor who just piles the ducks he shoots high on his back porch during freezing weather. But many of the lake residents have their own, simple—though somewhat illegal—method of procuring fresh duck for the table. Mallards are incorrigible gluttons and, if fed regularly, will eat bread right out of a kind person's hand. Once they're that close and that tame, it's but a short step to a quick grab, a wringing of the neck, and duck breast in wine sauce for dinner.

Back in the depression, when the Northern Pacific Railroad still ran around the lake, our neighbor Bill worked as a guard and he often managed to drop a bag or two of corn into the ditch as the train passed his backyard. The grain was fed to the mallards—a whole flock of them lined up at the trough at a regular feeding time—and whenever Bill's wife Heather needed a duck for dinner, she'd just bait a big, stout fishhook with a kernel of corn. A rash gobble and a quick wring later, she had meat for dinner.

Fishhooks are still baited with corn by Lake Whatcom residents—not to trap ducks (or at least not overtly), but to catch fish. Our lake, like many other lakes in the Pacific Northwest, has a large population of small kokanee (or "silvers" as they are known locally) that just dote on milky corn kernels. No one seems to know just why, because the kokanee are, after all, plankton feeders. Now, a rainbow trout or cutthroat will act like a fish and strike on angleworms and marshmallows, but a Lake Whatcom silver must have corn or you might as well not try to fish for these tasty, finny morsels. Our silvers are landlocked sockeye salmon, smaller than their seagoing cousins, reaching an average length of only ten to sixteen inches, and their flesh is light pink instead of dark red. They may easily be the tastiest fish on the Coast—unless you prefer young saltwater silver salmon (not the same as freshwater "silvers"), which are also exceptionally tasty and delicate, especially in the young "shaker" stage.

The season for all of these delectable fish coincides with that for fresh vegetables and blackberries and, though you cannot dig up clams or collect mussels during the summer months because of regular outbreaks of "red tide," you can still catch nimble rock crabs and the large, flavorful Dungeness to accompany your midyear feasts.

Whenever the economy of the Pacific Northwest has faltered, its hungry residents—with the possible exception of metropolitan urbanites—have ever been quick to turn to the profusion of foods from field, garden, forest, river, lake, and seashore. Oysters, clams, crabs, and fish have been ready companions to the copious amounts of vegetables grown in kitchen gardens and window boxes. Best of all, Northwesterners have always shared their culinary bounty with their less fortunate neighbors.

When my wife Victoria and I first moved to the Northwest in the mid-1970s, we were confronted by a series of personal economic hardships (I would not counsel anyone to move to the Northwest and try to make a living as an artist), but we did not starve. During our first summer and fall, we picked large quantities of wild apples and blackberries to supplement the family larder; but very soon, our neighbors taught us how to fish, dig clams, and catch crabs. Things became simpler after that. Early in the morning, after a foraging hike

through the woods, I would row onto the lake and troll for silvers until I had at least sufficient fish for breakfast; later in the day, I would go out again and catch fish for lunch and
dinner. Any surplus fish—especially the less delicately flavored cutthroat trout—were
smoked or frozen. Every weekend we would descend upon a small cove along the
Chuckanut shore, trap crabs, dig clams, and gather small marine crustaceans, molluscs,
clams, mussels, algae, and shoreside vegetables such as sea rocket and pickleweed. Friends
kept us well supplied with potatoes and garden vegetables, and a commercial fisherman
neighbor shared an occasional salmon, rockfish, greenling, or sole. What more could we
ask for?

Only once was our food gathering put to a severe test. Claude and Nadia, two friends
from California who had known me during one of my successful, rising-young-artist stages,
announced their imminent arrival. In less than twenty-four hours, we would be host to them
and to their two teen-aged children. There was only one problem with this: we were flat
broke. But some quick thinking solved the problem. Only in the Pacific Northwest could we
have taken care of our commissary problem as smoothly and efficiently as we did—without
spending an extra penny to entertain and feed our guests.

First, I took several frozen cutthroat trout from the freezer and placed them in a salt
and brown sugar marinade. Just then, some gardener friends arrived with several boxes of
fresh produce: greens, potatoes, carrots, and yellow Transparent apples. I invited them to
dinner the next day, too, figuring we now had more than enough food for a party. I next
grabbed my gear and went out onto the lake to catch some fish. Several hours later, after I'd
caught a dozen or so silvers, I returned, put the fresh (cleaned and bled) fish on ice, and
placed the marinated cutthroat into the smoker. While the trout smoked slowly over alder-
wood chips, I collected a bucket of ripe blackberries from the vacant lot bramble bushes and
made jam.

The next morning, I awoke early and went out for a couple of hours to catch more fish.
When Claude and Nadia and the children arrived, Victoria had lunch ready: new potatoes,
fresh, crisp vegetables, poached silvers, smoked cutthroat trout, summer apples, homemade
bread, and fresh blackberry jam. In the afternoon, all of us, accompanied by local friends,
went down to the Sound to trap crab. We did so in comfort, on some offshore rocks where
we had a great party, nibbling on homemade bread, smoked fish, crisp apples, and sweet
berries, while our baited pots caught crabs for us.

That night we ate freshly cooked hot crab, potato salad, vegetables, and fruits by the
campfire we had built in the vacant lot and drank wine until late into the night. For the next
day's meals, we finished up the previous day's leftovers: cold, cracked crab, silvers in aspic,
and smoked trout pâté.

Claude and Nadia never learned how destitute we were at the time of their visit. We
saved face not only because we could procure some of the best foods of our region at a moment's notice, but also because we did not have to worry about fancy ways of preparing the
meals or about the addition of expensive, rare, or exotic herbs and spices, since the cuisine
of the Northwest, in its best and most authentic form, is surprisingly simple.

The great French chef Escoffier once maintained that the culinary art reaches a considerable development in those regions where the life is easy and comfortable. This has, until
quite recently, not been true for the North American continent. Part of the lack of refinement in the art of fine dining in America may be blamed on those old, by now rather mangy
and bedraggled scapegoats, the Calvinist consciousness and the puritan ethic. But large

parts of the blame also fall to the American predilection for speed in everything, even in eating, coupled with an almost pathological demand for nutritional quality and balance in every meal (a national habit that was criticized with perfect irony by M. F. K. Fisher in her 1940ish tome *How to Cook a Wolf*, and by Ronald Deutsch in the 1970ish *The New Nuts among the Berries*). This has led to the development of peculiar dishes, food that may be eaten quickly and that attempts to provide the minimum daily requirements of roughage, nutrients, vitamins, and minerals in one fell gulp. Thus we have developed "liquid diets" and "fast-foods," concepts unknown in other countries until they were introduced by globe-trotting Americans. We are the first nation to have combined a wimpy roll, crisp lettuce, crunchy, fresh onion, denatured condiments, and a greasy chunk of meat into one dish, called the fast-food hamburger, a meal that with all of its variations in taste and quality epitomizes the American attitude toward food.

The cuisine of the Pacific Northwest, on the other hand (though our area, too, is not free from food fads), is based on a different set of principles. Foremost among these is the concept that superior natural, locally produced foods such as, say, salmon, oysters, clams, and mussels, may (but don't have to) be enjoyed by themselves, without the addition of various starches or red, yellow, and green vegetables. The enjoyment of fresh local food, prepared with sauces and condiments that enhance rather than mask its taste, is a true northwest phenomenon and, unlike classical French or Japanese cooking and the new "California Cuisine," it is not limited to just a few members of the upper social classes. Food-gathering—whether done as a daily necessity or as a luxury—permeates society in the Pacific Northwest, from the lowest to the highest social stratum, and is shaped by recurring natural cycles.

Smelt and eulachon, slender little oily fish which enter the rivers in the cold months from January to May, inaugurate the annual food cycles of the Pacific Northwest. Later in the spring, after thousands, perhaps millions of silvery smelt have been jigged or dipped from the water, everyone eagerly awaits the appearance of the first local (commonly Yakima) asparagus, and every purveyor of foods, from supermarkets to fancy restaurants, will downplay other vegetables while these succulent green spears last. In April and May (sometimes as early as March or as late as June), a great whispering arises: the morels have arrived. Many families jealously guard the locations of their favorite morel spots, whether they be in old burns, orchards, fields, or backyards, under aspens, cottonwoods, or apple trees. This pale brown delicacy, with its deeply pitted and ridged cap, is one of the world's most delicious mushrooms and, though rare, is much more common in the Pacific Northwest than in other parts of the country. In recent years, morels and other tasty mushrooms, especially chanterelles and boletes, have been served in the better restaurants of the Pacific Northwest and make an occasional (albeit expensive) appearance in our farmers' markets.

At the height of the asparagus and morel season, the fishing for trout and other tasty freshwater fish opens on our inland lakes—an event eagerly awaited by thousands of avid fishermen. And, as the waters warm up, the delectable, easily trapped, crawfish begin to stir. Fishing west of the Cascades may be slow this early in the year, but many west-side families travel to their favorite lakes east of the mountains to catch their limits of trout, bass, crappie, walleye, and, sometimes, catfish, burbot, and carp. Fishing is commonly so good east of the Cascades that I may have eaten almost as much eastern as western Washington fish—though I have never even caught a minnow east of the mountains: all of them were surplus fish distributed by friends.

The journey to the eastern lakes is only the first of several seasonal migrations across the Cascade passes in search of fresh, tasty food on the dry side. It will be followed later in the year by weekend treks to the cherry pickings, the apricot and peach harvests, the cornfields, the apple orchards, and to the increasing number of wine festivals. In Oregon, similar migrations take advantage of the natural bounty of the Hood River region, of the fruits and vegetables of the Willamette Valley, and of the larder of the seacoast, where excellent berries, molluscs, fish, and crabs may be procured in season.

Toward the end of the local asparagus season, winter cauliflower and broccoli become available for a short time, followed by spinach, lettuce, edible pod peas, green beans, cabbages, squash, summer cauliflower and broccoli, corn, tomatoes, Chinese greens and, last but not least, another vegetable, a noble globe, whose eagerly awaited arrival has become somewhat of an annual ritual: sweet Walla Walla onions. The first of the new potatoes, crisp White Rose, buttery yellow Finn, and sweet purple, and the luscious shell peas of the Skagit and Nooksack valleys come with our region's tender spring lamb and the first of the sea-run salmon.

Salmon, more perhaps than any other food, help determine the seasonal cycles of eating in the Pacific Northwest (nor can they be supplemented by any "equivalents" from other regions during the off-season). The spring salmon arrive first, large chinook which begin to enter the rivers in late May and early June (and as late as September). Next come the sockeye, then the pink, our most plentiful salmon, then the coho (silver), and finally the chum (silverbright). In the Columbia River, the chinook are accompanied by large masses of shad on their upriver migration; south of the Columbia, in the coastal rivers of Oregon and in the Klamath River of northern California (the southernmost boundary of the Pacific Northwest), the chinook share the rivers with spawning striped bass.

As the weather turns fine, large numbers of bottom fish and rockfish are taken by longliners, gill-netters, and trawlers and rushed to market. Local shrimp and squid, both commercially and sport caught, become available for a short season. The tasty oysters of winter and spring lose their fine flavor during the warm weather and turn mushy as they prepare to spawn, but razor clams, cockles, and mussels retain their crispness and taste.

The season of fresh fish is also the season of fresh fish roe, a delicacy appreciated by increasing numbers of Northwesterners. Starting early in the year with smelt and burbot eggs, the roe fancier will follow up these tasty ova with herring and rockfish eggs; then, in spring and early summer, with the roe of lamprey, carp, sturgeon (ah, caviar!), shad, and with the eggs of large-roed salmon species—first chinook, then coho, and finally the tastiest of the salmon roes, the delicate, firm eggs of the chum; and, late in the year, with golden whitefish roe.

Winter in the Pacific Northwest is a good time for catching tasty crabs—mostly because few other foragers will be out to compete for these delicate crustaceans—and it is the best time for eating oysters, whether they be tiny native Olympias, succulent Pacifics, or sweet and salty European flat oysters (which are now grown successfully in several inland water bays). Winter is also the time for inveterate (and perhaps a little masochistic) steelhead anglers to don their heavy waders and foul-weather gear to enter ice-cold rivers in pursuit of their favorite prey. Steelheading is true gourmandism—there is perhaps no other food in our region which is as difficult to procure. Nevertheless it is easy to understand why a successful steelheader will expose himself to the raging elements of winter over and over again: the steelhead, large ocean-run rainbow trout, are exceptionally good to eat. Winter also brings us tasty vegetables, even when snow covers the garden. Parsnips, turnips, and rutabagas can be left in the ground all through the winter and harvested as needed, and both brussels sprouts and kale develop their best flavor after they have become exposed to the mild frosts of our region.

The seasonal food cycles of the Northwest are also closely tied to the superb fruits produced in our region. Everybody eagerly awaits the ripening of the first crop of luscious northwestern strawberries in late May and June and, as school-age children earn spending money picking berries, many families descend upon U-pick fields to gather a year's supply of strawberries. When the strawberries cease to produce, the raspberries ripen, followed by tart salmonberries, deep-flavored thimbleberries, piquant wild dewberries, and domestic blueberries; then come the large Himalayan blackberries, wild huckleberries and, finally, mountain blueberries and wild and domestic cranberries.

Cherries begin to ripen by mid-June, apricots by July, and peaches and plums start their season in mid-July, keeping gourmets happy for two long, flavorful months. The first of our summer apples, fragrant yellow Transparents, become available in July, in August the crisp Gravensteins and juicy Tydeman Reds reach their perfection, and the McIntosh come into their own in September, followed by fall and winter apples: Jonathans, Newton Pippins, red Romes, Spartans, Winesaps, and red and Golden Delicious. The late-ripening Northern Spies, Spitzenbergs, and winter bananas are frequently left on the trees until January and picked as they are needed. And, as the apples ripen, so do the wine grapes, and in late fall the delicate scent of fermenting must wafts across the wine country of Oregon, Washington, and British Columbia.

The variety of comestibles produced in the Pacific Northwest is great, but it is primarily the superb quality of its foods that sets the Pacific Northwest apart from the other food-producing regions of North America.

The climate of the Pacific Northwest is mild (it is officially classified as moist to dry Mediterranean), with just enough winter frost to vernalize fruit trees and shrubs. The growing season is long, but the cool summer days (much cooler than those of other American agricultural regions, paralleling those of the best food-growing regions of western Europe) and the long northerly days of the midyear growing season, plus an ample supply of natural (or irrigation) water, combine to grow some of the tastiest produce in the world.

Best of all, the metropolitan centers of the Northwest are all located in proximity to truck gardens, orchards, vineyards, poultry farms, sheep enclosures, and cattle ranches, making the fresh products of the land accessible to everyone. Seattle's Pike Place Market, Vancouver's Granville Island, and the numerous farmers' markets which spring up during the growing season from Victoria to Bellingham and Spokane, from Sicamous to Yakima, Eugene, and Medford, are showcases for the region's fish and fowl, meats, vegetables, and fruits.

I came to discover the sumptuous bounty of the Pacific Northwest in a roundabout way. Raised in the Franken district of southern Germany—the only region in that land of dour eaters where the natives have developed a fine (almost "French") sensibility for good food—I was exposed early in life to the best of vegetables (in particular the plump, white, local asparagus), fruits, grapes, wines, river fish and farm fowl, pork, lamb, and beef. Later in life, repeated travels to other regions of Europe expanded my food horizon—to Holland for cheese, herring, and genever; to Belgium for mussels, beer, and rabbit; to the Rhine and Moselle for salmon (that is, before they had been killed off by pollution), and trout; to

Westphalia and the Münsterland for hams and sausages; to the French Channel Coast for mussels, oysters, saltmarsh lamb, and Camembert; to the Loire for wine, shad, pike, chicken, country bread, and butter; to Burgundy for poultry, escargots, crawfish, goat cheese, black currants, and chardonnays and pinot noirs of unequalled excellence; to the Alsace for gewürztraminer, carp, riesling, charcuterie, pinot gris, pâté de foie gras, quetsches, mirabelles, and bream; to Bavaria for cheese, butter, and beer.

Then, at the ripe old age of twenty, disaster struck. I moved to southern California, to a jungle of fast-food places and taco huts, pretentious restaurants and greasy-spoon eateries. Oh, there was some succor now and then: tree-ripened oranges, lemons, grapefruits, and avocados; fresh fish from the Newport Beach dory fishermen, rock crabs at Dana Point, waterfowl from the Salton Sea; the tasty Gulf blue crab from the Sea of Cortez; fresh shrimp and clams at San Felipe; and the luscious tropical fruit drinks of Mexicali. But on the whole, I remained dissatisfied. I submerged myself in the barrios of Los Angeles and Orange counties, surviving on the ethnic cuisines of Mexico, with occasional forays to Basque or Italian eateries recommended by friends (the kind of places that made their own wine, storing the casks in the cellars beneath the restaurants) and to—believe it or not—Pierpoint Landing in the port of Long Beach for the world's best chili dogs, handmade foot-long monsters with a sublime relish and the hottest of hot, pickled güero peppers; or to San Pedro to scrounge fish from fishermen.

It was during this long period of dissatisfaction that I began to formalize my notions about taste and to cultivate a taste memory. The cultural shock caused by the wide gap between the quality of fowl, beef, and produce to which I was accustomed in Europe and the pale supermarket produce of southern California made me search for foods of better taste, texture, and aroma. Starting in the markets of northern Mexico, I worked my way slowly north to San Francisco through both the San Joaquin Valley and along the Coast. The food improved as I traveled north, but the weather during the growing season was simply too hot. Fruits and vegetables matured before they could develop a rich, complex flavor; lamb and beef lacked the richness of cattle raised in cooler climes. Only the ocean fish and crustaceans were satisfying—that is, if I could get them fresh from the water. But even here, the freshness and taste of foods was frequently ruined in the kitchens of even the finest restaurants. Fish and meat and vegetables were overcooked, oversauced, and spiced to death. This "food abuse" appeared to have diminished some when the new "California Cuisine" was invented. However, an increasing number of the young chefs in this movement who experimented with the natural flavors of food and who achieved a certain amount of finesse in their cookery are now returning to the heavier, strongly spiced, and oversauced cooking of the Coast. In the long turn, only the ingredients have become more varied; the cooking itself has remained coarse.

In the late 1960s, graduate work took me to the University of California at Davis. I now had a new home base from which to explore the foods of the West Coast. Victoria and I traveled extensively: east to the Sierra Nevada, north to Oregon, to the beef and sheep ranges of the dry southeastern mountains, to the fertile Rogue and Willamette valleys, and to the Coast, and from time to time, south to Monterey, Santa Barbara, and Los Angeles.

We quickly learned that many of the superb foodstuffs hailed by the chefs of California as indigenous were either so uncommon that only one or two favored restaurants might obtain a fresh supply (because everything, from lamb to pigeons, from rabbits to oysters, requires special care in the hot California summer climate), or came from the Northwest, from Oregon and from Washington states.

We extended our travels farther and farther north in search of good food and found a culinary paradise in the Pacific Northwest. The restaurants, to be sure, still clung to greasy-spoon and fast-food cookery, but the raw materials! What raw materials! With the rising food consciousness which was now beginning to sweep the country, it was only a matter of time before the chefs of the Northwest would amend their methods and learn to make the best use of the superb local foods. In the meantime, there was only one thing for us to do: we packed our belongings and moved to Bellingham in northwestern Washington to be right in the middle of all these exciting developments, among the oysters of the Olympic Peninsula and the San Juan Islands and the apples and peaches of the Okanogan and Methow valleys, among the shad, striped bass, and chinook salmon of the Oregon rivers and the superb sockeye of the Fraser River. We needed to be close to the crabs, shrimps, mussels, scallops, and fish of the inland waters and to the delectable vegetables, berries, and cream and butter of the Skagit, Nooksack, and Fraser valleys.

Once we transcended our early poverty, we began to explore the region and discovered hitherto unsuspected delicacies: Wenatchee apricots; Alberni Canal and Hood Canal shrimp; Similkameen, Kittitas, and Yakima valley beef; San Juan Islands, Metchosin, and Saltspring Island lamb; Pleasant Valley cow cheese, Okanogan Highland and Briar Hills goat cheeses (and the delectable soft goat cheeses of the now-defunct Kapowsin Dairy); the tasty farm-raised chickens and turkeys of western Washington and Oregon; Tarheel pork, vegetables, pickles, and moonshine from Skagit and Snohomish counties; the delicious small molluscs and crustaceans of the inland waters and outer coast; the various fish roes produced in the Northwest, especially the sublime Columbia River sturgeon caviar; the meltingly tender kokanee from Lake Whatcom; and many other delicacies too numerous to mention. Last but not least on this list are the crisp and fruity wines produced in the Pacific Northwest.

I grew up in a German riesling and sylvaner vineyard and later managed to taste my way across much of Europe, trying both the local country wines and the well-aged treasures of renowned châteaus and vintages. I continued to search in this fashion—more from force of habit than to pay homage to the locally produced wines—when I moved to southern California. As I slowly extended my travels to the north to taste the foods, I also sampled the wines. I came to the Napa Valley quite early, before the arrival of the boutique wineries, before Robert Mondavi built his showcase wine factory, at a time when Joe Heitz still sold his luscious cabernet sauvignons in barrels to valley restaurants. From my home base in Davis, I was able to explore the expanding California wine districts from the Mendocino Valley in the north to Monterey and San Luis Obispo counties in the south, from the Sonoma Valley in the west to the mountain vineyards of Amador County in the east, with the torrid, overirrigated vineyards of the Central Valley and the urbanized vineyards of smog-bound Livermore Valley in between.

I tasted the development of California wines from their sweet Skid Row stage through their later incarnation as pleasantly dry, very simple table and party wines, to their achievement of a full-bodied, more complex character and international acclaim. But I was never satisfied by the quality of California wines. They were either too big or too flat and sweet. Only in the vineyards of western Oregon and eastern Washington did I find wines with enough finesse and with the right amount of fruitiness, acidity, and complexity. In the intervening years, the wines of the Pacific Northwest have continued to improve, while those of

California have become heavier and higher in alcohol—a style that pleased for a while as a novelty—and less complex and satisfying with each new vintage. The steadily increasing quality as well as the diversity of northwest wines may turn the Pacific Northwest into the nation's foremost wine-producing region within the next decade or two.

An accomplished regional cuisine depends not only on the quality of its raw materials, on its meats, fish, fowl, shellfish, molluscs, vegetables, fruits, and wines, but also on one other major element: a refined method of cookery which matches the flavors and textures of its foods. I was reminded of the truth of this assertion quite soon after our arrival in the Northwest. We had invited several friends to dinner and, still in the thrall of my California cooking skills, I decided to honor them with a number of special dishes which would combine the foods of one region with the cooking methods of the other. I have mercifully forgotten some of the things I concocted that night, but two of these dishes remain unforgettable: tacos and enchiladas made with pink salmon. Observing the silent suffering of our friends, I learned then that the exquisite foods of the Pacific Northwest may suffer from excessive cooking and spicing, and that the ideal in cooking is to do as little to the food as possible.

This simple approach to cooking does not mean that the cuisine of the Pacific Northwest is a primitive cookery. Far from it. It is a very complex, subtle cuisine, based on natural flavors and on sauces, condiments, and spices which enhance those flavors. Its strategy is to serve foods with contrasting flavors next to each other, instead of blending them into an amorphous whole. In some northwestern dishes, the influence of other cuisines can easily be detected. This is no surprise, since the settlers who peopled our region came from various ethnic and cultural backgrounds: we can find salmon smoked hard in the Indian fashion next to delicate slices of chinook smoked in the light Scottish tradition; dishes flavored with Mediterranean spices next to foods herbed with basil, dill, or tarragon; vegetables (always cooked only until they are barely done but still crisp) bound with a French-style cream sauce next to crunchy greens seasoned with an oriental oyster sauce. But in each case, the "foreign" herb, spice, or sauce has been transmuted into something new, uniquely Pacific northwestern. Several of the small restaurants of our region, excellent eateries, where the owner-chefs bestow special attention on food and guests alike, have refined this approach to a fine art, creating soups and sauces of high complexity and exquisite flavor. But this special attitude toward cooking permeates the northwest kitchen, in private homes as well as in restaurants. It may even affect those time-honored and rigidly structured American institutions, the picnic, barbecue, and clambake.

A recent picnic, for example, a simple hamburger and hot dog affair on the Bellingham waterfront, was transformed when one guest arrived by boat, bringing a load of large, freshly gathered limpets. It mattered little that most of the picnickers had never eaten a limpet before (nor had they thought of it as a food). The limpets were rinsed, placed upside down on the barbecue grill, and eaten hot from the shell. A clambake of fresh clams also showcased the inventiveness of Northwesterners when it comes to food: a matting of wet eelgrass was spread into the bottom of the pit, over the hot rocks; clams and cockles of different species, several chickens, and a stag's worth of deer ribs were spread on top; the food was enclosed with more eelgrass, wet burlap, and soil and covered with a sheet of plywood. As the clams steamed, our host barbecued several fresh silver salmon. Guests had brought fresh bread, berries, and crisp vegetables. The feast was a success. I garnered the culinary prize of the day: a female pea crab heavy with roe which we found in one of the steamed butter clams.

The cuisine of the Pacific Northwest can be as simple as a barbecued salmon, dotted with butter and garlic, and sprinkled with salt and pepper, or as complex as the exquisite sauces prepared by some of our outstanding restaurant chefs. It may concentrate on one or two simple foods, served in a plain fashion, or it may be a series, a symphony of different foods, served side by side, a harmony of matching flavors or a stimulating arrangement of opposites in texture and flavor.

There is as much emphasis on the texture and color of food in this cuisine as there is on taste and aroma. That is not to say that taste and aroma are unimportant—they are the underlying raison d'être of northwest cookery. Unless the raw materials are of the highest quality and impeccably fresh, unless taste and aroma are at their most exquisite stage, there is little reason to worry about texture and color. Northwest cuisine is based on the fresh quality and character of local foods to such a degree that it cannot be replicated elsewhere, since it is impossible to translate the unique taste of the Northwest's fresh ingredients into other raw materials—especially not into foods which are too old and which have lost their natural aromas and flavors. There are only two ways to enjoy northwest cuisine: come to the Northwest, buy the ingredients, read our recipes, and cook; or eat at the excellent small restaurants in the region whose chefs specialize in producing the best of the Northwest's cooking.

In the following chapters, I have tried to stress the important features of the raw materials which shape the cuisine of the Pacific Northwest, together with providing a few select recipes which show how our region's chefs and home cooks treat these foods. This is followed by a guide to some of the small restaurants in our area that specialize in northwest cuisine, and by a list of sources and addresses which will allow visitor and resident alike to find the best foods the Pacific Northwest produces. Bon appetit!

Vegetables

T he other spring, as I bought the first of the season's fresh strawberries, I had a talk about vegetables with my favorite farmer. Each year in the past, the perfectly ripe, juicy berries on her sales stand had been flanked by tender young spring vegetables: fist-sized cauliflower and broccoli, slender Chinese greens, curly-leaved lettuce, and crisp snow peas. But now, there were only berries. I asked her if the bugs and slugs had destroyed her spring vegetable crop. "No, the home gardeners did. How can you expect me to compete when every green-tinged thumb in the region grows too many vegetables and then gives them away—free!"

Well, I don't grow my own vegetables, but I shamelessly take advantage of the bounty offered by friends who grow more than they are able to eat, can, freeze, or even give away. This seems to be a uniquely northwest phenomenon, for nowhere else will a garden produce such a splendid surfeit of produce with so little effort. All you have to do is clear a piece of ground, stick seeds into the soil, and wait. Nature will do the rest. Sometimes you'll have to water your garden a bit, of course, and clear it of weeds. But then many of the "weeds" themselves, chickweed, bracken, portulaca, sheep sorrel, daisies, dandelion, curly dock, plantain, fireweed, amaranth, nettle, lamb's-quarters, pigweed, burdock, shepherd's purse, thistle, et al., are quite edible and delicious (especially in their juvenile stage, when they are most annoying to the gardener) and are just great for delicate salads and fragrant soups. In the Northwest, we don't have to worry much about some of the more serious garden pests, such as bind weed, cocklebur, star-thistle, tumbleweed, and mallows, that plague our neighbors to the south—well, at least not as much as they do. As for snails, eat them, and for slugs, do what Eugene Kozloff recommends—squash them—or, if you're really brave, clean, fillet, and eat them.

Food sharing has been and still is one of my favorite northwest traditions, whether it be fish, crab, clams, or vegetables. The latter seem to predominate by sheer quantity alone: a walk down any residential street in spring and summer will reveal a multitude of small gardens, tucked into sunny corners of backyards and front lawns. Here manicured flower beds have been replaced by flamboyant clumps of leafy corn and tidy rows of cabbage, beans, lettuce, beets, and peas. One friend, an exceptionally avid gardener, has worked out a successful dual-production system, planting shade-tolerant peas, greens, and beans in a secluded Whatcom County woodland hill plot, and tending sun-loving zucchini, corn, peppers, and tomatoes in his parents' backyard on the Skagit River floodplain. He gets the best of both flavor and quantity this way.

Fortunately, he always plants much more than he can possibly use for his extended family—and we have quite liberally benefited from early spring, when he plucks the first tender greens from the cold frame, to late fall and winter, when tasty brussels sprouts and kale overwhelm his garden.

Some gardeners have gotten quite sneaky about distributing their excess produce (short of recycling it through the compost heap). You'll be sitting down to a good book, or dinner, or a well-deserved bottle of wine when, suddenly, the doorbell peals furiously. Checking on the commotion, you'll inevitably be confronted by a large sack or box of vegetables (except on those occasions when an errant newsboy, stray preacher, or out-of-town friend makes an unscheduled appearance). You'll stumble over a great heap of celery, carrots, chard, potatoes, cabbage, or whatever happens to be in season and is thriving in a friend's garden. There is, of course, no visible donor by the time you reach the front door. So you may never learn where the delectable pile originated—unless you can tell by the taste, for an educated palate can distinguish between vegetables grown in different gardens.

But good northwest vegetables are not only tasty, they are also beautiful, even when unceremoniously abandoned on your doorstep.

Behold an asparagus bud, a perfectly formed spire of green, rising smooth from a stocky base and merging into a scaly, greenly-purplish tip. Or look at the yellow-green or reddish-brown translucent leaves of lettuce and sui choy, at the luminous pods of pea and verdant bean, at the white curd of cauliflower, the forest green of chard and spinach, or the affected reds of radish and tomato.

Examine a common garden beet, its glossy maroon globe sprouting sea-green, purple-veined leaves, plumed like the bonnet of a Tyee warrior. Admire the multicloved, paper-veined garlic head, a cupola of wedged delights, or the perfect shape of an onion bulb, a globule of glowing red or royal purple, of striated gold or pearly tegument. Touch the velvety caps of champignons, shiitaki, or cèpes, or meditate upon the ethereal forms of oyster mushrooms and fresh sprouts. Brighten up your pantry and your meals with the orange of chanterelles and carrots or with the yellow of ripe crookneck squash.

Search out the works of master artists, painted during the last thousand years or before, and you will find the noble vegetable honored by their brushes. You will discover your favorite greens and roots and stalks in the proud company of fish and fowl, of flowers and birds, of lords and ladies, of nudes and saints and mythological beasts. I have, for as long as I can remember, pursued fresh vegetables with a passionate palate, yet I am not now able to tell whether I first became enchanted by their forms or their flavors. Vegetables, more than any other food, exert spiritual sway: they take us back to our evolutionary roots, providing us with nourishment directly from the earth, and they imbue us, over a period of culinary time, with the essence of the land on which we live.

I must have seemed eccentric to other children when I was growing up, because I feverishly began to search out vegetables as soon as I was weaned. I devoured carrots, cabbage, cauliflower, kale, kohlrabi, turnips, beets, brussels sprouts, even raw potatoes—and whatever other vegetable I could find. I was a plague, a ravenous biped rabbit in my grandfather's vegetable garden. You name 'em, I loved 'em, and I still do. Raw or cooked, as long as they are fresh.

Besides fresh, civilized vegetables, I also cherish the less couth wild greens, from amaranth to zingy nettles. I especially like nettles, though these irritating shoots must be properly steamed lest they zap you harder than the firiest chili pequin. I have even had my mouth full of raw nettles (the memory still pains me), for as children we indulged in tossing each other into lush nettle beds in our recurrent fits of puerile sadism. Still, in spite of many such painful experiences, I have never tired of eating this herb.

The nice thing about vegetables is that you have so much to choose from and that their quality can be so high. The vegetables planted by modern gardeners, whether from a small backyard plot, a suburban truck garden, or a large commercial field, tend to be pretty much alike throughout the civilized countries of the Northern Hemisphere. The Chinese and Japanese once had quite an advantage over us in the sheer number of planted varieties alone, but modern economics have reduced the bounteous variety in Asian fields and gardens, and many popular oriental vegetables, from bitter melon to gai lan, are now planted in the Northwest. The main difference lies in the quality of the soil and the environment: vegetables grow well almost everywhere, but they achieve an exquisite taste in only a few especially favored areas. Western Europe, Japan, and the Pacific Northwest produce the best vegetables in the world; only the Northwest does so consistently. Seeds and cuttings of high-yielding clones and productive cultivation methods are readily exchanged between vegetable growers and nations, but the quality of what goes into the soil may have little effect on the quality of what comes out, if environmental conditions do not favor the vegetables.

Take the Skagit Valley, for instance: a large share of the vegetable seeds marketed in the United States are grown on the fertile flats of the Skagit River delta. Yet, no matter where in the country these seeds are planted—unless it is in other areas of the Pacific Northwest—the vegetable plants which sprout from them cannot reach the quality of the vegetables grown in the Skagit Valley. It is simply a matter of soil and climate—and latitude: the long daylight hours of summer help to put flavor into the vegetables. I was raised on European vegetables, luscious in their own right, but not as tasty as the vegetables from the Pacific Northwest. Even so, our vegetables came from small gardens—where they were raised with painstaking care—and sometimes from truck farms or small fields, and I never doubted that their delicious savor was largely due to the fortuitous combination of climate and soil.

Our climate was similar to that of the Pacific Northwest—mild and moist, not hot and dry as in California or hot and muggy as on the East Coast, during the growing season—and our soils were of two predominate types: alluvial (or glacial) deposits or loess, both heavily enriched with organic materials (again somewhat like the Pacific Northwest). No wonder European chefs rave about the quality of their vegetables. Yet the Northwest has that little extra, that indefinable ingredient that makes a difference in taste, texture, and handling quality.

Europeans, however, had one important advantage: their vegetables were picked fresh daily. The Northwest, like other areas of the North American continent, suffers from an inadequate distribution system for fresh produce. Centralization of the distribution system has made large-scale vegetable farming possible and has helped keep the prices of produce low, but at a cost to freshness and eating quality. Europeans are still able to buy their vegetables at the daily farmers' market in each town's market square. Here, we must scour the countryside and look for farmers' produce stands to find fresh produce. Only Seattle, Vancouver, British Columbia, and Victoria now have daily farmers' markets where produce is brought in fresh by local farmers. Other population centers, Portland, Yakima, Bellingham, et al., still have only weekly markets; their residents must depend on supermarkets in the interim.

How fresh and tasty vegetables are matters little, however, if they are prepared improperly. My mother once held a belief (long since abandoned) that fresh vegetables are palatable only if they are cooked, cooked, cooked, and then ground up in a meat grinder, mixed with a brown roux (made with flour and lard), and cooked again. When the roots, stalks, or greens had been reduced to a stiff, amorphous vegetable paste, devoid of even a trace of fresh flavor, they were deemed fit to eat—well, at least by the rest of the family. I insisted on eating raw vegetables. Or I begged for pieces of the freshly (over-) cooked vegetables before they were stuffed into the meat grinder. Needless to say, the rest of the family thought me strange, for who would willingly eat "improperly" prepared or "raw" vegetables, unless he was a little weird. By the time I was ten, I had learned to cook my own vegetables and, with time, I have had the satisfaction of seeing the rest of my family (with the exception of my father who will eat only canned vegetables) come around and learn to prepare their vegetables in a more civilized fashion: quickly cooked until they are tender, but still crisp, without loss of their fresh color.

I was very excited about moving to California, because I was young and had not yet learned to see through the hyperboles of press agents. The Golden State, more than any other place in the world, had a reputation for the best and the tastiest of vegetables. My disappointment came quickly. None of this produce even remotely approached the quality of European vegetables. The insipid greens, spongy roots, and vapid stalks sold by the greengrocers and truck farmers of southern California were an insult. They had been raised in a clayey, irrigated soil where a hot sun (and an excess of fertilizer) allowed them to grow rapidly to marketable size, soaking up water and alkali instead of flavor.

Some vegetables had been raised in cool coastal valleys, where fogs and sea clouds blocked out the hot rays of the southern sun; but these, too, lacked savor, for cool-climate vegetables (which is what most of our varieties are) need the long daylight hours of the cool summer days in the northern latitudes for their best development. I had to wait for several years, until I made my first forays to the Oregon vegetable fields, to taste excellent vegetables once again. And only later, after I moved to the Puget Sound region, could I return to eating such vegetables daily. California does a few things well, however. Artichokes, which thrive in the cool, mild, foggy seaside fields (though the west coast of Vancouver Island has a much better potential for growing superb artichokes, few are grown in our region), and tomatoes, which do best in the scorching dry heat of the interior valleys (I once harvested tomatoes in the Central Valley when the outside temperature was 117 degrees in the sun), surpassed my expectations.

But I soon learned to explore the tastes of strange, exotic, and very American vegetables. There were a few adjustment problems. I pride myself on liking every vegetable when it is fixed properly, yet I found it difficult to get excited about vegetable marrows or chayote. Nor do I much care for either summer or winter squash—with the exception of crispy young zucchini. Only recently have I begun to enjoy butternut squash, but solely when it is prepared with ginger sugar.

Having grown up in western Europe, I had never seen any squash, other than a pumpkin, until I moved to the West Coast, and I avoided eating squash for quite a while, simply because I didn't know what to do with it (none of my newly acquired friends cared for squash). Yet, as always, curiosity finally got the better of me. Attracted by a particularly shiny, dark-green and golden, deeply fluted acorn squash—a painter's dream of how a tasty vegetable should look—my resistance melted and I took the plunge. I quickly learned that I had approached this vegetable with a decidedly improper attitude. I should have known better, of course, but I had somehow conceived the notion that acorn squash was some kind of exotic tropical fruit. After all, the ancient Aztecs had eaten large quantities of squash with gusto.

I carefully wrapped my purchase in tissue paper, to make sure it would not get bruised, and packed it for lunch. I shall never forget the experience: it was a lovely, sunny spring day (the smog was kept well offshore by a land breeze) and I was sitting with a number of friends on a well-groomed lawn in the shadiest corner of the college quad when I unwrapped my prize. My friends couldn't help but stare: "Are you eating a squash for lunch?" "How did you cook it?" "Cook it?" I sneered disdainfully and took a big bite. I chewed the piece carefully and, friends or no friends, spat violently amid hoots and bellows. A piece of raw winter squash is a horrid object, a culinary disaster of the first magnitude (surpassed in distaste only by the first hearty, mouth-puckering bite I took out of an unripe avocado, skin and all).

But unfamiliarity does not always lead to a permanent estrangement. As I traveled along the Coast, I took to several other unfamiliar vegetables with gusto: gai lan, bok toy, sui choy, daikon, bitter melon, shiitaki, enokidaki, plantain, chrysanthemum leaves, seaweeds, gobo, bean sprouts, lotus roots and leaves, sweet corn, and, especially, fresh gingerroot and chilies. And I discovered new and pleasant taste sensations among wild greens and roots: mallows, wood sorrel, miner's lettuce, prickly pear cactus, mountain sorrel, epazote, saltbush, pigweed, bracken shoots, milkweed flowers and buds, waterleaf, and pickleweed. I also tried the native roots: watershield, yellow pond lily, cattail, amole, camas and, later, bitterroot. But I continued to prefer potatoes, if only because they were more plentiful, had no pretty flowers which needed to be sacrificed before the tubers could be cooked, and because they were easier to prepare. Only brodiaea bulbs really caught my lasting fancy—their sweet, nutty taste is inimitable—and I singlehandedly ate many a meadow (always making sure to return the tiny satellite bulbs to the soil to propagate this delicacy).

Perhaps my fondness for tubers of all sorts stems from the fact that I was raised on potatoes, yet I have always had a bit of a love and hate relationship with them: as a child I was fed potatoes and more potatoes *ad absurdum*. Every fall, my parents would order a couple of tons of country spuds (a variety of somewhat vague ancestry) from a local farmer to serve as the family's main staple for the coming year. As I grew older, I inherited the chore of unloading these tubers from the farmer's horse-drawn cart. This meant packing the mud-stained spuds into pails and carrying them, pound by pound, down a narrow stone stairway to the holding bin in our ancient cellar. But it was well worth the labor, for we could feast on new potatoes—boiled, baked, fried, etc., etc.—to our hearts' and bellies' content.

Potatoes store well in cool, dry, dark cellars, but even under the best of conditions (and in the absence of chemical treatment) quite a few spuds will begin to rot by late spring and early summer. As potato carrier, I was bequeathed the additional chore of descending into the holding bins several times each spring—whenever the sickly odor of decay began to waft through the gothic vault—to turn over the tubers and separate the good potatoes from the rotting ones. Thus the hate part of my relationship.

German highland potatoes have good texture and flavor, but do not reach the exceptional quality of potatoes grown in the Pacific Northwest. Nor do the spuds grown elsewhere on the North American continent attain the same refinement in taste and texture. Potatoes come in a great number of species and in almost unlimited varieties (some of which, like the gnarled "asparagus" potato, are not easily recognized as spuds but look more like discolored, withered roots). Yet the average American (and Pacific Northwest) consumer is concerned with only a handful of varieties. Few supermarket produce managers—and even fewer potato eaters—care about providing variety for the home table beyond the readily available standard types of spuds. We can always count on finding a good assortment of white- or red-skinned tubers, thin-skinned, waxy boiling and frying potatoes, or thick-skinned, mealy baking spuds at our greengrocer's.

The Northwest grows a fair variety of potatoes—red LaSodas, Pontiacs, and Norlands for boiling; white Superiors for frying, boiling, and baking; Kennebecs for chips and fries. Yet a single variety dominates the potato fields of eastern Washington, southern Idaho, and eastern Oregon: the Burbank russet, a white potato that is excellent for both baking and deep-frying, but which has gained its prominence because it can be easily converted into processed fast-food french fries. It is the potato that almost single-handedly props up the American convenience food market. In the porous, sandy loams of Transcascadia, the Burbank russet grows into large, fairly even-sized, long, mealy tubers. It has become so successful that it makes up more than 40 percent of all potato plantings in the Northwest (accounting for about 75 percent of the baking and processed potatoes sold in the U.S.). Despite its popularity and commercial success, it is not our best potato. And there are indications that it may not be around for much longer.

Potatoes are propagated from bud (eye) sections of tubers, not from seeds, to assure a perfect reproduction of the desirable characteristics of a given variety and to avoid mutants caused by hybridization and cross-fertilization of the seeds. All potatoes of a particular variety are thus direct cellular descendants or "clones" of a common ancestor. While this assures an exact transmission of the ancestor's desirable qualities, it also causes a weakening of the biological resistance to destructive pests and diseases as a potato variety ages. The Burbank russet is getting quite old—it has been around for more than a hundred years now—and it is beginning to show signs of strain.

One potentially devastating pest, late blight, is making greater inroads each year. In 1982, for example, it affected more than 35,000 acres of eastern Washington potatoes. Late blight is a fungus causing devastating spoilage, especially among stored potatoes. It can be controlled by a judicious (and expensive) application of fungicides but, as the variety grows older, control of the blight becomes increasingly difficult. There is quite some cause for worrying, because this is the blight which caused the Irish potato famine of the 1890s. Not a pleasant prospect for baked potato and fries fanciers.

The Burbank russet also suffers from "hollow heart," a large, irregular cavity near the center of large tubers. The walls of this cavity are usually discolored and brownish. Hollow heart is not rot and no decay occurs unless the hollow extends to the surface of the spud. It occurs when potato tubers grow too rapidly, especially when they are overirrigated. Or it may be caused by cold wet soil in the fields when the tubers begin to form. It may not be rot, but it nevertheless makes the spuds taste awful. Another sign that potatoes have been subjected to stresses and uneven growing conditions, especially extremes of soil moisture caused by sloppy irrigation, is an excessive knobbiness of a Burbank russet's surface.

I once might have worried about the quality and fate of the Burbank russet, because I do like to eat an occasional (well-buttered and herbed) baked potato. But then, a couple of years ago, I was served a potato that changed my mind. It was an absolutely perfect baked potato, the best spud I have ever tasted. Commenting on the restaurant's assiduousness in obtaining such excellent Idaho potatoes, I was quickly informed that this was no import, but a local potato, a Netted Gem (a variety very closely related to the Burbank russet) from Skagit County.

This called for a closer investigation of the potatoes grown in western Washington and it led, in the end, to a complete reevaluation of my attitude toward northwest spuds. I learned that northwestern Washington, especially the well-drained, gravelly farmland of the Nooksack Valley, is the number-one producer of seed potatoes in the country, growing potatoes too precious for mere eating. Some of these sumptuous spuds can be bought locally, direct from the farmers, but they rarely enter wholesale channels. I have become particularly fond of Netted Gems, Kennebecs, Nooksacks, and red LaSodas. I have also learned, however, to be very particular about these potatoes' exact place of origin.

Northwest Washington potatoes grown on dry, well-drained uplands are of superior texture and flavor; potatoes grown in damp (sometimes even marshy) bottomlands have a very inferior taste, a watery consistency, and spoil quickly in storage. It helps to know your potato seller well if you expect to eat spuds of consistently high quality.

The best potatoes grown in the Pacific Northwest (and my unqualified favorites) are produced in small quantities only. They are unavailable from either large farms or supermarkets, but are sold in season at local and regional farmers' markets. The yellow "Finn" potato—actually a very buttery Swedish spud—is superb for both boiling and frying. I like to buy these when they are about the size of large prunes and boil and serve them whole. Purple potatoes look quite strange—they are a deep purple hue and keep much of their color in cooking—but are very delicious to eat. They have a richer, sweeter taste than our commercially marketed spuds. I like to parboil these thin-skinned tubers and then sauté them in freshly made butter until they are done. Or I may toss them in the butter with bits of rendered bacon, sliced chanterelles, tiny new onions, and a sprinkling of fine herbs.

The cultivation of tasty spuds is undergoing major changes in the Pacific Northwest at the present time. We will always have our large producers who grow potatoes for both the bulk fresh market and for the processors (more than half of the potatoes consumed in the U.S. are eaten as processed french fries, potato chips, or frozen or dehydrated preparations), but the culinary excitement of the future lies with small truck farmers who are experimenting with rare or unusual varieties, ranging from stolid Dutch spuds to weird asparagus potatoes.

Potatoes go very well with onions and, fortunately, our region also excels in the production of these pungent lily bulbs and greens. The Pacific Northwest produces superbly flavored chives, green onions, leeks, yellow onions, white onions, red onions, shallots, and garlic. Especially garlic. The cultivation of these strong-flavored bulblets has only recently reached commercial levels in western Washington—after it was discovered that garlic grown in the well-drained, gravelly soils of the Puget lowland possesses a taste superior to that of the garlic grown in hot, arid southern climes.

Fresh garlic is beginning to play an increasingly important role in the cuisine of the

Pacific Northwest, and even California gourmets (especially restaurant chefs) now import their garlic from the Northwest. But our most famous—and some say our tastiest—member of the onion tribe is the justly renowned Walla Walla sweet onion.

The Walla Walla onion is very large, very sweet, and very low in those sulphurous compounds which give pungency to other onions and bring tears to cooks' eyes. Some aficionados claim that this onion is a special variety; others maintain that it is just a common onion which achieves its renowned quality only when it is grown in the sandy soils of the Walla Walla Valley.

Curiously enough, the Walla Walla onion farmers—the ones who have the most to lose if their "unique" onion can be grown successfully in other parts of the Northwest—are also the ones who maintain most avidly that the Walla Walla onion is a special variety. The progenitor of this onion, or so the story goes, was discovered by a French soldier named Pierre (Pete) Pieri around the turn of the century on the island of Corsica. Pierre secured some seeds of his favorite onion before he immigrated to the Walla Walla Valley. He successfully planted the seeds on his new farm. His Italian immigrant neighbors soon discovered that Pete's onions were superior to their own—they grew to greater size and matured earlier—and they in turn obtained some seeds from one Guiseppe Locati, who happened to be working for Pieri at the time. This onion was soon widely planted in the valley. It evolved through a lengthy selective breeding period until it emerged as today's Walla Walla sweet.

The Walla Walla onion is an onion possessed of a superb eating quality, but it is very high in water and will not dry and store very well. It can thus be enjoyed for only a very short period each summer (though it may be frozen); but this does not deter the region's Walla Walla onion fanciers from eagerly awaiting each new crop. For the Walla Walla onion is very sweet.

Onions are commonly sold by the bulb, but the Walla Walla sweet is marketed in twenty-five- or fifty-pound bags. I buy a few bags each year and, for several glorious weeks, Victoria and I eat a lot of onions—raw, sautéed, baked, on sandwiches, in pies, in quiches, and in stews. I particularly enjoy these onions in an onion/apple/chili sauce.

For many years, the Walla Walla onion growers have claimed that theirs is the world's sweetest onion. This blatant appeal to the well-documented sweet tooth of the American consumer did help increase sales for a while, but the Walla Wallans have recently lost out to an upstart onion from Vidalia, Georgia, in a series of blind sweetness tests. This by no means makes the Walla Walla an inferior onion nor does it take away from its claim of having a superior taste, for mere sweetness in an onion makes it insipid. Like a sweet wine, a sweet onion needs a healthy amount of acid to balance the bulb's sweetness, or it will taste flat and cloying. And that is precisely the Vidalia's main problem: it is an insipid onion that has nothing but sweetness going for it. The Vidalia onion growers have overcome this fault by packaging and selling their onions in a vinegar pickle. The Walla Walla sweet onion, on the other hand, needs no pickling juice to make it palatable.

This still leaves us with the question of the effect variety and location have on the onion's taste, however. Does the Walla Walla sweet reach its best development only in the Walla Walla Valley, or can it achieve perfection elsewhere in the Northwest? I have tasted Walla Walla sweets grown in different parts of our region, and I am firmly convinced that its excellence is not limited to just one location. The onion's special taste may, however, be closely related to the quality of our soils, to the length of the northern growing days during the summer, and to the relative mildness of our climate—which is much cooler (and less muggy) than the weather in either Georgia or Corsica. Desert soils may, on the other hand, play some role in this onion's taste: some of the best "Walla Walla" sweet onions I have tasted have come from the Yakima Valley.

Several other vegetables I like also grow best in the Yakima Valley, but do not do as well west of the Cascades. I liked sweet corn and hot peppers so much that I experimented with growing my own. I had, of course, been quite familiar with the plump yellow kernels of maize before coming to the U.S.—as chicken feed and hog slop, not as gourmet fare. Maize is grown for human food in Europe only along the Mediterranean fringe and in the Balkans, but it does not prosper in the cool climates of western and northern Europe.

Yet I needed only one taste of sweet corn, freshly picked, cooked right away, and served piping hot, with fresh butter, to recognize that I had, so far, missed a supreme delicacy. Unfortunately, this first taste also prejudiced me: it had been so perfect, of such a delicate natural sweetness and fresh corn flavor, that I found it difficult to settle for the inferior "sweet" corn sold by greengrocers.

Sweet corn is picked and eaten when it is still milky and thus botanically green. Its kernels are tender because their sugar has not yet been converted into the starchy embryo of the ripe seed. Once an ear of corn has been separated from the stalk, this conversion of sugar into starch accelerates and the corn's culinary quality deteriorates by the minute. This is why sweet corn must be eaten as quickly after picking as possible. It will, of course, remain edible for several days, but it may not be worth eating. There is only one good way of preparing fresh sweet corn (though there are several acceptable ones), and it depends on the strict observance of several important steps.

First, plant your sweet corn, nurture it (I have yet to succeed in doing this successfully, but there are always friends who are very good at growing corn), tend it carefully until the ears are ready to cook. Gardeners once upon a time diligently twisted off the suckers (the small side shoots which form at the base of the stalks), believing this was necessary to obtain good ears of corn. This time-consuming exercise has been abandoned by most modern-day gardeners (after a series of scientific experiments showed that suckering did not lead to an increase in the quality of the ears); only the Tarheels living in the foothills of the North Cascades still indulge in this tedious practice. And, of course, they claim that their corn tastes better than anybody else's. They are right, but for the wrong reason: Tarheels do not raise corn—or other vegetables, for that matter—from commercial seed, but from seeds which have been handed down through several generations of families and gardeners, seeds which are saved from the harvest and which are freely traded among the foothill people from Sedro Woolley to Darrington. The Tarheels eat a lot of fresh corn and they freeze and can large quantities for winter consumption, but they always make sure to have as little distance as possible between the corn patch and the kettle.

Second, heat up a kettle of water and, when the water seethes and burbles, go to your garden, pluck the corn ears from the stalks (take only as many as you can cook at once), rush to the kitchen, shuck the ears (you'll save time and precious taste if you learn to do this on the run—you can always sweep up the mess later), and drop them into the boiling water.

Third, while the corn is cooking, make fresh butter in your food processor, and grind salt and pepper. Do not overcook your corn. Boil it for a maximum of five to ten minutes, depending on the size of the ears. Or, if you're still afraid you'll overcook the corn, use this simple method: drop the shucked ears into boiling water (salted, if you must) and bring the water to a boil again. As soon as it bubbles vigorously, cover the pot with a tightly fitting lid and turn off the heat. Let it sit for ten minutes. Remove the corn from the water and serve it immediately with the fresh butter. If you are going to eat it later, chill the corn under cold water right after it comes from the pot, to arrest the cooking process. Once you have eaten corn this fresh, tender, sweet, and tasty, you will find it difficult to settle for second best ever afterwards.

The one problem Northwesterners have with sweet corn is that it likes heat—and must have it to be sweet—but it also needs lots of water. Too much dry heat, combined with an excess of irrigation, makes the kernels tough and flavorless; a lot of warmth makes them watery and flavorless. Much of the corn grown in western Washington suffers from the latter, but sweet corn raised in the warmer parts of Oregon's Willamette Valley and in Washington's Yakima and Walla Walla valleys is sublimely delicious. There is only one obstacle: you must travel to those valleys to get it when it is in season.

Sweet corn shipped from one of these growing areas to a supermarket spends at least one day in transit—under the best of conditions—and, as I have emphasized, every minute counts. There are several ways in which sweet corn addicts can fulfill their quest for freshness and taste, however: they can move to one of these valleys, or visit a friend already living there during the fresh corn season, or rent a hotel/motel room with a kitchenette, or set up camp and cook the fresh ears on a camp stove.

If I cannot get my corn that fresh, I actually prefer to eat sweet corn that has been frozen right after it was picked (and thus had its sugar "fixed") to "sweet" corn that has been shipped by slow truck to Seattle, Portland, or Vancouver (where the sugar has converted to starch in transit). Frozen corn should never be thawed before it is cooked and should not be kept for more than a few months after the harvest. If you insist on eating sweet corn in, say, the middle of January, don't expect it to be especially sweet or tasty. The odds are simply against you. Eat a fresh winter vegetable instead and dream about the next summer's fresh corn season.

One vegetable that is often served with sweet corn and which grows well in the same garden patch (its vines can be trained to climb cornstalks for support) does not need to be handled with equal celerity; it does well even when corn fails to mature. Green beans are, of course, best when they are eaten right after they are picked, but they keep their freshness and taste much longer than sweet corn. Mature shell beans, which turn into dried beans when they are shelled and stored, are very good to eat at harvesttime, yet they are still very flavorful a year or two later (if they have been stored properly).

Shell beans, like dry peas and lentils, need heat to mature, but green beans do very well in a mild climate. They need some heat during the early stages of growth, or they may not set fruit; but once the pods have formed, the beans can reach full flavor, even in the cool, rainy coastal gardens of our area and in the tree-shaded valleys of the northern Cascades and Coast Mountains. These beans ripen (and thus harden) very quickly when they are exposed to too much heat. Their pods may be quite tough and stringy even in the green, edible state. It is much better to let them ripen and enjoy them as good shell beans instead of as inferior green beans.

Hot dry climates, like that in the Palouse or the Walla Walla and Yakima valleys, grow excellent dry legumes; but it takes a cool climate with a long growing season, yet with enough warmth during the summer months, to put flavor and succulence into green beans. Little wonder green beans, both the bush and pole varieties, sprout luxuriously along the Oregon coast and in western Washington and British Columbia. Even the old scarlet runner bean, which has succumbed to the onslaught of modern, more productive varieties elsewhere in the country, still holds its own along the Pacific Northwest coast. Beans raised in our cooler areas need the special care of dedicated home gardeners, however, for their best development, and they should be planted in sunny spots. They may not set much fruit in cold years, but whatever pods they produce are well worth struggling for.

The best green bean growing area on the West Coast, if not on the continent, is in the northern Willamette Valley, however. It is surprising that the green bean was not native to this area and was unknown to the indigenous population until white settlers—the Astorians—brought it with them from the East Coast. It is strange, because the northern Willamette is bean growing country par excellence, producing luscious, tasty pods of unsurpassed flavor.

While green beans do exceptionally well in the coastal areas of the Pacific Northwest, tender peas do even better. There seems to be some argument about where the pea originated (there is none about the bean—it's an "All-American"). Earlier notions that it came from the Middle East have now been discounted, for, as Waverly Root states so aptly, the pea "flourishes in cool weather and perishes in heat." This is one reason Europeans, especially the French, have enjoyed such excellent peas, and why Americans have had such tasteless, primarily dry peas. Throughout much of the continent, from Quebec south to Florida and west to California and Idaho, cool or cold winters are followed by short, warm springs, which in turn are rapidly driven out by long, hot and muggy summers. Peas just don't like that kind of weather. They go to seed very quickly, and they toughen before they can develop much flavor.

It's a totally different story in the Pacific Northwest. Our climate, with its long gentle springs and mild summers, is just made for the proper growing of peas. It may sound chauvinistic, but there are no peas like ours, for no one else has our perfect pea growing weather. And of all the pea growing areas on the continent, there's nothing like the Skagit Valley. Here the rich alluvial soils and the long, cool summer days literally make peas happy.

Sugar peas, the edible pod pea of the Chinese and Vietnamese, the "mange-tout" of the French, have been around for a long time, but the sugar snap pea is a very recent development. It has been known for only a few years, the fortuitous result of a genetic accident, but it has taken the Northwest by storm. Snow peas (or sugar peas) are flat, more pod than pea; they looked very strange to me when I first encountered them in a Chinese eatery (long before they were "discovered" by Caucasian gourmets). Sugar snaps have nothing exotic about them. They look just like normal peas, round-shelled, or maybe like tender beans. But like snow peas (and quite unlike shell peas), they may be eaten pod and all. And they are very sweet and tasty. I planted my first sugar snap peas as a jest among the flower pots of my apartment deck. It kept me busy all summer long, for the peas were so tasty, I searched for them daily. But it didn't matter if I missed a pod or two during my diurnal quests, because sugar snap peas grown in the Northwest stay sweet and tender until they are fat and plump.

I like to travel through the cool coastal areas of Washington State in late summer when the inland heat has wiped out all of the tender vegetables of spring and early summer, when cabbage and spinach, gai lan and siu choy and all of my favorite wild greens have bolted and gone to seed, to see if any of the delicate greens have survived in the mild environment of the maritime fringe. I usually succeed in finding my favorite vegetables in unexpected places: snow peas and lettuces in a farmers' market, spinach and tender, young bok choy in a friendly gardener's backyard, and tender wild greens on the coastal bluffs.

We have become too concerned with quantity instead of quality. Our farmers produce for the sake of producing; they have little concern for the taste and texture of what they grow. But even as I write this, I pause and reflect, for it is precisely the intensive approach to agriculture which has created three of the Northwest's most delectable vegetables: Yakima Valley asparagus and Skagit Valley broccoli and cauliflower.

I was raised on asparagus, on the big, fat white stalks which thrived in the soils of Franconia, and which were cut fresh every morning and taken to market the same day. I had very fond memories of this asparagus, of its luscious taste which seemed more meat than vegetable—a very delicate meat to be sure, unlike that of any known animal. When I came to California, I found temporary solace in the white asparagus of the San Joaquin Valley—until economic expediency drove it to extinction. But I was never very fond of green asparagus.

For one glorious long summer, I lived close to an abandoned asparagus patch, and I would rise early every day to cut fresh green asparagus for my morning omelet. I enjoyed the culinary exercise, and the asparagus was tasty enough, but it wasn't anything to warm your heart and make you break out in lyric exclamations.

It was not until I came to the Northwest that I began to appreciate fully the lovely taste of Yakima Valley asparagus. And I began to participate in the annual asparagus lover's ritual: first comes the Mexican asparagus—sometimes as early as January—then, in early March, the California asparagus. But early March in a California asparagus growing area— I have been through it and lived to tell the tale—is quite unsuited to growing delicate vegetables; it's just too hot and dry. Finally, sometimes as early as April, the long wait is over. The first of the Yakima asparagus reaches the market. Many aficionados have already jumped the gun, however. In eastern Washington, asparagus has gone wild with a vengeance. It grows profusely along roads, ditches, and in orchards, attracting a pilgrimage of avid "weeders" equipped with sharp knives and eager palates. There would be much more wild asparagus in eastern Washington if so much of it were not eagerly devoured by knowledgeable gourmets. But I am hoping the pilgrimage will continue, for the fruit growers and county road departments care little for the tasty vegetable, and they will be more than ready to control the rank growth of wild asparagus with a spray of herbicides if the annual migration fails to control this bounty.

After discovering the pleasures of Yakima Valley asparagus, I thought often of the white asparagus of my youth and wondered if it was as good as I remembered. Then, in the spring of 1981, the long-awaited opportunity came: within a few days of each other, I was able to taste the best of the white Franconian asparagus—we bought a few bunches and cooked them on our camp stove—and the best of Yakima green. I must admit that I prefer the Yakima green asparagus. It simply has a richer, fuller flavor, and, best of all, it tastes like a vegetable. The white European asparagus seems to have problems making up its mind whether it is plant or fowl. Besides, where but in the Northwest do you have restaurants which will serve no other vegetable but the fresh local asparagus in season simply because it is so good and because there is nothing else to match its taste and quality?

Asparagus is grown throughout the Northwest, if not always in marketable quantities. Walla Walla asparagus may be the only one I do not like very much. It has a muddy taste and it reminds me more of California asparagus than of the best our area can produce. But I am in love with Yakima Valley asparagus. I like it so much that I have tasted very little asparagus grown west of the Cascades. But, as I learned to my surprise, west-side asparagus is not to be scorned. Victoria and I had dinner with Rick O'Reilly (of La Petite Maison in Olympia) and Rick's wife Donna at their beach cabin on the east shore of Camano Island during late spring. Rick had cooked a superb roast of northwest beef for us and he had planned to accompany it with some asparagus he had bought on his way up from Olympia. At the last moment, just before the dinner was ready, he remembered that there might be a few asparagus stalks left in the old asparagus patch behind the cabin. We went to take a look and were in luck. Enough asparagus buds had risen above the beach sand to furnish us with a sumptuous repast. This asparagus was very tasty, very tender, and on a par with Yakima green.

I have since learned that asparagus production on the west side of the Cascades is on the increase. But it may be several more years before we can reap the full benefit of these experiments, since asparagus plants take at least three years to reach full production. One attempt that is bound to be crowned with success is taking place at the Sooke Harbour House on Vancouver Island. Sinclair Philip, one of our area's most sophisticated chefs, has just put in his first asparagus beds (the entire production is reserved for his restaurant), and inn guests will be able to experience the ultimate in fresh flavor—Sinclair's vegetables are often picked only minutes before they are served to the inn's guests.

Asparagus is not the only vegetable that is eagerly awaited each spring. Skagit County winter cauliflower has an equal number of avid fans. Unfortunately, most of them are in California. For some strange reason, the produce wholesalers of the Pacific Northwest refuse to pay the few extra pennies our local cauliflower is worth and ship in cheap California cauliflower instead. California wholesale producers, on the other hand, buy up all the northwest cauliflower they can, because it is so much better than anything California can produce. Besides, California restaurants and gourmets gladly pay more to get the best cauliflower in the country. The same story is repeated a few months later with spring cauliflower and with broccoli.

But not all is lost. Our farmers produce enough cauliflower to sell some at roadside stands and farmers' markets, and it is well worth a drive into the country to buy it fresh during the harvest season—usually about April for the winter cauliflower, July for summer cauliflower, and August for broccoli. It is easy to tell cauliflower and broccoli grown in the Northwest from their inferior California cousins: our cauliflowers have bigger, denser heads—they are rarely thin and straggly—and our broccolis are also very dense and of a bluish-green tint (not the faded yellow-green so common among California broccolis). If you cannot tell the difference by color and appearance, you will be able to taste it: our cauliflower and broccoli have a rich full taste; the cauliflower and broccoli imported from California taste insipid.

It would be easy to laugh off the competition between the California and northwest produce industries as insignificant. Yet during the summer of 1982 I watched a constant stream of trucks head for the British Columbia border. They were carrying cheap California cauliflower to Vancouver in open trailers. These inferior vegetables—even after transportation costs and customs duties had been added, they were still cheaper than the exquisite, but more expensive, cauliflower produced in British Columbia—were dumped on the market at such low prices that they may have permanently damaged the vegetable growers of the Fraser Valley. Fortunately, in Vancouver, as elsewhere in the Pacific Northwest, the general trend in consumer preferences is away from the supermarkets and back to small farmers' markets for the freshest of produce. Our farmers may yet survive the onslaught of California's agribusiness.

But there is hope on quite another front. The recent influx of Chinese immigrants and Southeast Asian refugees into our region has led to a revived interest in the growing of specialty vegetables. These new farmers and truck gardeners quickly learned that many of their favorite vegetables, especially cruciferae, did exceptionally well in the cool climate of the Pacific Northwest. They have also been very successful in marketing their produce. This is why we can now find such dainties as baby bok choy, choy sum, gai lan, gai choy, lo-bak, bitter melon, and edible chrysanthemum leaves in our farmers' markets. But the oriental influence also shows itself in the greater freshness available at the greengrocer's. Chanterelles and morels, almost unknown to any but the most avid mushroom hunters just a few years ago, are now commonly sold during the season (for a price); shiitaki and enokidaki can now be found, fresh and fragrant, even on supermarket produce counters; and fresh water chestnuts are easy to find.

Further hope for a better supply of fresh local vegetables comes from the back-to-the-land small farm movement, which is especially strong in western Washington. It is these small farmers, enthusiasts like David Skinner, who is trying to grow truffles on San Juan Island, or Mark Musick of Arlington, who gathers wild greens for Seattle's fancy restaurants, or Darlyn Del Boca of Lynden, who grows odd and interesting vegetables, many of them as yet untried for our area, who will help determine the future development of northwest agriculture and point the way to the kind of greens, stalks, and roots we may be eating in the near future.

Let us never forget the prime advantage we have over vegetable growers in other parts of the country: because of our mild, moist climate and superb soils, our vegetables will prosper and thrive and multiply, even if left to themselves (many have in fact escaped from cultivation and can now be found growing wild throughout our region); in other parts of this continent, these vegetables would wither, shrivel, and die if their steady diet of irrigation water, fertilizers, and pesticides were removed.

The Pacific Northwest is fortunate indeed in having such superb vegetables. I just wish there were more of them!

Mushrooms Gewürztraminer

Here's a tasty appetizer from Louise Rauner of the Yakima River Winery in Prosser.
Serve with a well-chilled Yakima River gewürztraminer.

Bulk sausage ¼ pound
Yakima River gewürztraminer ¼ cup
Unsalted butter ⅛ cup
Small onion 1, diced
Mushroom caps 12, 1-inch diameter
Sharp Cheddar cheese ⅛ pound, shredded

1. Cook sausage with wine in covered pan for 10 minutes.
2. Remove cover and continue cooking over low heat until sausage is a delicate brown.
3. Mix sausage with butter and diced onion.
4. Brush mushroom caps clean, fill with sausage mixture, and top with grated cheese.
5. Bake at 325° for 10 minutes.

Serves 4

Caviar-Stuffed Mushrooms

This recipe works best with the delicate meadow mushroom, Agaricus campestris, *but com-*
mercial mushrooms may also be used—if fresh.

Salad oil ¾ cup
Cider vinegar ¼ cup
Garlic clove 1, coarsely chopped
Black pepper dash
Medium mushrooms 30 to 36
Cream Cheese (see Index) 8 ounces, softened
Mayonnaise ¼ cup
Onion 3 tablespoons minced
Salmon caviar ½ cup

1. In a shallow bowl, combine oil, vinegar, garlic, and pepper.
2. Brush mushroom caps clean and remove stems. Coat caps with oil-vinegar mixture, and set aside, hollow side up.
3. Combine Cream Cheese with mayonnaise and onion. Fill mushroom caps with cheese mixture.
4. Top each mushroom with a rounded ¼ teaspoon of salmon caviar and serve.

Serves 6 to 8

Rick O'Reilly's Mushroom Pie

This recipe can be made with either commercial mushrooms or with such tasty wild mushrooms as chanterelles.

Pie shell   one 9-inch, prebaked
Mushrooms   1 pound, chopped
Unsalted butter   ¼ cup
Salt and pepper   to taste
Port wine   ½ cup
Cream   1 cup
Swiss cheese or aged Marblemount goat Cheddar   1 cup grated

1. Bake a pie crust using any crust recipe. (Or bake small shells for individual servings.)
2. Wash and drain mushrooms and sauté in butter, with salt and pepper, until all juices are reduced.
3. Stir in port and whipping cream and cook over medium heat until well reduced and thickened (about 10 to 20 minutes).
4. Add grated cheese and pour mixture into pie shell. Place pie in 425° oven for a few minutes, until cheese melts, and serve hot.

Serves 4 to 6

Marinated Garden Salad

Here's a recipe from Virginia Fuller of Tualatin Vineyards. While this salad may go well with a chilled wine like gewürztraminer, I like it even better with a frosty lager beer, say, a Henry Weinhard's Private Reserve.

Virgin olive oil   1 cup
Sugar   1 teaspoon
Salt   2½ teaspoons
Italian seasonings   2 teaspoons
Gewürztraminer   ¼ cup
Rice vinegar   ⅔ cup
Cumin   4 teaspoons
Freshly ground black pepper   ¼ teaspoon
Cayenne   dash
Garlic cloves   2, slivered
Fresh lemon juice   2 teaspoons
Cilantro   1 tablespoon chopped
Assorted vegetables (cucumber, onion, green pepper, mushroom, water chestnuts, peas, green beans, corn, firm tomato)   10 cups cubed

1. Combine all ingredients except vegetables. Blend well.
2. Pour over cubed vegetables, reserving tomato. Chill. Add tomato just before serving.

Note: This recipe allows for quite a number of substitutions: instead of water chestnuts, you can use Jerusalem artichokes or even brodiaea bulbs (make sure to return the tiny satellite bulblets to the soil); you can use store-bought mushrooms or morels (if you can get them), and later in the season meadow mushrooms, oyster mushrooms, or chanterelles, and so on.

Serves 10

Fraser River Potato Salad

Serve with chilled sauvignon blanc, aligoté, semillon, or a British Columbia cottage winery gewürztraminer.

Medium purple potatoes*   6 cups thinly sliced and quartered
Vegetable oil   6 tablespoons
Vinegar   2 tablespoons
Fresh lemon juice   1 tablespoon
Onion   ¼ cup chopped
Powdered dill weed   ¼ teaspoon
Salt and freshly ground black pepper   dash
Salmon caviar   3 tablespoons, plus additional for garnish

1. Cook potatoes in boiling salted water until barely tender. Drain.
2. In large bowl, combine oil, vinegar, lemon juice, onion, dill, salt, and pepper. Add potatoes; toss to coat.
3. Gently fold in caviar, making sure not to break the "berries."
4. Cover. Keep cold. At serving time, garnish with more caviar (either salmon caviar or, as a variation, golden whitefish caviar).

* Purple potatoes have become regularly available in our area only during the last few seasons, but even now they are mainly found at farmers' markets. This recipe also works well with the long, skinny asparagus potatoes raised in the peaty soils of the lower British Columbia mainland.

Serves 8 generously

Grandpa Manca's Salad Dressing for Wild Greens

This is one of my favorite salad dressings—it's perfect for fresh spring greens such as wild mustard, wood sorrel, shepherd's purse, or dandelion.

Fresh mint (preferably peppermint, but spearmint will do)   1 cup
Large eggs   2
Cider vinegar   1½ cups
Strawberry vinegar   ½ cup
Honey*   2 tablespoons
Salt and freshly ground white pepper   to taste
Olive oil (preferably Tuscan extra virgin)   3 cups

1. Chop mint, place in food processor, and add all remaining ingredients, except oil.
2. First blend a little bit (pulse), then turn processor on full. Pour in olive oil slowly until well blended.

* Martin Hahn prefers Greek honey. I have found that the cascara honey available on the west side works well.

Makes 6 cups

Lamb's-quarters Soup

This is one of the excellent dishes made by Dan Ripley at M'sieurs Restaurant from seasonal vegetables.

Lamb's-quarters   2 bunches
Very small onion   1, finely diced
Unsalted butter   4 tablespoons
Medium chicken stock*   1½ cups
Bay leaf   1
Salt and freshly ground pepper   to taste (use no salt if using commercial, presalted stock)
Heavy cream   ½ cup (or more)

1. Wash lamb's-quarters in cold water, strip off leaves, and discard stems.
2. Gently sauté cubed onion in butter over low heat until onion is almost transparent (make sure it does not brown and burn).
3. Add chicken stock, lamb's-quarters, bay leaf, salt, and pepper. Simmer for about 10 minutes.

4. Cool. Remove bay leaf. Puree soup in food processor or food mill.
5. Let soup sit for about 24 hours for better flavor. Just before serving, add cream. Heat gently. Serve.

* By "medium" chicken stock, I mean a stock that is not too strong and that will not overpower the delicate lamb's-quarters.

Serves 6 to 8

Green Soup

Virginia Beck is one of those people who just have a knack for cooking. She invented this dish one evening when she was expecting guests, but had forgotten to plan ahead for a soup. She quickly made it up from vegetables growing in her patio planters (with a little help from the refrigerator larder).

Spinach   3 cups washed and chopped
Sorrel leaves   ½ cup washed and chopped
Parsley   2 tablespoons chopped
Small onion   1, chopped
Unsalted butter   3 tablespoons
Boiling potatoes   ¾ pound, boiled and thinly sliced
Chicken stock   4¼ cups
Freshly grated nutmeg   to taste (about ¼ teaspoon)
Dry sherry   2 tablespoons
Cayenne   pinch
Heavy cream   1 cup
Fresh chives and parsley   garnish
Crème Fraîche (see Index)   6 tablespoons

1. In a food processor fitted with the steel blade (or in a blender), mince together spinach, sorrel leaves, and 2 tablespoons parsley.
2. Place onion and butter in saucepan over moderate heat, stirring until onion is softened.
3. Add potatoes and continue stirring for 2 or 3 minutes.
4. Add chicken stock and nutmeg and continue cooking until potatoes are soft.
5. In a food processor (or in a blender), puree potato mixture in batches, transferring them to a larger saucepan after they are pureed. Bring puree to a slow simmer over moderately low heat.
6. Add sherry and cayenne and continue to cook for 2 or 3 minutes.
7. Add cream and continue to heat slowly, but do not allow to boil.
8. Serve with chopped chives and parsley and a tablespoon of Crème Fraîche for each serving.

Serves 4 to 6

Fresh Yakima Valley Hop Shoots I

Water 1 gallon
Salt 1 teaspoon
Fresh hop shoots 2 pounds, cleaned and trimmed into 4-inch lengths
Fresh lemon juice from ½ lemon

1. Bring water and salt to rapid boil.
2. Drop hop shoots into water, boil for about 3 to 5 minutes, or until shoots are tender, but still crunchy.
3. Remove immediately and rinse under cold, running water.
4. Place on platter and sprinkle with lemon juice. Serve.

Serves 4 to 6

Fresh Yakima Valley Hop Shoots II

Unsalted butter 3 to 4 tablespoons
Fresh hop shoots 2 pounds, cleaned and trimmed into 4-inch lengths
Salt and freshly ground pepper to taste
Crème Fraîche (see Index) ½ cup

1. Heat butter in large heavy skillet. When butter begins to foam, add hop shoots. Sprinkle with salt and pepper, turning shoots often to coat with spices and cook evenly.
2. When shoots are tender but still crisp (about 3 to 5 minutes), remove from pan to platter.
3. Add Crème Fraîche to pan; combine with butter by stirring with wire whisk. Pour over hop shoots. Serve hot with cold beer.

Serves 4 to 6

Dan Ripley's Sautéed Red Cabbage

Dan believes in keeping the vegetable dishes at M'sieurs as simple as possible. He is one of the few chefs I know who is consistently able to cook vegetables to just the right degree of doneness: crunchy but not undercooked. This cabbage dish is excellent with fall and winter meat dishes, especially pork and sausage.

Small red cabbage   1
Boiling salted water   6 cups (or more, as needed)
Unsalted butter   3 tablespoons clarified (or more; use 1 tablespoon for each 2 servings; adjust to size of cabbage)
Red wine vinegar   6 tablespoons (1 tablespoon per serving)
Salt and freshly ground white pepper   to taste
Fennel seed   1 or 2 pinches

1. Clean and trim head of cabbage. Split and core; cut as for coleslaw into 1- to 2-inch by ¼-inch pieces. Allow ½ to ¾ cup per person.
2. Pour boiling salted water over cabbage to cover in noncorrosive pan or bowl. Set aside for 20 minutes, then rinse under cold running water and drain well. (Up to here, recipe may be done ahead of time.)
3. Melt clarified butter in large sauté pan; add vinegar, salt, pepper, and fennel seed. Add cabbage to pan and sauté gently, tossing or turning cabbage frequently until cabbage softens and is totally heated through, but not browned. (Cabbage will go through color changes because of acid in vinegar. Tossing until cabbage is coated with vinegar and butter will bring color consistency.)
4. Serve when hot and beginning to wilt.

Serves 6

Cucumber Sauce

This is a cucumber sauce that may be served hot over fish or potatoes. It calls for tough-skinned American cucumbers, which need to be skinned to be palatable, since their skins are waxed. I would recommend using the thinner-skinned Japanese kyūri cucumber (which also has smaller seeds), available at many of our farmers' markets.

Large cucumbers   2
Small onion   1
Celery stalks with leaves   2
Light fish stock   ½ cup
Lemon juice   1 tablespoon
Parsley Butter   2 tablespoons

1. Peel cucumbers and onion; wash celery stalks. Chop all 3 into small pieces.
2. Place with stock and lemon juice in a heavy saucepan and simmer until cucumbers are translucent and soft enough to be mashed with a spoon. Puree everything in a food processor.
3. Reheat and swirl in Parsley Butter.

Makes 2 cups

Parsley Butter

Unsalted butter   3 tablespoons
Parsley   4 tablespoons minced
Fresh lemon juice   1 tablespoon
Salt and pepper   ¼ teaspoon each

Cream butter in warm bowl and beat in parsley, lemon juice, salt, and pepper. Chill until ready to use.

Makes ½ cup

Green Sauce

This is an excellent sauce to serve with cold poached fish on a warm summer evening, and it is just as good with crisp raw or parboiled vegetables. I would not serve a fancy wine with this sauce, since it is quite high in acetic acids that might upset a wine's balance. Serve it with a generic white, like Hinzerling Vineyards Ashfall White or a Knudsen Erath blanc de blancs, or better yet, with a good, well-chilled, lager beer.

Parsley   ⅓ cup coarsely chopped
Onion   ⅓ cup coarsely chopped
Chives   2 tablespoons coarsely chopped
French tarragon   1 teaspoon chopped
Garlic clove   1, finely minced
Olive oil   ½ cup
Wine vinegar   3 tablespoons
Dijon mustard   1 tablespoon (optional)
Hard-cooked egg   1, quartered

1. Combine first 8 ingredients in the work bowl of a food processor. Blend with steel blade until herbs are finely chopped. Do not overblend; the ingredients should retain some texture.
2. Add egg and process briefly until coarsely blended.

Makes about 1¼ cups

Fruits

Two furlongs from my apartment lives a very special wild apple tree. It is small, as apple trees go, and it has chosen an odd place to grow and bear fruit—in the shade of tall cottonwoods and dense alders, surrounded by a thicket of salmonberries, its arching branches partially overgrown by wild blackberries.

This hidden apple tree grows only a few feet from a busy arterial street, yet its presence is largely unsuspected by the hurried commuters, schoolchildren, or joggers who pass within easy reach of its outlying sprigs. In summer, when the tree is showered with green light from the cottonwoods, grouse slink through its branches to taste the blackberry clusters which droop from the climbing vines, to peck at the ripening pomes which crowd the branches, or to nibble on the dewberries which sprawl across the forest floor. Later, raccoons and deer beat a path to the tree to harvest the fruit. I gingerly follow in their tracks to collect my share: any apples the wild animals cannot reach are mine.

I have been unable to determine to what named variety, if any, this apple tree belongs (nor do I much care). Who knows whether its parental core was surreptitiously flung from one of the electric streetcars which once passed this spot, hurled from a logging railroad which crossed Whatcom Creek only a dozen rods from the thicket, or tossed from a bouncing Model T? It is an old, heavy-trunked tree, bent and twisted from its life amid uncouth forest trees; but it is impossible to tell for how long it has flourished here in undisturbed seclusion. Created from a table scrap of human appetite, it now satisfies no human hunger but mine.

Apples fall into several major categories: summer apples which must be eaten soon after they ripen, for they will quickly lose their crispness and flavor, and winter apples which can be stored for long periods of time. The yellow Transparent, the McIntosh, the Gravenstein, the Astrachan, and the Tydeman red (along with many others) are all early ripening summer apples; the Northern Spy, the Spitzenburg, the russet, the Newton Pippin, the red Delicious, the Winesap, Spartan, Rome Beauty, Golden Delicious, Snow, et al., are winter apples.

We further divide apples by their cooking and eating qualities: some apples, like the Jonathan, Gravenstein, and Golden Delicious, are excellent for pies and sauces; others, like the red Romes, are best for baking; while a few, like the red Delicious, lose their flavor in cooking and should thus only be eaten raw. Much of the dissatisfaction voiced by consumers and food writers about modern apple varieties stems from their unreasonable demand (which would have appalled their grandparents) that each apple must be an all-round fruit, equally good for eating fresh, saucing, cooking, and baking. Such a demand arises from our newly acquired habits of supermarket shopping; we grab whatever is cheap, looks good, and is available all year long. We rarely stop to think about quality and seasonal peaks any more. Our forebears were more flexible in their attitudes: they planted different varieties of apples in their gardens to meet different culinary needs, harvesting the fruit as required, drying or canning any that would not keep.

I first encountered my favorite apple tree early one August, when I searched for a tart (unripe) cooking apple to add to a special cabbage dish. The yellow Transparents available in the markets were too sweet for my purpose, but I expected little trouble in finding what I needed. Within walking distance of my apartment, quite a number of wild apple trees push their branches through the oceanspray, alder, ninebark, thimbleberry, and crabapple underbrush which lines the forest edge. I explored their maturing fruit with probing fingers and a sharp knife, but none of them would do. Some showed their yellow Transparent ancestry by their early ripening—I ate a couple on the spot. Others, like the Snow hiding in the brambles across the street from our driveway, had fruit which was still too young and woody even for the cabbage pot.

A nervous ruffed grouse, undetected until it burst from a thicket with a noisy rush of wings, directed my attention to a corner of the woods where I had never before suspected an apple tree's existence. Yet here it was, heavily hung with large, yellow-green fruit. I plucked an apple, cut it in half, tasted its unripe flesh, and recognized that I had come to the end of my search. I filled my pockets with apples and returned home.

These apples surpassed my expectations. They cooked up firmly, keeping their shape well even when simmered with the red cabbage, and they had a deliciously tart flavor. I had picked more than I needed for dinner and stored the remainder in a plastic bag. Somehow the bag slipped out of sight behind a flour bin. The apples and the apple tree were forgotten until I rediscovered the bag some two months later, in October. I took a close look at the apples, expecting to find nothing but rotted mush. To my surprise the fruit had ripened to perfection. The apples were a rich green-tinged golden color now, still crisp and very tasty.

I quickly took a walk across the street to inspect the apple tree. Sure enough, it was loaded with ripe apples, all of them delicious and fragrant. The deer and raccoon had eaten their share from the lower branches, and I harvested the remainder. These apples stored well, but they did not last very long: they had such a nice flavor that Victoria and I could not resist the temptation and ate all of them in a very short time. The next year's crop was not quite as tasty—the summer had been very chilly—but in the following year the crop was once again of superior quality.

Weather plays an important role in the proper ripening of temperate climate fruit. Some, like apricots, nectarines, and peaches, like it warm and dry; others do best when the days are pleasantly warm and the nights cool. Most need an extended period of winter chilling to set good, tasty fruit in the following year.

A dozen years ago I translated a medical text written by a German naturopath doctor into English. It consisted primarily of dietary prescriptions for patients suffering from severe arthritis. Apples made up a large part of this healthful diet, but the good doctor warned with pronounced vehemence that his patients were to avoid both California and northwest apples at the risk of spoiling the efficacy of the treatment, because both of these regions were known for producing unhealthy, watery apples in overirrigated hot-climate orchards. This doctor had no notion, incidentally, of where California ended and where the Northwest began. He did, on the other hand, recommend British Columbia apples with fervor.

The whole treatise was amusing, because it showed to what an extent Europeans have become dependent on West Coast produce. But the doctor raised one objection which I have since heard reiterated over and over again: he cursed the red Delicious apple. Critical antipathy to this shiny red apple has risen to a shrill crescendo of distaste during the last several years, but neither the red Delicious apple nor the general quality of northwest fruit are at fault. I fear that our farmers and their produce may fall victim to the machinations of New York and other East Coast apple growers.

Even James Beard, the Northwest's best-known culinary native son, jumps on the bandwagon. He clearly voices his opinion in *American Cookery*: "I find that the apples shipped from Canada are often much better in New York than those shipped from the Northwest." Waverly Root, who lived in France for much of his life and who may never have tasted a fresh red Delicious from a prime orchard, also belittles our most popular apple. New York apple specialist Fred Lape waxes venomous when he discusses the red Delicious, calling it "beautiful red, slightly flavored sawdust." Which says more about Mr. Lape than it does about the red Delicious—one wonders how old the apple was which Mr. Lape ate.

The most interesting thing about the red Delicious in this context is the curious fact that it does not grow well along the East Coast. The Delicious does not develop its bright color until late in the season, and, under the sultry climatic conditions of the New York and New England orchards, this apple loses its crispness by the time the color has developed fully. Besides, which strain of the red Delicious do the critics condemn? When Washington State University counted the commercial strains of this apple back in 1969, there were more than one hundred and thirty different sports (variations) in common use—there are probably quite a few more by now—all with somewhat different characteristics.

This is not to say that the red Delicious is our best apple—it definitely is not—but to show that it has been maligned unjustly. The Northeast's main challenger to the primary status of the red Delicious in the heart of the American consumer has been the McIntosh. The McIntosh, also a deep red apple, is good for eating fresh as well as for baking and cooking, but it does not stay fresh and tasty for very long once it has been picked.

The red Delicious had been my wife's favorite apple for a number of years (until she discovered the Spartan), and a New York-born friend constantly teased her about this strange preference. Why, she asked, eat an inferior apple, when you can enjoy a good New York McIntosh? Well, we couldn't find any fresh New York apples in our markets, no matter where we searched, but later in the year our friend's parents came west from New York, and they brought a good supply of New York McIntoshes along. We tasted these apples: they were mealy and insipid. "Well," our visitors said, "what do you expect? They were picked a week ago. They can't be crisp anymore. But you should come to New York and try them fresh from the tree!"

And this is precisely where the much-maligned red Delicious has an advantage over the McIntosh and several other winter apple varieties: it keeps quite well in atmospherically controlled cold storage (where the temperature is kept low and most of the oxygen is replaced with carbon dioxide to arrest the apples' respiration), and, if handled properly, it will stay crisp and shiny for long periods of time. But this apple deteriorates rapidly once it is taken from its controlled storage environment; it may become mealy and flavorless within a period of a day or two. And this is where, in part, the red Delicious got its bad reputation. Fruit merchants and greengrocers should take only as many apples from the cold room as they sell in, say, half a day to make sure these apples stay fresh and crunchy.

When red Delicious apples are shipped from the Northwest to other markets, proper storage control must also be maintained at all times, or the apples will spoil en route. Here some unscrupulous operators may have done serious damage to the reputation of northwest apples. In recent years, large California processing houses have invested heavily in eastern Washington orchards, often planting new apple trees on land unsuitable for good fruit production. The apples from these orchards are frequently shipped to Japan, Taiwan, and China by slow freighter in noninsulated containers. Many of these shipments arrive as inedible mush—especially if the ship has crossed tropical waters—and many Asian importers, who feel rightly cheated, are beginning to buy their apples elsewhere from more conscientious growers and shippers.

Several years ago, I stopped eating commercially processed Washington apples for a similar reason. I just couldn't find anything but mushy, insipid, or mealy fruit in our markets. I still got my fill of apples, however. I learned to scout for wild apple trees, to eat my fill during the season, store what I could, and do without during the rest of the year. Starting in the coast ranges of northern California, I slowly ate my way north to British Columbia. I consumed a great number of apples—pippins, Gravensteins, and odd hybrids—and became convinced that the only good apples in the Northwest grew west of the mountains, whether this be in the Rogue River, Umpqua, or Willamette valleys, or along the inland waters of Washington and British Columbia, or in the hidden dales of the northern coast ranges and Cascades. I did make an exception for the Columbia Gorge and the Hood River Valley, but only because even the easternmost orchards of this fruit-growing region are still under the occasional influence of cool maritime air.

I had noticed with surprise that the farther north I traveled, the crisper and tastier the apples became. Yet I was also aware that during cool, wet years the apples grown on the west side of the Cascades did not reach their full flavor potential. There was just not enough warmth and sunshine to ripen them properly. About this time, I discovered wines made from Yakima Valley grapes. I had thought of the Yakima Valley as the "Yakima Desert," a torrid valley nestled in the arid interior regions, where heat and excess irrigation combined to produce watery fruit. Well, I now had to reevaluate my position, for I knew that a region which could produce fruity, delicate rieslings couldn't be all bad. This called for further research, and I finally paid the Yakima Valley a visit.

It just so happened that on the way to and from a barrel tasting at Hinzerling Vineyards in Prosser, I also ran into a lot of fruit orchards and stopped to buy some fruit fresh from the tree. It was at precisely this point that I stopped blaming Yakima growers for the inferior fruit I had previously suffered through, and began to blame the processors and shippers instead. I now mounted a series of trips through eastern Washington and British Columbia during the harvest seasons, trying to find the perfect apple. Despite a few positive surprises, I found that the summer climate of the Walla Walla Valley (and eastern Oregon, for that matter) is too warm to grow good apples. But the Yakima Valley was much better. I really took a liking to the apples grown in the western part of the valley, where the lowlands slope upward toward the Cascade foothills; even the orchards near Selah and in the Wenas Creek drainage produced good fruit, despite the scorched appearance of the encircling hills and ridges.

Yet the farther north I traveled in the Cascades, the better the apples grew. I had to discard several misconceived notions. The east side of the Cascades was neither as dry nor as consistently hot as I had been led to believe. The best growing regions offered a good mix of warm days and ample sunshine to ripen the apples, and cool nights to keep them crisp. I thus discovered that Wenatchee apples were crisper, fruitier, and had a richer, fuller taste than Yakima apples—though those from Peshastin, which is a little higher in the hills than Wenatchee, were even better. But even this far north, the apples grown on the hot plateaus, away from the mitigating influences of the Columbia River and the Cascades, were of lesser quality. I found my favorite apples, apples I liked even better than the best I had eaten on the west side, in the highland orchards bordering the Okanogan and Methow rivers. Here at last were apples to satisfy the pampered palate of a serious connoisseur.

Excellent apples are also grown north of the U.S. border, in the lake countries of the Okanagan and Columbia rivers. But the quality of British Columbia apples depends very much on the climate (and on the amount of irrigation water the individual horticulturalist allots to his trees—even in a cool climate too much irrigation may make the apples watery and tasteless). During cold years, British Columbia apples may lack sufficient sugar and fruit, but in warm years, when Oregon and Washington apples may suffer from excessive heat, the Canadian apples are at their best. In very hot years, the apples grown in the northern Okanagan, in the Spallumcheen Valley, and in the Shuswap country are superb. Even the temperamental McIntosh flourishes here, developing its best taste (much better than that of New York apples) in the orchards to the north of Kelowna.

I discovered two of my favorite apples in the Methow and Okanogan river orchards: the Tydeman red, a large crisp, summer apple—far superior to the McIntosh—does exceptionally well near Omak and Tonasket. Unfortunately, it does not keep long and must be eaten fresh during its short season of less than a month (from the end of August to about the middle of September). But it is well worth searching out.

The Spartan, a red (or reddish/brown) Newton Pippin/McIntosh hybrid, keeps just about as well as the red Delicious, but it stays much crisper and has a far better taste. It ripens late, but stays commonly available until the next season's crop is picked. Ah, for the miracle of cold storage! Its closest competitor, the red Delicious, on the other hand, keeps so well in cold storage that fruit growers may continue to sell the last year's crop after the new crop has already been picked. The current crop just goes into storage, too, until all of the old crop is sold. Only the consumer suffers. You may think you are buying a fresh apple, new from the harvest, when you are actually buying fruit that may be a year old, or even older.

Washington State is the largest commercial apple producer in the nation, with an estimated sixty-five to sixty-seven million bushels produced in 1982. In an average year, Washington State grows two-and-a-half to three times as many apples as its closest competitor, New York State. One reason for this astounding success is that a great number of different apple varieties do well north of the Columbia River. Apples show a greater variability than most of the other tree fruits (there are several thousand named varieties of apples), and more than a dozen are commercially significant in our region.

The red Delicious is by far our most popular apple, followed by the (unrelated) Golden

Delicious. This is another much-maligned apple. It fails to reach its best development in New York State, but it does well in the Pacific Northwest and in Europe (more than 50 percent of the apples produced in France, for example, are now Golden Delicious). It is a good all-purpose apple that makes good applesauce, holds its shape well in pies, and is truly delicious when eaten fresh—and ripe—from the tree. The Winesap, our third most common variety, is also an excellent all-purpose apple, but its tart, vinous flavor makes it especially good for cider. The Jonathan, McIntosh, Granny Smith, Northern Spy, and Spitzenburg are all good multipurpose apples. The red Rome and the Newton Pippin are very good for baking, the Gravenstein is unsurpassed for applesauce, and the early summer varieties— Lodi, yellow Transparent, Viking, and Summer Red—are best for eating fresh.

Apple growing is not a static pursuit. New varieties are constantly introduced. Besides the Spartan and Tydeman red, several other new and promising apples have been planted extensively during the last decade: the Golden Criterion and the Jonagold show particular promise. But so do the wild, naturally hybridized apple trees. As much fun as I have visiting fruit stands, farmers' markets, and orchards in my continuing quest for tasty apples, I still prefer to look for wild apple trees along streams, in pastures, and along country lanes. I never know what different taste sensations and textures await me, and I get to savor the excitement and anticipation of a personal "hunt" for the perfect apple.

Despite the large quantities of apples locally available west of the Cascades, many northwest apple fanciers still believe that all of our commercially grown apples are produced east of the mountains. This has never been true, of course. Small orchards persist throughout many of our valleys (not to mention the Willamette Valley), and during the harvest season the itinerant gourmet will find copious quantities of fresh local apples for sale—in front yards, garages, and fruit stands—along most of the highways leading into the high country, or along the winding roads which cross the Coast Range to the beaches. While the commercial orchards, even the best, must concentrate on a few varieties that will sell well and store well, the small growers and home growers will often experiment with peculiar or uncommon varieties. I buy such rare apples as Northern Spies and russets from a local farmer (though the Northern Spy will not do as well in the Northwest as it does in the Northeast: it needs the hot, muggy evenings of East Coast summers to ripen properly and develop fruitiness and sugar). Scanning produce ads in regional newspapers will often lead the apple fancier to tasty varieties whose presence in our region would be otherwise quite unsuspected.

Commercial tree fruit production was once common in the San Juan Islands and on the lowlands of the Puget Sound Trough, before the large corporate farms of the Yakima Valley captured the market with inexpensively produced fruit and made it impossible for west-side farmers to grow apples economically. The San Juan Islands' orchards have lain idle for several decades, producing their apples only for deer, raccoon, and those fanciers who were willing to search them out and pick them. But during the last several years, a new interest in small-scale farming has led to a resurrection of the old orchards and to new plantings, especially on Orcas and Lopez islands, in northern Whatcom County, and in the Skagit Valley. Many of these orchards are planted to Lodis, yellow Transparents, Gravensteins, and other early apples; but Winter Bananas, Pearmains, Kings, and Cox's Orange Pippin (of which Waverly Root says "the British boast that it is the finest dessert apple in the world") are also grown. Many new and tasty varieties, plus some rediscovered old ones, should be available in years to come.

Pears, closely related to apples, have also spread throughout our area in both orchards and woodlots. But they are more finicky about their environment than the apple and are thus not as common in the wild. Nor do wild pears taste quite as good as wild apples do, for pears will not produce prime fruit unless they are well tended. There is, furthermore, one other big difference between apples and pears: our domesticated apple trees are derived from wild apple and crabapple trees, whose fruit is very tasty, though it may be somewhat small and astringent. The wild pear, on the other hand, is small, hard, and bitter (this harshness disappears in cooking), and all but inedible. Oh, I've tried to eat them, but I commonly gagged after a bite or two; and I've also tried to ripen them off the tree, but without success. Wild pears are good pickled in brandy (drink the brandy and throw out the pear).

Ripening the fruit off the tree is, strange as this may seem, the only way of getting excellent, soft pears (you want your apples crisp, but your pears soft). Pears are an exception to the rule that tree-ripened fruit is best. All pears have grit cells (also called stone cells) in their flesh, which are produced more plentifully as the pear ripens on the tree. The longer a pear stays on the tree, the grittier it may be. Picked after it reaches its maximum size and separated from the source of its vigor, pears stop growing grit cells (and may even reabsorb them) and become soft and tender—and sweet. The grit cells also seem to be the source of bitterness in pears, for the wild, tree-ripened pears are very bitter as well as coarsely gritty, while our more luscious commercially grown pears, plucked before they are mature and ripened in a cool, dark environment, become very toothsome—much sweeter than the fruit would be had it been left on the tree to ripen in the sun.

The Pacific Northwest is pear country par excellence. Somehow the climate and soils combine to make this the world's greatest pear-growing country. Pears are also grown in northern California, and in considerable quantities, but the quality is just not the same. California pears grow too fast. Overwatered and exposed to an excessively hot climate, the fruit matures long before it has a chance to develop a good flavor. California pears have lots of sugar, but no taste.

Pears are trees of the northern temperate zones: most must undergo a period of winter chilling, or they may not flower and set fruit in the coming growing season. The gritty little Kieffers and La Contes will grow and produce fruit in mild winter climates, but even the adaptable Bartlett pear likes its winters frosty. Pears can tolerate hot summers (though their fruit will not), but they do best in cool to warm summer climates, with a few weeks of hot weather to raise the sugar levels during the ripening. About a dozen or so pear varieties are commonly grown in the Northwest, but only a few are marketed on a regular basis.

The Bartlett, also known as the Williams pear or Bon Chretien, is the standard pear of the Pacific Northwest (and the U.S.; it takes up some 75 percent of the pear plantings). It is a luscious pear, sweet and tender, and may be eaten cooked, baked, or raw. It comes in several models. The large, golden summer Bartlett is picked as early as August in some of our growing areas; the somewhat smaller winter Bartlett is ready to be eaten in October. The red Bartlett, a deeply reddish sport, is sweeter and sturdier than its golden ancestor, but it does not hold up as well in cooking. None of the Bartletts last long in storage. The tour de force of Bartlett-dom is, of course, the famous *Poire William*, a distilled pear spirit. It is often enhanced by a pear grown in a clear bottle: the pear is placed in the bottle when it is still young and very small, the ripe pear is detached from its branch spur in fall, and, after the bottle is filled with pear spirit, the ripe fruit continues to impart its essence to the liqueur.

The small, aromatic Seckel pear has a rich, liqueurlike taste of its own. It is good to eat raw (though it is somewhat gritty), but it is even better when it is pickled in brandy (drink the brandy and eat the pear). The soft and sweet Clapp's Favorite, the tart, speckled Forelle, and the savory Flemish Beauty are more often found in home gardens and small orchards than in city markets (look for these pears at farmers' markets and fruit stands), but the superb Bosc and d'Anjou are readily available.

The russet-colored Bosc is a strange-looking pear, long and lean, with a thin neck (somewhat like a crookneck squash). Its flavor can be sublime. This pear is good eaten raw and holds up excellently in cooking and baking. The Bosc keeps very well in cold storage, but it must be ripened at room temperature. The squat, juicy d'Anjou, which ripens as late as November in the more northerly parts of the Pacific Northwest, keeps exceptionally well in cold storage and may be found in our markets as late as April (or even later). It is also better if ripened at room temperature for a few days after purchase. The winter Nelis, the ugly duckling of peardom, hides a refined taste beneath its rough exterior. It is an excellent small pear that would be much more popular if it were graced with a more appealing appearance. The winter Nelis is not only delicious, but it also keeps well. Before the advent of modern storage methods, this hardy pear was planted widely throughout the Northwest because it would last for a long time without special treatment or the need for expensive cold storage.

All of these pears do well throughout our region, but the best commercial pears are grown in several intermountain valleys where cold winters and warm summers—with the necessary hot spell—combine to form ideal growing conditions. Cool, moist summer regions, like western Washington, or hot summer areas like Transcascadia, produce good, but not outstanding, pears. Washington pears are thus surpassed in flavor by Hood River and Willamette Valley pears, and these are in turn exceeded by the pears grown in the fat bottomland orchards of the Rogue River and its tributaries. It is here that the queen of pears, the sybaritic Doyenne de Comice, reaches its pinnacle.

The Rogue River Valley is, without doubt, not only the best pear growing area of the Pacific Northwest, but of the entire continent (if not the world). First planted to fruit in the 1850s and 1860s, the valley boomed with the arrival of the railroad in 1884. As in other parts of the Northwest, every agricultural commodity was tried out at least once, from vegetable farming to cheese making. The climate seemed favorable to the growing of tree fruits, and apples, pears, peaches, and even exotic almond trees (these didn't last) were planted. The apples had problems adapting to the heavy clay soils of the valley and, after 1910, most apple trees were replaced by pear trees, which grew well in the sticky adobe clay of the bottomlands and produced fruit of an exceptional quality. The quantity of the fruit produced on each tree has remained below that of the irrigated orchards of northern California and eastern Washington, but the quality is much higher. And the fickle, fragrant, velvety Comice just loves the Rogue River Valley.

Today, the orchards of southwestern Oregon are the last region in the world where this luscious pear is still grown in any quantity. True, there are plantings in Washington and in the Hood River Valley, but they are very small, and the quality of the pears is just not the same. In 1982, much of the Rogue River Comice crop was lost to windfall, but Hood River pears reached the market in fair quantities. It was easy to tell the difference, just by smelling a pear. The Hood River Comices showed the breeding of their variety, but they lacked the culinary nobility of the Rogue River pears.

The Comice is a very difficult pear to grow and send to market. Unless conditions are exactly to its liking, it will not produce fruit; unless the weather is just right, the fruit will not reach its best development; and after the pears are picked, they bruise with maddening ease. Comice pickers have to be specially trained: the pears are gently plucked off the tree, immediately wrapped in tissue paper, and carefully placed in boxes. They won't withstand even a breath of mishandling. A bruised Comice rots very quickly. Twixt the tree and the consumer, the growers and shippers are plagued with constant fears of spoilage. For this reason, most Comice pears today are shipped by mail order only—the shippers send them out when they are still firm enough to handle but not so ripe as to liquify in transit.

Little wonder the Comice has become exceedingly rare and expensive—most growers just cannot handle the labor and expense of producing this fragile pear. Even the French, who love the honeyed Comice above all other pears, now have to order theirs from Oregon. While the Comice is not inexpensive, it is worth its high price. It is inimitable: tender, juicy with a nectarlike sweetness, perfumed with an ambrosial, very delicate yet distinct fragrance of pear, and it is unbelievably tender and delicious. Every true pear fancier must eat it at least once a year. If you don't trust the shippers, drive to southern Oregon in late October and buy the pears directly from the growers (culls and less-than-perfect fruit sell for ridiculously low prices). It will be a very rewarding trip.

One other pear is making inroads into Pacific Northwest orchards. The Chinese sand-pear, an apple-shaped, gritty russet pear, has been around for a long time, but until recently it has been unpopular among western connoisseurs because of its somewhat coarse texture. Part of the problem lies in the handling: this oriental pear must be fully tree-ripened before it may be eaten. When it is picked in the subripe state, like other pears, it will be (and will stay) watery and insipid. But when it is picked at the peak of its ripeness, it is surprisingly tender, only slightly gritty, and very flavorful and aromatic.

I had no idea of how good an oriental pear could be until I bought several from a Japanese gardener at Seattle's Pike Place Market in the fall of 1982. The pears were available for a scant two weeks and, though I searched for them afterward, I could not find any more. I purchased several underripe oriental pears at markets in Portland, Seattle, Bellingham, and Vancouver, but none of these ripened properly in storage. They were very gritty and insipid when I bought them, and they were mushy and insipid when I threw them out a few days later. Several Bosc and d'Anjou pears kept in the same basket had ripened to perfection during the same period of time.

Besides pears, among the fruits grown on the West Coast, (tree-ripened) apricots are among my favorites. Until quite recently, I would have wholeheartedly agreed with Waverly Root, who claims that California produces the best apricots in the world for eating fresh. I have spent quite a bit of time in California apricot orchards, eating the ripe fruit fresh from the tree (they ripen just before the pears) and I was firmly convinced that I knew perfectly well how the best apricots should taste. My early experiences in the Pacific Northwest only served to confirm my bias. Apricots never reach their full flavor if they are picked before they are ripe, and I could only find underripe and insipid apricots in west-side markets. After repeatedly tasting these mere shadows of apricots, I had a very low opinion of the quality of northwest apricots. They just weren't worth the bother. They might be good enough for making sugared "cotlets," but they shouldn't be eaten fresh.

It was at about this time that I happened upon my first tree-ripened Washington apricots. Victoria and I were returning from a trip to eastern Washington and before we crossed Stevens Pass to the west side, we stopped at a small orchard fruit stand in Peshastin to restock our snack box. I dubiously eyed some local apricots, but when the proprietor insisted I try one, I grudgingly submitted to the ordeal. It was quite an experience. Expecting a watery, flavorless mush, I was instead overwhelmed by the burst of flavor that expanded in my mouth. This apricot was unlike any I had ever eaten. It was sumptuous, honeyed, and fruity, yet firm-fleshed. It was, in short, delicious! I had just experienced my first Wenatchee Moorpark.

This called for further exploration. During the rest of the apricot season, I discovered Perfections, which deserved their name; these irregularly, lump-shaped apricots had a very concentrated taste—almost like the best of dried apricots, intense yet fresh flavored. But I came to like the tree-ripened Tiltons the best. These very small, plum-sized apricots with firm, medium-orange flesh surprised me with their flavor, more delicate and balanced than the Perfection, a fat apricotness with a delicious undertaste of ripe Mirabelle plums. These Tiltons came from the Yakima Valley, and, though I spent some time buying different batches of apricots and tasting back and forth, I have as yet not decided whether I like these the best or the Wenatchee Moorparks.

The excellence of tree-ripened northwest apricots should have come as no surprise to me. Apricots are no southern trees; they are native to northern China (the prototypes grow wild in mountains near Beijing), and they should thus do best in moderate climes. There are a few problems with the cultivation of apricots on our continent, however. Apricots dislike cool, wet weather—they develop brown rot and blight—and they cannot take excessive winter cold. The trees need some frost during the dormant season before they will bloom the next spring, yet their blooms come very early and are damaged by late spring frosts. Their sumptuous fruit reaches its best development when ripening in moderate heat and in the long hours of summer sunshine found in the northerly latitudes of the Pacific Northwest, but it quickly turns flat and insipid or even watery if the trees receive too much heat and irrigation water. The quality of apricots, like that of wine grapes, varies from year to year.

Peach trees and nectarines (which are basically smooth-skinned peaches) have even more problems than apricots. Most varieties need a minimum of two months of freezing weather in the winter to set good fruit the next summer, but they also like hot, sunny summers. They have thus done very well on the East Coast, and tasty varieties have even been developed for different mild-winter Californian climates. The Pacific Northwest produces large quantities of excellent peaches, but it is hard to tell if their quality exceeds that of peaches grown elsewhere. The only peaches and nectarines from the Northwest I have tasted that seemed exceptional came from the Methow Valley; more precisely from orchards planted on glacial kame terraces above the lower Methow River. Both were, of course, tree ripened. The peaches were small, somewhat lumpy, Red Havens. They were powerfully fragrant with an intense, peach and flower aroma, and a deep, complex, almost liqueurlike flavor. The nectarines were Red Golds picked fresh from the tree on a hot day in mid-September. They were juicy and had a depth of flavor which I had hitherto missed in nectarines. This just goes to show that I have to work on my peach and nectarine taste threshhold—who knows what else I may find down the seasons.

Plums and prunes also produce excellent fruit in the Pacific Northwest, on both sides of the mountains. The Willamette Valley and the lower Columbia River region once supported an extensive prune industry, and vast prune orchards and tall prune driers (large barns filled with shelves for drying prunes) once dotted the landscape. But the northwest prune industry was eclipsed by competition from California (where prunes were produced more cheaply), and today most of our prunes are grown for the fresh market. This is quite a gain for the lover of fresh fruit, for our prunes are superbly flavorful. California may have captured the market for dried prunes, but it has not succeeded in matching the exquisite flavor of our fresh prunes and plums.

Three prunes in particular rise to the apex of culinary heights in the Pacific Northwest. The small, blue-black, green-fleshed Damson plum (which makes excellent jams, jellies, and tarts), the delectable Greengage (or reine claude), by far my favorite plum, and the runner-up of my fancy, the big, plump Italian prune, purplish-black like the Damson, but fat and sweet instead of tart.

The West Coast's only wild plum, the shrubby Klamath plum, a tart but tasty little fruit, only grows as far north as the Willamette Valley. It is too astringent for most people to eat raw (unless the summer was exceptionally warm and the fruit has ripened out with extra sugar), but it makes superb preserves and sauces. The domestic plum (the Damson plum and its relatives) has occasionally escaped from cultivation in the Pacific Northwest, especially in western Idaho and along the Snake River, but the only introduced plum which I have found growing wild in different parts of the Northwest is the blackthorn, better known as an ingredient in sloe gin than as a table fruit.

Other regions may dispute the primacy of the Northwest's plums and prunes, but none can match the quality of the sweet cherries grown in our region. I can speak from long and thorough experience, because I have tasted cherries from the best of the world's growing regions, and I have found none to be as delectable as the luscious cherries grown in the Pacific Northwest.

I began to like cherries early in life and have maintained an active culinary interest in this toothsome drupe ever since. In my early teens, I made a precious discovery—a sweet cherry tree which had sprung up in a remote woodlot, tall and majestic, and partly overhanging a cow pasture. Over the years I developed a proprietary interest in this tree, waiting for it to bloom each spring, taking sprigs of its blossoms home with me and, as the season advanced, visiting it several times a week to check on the ripeness of its fruit. Then, when the cherries were ripe and red and juicy, they all belonged to me—and to the birds. Birds just dote on cherries, and the ripe fruit rarely survived their predacious incursions for more than a few days. I consumed my share amid a cacophony of twitters, trills, warbles, and chirps. For a few glorious days, the birds and I feasted on fresh, sweet cherries, and then it was all over until the next year.

Only in the Pacific Northwest did I once again find cherries whose flavor matched that of the special cherries of my youth (a flavor which is entrenched in my taste memory, perhaps embellished, but vivid nevertheless). Yet in the Northwest I was suddenly confronted with an embarrassment of riches. The Northwest's fresh cherry season lasts only for about a month and a half, but during this period one variety after the other tempts the palate.

First come the Burlats, then the Deacons and the sweet yellow, pink-blushed Rainiers and Royal Anns. These are followed by the deep red Chinook, the black Tartarian, the Van, and, finally, the noble Bing. The deep red, intensely flavored Bing is a hard cherry to follow, but the black Republican tries, and the late-ripening black Lambert (perhaps the most perfect incarnation of sweet commercial cherrydom) even surpasses the Bing. It is larger, firmer, has a more intense flavor with a tart undertang which makes it a more interesting fruit than the often subacid Bing. Together the Bing and the Lambert dominate the northwest cherry industry, making up 95 percent of the crop.

Our sweet cherries grow best in warm-weather regions, the Willamette Valley (the Bing was developed near Portland by a Chinese gardener), the Hood River Valley, along the Columbia River near The Dalles, in the Yakima Valley and from the Wenatchee River Valley. The best of these cherries come from the small orchards which perch high above the Columbia Gorge on cliff-top terraces. Cherries grown on the east side of the mountains may fail to develop sufficient acid and thus remain flat in taste during excessively hot years. At such times, the best sweet cherries in the Northwest are produced in the Shuswap country of British Columbia. Sweet cherries are very susceptible to climatic variations: rain falling at the wrong time can quickly destroy a ripening crop of Bing cherries, for example. The cherries soak up too much water and burst.

Pie cherries, also known as "sour" cherries, do not face that problem, nor do they need the large quantities of sunshine necessary for producing high levels of sugar, and they thus do well on both sides of the Cascades. Sour cherries are seldom available in our city markets, but U-pick orchards are spread throughout our region, and sour cherries are often found at farmers' markets and fruit stands. Our native cherries are even tarter than the sour cherries. Aptly named chokecherries and bitter cherries, they can add an interesting flavor to pies, jams, and preserves, but they are too astringent to be eaten by themselves. Both the sweet and sour domestic cherries have occasionally escaped from cultivation, but we lack the abundance of wild cherries (and plums) enjoyed by the East and Midwest. What our region lacks in tasty wild cherries, it more than makes up for in a splendid abundance of wild berries.

Several years ago Victoria and I quite literally stumbled upon one of our region's most exquisite delicacies. We were ambling along a coastal bluff in southern Oregon, looking at wild flowers, butterflies, bees, and birds, when we spotted a large colony of leather-leaved coastal strawberries (*Fragaria chiloensis*) among the seaside daisies and cliff grasses. We were in luck; the plants were loaded down with large numbers of small, red fruit. These tiny berries were sweet, juicy, and flavorful. We just sat ourselves in their midst and ate our fill. A few years later, we discovered the equally tasty common wild strawberry (*Fragaria virginiana*) growing on the bluffs and prairies of Whidbey Island and, later still, the wild field strawberry (*Fragaria vesca*). But you need not worry about which of these wild strawberries you encounter; they are all equally delicious.

The Pacific Northwest grows not only exceptionally flavorful wild strawberries, but delicious commercial strawberries as well. Domestic strawberries will grow almost anywhere; but they demand special growing conditions to bring out the best in their flavor. They need warmth for sugar and fruitiness, but they do not prosper in very hot climes. They need water, but they will turn insipid with too much irrigation, and they will rot during long spells of wet weather. They also need our long northern summer days for good flavor development. Within certain limits, the farther north strawberries are grown, the better.

Commercial strawberries are grown in both the Willamette Valley and the Puget Trough, but it is difficult to determine where precisely our best strawberries originate. A lot depends on the weather which predominates in a given year, on the variety of berry grown, and on the way the berries are treated, both before and after they are picked.

Strawberries do exceptionally well in the warmer parts of the Puget Sound region, in valleys opening from the mountains onto the lowlands, and on islands where the sky will be sunny, by some climatic and geographic quirk, while it rains elsewhere. The Puyallup Valley, Bainbridge Island, Whidbey Island, and the Nooksack and Fraser valleys all produce excellent berries. But our best strawberries may well come from the Sequim region of the northwestern Olympic Peninsula, and from the sunny fields of southwestern Vancouver Island. Both areas receive more than their share of summer sunshine because they lie in the rain shadow of high coastal mountains, and they are far enough to the north to get the benefit of the long summer days. Farther to the south, strawberries are commonly grown during cool spring weather when the temperatures are mild. Yet this also means very short days: no wonder California strawberries have so little flavor. In the Northwest, strawberries ripen in June, at about the time of the summer solstice, when the daylight hours are at their longest (during summer, northern Washington and southern British Columbia have about two more hours of daylight than central California does).

The question of strawberry varieties is even more complicated. Growers prefer to raise berries which ripen all at once, at the time when school lets out for the summer. This assures a ready supply of eager, inexpensive labor for picking (no one has yet discovered an effective method for harvesting strawberries by machine). The home gardener here has an advantage over the farmer, because he can grow Quinault berries, which bear delectable fruit over a long period of time. As long as the weather stays warm, there should always be a few ripening berries in the garden.

The commercial grower also has to select berries that will survive handling, shipping, and processing (mostly freezing), and which are resistant to diseases. Unfortunately, strawberries are very susceptible to such diseases as leafspot, red stele, root rot, and verticillum wilt, not to speak of slugs and bugs. To make things worse, even disease-tolerant varieties often lose their resistance after a period of time and must be replaced with new, still-resistant berries. Thus the excellent Marshall was replaced by the Northwest, and the Northwest is in turn giving way to the Shuksan.

There are some berries that stand out because of their quality (though I sometimes wonder if the place of origin is at least as important as the variety). Hood strawberries in Oregon, and Rainiers from Washington are always good buys. But there are many other excellent commercial varieties. They all show slight variations in their adaptation to soils and climate, and a berry that is excellent in one year may have to concede "best of show" to a different variety in the next, because of the unpredictable variability of our climate.

One summer I liked the Rainiers grown in the Puyallup Valley the best. The next summer we held a tasting of Oregon and Washington berries and decided that we preferred the Bentons grown in northern Whatcom County (the Benton, originally an Oregon berry, is incidentally also an excellent berry for the home garden), followed by Puget Beauties, Shuksans from the same area, Puyallup Rainiers, Sauvie Island and Willamette Valley Hoods and, in last place, Totems, a low-acid, low-flavor British Columbia variety. But then, a few weeks later, a friend brought some Shuksans from Sequim, which were so tasty that they eclipsed any of the berries we had previously sampled. And, of course, the taste of strawberries may vary not only from season to season, and from area to area, but also from grower to grower and sometimes from one day to the next (a single rainstorm can make a difference). So, there is just one thing to do: a true strawberry fancier must keep up a constant search for the perfect berry and eat as many of these juicy morsels as possible, year after year.

Our strawberry season lasts for only a few weeks but, as luck would have it, it is followed right away by the raspberry season, which is in turn followed by the blueberry season. This takes us from early June all the way to October. And once the fresh berries run out, we still get to enjoy frozen ones.

Idaho and eastern Washington have two species of savory wild raspberries, but throughout most of our region we must do with two "lesser" raspberries: the salmonberry and the thimbleberry. At least we have a flavorful black raspberry west of the Pend Oreille and Palouse. Our tastiest wild raspberry is, unfortunately, also our least common, and it is not grown commercially. Even where it is common, it does not produce much fruit unless conditions are just right. Victoria and I encountered this delectable berry as soon as we moved to the Puget Sound region. It grew right outside our first house (along with tiny wild blackberries), and we had a good supply for one long, glorious summer. However, we haven't been that fortunate since.

Red raspberries are grown commercially throughout the Pacific Northwest (the best come from the Fraser Valley, where more than 50 percent of the North American raspberry crop is grown), but not many farmers bother with the domestic blackberry. This berry, also known as the Himalayan blackberry (nobody seems to know why), has escaped from cultivation and adapted so well to our region that it is well on its way to becoming the most common shrub west of the Cascades (what the Kudzu vine is to the South, the Himalayan berry is to the Northwest, but the berry tastes better than the Kudzu). It is much easier to pay pickers to gather these "wild" berries than it is to grow them in well-manicured rows. The supply of these large, tasty (though somewhat seedy) berries is more than sufficient for all comers.

This berry reaches its best development, in both size and flavor, in coastal Oregon and in western Washington and British Columbia. It is not as delectable as the small, sprawling native blackberry (dewberry) and it does not hold its shape as well in pies, but it is still a very good berry. I like to mix its fresh juice with sugar and kirsch, to make a deeply colored, flavorful cordial.

Another introduced blackberry, the Evergreen or cut-leaf blackberry, has also become very common (it is currently infesting my flower bed). Its berries, which ripen later than the other blackberries, are very firm and have a rich, vinous taste. They hold up better in pies than the Himalayan berries, and they also make an excellent syrup and cordial.

The Pacific Northwest has several species of small, mostly high-mountain blackberries, but our most common and most beloved berry is the small-fruited dewberry (or Pacific blackberry). It is abundant west of the Cascades in clearings, meadows, logged-over areas, at the edge of thickets, in open woods, and sometimes even in dense forests. This tart (sometimes, though rarely, it is even sweet) little blackberry (about a quarter the size of the Himalayan berry) is the pie blackberry par excellence. Sugaring and baking really bring out its flavor, but I also like to eat it fresh from the vine.

The dewberry does not make as good a syrup as either the Himalayan berry or the Evergreen blackberry, because it is so firm, but then very few cooks are able to pick it in sufficiently large quantities to indulge in such a luxury. Not only are the berries spaced sparsely along the sprawling vines, but this blackberry has both male and female plants—the male produces flowers, but no fruit. Many berry fanciers have returned to a berry patch they marked out when it was in full bloom, only to find no berries later in the season because the entire patch consisted of male plants. Experts can tell the difference between the male and female flowers, but I find it easier to remember the spots where I have once picked the wild blackberry in profusion and return year after year to gather my share.

Early last summer, as the small, wild blackberries were just beginning to ripen, and when the local raspberries had just reached their peak of perfection, we bought a flat of luscious Puyallup raspberries and a box of early loganberries. Since the loganberry (like the raspberry) is a cross between the blackberry and the raspberry, Victoria decided to conduct a taste test to see which of these berries had the best flavor. She baked six tart shells, and we set out to find some wild blackberries. We were able to gather a more than sufficient quantity in a very short time and, since the weather was fine and berry picking was such fun, we added two wild raspberries to the test: thimbleberries and salmonberries. Then, just for contrast (and because they were ripe), we also picked a mess of red huckleberries (we looked for blackcaps but couldn't find any, and the Himalayan berries and the Evergreen blackberries were far from ripe). We now had six different berries to compare.

Victoria filled the tart shells with the different berries and finished them off with a simple fruit glaze (berry juice, sugar, cornstarch). The results were in part predictable, in part unexpected. The small wild dewberries lived up to their reputation. The raspberries were delicately fruity; the loganberries less so. The salmonberries were disappointingly insipid, with a bitter undertaste. The red huckleberries had become transformed in the light cooking provided by the gentle heat of the glaze. They were still pleasantly tart, yet had acquired a fruitiness and complexity of which the raw berries had shown only a hint. But the thimbleberries brought us the greatest surprise.

Thimbleberries are very fragile, and they crush easily. Victoria had packed as many of them as possible into the tart shell by squishing them down with the back of a spoon. The glaze gave off just enough heat to bring out the full flavor of the berries. They were superb, with a rich, mouth-filling brambleberry taste.

The little red huckleberry which did so well in our tasting is only one of some fourteen representatives of its genus that grow in the Pacific Northwest. They range from the small, native cranberry (and the larger, commercial cranberry) of our coastal bogs to the bright red grouseberry of alpine slopes, from the shot-sized purplish-black Evergreen huckleberry of the Coast to the big black, high-bush huckleberry of the mountain forests and the small, exceptionally tasty blueberries of alpine meadows, lakeshores, and bogs.

The large, thick, and somewhat mealy commercial cranberry is grown extensively in specially prepared bogs along the Oregon coast and in southwestern Washington. It is a nice berry, good for being cooked with sugar to accompany a Thanksgiving dinner, but it lacks the character of the small native cranberry. The commercial growers harvest their cranberries in the fall by flooding the bogs. The ripe berries break off the branchlets, float to the surface, and are scooped up by man or machine.

Harvesting the wild cranberry is not that simple. I have spent long hours on my knees, gathering wild cranberries from the tiny shrubs which hide among the lichens, willows, and labrador tea of protected dune slack areas, where small patches of highly acidic humus allow the cranberries to flourish. And I have gingerly traipsed along the edges of sphagnum bogs in search of these delectable tidbits. There is no commercial supply of these berries and you must collect your own if you want to enjoy them. This is hard work, but definitely worth the effort (and the inevitably wet feet).

Blueberries are grown commercially throughout our region. They are generally very tasty, far superior to the commercial berries grown elsewhere. The best blueberries are produced in the cool, long summer daylight of the Nooksack and Fraser River valleys. As with cranberries, a large size can mean a lack of taste in the berries, but the growers prefer to plant their fields to the bulkier, easier-to-harvest large berries. Besides, blueberries are commonly sold by the box, not by weight, and it is easy to see that it takes fewer large berries to fill a box.

The consumer suffers, because the large berries don't have a full blueberry flavor. But a number of conscientious growers have solved this problem by planting their fields to several different varieties of blueberries, from very small, highly flavored berries to large, mild-tasting ones. Up to three of these varieties are sometimes mixed together. This allows the producer to achieve a fair amount of bulk, but it also presents the blueberry fanciers with a good overall flavor in the berries they buy (this is especially important when these berries are used in pies, pancakes, or other dishes).

But no matter how good some of our commercial blueberries taste, they are still no match for their wild cousins. Our best blueberries grow on the low, creeping shrubs of the high mountain meadows. One of these, the Cascade blueberry, which ranges from southern British Columbia to northern Oregon throughout the high Cascades and Olympic Mountains, is so tasty that botanists have bestowed the specific name *deliciosum* onto this flavorful berry. There is as much difference in taste between this blueberry and the black huckleberry of the lower slopes as there is between the latter and the commercial blueberry.

Fortunately, northwest blueberry fanciers can enjoy both berries, without a conflict in their picking schedules. Depending on the altitude, the black huckleberry ripens from August to September; the Cascade blueberry is commonly ready from September into October, often staying on the shrub until just before the winter's first snowfall covers the plants.

Each year, Victoria and I make a special effort to pick as many wild berries as possible, starting with shoreside strawberries and finishing with wild cranberries and alpine blueberries. There is only one berry I enjoy which Victoria refuses to eat. And it's all my fault.

A decade ago, on one of our early forays into the Puget Sound country, we camped at Deception Pass State Park. Our secluded campsite was enclosed by lush salal bushes, just festooned with ripe berries. We had traveled far that day, and we were very hungry. I did the cooking. I felt like experimenting (in spite of my tiredness—or perhaps because of it), picked a large quantity of salal berries, and mixed them into our rice. I don't remember the exact quantity, but it was at least half and half. The rice was now deeply purple. We quickly learned that salal-flavored rice and barbecued salmon steaks do not go well together, but we were so hungry, we ate the entire awful mess. Victoria hasn't eaten any salal berries since (nor can she stand to watch me eat them).

I have never ceased to enjoy these blackish, somewhat resiny, and very common berries. I often pick them as I gather wild apples. But then I like to eat every one of our superb northwest fruits, whether they be pomes, berries, or drupes, as frequently as possible, preferably in season. And I commonly make a point to serve the best and freshest of our fruits as dessert whenever I have dinner guests from other parts of the country (especially from California). It's just plain fun to show off with our superbly delicious fruits.

Late-Harvest Riesling over Peaches

Here's a simple but tasty Yakima Valley dessert recipe from Louise Rauner, wife of Yakima River Winery wine maker John Rauner.

Tree-ripened peaches 4
Cherries 8, pitted
Late-harvest riesling 1 bottle

1. Peel and quarter peaches.
2. Place one peach quarter in a champagne glass.
3. Top with a pitted cherry.
4. Fill glass with riesling. Serve chilled. Accompany with remaining wine (or top off glass from time to time, as you sip).

Serves 8

Dried Fruit Whip

Several of the fruits grown in the Pacific Northwest dry well: apples, apricots, peaches, prunes, et al. Dried fruit can be reconstituted in water, but it is so much better when it is reconstituted in a spicy wine, like the Oregon muscat produced by Tualatin Vineyards. Here's a recipe from Virginia Fuller of Tualatin that contains a great suggestion on handling dried fruits. Serve with well-chilled muscat or late-harvest wine.

Pitted dried apricots, peaches, or apples 1⅓ cups
Muscat wine 1 cup
Sugar ½ cup
Gelatin ¼-ounce package
Pure vanilla extract ½ teaspoon
Orange peel 1 tablespoon grated
Hazelnuts ½ cup chopped
Whipping cream ¾ cup, whipped
Egg whites 4, beaten stiff

1. Place dried fruit, wine, and sugar in heavy saucepan. Heat to a boil, reduce heat, and simmer 15 minutes.
2. Remove pan from heat. Strain liquid and reserve.
3. Sprinkle gelatin over liquid (to let it soften).
4. Pulverize fruit, mix with liquid, vanilla, orange peel, and hazelnuts.
5. Stir in whipped cream and carefully fold in beaten egg whites, using an over and under motion with a spatula.
6. Spoon into serving goblets and chill.

Serves 6

Jerilyn's Blackberry Cobbler

Jerilyn Brusseau calls for freshly picked wild blackberries in this recipe, but you can make do with commercially available frozen berries.

Ripe wild blackberries   6 cups
Sugar   1¼ cups
Cornstarch   ⅓ cup
Topping
Sugar and freshly ground nutmeg   as desired
Cream or ice cream

1. Rinse blackberries very gently, then sprinkle with 1 cup of sugar. Let stand 1 hour at room temperature to allow berry juice to flow freely. Drain, reserving juice.
2. In a large saucepan, combine remaining ¼ cup sugar with cornstarch and reserved blackberry juice.
3. Cook this mixture over medium heat until thickened and clear. Let cool slightly, then stir in blackberries.
4. Pour mixture into a greased 9 by 13-inch baking dish, then prepare Topping. Spoon Topping carefully over berries. Be sure to spread Topping to edges to prevent excessive bubbling over. Sprinkle Topping liberally with nutmeg and sugar.
5. Bake cobbler at 350° for 35 to 40 minutes until golden and filling is bubbling. Remove from oven, cool slightly, then spoon into serving dishes.
6. Top with fresh cream or with a well-chosen ice cream.

Serves 12 to 15

Topping

All-purpose flour   2 cups
Sugar   1 cup
Baking powder   1 tablespoon
Salt   1 teaspoon
Milk   1 cup
Butter   ½ cup, melted
Sugar   2 tablespoons
Freshly ground nutmeg   ¼ teaspoon

1. Stir flour, sugar, baking powder, and salt well; then add milk and butter all at once.
2. Beat with a wire whisk until smooth.

Jerilyn Brusseau's Whole Wheat Apple Cider Muffins

This is a regionally renowned dish.

Light cooking oil 4 tablespoons
Honey (blackberry honey, if available) ½ cup
Fresh apple cider* 2 cups
Eggs 2
Stone-ground whole wheat flour 2½ cups
Bran 1 cup
Coarsely ground cornmeal 1 cup
Soy flour ½ cup
Baking powder 3 teaspoons
Fresh or frozen blackberries 2 cups

1. Blend together oil, honey, cider, and eggs. Set aside.
2. In a medium-sized mixing bowl, combine remaining ingredients except blackberries.
3. Pour liquid mixture over dry ingredients.
4. Blend very briefly, then gently stir in blackberries.
5. Spoon mixture into muffin pans and bake 25 to 30 minutes at 375°.

* Jerilyn Brusseau recommends Wax Orchards cider because it has a special consistency.

Makes 24

Captain Whidbey Apple Cake

Eggs   3
Sugar   2 cups
Vegetable oil   1 cup
All-purpose flour   2 cups
Cinnamon   2 teaspoons
Baking soda   1 teaspoon
Salt   ½ teaspoon
Vanilla extract   1 teaspoon
Walnuts   1 cup chopped
Tart apples   4 cups peeled and thinly sliced
Cream Cheese Icing

1. Beat eggs with a mixer until thick and light.
2. Combine sugar and oil; pour into eggs with mixer on medium speed.
3. Stir together flour, cinnamon, soda, salt; add to egg mixture with vanilla; beat to mix.
4. Stir in walnuts.
5. Spread apples in a buttered 13 by 9 by 2-inch pan. Pour batter over apples, spreading to cover.
6. Bake at 350° for 1 hour. Remove from oven to cool. Spread with icing. Refrigerate.

Serves 12 to 15

Cream Cheese Icing

Cream Cheese (see Index)   6 ounces, softened
Butter   ¼ cup, melted
Powdered sugar   2 cups
Fresh lemon juice   1 teaspoon

1. Beat Cream Cheese until fluffy; beat in butter, then sugar and lemon.

Makes 1½ cups

Birchfield Manor Strawberry Almond Brandy Torte

At Birchfield Manor in Yakima, everything is made from scratch. However, for the convenience of the less experienced pastry cook, Wil Masset has written this recipe in such a way that you can prepare the parts from your favorite recipes or even purchase the various parts and just assemble them. Either way, this is a very delicious torte. Serve with a rich, sweet Yakima Valley late-harvest riesling or gewürztraminer.

Pound cake made with fresh lemon   1, sliced lengthwise into 1-inch-thick slices
Simple syrup*   ¼ cup
Cooked custard (Bavarian cream)   1 cup
Vanilla butter cream icing   1½ cups
Almond paste   ¼ cup, softened and mixed with butter cream icing
Very ripe dark strawberries   2 cups
Strawberry jelly (not jam)   ½ cup
Brandy   2 tablespoons
Slightly sweetened whipped cream   1 cup
Toasted slivered almonds   garnish

1. Place a slice of pound cake on cutting board and brush with simple syrup.
2. Spread layer with custard cream and place another slice of cake on top. Brush second layer with simple syrup. Repeat until all slices are coated and layered. Refrigerate to cool.
3. Spread sides and top of cake entirely with butter cream icing/almond paste mixture, about ¼-inch thick. Cover top with cleaned and trimmed whole strawberries. Refrigerate. (When cold, the butter cream should hold the berries firmly in place.)
4. To serve, mix jelly and brandy together. Brush mixture on top of refrigerated torte. Slice while cold and pipe on whipped cream with a pastry tube. Garnish with toasted almonds.

*   To make simple syrup, boil ½ cup water plus ¼ cup sugar and cool. Mix in 3 tablespoons brandy.

Serves 12

Chuckanut Strawberry Ice

This is a recipe from Bob Meade's Le Cuisinier Cooking School in Bellingham.

Fresh strawberry puree*   4 cups
Fresh lemon juice   from 1 lemon
Salt   ¼ teaspoon
Curaçao or other orange liqueur   ⅓ cup
Water   1 cup
Sugar   ⅔ cup

1. Make puree by lightly cooking enough strawberries to make 4 cups (strain or blend if desired).
2. Add lemon juice, salt, and orange liqueur to puree.
3. Heat water and add sugar. Stir until sugar has dissolved. Add to strawberry mixture.
4. Freeze in ice cream freezer, according to manufacturer's directions, for best results. (If you do not have an ice cream freezer, place mixture in freezing tray until ice begins to form; remove from freezer and beat vigorously. Return to freezer; repeat the intermittent beating process at least 3 times. Allow to freeze again. Beat 1 more time and serve.)

* It will take about 2 quarts of fresh strawberries to make cooked puree.

Makes about 1½ quarts

Fish

Winter is not a good time for buying fresh fish in the Pacific Northwest. Though our waters teem with delectable fish all year long, many fishermen prefer to lead a seasonal life, pursuing salmon when they get ready to run up the rivers or catching herring preparing to spawn in coastal kelp beds. They do not much enjoy the backbreaking labor of trawling for cod, hake, or bottom fish and rockfish. Only during the last decade, when income from salmon fishing has declined, have fishermen sought other less desirable species of fish. But fishing during inclement weather can be quite hazardous, and because the majority of our fishing boats are small and antiquated, several boats and men are lost each year. It is difficult to determine how many of these losses are caused by failing gear, human error, or just plain inexperience.

The gourmet's concern, however, is the availability of fresh fish. Processors and fishmongers are only too willing to substitute frozen and then thawed fish for fresh fish. This allows them to buy fish cheaply during times of abundance—there are always more fish caught in summer, when the weather is fine, than the market can use—and sell them at a high price in winter, when supplies of fresh fish are low. The frozen stores also permit merchants to hold down the price of fresh fish during times of dearth, shortchanging the fishermen. The latest fad in the fish trade is the importation of fresh foreign fish, flown in from as far away as Norway. This depresses the gourmet market for fresh local fish, allowing few fishermen to make a decent living during the off-season. But the problem relates at least in part to a slowly changing cultural phenomenon: local food preferences.

Despite our superabundance of fish varieties, Northwesterners have only recently learned to enjoy eating fish other than salmon or trout. The past reluctance to eat anything but salmonoid fish is one of the reasons why the winter steelhead, a sea-run trout, has been pursued so vigorously, as if no other fish would do. The steelhead, closely related to the Atlantic salmon, is, of course, very tasty, but I'm afraid that most of the northwest gourmets who insist on having it grace their tables had less concern for its flavor than its family. This is readily noticeable today when Indian-caught steelhead, fish that has often suffered from careless handling and a subsequent loss of flavor and firmness of flesh, brings a high price in seafood markets, though it may not be fit to eat.

Yet the steelhead, whose small numbers could never make up for the lack of salmon during the off-season, has been overfished so ruthlessly that it has become extinct in some rivers and hovers on the verge of extinction in others. At the same time, tasty ocean fish—flounder, sole, greenling, and rockfish—have been consistently underfished. This has changed somewhat during the last decade, but even now most of the delicious white-fleshed fish caught in the Pacific Northwest are shipped to other parts of the continent and to foreign countries, instead of being eaten with gusto by regional aficionados.

Too many Northwesterners are unaccustomed to eating different varieties of fresh fish (though many will eat all kinds of odd marine creatures when these are disguised in processed fish sticks). Despite the belated acceptance of the fillets of white-fleshed cod and sole or pink-tinted rockfish (the latter are often sold as "red snapper") by our region's consumers, many of the smaller and more interesting fish still find few buyers. The superbly rich and velvety sablefish ("black cod") and the delicate lingcod are now popular, but most greenling, sculpin, and sea perch are still not as widely enjoyed as they deserve. It seems odd that northwest consumers would rather eat defrosted, and thus often spongy and insipid, salmon than our more exotic fish species. The main reason whitefish is eaten at all in our region seems to be its low price, not its superb flavor. I am always surprised to find how few connoisseurs in our fish-rich region know how to judge the flavor of fish—beyond white or pink, firm or soft—and how few can or even care to differentiate between the different types and species of fish.

The situation is even more peculiar when we consider freshwater fish. Apart from an occasional offering of fresh, river-caught steelhead and fresh Columbia River smelt, only flabby pond-raised rainbow trout, farmed *en masse* in Idaho and Montana, are regularly available in our fish markets. The nonangling gourmet may have to do without such delicacies as carp—though this plump fish is caught commercially in Moses Lake, Banks Lake, Sprague Lake, and the Columbia River. Carp is available fresh (and it must be impeccably fresh or it will be inedible) only in ethnic and specialty markets (including Seattle's Pike Place Market fish shops). Whitefish, sucker (the longnose sucker is prized in the Great Lakes region as "mullet"; the large-scale sucker sometimes makes it way incognito into fish-and-chip shops), and burbot (whose eggs are frozen and shipped to Europe and Japan) are also hard to find. The delectable shad, which runs up the Columbia and other northwest rivers in ever-increasing numbers, is not caught commercially, nor are the tasty striped bass (common to the Umpqua River, scarce farther north), the walleye, yellow perch, or channel catfish. The sublime kokanee, flavorful cutthroat trout, and all sunfish, from black crappie to largemouth bass to pumpkinseed, call for expert fishing skills on the fish fancier's part.

Let us not forget the fat and juicy lamprey, a delectable parasitic fish that has been so neglected by North American gourmets that it has multiplied and attacked and damaged healthy fish populations. Lampreys run up our rivers to spawn, like their prey, salmon and shad (though they have been known to suck the juices of whales), and can be seen ascending the fish ladders on the Columbia River dams in large numbers, using their suction disks to attach to the concrete walls as they fight the turbulent currents of the chutes. Romans, renaissance Italians (see Boccaccio, *Decameron,* LX:8, where Ciacco avenges himself because he is served mere tuna at a dinner, instead of lampreys), and Northwest Coast Indians doted on lampreys. The coastal tribes liked them especially when smoked over alder wood fires and considered the rich meat a delicacy.

Unless you are an expert with rod and reel and baited hook, or perhaps are fortunate in knowing a fisherman who catches more than he can use, you must do without all of these gourmet delights. Yet you may find partial succor in oriental fish markets. Americans and Canadians of Japanese, Vietnamese, and, in particular, Chinese descent, insist on a large variety of fresh fish for their tables, and the markets catering to their needs have a year-round supply of the freshest fish available. The fish for sale in these stores will not always be halibut, trout, or salmon, of course, but they will be fresh and, with proper care and preparation, any fish can be delicious.

Having tried (and failed) to find fresh fish in Bellingham seafood markets during winter, I was overwhelmed by the variety and quality of the fish sold in Vancouver, B.C.'s Chinatown fish markets. Large tanks held live rockfish, greenling, and carp. Freshly butchered sturgeon, shiner sea perch, rockfish, sole, flounder, and sculpin (their poisonous spines removed) lay stretched out on crushed ice. Just about anyone in our group would have unhesitatingly bought any of the fish we inspected. But, as we quickly learned, the Chinese are much more fussy and selective.

The difference in the Chinese approach quickly became obvious to us as we watched a young couple buy fresh fish for their dinner. They were peering intently into a large salt-water tank, discussing the merits of this rockfish or that, as a fishmonger holding a large dip net stood by. The whole process reminded me of the days when I bought goldfish at the corner drugstore—only these fish were bigger.

The couple had finally agreed on a particular fish and pointed tentatively at its shadowy form. The salesperson pounced with the dip net.

"Nice fish?"

"No, not that one, you missed the one we wanted; this one."

"Oh, sorry."

"No, you've gotten the wrong one again."

"Yes, that one. . . . What do you think, darling?"

"Not very lively, is he? And look at all the scales he's missing."

"Let's try that one instead."

"Oh. . .look at his fins. They're moldy. . . . And his gills look slimy."

"Maybe he's sick?"

"Do you think he has some disease?"

"And just look at those eyes; they're all milky and dull."

"Maybe all of these fish are sick. Look how they're gasping for air!"

"Come to think of it, the water doesn't look that clean and it doesn't smell that good. Maybe there's something in the water."

"Let's go to Win Fung instead."

At this announcement, the fishmonger cut in aggressively: "All of our fish are healthy. Just look how happy they swim. Nothing wrong with them. Healthy!"

"Sorry, but we're going to have steamed five willow fish for dinner. You know as well as we do that you've got to have perfectly fresh fish if you're going to steam it. I don't want to smell up my house with a sick mudsucker. Besides," she pointed to a particularly wobbly rockfish, "I wouldn't dare serve *that* to my mother-in-law!"

The couple indignantly left the store, walked down Main Street for a few blocks, and entered another fish shop. We followed to see what would happen. But here they found what they wanted without much ado and they had the fish of their choice removed from the tank, cleaned, scaled, and wrapped.

Buying live fish in a Chinese fish shop is a somewhat singular experience, quite unlike buying your fish prewrapped at a supermarket. Once you have selected your fish, there seem to be several different ways of getting them ready for the table: you may have your fish wrapped live, to take home and deep-fry it (without, of course, killing it first). If you like your fish fresh but dead and dressed, you may find that, depending on the fishmonger's preference, your fish may be scaled and have its fins chopped off while it is still alive, killed only as it is bled and gutted, or killed by being bopped on the head before it is dressed. If the first method seems a bit cruel to you, just consider what happens to fish who are caught in gill nets, purse seines, and dragnets. In most cases, the fishermen are too busy to kill the fish they have caught; they simply dump them into the hold where they die a slow, agonizing death by suffocation—all the while pumping enzymes into their flesh, which drastically reduces their culinary value. Or you may subscribe to the theory that fish have such a primitive nervous system that they can't feel a thing anyway, no matter what is done to them (even if, as Jean-Pierre Rampal narrates, a slice is cut from their living body, before they are returned to a tank, to make sure their flesh is perfectly fresh for sushi).

I like fresh fish better than fish in any other form. I do enjoy fish preserved by smoking if it was fresh before it entered the smoker and if it was smoked over alder, cherry, or apple-wood instead of the coarser flavored hickory. Sometimes, when nothing else is available, I even eat frozen fish. But I find this acceptable only if it has been flash-frozen and properly handled and stored and if it has not been thawed before cooking. I have also eaten canned fish in the past, because fresh fish was not available and frozen fish was such an inferior product. The technology for freezing fish successfully without much damage to flavor, texture, and moisture has improved considerably in recent years, but the best freezers cannot turn out a good frozen product if the fish was maltreated on its way to the plant. Frozen fish should always be glazed, that is, encased in a protective sheath of ice to preserve its moisture and flavor.

Fish should never stay frozen for more than a couple of months or it will lose all flavor and firmness. Thawing a frozen fish before it is cooked will drastically reduce its quality. It is thus best to cook all frozen fish while it is still frozen—just increase the cooking time. The worst thing that can be done to frozen fish is to thaw it, pack it onto a plastic meat tray, wrap it tightly in plastic film, and place it in a supermarket cooler, usually accompanied by something like: "This product has been thawed for your convenience." This product will not kill you when you eat it, but it will certainly do nothing to please your taste buds.

I still cannot claim, however, that I really enjoy eating frozen fish. Even the best suffers from a lack of flavor when compared to truly fresh fish. The texture of the flesh tends to be much softer and may be quite spongy if the fish has been frozen improperly. My own experience has shown me that a fish must be bled and cleaned right after it is taken from the water to retain flavor and retard decay. Freshly caught fish is best when eaten within twenty-four hours after landing. And, of course, frozen fish is best when it is processed within this time period.

Freshness in fish is an elusive phenomenon to many people, something esoteric that seems difficult to ascertain. Yet it is actually quite easy to distinguish fresh fish from fish that is too old to enjoy (and has, perhaps, become unsafe to eat). Unlike beef and lamb, fish does not improve with age. Part of the continuing problem with the quality of fresh fish stems from the supply and marketing practices of the past: very few people have had access to truly fresh fish and few can tell what it should taste like. And unless you have a taste memory of fresh fish, you have no standards by which to judge the often inferior products sold in supermarkets and fish shops. Yet once you have tasted the pleasures of fresh fish, you will never again settle for less.

The first thing a gourmet must consider when setting out to buy fresh fish is the season. A fish sold out of season will not be fresh (unless it has been caught illegally). Or it may not come from the waters of the Pacific Northwest at all, but from some foreign country, like the king salmon now flown in from Norway. I am always surprised at how many people assume that the salmon they buy in a supermarket in midwinter is really "fresh." Other seasonal fish besides salmon are also caught only when the fish enter rivers or estuaries to spawn: shad, smelt, lamprey, steelhead, and cutthroat trout all have short runs during which they are plentiful, followed by a long dearth which lasts till the next spawn. Some fish, such as rockfish, greenling, sole, sea perch, farmed silver salmon, pond-raised trout, and sculpin may be available year-round—unless, of course, the weather is forbidding. Some fish, like halibut, may only be taken during a short open season (usually from May through October), or fish may be out of season for only a few months, like sturgeon, which is not taken from about May through July.

Be sure to buy fish you know to be in season and keep in mind a few simple points. Always take a good look at the way the fish is stored. It should lie on, and preferably be surrounded by, crushed or shaved ice to keep it at thirty-two degrees Fahrenheit at all times. Under optimum conditions, most dressed fish will have a shelf life of up to two weeks. This means that fish which has been bled and cleaned within minutes after hitting the deck and which has then been put into a cooler immediately and kept at a storage temperature of thirty-two degrees may remain edible for a fortnight—if the storage temperature never rises. On the other hand, fish will lose a day of shelf life for every two degrees above thirty-two degrees that the temperature is allowed to rise during a twenty-four-hour period.

Since it is impossible to tell, even for an expert, how long a fish fillet or steak has reclined in a fishmonger's cooler before it attracts your fancy (unless it is moldy, of course), you are much better off buying a whole fish. If you want steaks or fillets, have the fishmonger cut the fish for you or do it yourself later. Once you have been attracted to a whole fish, look it firmly in the eyes: they must be clear, not hazy, and slightly bulging, not sunken. Next take a look at the gills. They should be red, not vaguely pinkish, white, gray, or brown, and they should be free of slime or mucus.

Check the fish for firmness. Poke the sides and the stomach with a finger. Both must be firm and elastic; your probing poke should leave no dimple behind. Then look at the fish's color and compare it to what you expect the species to look like (you need to become familiar with the appearance of the different food fishes; sorry, there is no shortcut). The color should be bright and as lifelike as possible, never dull or leaden. The belly should be silvery-white and not show any yellow stains or other signs of discoloration. Look into the fish's stomach cavity. It should look clean and have no bits and pieces of internal organs attached to the spine or ribs.

Your sense of smell may be even more important than your sense of sight when you judge a fish for its freshness. Take a good sniff at the fish you plan to buy. A fresh fish will not smell fishy. This cannot be overemphasized. A strong, fishy odor is a telltale sign of decay. Yet even in the Pacific Northwest, few consumers are aware of this. I have often smelled fish in fish shops that was obviously too old. Standing at a fish counter, I have been able to smell its penetrating odor from several feet away, yet I have watched people buy it.

Never go to a market with a preconceived notion about what seafood you want to have for dinner, until you see what is available fresh. Always prepare your fish on the same day on which you have bought it; if you can't, your shopping excursion has lost its purpose and you might as well buy a frozen product. And never let a fishmonger persuade you that a fish will stay "fresh" for several more days. In the end, only experience will tell you what a fresh fish looks like and how it tastes. I have been fortunate in knowing several experienced anglers who taught me that there is no reason why anyone should settle for less than the best and freshest fish—even if you have to catch it yourself.

I have caught large numbers of fish myself, mainly meltingly tender kokanee (also known as "silvers"), cutthroat, Dolly Varden, rainbow trout, carp, sculpin, and a few salmon and odds and ends. Living next to a large lake has made fishing easy, but I got the biggest lesson about northwest fish on my very first fishing trip on the inland waters.

Bill, Lanny, and I had picked a good time for the excursion. August in the San Juan Islands is often blessed with brilliantly clear and hot days. The sun bathed us in pleasant warmth. The short, frothy chop of the tide rip whitecaps knocked against the *Grampus*'s wooden hull with quick, hollow thuds as we lolled in the two-knot current, trailing bright plastic squid behind the boat, trying to catch some salmon for dinner.

The fish were biting: fat, shiny, silver-sided coho salmon, ranging in size from about eleven to fourteen inches. Bill was furious. "They're not legal!" he shouted, "We've got to throw them back!" He stomped up and down the small poop. "I was just out here two days ago and we caught lots of silvers. All of 'em more than fifteen inches long. I don't know what happened!" Bill had promised us a great fishing trip with lots of fish, and here we were catching nothing but undersized shakers. And the fish kept biting. But this fishing trip was jinxed. We caught more than fifty salmon within a period of two or three hours, but none reached fifteen inches—not even when we tugged on their blunt tails a bit. We just didn't have the luck. But I did learn one important lesson from this ill-starred expedition: always read your fishing regulations, no matter how experienced your skipper and guide is, because even the best of men become set in their ways, but fishing regulations change.

Several days later, when we had returned, I narrated the details of this fishing trip to my neighbor and fishing mentor Bob Grieves. Bob has spent some sixty years fishing the waters of the Pacific Northwest, both inland and offshore, and, though he now felt too old to go out onto the salt chuck, he always kept track of things. "You threw back how many fish?" he asked incredulously. "More than fifty," I replied. "You've got to be kidding," he snickered. "Wait! Let me show you something!" He vanished into his apartment and instantly returned with the current copy of the saltwater fishing regulations. "Read!" I read! The fifteen inch rule had been abolished, and all of the fish we had thrown back had been perfectly legal. We could have had fresh salmon for dinner, after all, instead of settling for canned sardines.

We did learn one additional lesson on a later leg of this same fishing venture: how to clean a rockfish. We caught a beautiful black rockfish with a characteristically big head—about one-third of its body length—and a body that was widest near the gill cover, tapering rapidly toward the tail fin. Fish is fish, we thought, and we proceeded to clean this rockfish the way we would have dressed a trout. That, we learned quickly, was a mistake. Gutting a rockfish is both necessary and laudable when you are going to cook your fish whole, either poached or in a seafood stew—unless you do as the Vancouver Chinese sometimes do and throw your live fish in seething oil for a couple of minutes and then eat it, the outside cooked to a crisp, and the inside still quivering. If, on the other hand, you want only the fillets—the fish's body is too compressed to allow for the cutting of steaks—you do not have to dress the fish. Just lay the fish onto a cutting board, hold it down tightly, and cut off the fillets by running a very sharp knife along the backbone, from head to tail. Do not cut through the skin at the tail. When you have reached the tail, flip the fillet and, using the attached piece of skin as an anchor, cut off the skin. Because these fish are so compressed and have such a large stomach cavity, there is surprisingly little flesh, for its size, on a rockfish, and our twenty-four-incher brought us two meager pieces of fillet—just enough for one dinner for two.

I am afraid that Lanny's rockfish haul did little to raise the spirits of a crew that had been bent on a cache of salmon. There appears to be an ongoing argument among Pacific Northwest gourmets about which of our salmon species is the tastiest, the chinook or the sockeye. James Beard opts for the chinook; I claim the sockeye. We both have good reasons for our preferences.

James Beard, in naming his favorite, is not concerned with all chinook salmon ranging from the rivers of California north to Alaska and west to northern China and Japan, but with only one limited population, the Columbia River chinook. He has a point, for he grew up in Portland, Oregon, and the chinook was the tastiest fresh salmon Oregonians could obtain. Chinook salmon headed for the Columbia River were the fattest of our fish because of the tremendous length of river they had to ascend before they could fulfill their life's terminal function and spawn—some twelve hundred miles of currents and rapids and low waterfalls. This salmon was plentiful during Mr. Beard's childhood—until a combination of overfishing, poaching, and the insurmountable barriers of obstructive dams reduced their numbers to the vanishing point.

Unlike pink, coho, and chum salmon, which spawn close to tidewater, the chinook salmon and the sockeye spawn in the headwaters of rivers or in mountain lakes far from the sea and thus need to acquire a large store of fat to provide energy for upstream travel. Because access to the upper Columbia River has been cut off by Grand Coulee Dam, the great, fat, upper Columbia River chinook, so prized by James Beard, have ceased to be. The only chinook salmon of comparable—and those who have tasted both, say of superior— flavor come from Alaska's Yukon River, where the salmon have to store up sufficient energy for some eighteen hundred miles of upriver travel. Chinook salmon from the limited runs of our shorter coastal streams do not have the fat and firm muscles—and thus not the flavor—of chinook from the longer rivers, though these salmon may also reach a huge size (up to 125 pounds).

The chinook, like other salmon, do not feed during their upstream migration to the spawning gravels. They are thus fattest and have the best muscle development (salmon use their entire bodies to propel themselves forward, not just their fins) when they are taken in salt water, near river mouths and in estuaries. They lose flavor as they burn up energy fighting their way upriver, against currents and rapids, and become skinny before they reach their spawning grounds. Finally, they cease to be edible when they finish their spawn, their spent and dying bodies drifting downstream and piling up along the shores in banks of decaying flesh. At this point, they are a treat only for bears and ducks and eagles, who gorge themselves on this mushy carrion. The decline in the quality of the salmon's taste as it moves from the ocean to freshwater is one reason why offshore trollers can demand such a high price for the salmon they catch.

Commercial trollers operate on the same principle as sports fishermen and use similar gear. The main differences lie in the longer poles used by commercial fishermen, the larger number of hooks and lines per pole—an average of three or four lines and up to eighteen "spreads" (leader, lure, and hook) per line, and the use of power gurdies instead of hand-operated fishing reels. But the principle is the same: a lure or baited hook is trolled behind the boat to catch fish. Offshore trollers also command a higher price for their fish because of the great care they bestow on their catch: the fish are killed, gutted, and iced right after they are landed aboard the fishing boat. The quality of these salmon does depend on how long a troller stays out: if he stays out a week or more, his fish will not, of course, be fresh. As a rule, troll-caught salmon are handled with care by processors, because they go to only the finest restaurants and fish shops (do not expect to see them at your supermarket, unless the season was uncommonly productive).

The chinook salmon have, on the average, a higher fat content than the sockeye (11.6 percent versus 9 percent), the second richest salmon species; but the red salmon have a slightly higher amount of protein (20.3 percent versus 20 percent). The sockeye salmon, like the chinook, ascend large rivers to spawn, but are even more finicky than the chinook in the selection of breeding gravels. They will spawn only in small creeks which run into lakes or along gravelly lakeshores, which in turn drain into large rivers. This is one reason why so few of our rivers support appreciable runs of sockeye, though this salmon occurs all the way from California's Klamath River to Japan.

Bristol Bay on Alaska's Bering Sea coast is the center of this salmon's abundance, but the tastiest sockeye—and no one seems to dispute this—are the ones that ascend British Columbia's Fraser and Thompson rivers to spawn in the lakes and creeks of the Shuswap country. These small salmon (their average weight is a mere 3.5 to 8 pounds, compared to the chinook's 10 to 50 pounds) have to build up muscle power and store fat for energy to ascend one of the continent's most treacherous stretches of rapids, in the Fraser River canyon between Yale and Lytton, and they have to traverse the cascades of the Thompson River before they finally reach their spawning grounds in the tributaries of Adams and Shuswap lakes. Other runs of sockeyes brave the second canyon of the Fraser between Lillooet and Williams Lake and climb to the high alpine lakes of the Chilcotin and Cariboo.

These salmon are exceptionally tasty when they are caught in Georgia Strait, just before they enter freshwater. They are the equal or better of any king salmon I have tasted. The superb flavor of these sockeye-salmon may depend less on fat and muscle development, however, than on diet. In contrast to the chinook, which feed largely on herring, sandlance, and squid, the sockeye feed mostly on tiny euphausids and other minuscule crustaceans, and it is this diet of pelagic, shrimplike plankton which gives the sockeye their special flavor, the little culinary edge, beyond size and fat and muscle texture, which creates their unique, rich, complex taste.

One problem gourmets have had with sockeye in the past was the way this fish was processed by the fishing industry because of its size: this tasty salmon had just the proper diameter for fitting into cans. But compared to the fresh fish, canned sockeye is a culinary abomination. However, things are changing. The sockeye is the favorite fish of the Japanese, the world's most knowledgeable lovers of seafood, and fresh sockeye is increasingly available in season in fish shops and restaurants. Fresh sockeye from the Fraser run has been readily available to me because I live in Bellingham. The sockeye destined for the

Fraser and Thompson rivers tarry in United States waters, in Rosario Strait, the San Juan channels, and the lower Strait of Georgia, while they wait for river conditions favorable to their ascent, and they are caught in large numbers by American fishermen. (This may change when the new United States/Canadian fisheries treaty is ratified. But this is of little concern to the northwest gourmet, for sockeye are readily available in Vancouver fish markets.) During the summer, fresh sockeye, bought directly from fishermen, have always been one of our most appreciated staples.

If you are fishing in the islands and have no luck catching the elusive salmon, you might try pursuing lingcod instead. The lingcod, an elongated, big-mouthed fish with a mottled body and a large head and formidable canine teeth, is one of our region's tastiest fish. As a result, it has been heavily overfished near urban centers, but is still plentiful in the northern San Juans and in British Columbia. The lingcod, which is neither a ling nor a cod but a greenling, may grow up to five feet in length and weigh more than sixty pounds (fish over six feet long and over ninety pounds in weight have been reported, but not verified). The lingcod's lean white flesh—it may be intensely green in juveniles, but the color disappears in cooking—is firm and delicious. It is a favorite of restaurant chefs because it slices nicely and holds up well in cooking. It has a light, delicate flavor which lends itself to enhancement by a variety of sauces.

Close relatives of the lingcod, the rock, kelp, painted, long-spine, and white-spotted greenling, are much smaller than the patriarch of the family, ranging from a foot to two feet in length and reaching a weight of up to five pounds only. The flesh of some greenlings may stay green even when cooked, but it is nevertheless very tasty, and fillets and steaks (green steaks!) of these fish look great on a platter when they are accompanied by a green sauce— such as a sorrel or chive sauce. Greenling is quite common around kelp beds and rocky shores, but it is too smart to be hooked easily on lures and bait. Commercial fishermen bring up many of these fish when they drag for bottom fish, but they commonly throw them back, because there is no market for green-fleshed fish. Unfortunately, these tasty fish do not take well to being net-caught and manhandled, and the trawlers often leave behind a long trail of dead or dying greenling (as well as small rockfish) in their wake.

The lingcod, on the other hand, is a highly desired commercial species in both the inland waters and along the outer coast. This fish is not always easy to net, because it likes to lie in holes, in deep depressions in the benthic floor, which are passed over by dragnets. I know several sports fishermen who claim to have found such holes accidentally, who have taken a compass reading to establish their position, and who are able to return to it over and over again to catch themselves a mess of these delectable fish. The lingcod is fond of deep water, down to below sixty fathoms and prefers areas of strong tidal currents. The precipitous eastern shore of Waldron, across President Channel from Orcas Island, is often just the right spot.

Waldron is a small, strange island that rises from the water like a cresting wave sculpted in living rock. Marshy meadows, flat grassy uplands, and low bluffs border the shallow waters of the western shore, but the eastern shore rises quickly to a sandstone height of almost six hundred feet before it tumbles into President Channel in a series of cascading cliffs and rockslides. Kelp hugs this eastern shore, because the water depth increases rapidly, from a narrow coastal shelf of nine to twelve fathoms depth to a channel bottom of five hundred feet or more. This may seem too deep even for a lingcod, but you can fish along the undulating edge of cliff and kelp, where this fish may lurk amid a maze of rock and seaweed, pouncing on passing schools of herring, tomcod, or hake with ravenous appetite.

Fishing this steep, rugged shore at a time of rapid tidal movements can be exhausting as you try to keep the boat off the rocks and the fish lines from tangling. Instead of trying to troll in these treacherous waters, you might want to mooch. Tie a heavy sinker and a strong hook baited with herring to the end of a line and lower it until the bait hangs suspended a few feet above the bottom. The rolling motion of the boat agitates the tip of the rod and jigs the bait up and down in the water.

I would have loved to have caught a large lingcod or even a rockfish or small greenling on our ill-fated salmon fishing trip, though secretly I harbored hopes of catching a cabezon, Red Irish Lord, or other large sculpin. When I mentioned this to Bill and Lanny, they thought I was nuts, for they consider sculpin ugly, squat, a bluntheaded creature of many spines and colors, a trash fish to be thrown back into the water when caught or perhaps cut up for crab bait. But I always eat mine—if I manage to catch one. Sculpin has white flesh that is quite tasty and compares well with that of rockfish and greenling, and it is indispensable, whole or cut up, in the great seafood stews known variously as bouillabaisse, bourride, or cioppino. For the lowly sculpin is akin to the "noble" *rascasse*, a fish that has fallen victim to more misunderstanding than perhaps any other fish.

Even cookery writers who should know better firmly state that this fish occurs only in the Mediterranean, when its close relatives do, in fact, live all along the European and American coasts. The name *rascasse* signifies nothing but a common sculpin (as Julia Child duly notes). This fish has become quite popular with American chefs in recent years (especially in New York and California). They have it flown in from France and other Mediterranean countries at great expense to flavor their versions of the Marseillaise fish soup, bouillabaisse, while its equally tasty relatives living in nearby waters are undisturbed by culinary experts who would rather ape a European stew than create a native one. In the Pacific Northwest today, sculpin is eaten regularly by the descendants of Mediterranean fishermen, the gourmets who invented the spicy seafood stews in the first place. And, while the big city chefs have their fish flown in from foreign climes, our fishermen happily adapt their traditional recipes to take advantage of the local supply of seafood.

There is a persisting misconception among American chefs and gourmets alike that a tasty seafood stew must contain expensive ingredients: the rarer and more precious the raw materials, the tastier the stew. Not so! We often forget how stews like bouillabaisse and cioppino came into being in the first place. A commercial fisherman, to make a living, has to sell the most marketable fish and crab he catches; he feeds his family on the unsalable rejects. This may be difficult to understand for northwest commercial fishermen who are still blessed with a bounty of high-quality fish, though the same principle applies in a different fashion: steelhead, cutthroat, and other sports fish which may not be netted legally are not generally thrown back when caught incidentally, but end up on a fisherman's table. The northwest fisherman's steelhead is the Provençal fisherman's *rascasse*. But these fish are rejects only in the eyes of fishmongers—they may in fact be tastier than the filleted and steaked fish of the luxury markets.

A good seafood stew uses fish that are too small or too bony to be filleted and steaked, and it will call for them whole or cut into large chunks. I consider it a waste to throw good fillets of white fish (or shrimp, clams, and Dungeness) into a fish stew, when a tastier dish can be made by using small and odd fish that do not lend themselves readily to dissecting with knife and fork (plus shore and kelp crabs, small limpets, periwinkles, and other minuscule marine snails). I have before me several fish stew recipes which blithely call for such delicacies (all better eaten by themselves as a main course) as flounder, cod, rockfish, striped bass, trout(!), fresh tuna, Dungeness crab, mussels, oysters, scallops, and crawfish. One recipe from a northwest cookbook suggests adding halibut cheeks and sturgeon to the fish soup. What a waste!

Few of these fish appreciate the liberal spicing and the intense cooking pressure of the stew; others will lose their unique and exquisite flavors. If these fish (and shellfish) are pre-cooked and added to the stew at the last moment, as some cooks suggest, they will add neither flavor nor interest to the concoction, but merely the snob appeal of expensive ingredients or, perhaps, a safe familiarity for conservative eaters. One cook states that though she feels luxury fish and shellfish have no place in such a stew, they add a "touch of class" and are popular in restaurant versions of seafood soups. . . . So much for the flavorful fisherman's dinner—it has become denatured and citified. Fortunately, the Northwest is one area where connoisseurs still know how to prepare a proper seafood stew, no matter what fancy "foreign" name they attach to it.

Had I caught a cabezon (or a Red Irish Lord or great sculpin, for that matter, but not any of the smaller members of the family) and chopped it up and used it in a stew it, too, would have been wasted. This fish gets to be respectably large—the cabezon may reach a weight of thirty pounds and a length of two and a half feet—and, like the greenling and like the large and small rockfish of the Pacific Northwest, it is excellent cooked whole, either baked or poached (it may also be stuffed).

I learned to catch the small sculpin of shallow shores and tidepools (and its freshwater cousins of streams and lakes) and use it and other small fish—gunnels, blennies (these must be soaked in vinegar and salt water to get rid of a strong fish odor, and they are best in recipes calling for lots of garlic and hot spices), midshipmen (these may also be baked or smoked), arrow gobies, kelp fishes, sea perches, and even dogfish (make sure to soak these overnight in a vinegar or lemon juice solution to get rid of the urea taste—the acids neutralize the urea)—instead. All of these fish work well in soups and if they are too small or bony, their bodies may be discarded after they have imparted their flavor and nutrients to the stew. The wolf eel, a large, oversized blenny (to eight feet in length) is also good eating—if you learn to handle it. Sluggish and even meek when left alone, it can turn vicious when attacked. But so can the lingcod. There is at least one verified report of a lingcod taking a good chomp at a swimmer's arm.

Once, while trolling in the San Juan Islands, we had given up our hopes of salmon, sculpin, lingcod, and the like, and pulled in our gear and headed for a large tide rip at the eastern end of Spieden Island. Here at least we got to see lots of fish, though we never had a bite. Two teen-age boys in an aluminum skiff fished the tide rip for herring and were very successful in catching these small silvery fish by a method we had tried earlier that morning (without success) while anchored in Fox Cove. Several multibarbed hooks are tied at intervals to a piece of fishing line, the line is weighted with a sinker, and the contraption is jigged up and down in the water to snare herring. (I'm not sure what we did wrong that morning, for we never impaled a single fish, though we could see their glittering schools pass beneath us in the clear water.) Herring, like their nobler relative, the shad, are delicious to eat. They are quite bony, however, and require special treatment. But they are well worth the effort. Pickled and smoked herring are particularly delectable.

A large share of the credit for raising the Northwest's consciousness of fresh fish—for now fish is handled delicately in our cuisine—must go to Chinese and Japanese cooks and gourmets among us. I learned a long time ago that, whenever I had a need for a truly fresh fish, I had to buy it from a Chinese fishmonger. Yet the Chinese in the Pacific Northwest, living in tightly knit enclaves, have shown little active interest, apart from operating restaurants, in changing the eating habits of the foreign barbarians amongst whom they have chosen to live. Culture change here took place by osmosis, not through active proselytizing.

The Japanese, on the other hand, have been very active in promoting their way of eating and in the process they may have wrought a most significant change in American, and especially in northwestern, seafood eating habits. By introducing sushi and sashimi, both of which call for raw, fresh fish, they raised and changed the taste consciousness of northwest gourmets. Some Americans had long been accustomed to eating certain fish raw: lox, gravlax, and pickled herring are heavily salted and eaten uncooked. Only the Japanese insistence on the freshest of fish and their appreciation of the delicate and complex flavors of raw seafood, however, led Northwesterners to appreciate the fine qualities of "freshness."

The Japanese have also purchased large quantities of fresh (and fresh-frozen) northwest seafoods, especially salmon, for export to Japan. But, in order to find fish that meets their stringent quality standards, they had to educate both fishermen and processors in proper fish handling techniques. This appears to be a continuing process, since many seafood professionals resist change with a peculiar stubbornness. But now the northwest consumer has also become involved. Tasting truly fresh fish for the first time at sushi bars, many Northwesterners are now demanding the same excellence in the fish they consume regularly.

The outlook for the future is very bright, because more northwest consumers are becoming aware of the quality and variety of fish available to them. And they are beginning to learn how to discern freshness. For example, I went shopping in Seattle's Uwajimaya Asian supermarket, an outlet for many hard-to-find Oriental foods and a good source of fresh fish and fresh and preserved fish roe and was pleased to see a number of non-Asians in the fish department, checking on the fish and commenting to each other on its quality and freshness. They did not limit their purchases to only the more common bottom fish or salmon and were buying some of the odder fish and roe as well.

But freshness in commercial fish is not the exclusive province of specialty stores like Uwajimaya, Jack's Fish Spot in the Pike Place Market, Peter Troy's seafood markets in Portland, et al., anymore. Small fish stores throughout our region are beginning to stock fresh fish (even a few butcher shops are now doing this, especially east of the Cascades), and here and there supermarkets are adding specialty fish counters. Restaurants like Ray's Boathouse in Seattle, La Petite Maison in Olympia, and the Sooke Harbour House on Vancouver Island serve only fish that is at its best and freshest, pleasing and educating their clientele at one and the same time. And once you have tasted fresh fish prepared by the hand of a master, you'll be loath to settle for less.

Fillet of Sole with Spinach à la Sylvia Henry

Scott Henry produces a superb chardonnay at his winery in Oregon's Umpqua Valley. His wife likes to use the family wines in her cooking. Be sure to make this recipe with Henry Estate 1979 chardonnay, and serve it with more of the same and some parsleyed new potatoes.

Unsalted butter   ¼ cup
Flour   ¼ cup
Milk   1 cup
Cream   ¼ cup
Chardonnay   ½ cup
Mushrooms   ¼ pound, chopped
Parmesan cheese   ¼ cup grated
Worcestershire sauce   ½ teaspoon
Salt and freshly ground white pepper   to taste
Spinach   3 cups cooked and chopped
Sole fillets   1½ pounds

1. Melt butter and stir in flour a little at a time, blending very gently over low heat until it bubbles.
2. Add milk, cream, and wine and cook over low heat, stirring constantly, until mixture is thickened.
3. Add mushrooms, cheese, Worcestershire sauce, salt, and pepper.
4. Spread spinach evenly over bottom of greased 8 by 12 by 2-inch baking dish.
5. Lay fillets on top of spinach and cover with wine-cream sauce.
6. Bake at 375° for 25 minutes or until fish flakes easily.

Serves 4

Dan Ripley's Sautéed Bottom Fish—The Basic Technique

This is a basic recipe that works well for a number of different fish types: large fillets of impeccably fresh sole and flounder, greenlings, and even rockfish. Ask your fishmonger for the freshest variety of the day. Allow 6 to 8 ounces per person. You may ask the fishmonger to remove the bone line present in most of these varieties. This will make eating the fish much more pleasant, and you'll lose only about an ounce per fillet.

Large rockfish, cod, ocean perch, or flounder fillets   2
Freshly ground white pepper   to taste
White flour   1 cup (or more, as needed)
Unsalted butter   4 tablespoons clarified

1. Trim and clean fillets. If necessary, rinse under cold running water, drain, and gently pat dry with paper towels. (Dan feels that any fish which has been out of the water for more than 24 hours should be rinsed.)
2. Keep fish cold until just before cooking. It may be removed from the refrigerator 5 to 10 minutes before cooking.
3. Sprinkle fillets with a bit of freshly ground white pepper. Salt is not necessary, especially if it is included in the sauce.
4. Dredge fillets lightly in flour and shake off excess.
5. Heat clarified butter in a sauté pan large enough to accommodate fish. You will need at least 2 tablespoons of butter per fillet. (Don't use too much, though, or you'll "boil" the fish in butter.)
6. Place fish "rough" side down in pan. Sauté until golden brown, then turn to other side. Sauté until visible flesh turns opaque, or until juices emerging from already cooked side begin to look somewhat opaque. Do not overcook! All fish should be just "cooked through."

Note: Do not try to sauté too much fish in one pan. If cooking for 4, it is far better to use 2 pans, one each for 2 fillets. Nor can you properly sauté fish for a crowd—the fish will not hold well under a cover (as many cookbooks suggest). Better to use small portions of fish as an appetizer if you're serving many people.

Serves 2

Dan Ripley's Basic Poached Fish Fillets

Water   enough to fill ⅔ saucepan
Bay leaf   1
Black peppercorns   10 to 12
Fresh lemon juice   2 tablespoons
Dry white wine   1 cup
Large garlic clove   1, unpeeled
Fish fillets (or whole small fish)   2

1. Select a large, deep saucepan (matched to length of fillets) with a tight-fitting cover. Fill pan ⅔ full with cold water, or at least up to 1½ times deepest thickness of fish.
2. Add all ingredients except fish and bring poaching liquid to boil; simmer for 10 minutes.
3. Have fish ready—trimmed, rinsed, and dried (if necessary), or rolled (sole/flounder). Carefully place fillets in poaching pan. Return pan to bare simmer over high heat with cover on, but do not leave unattended. Check frequently and adjust burner temperature to maintain a bare simmer for 10 minutes per inch of fish thickness. Adjust cooking times for different sizes of fish.
4. Remove fillets with long, flat turner to toweling to drain quickly (and thoroughly) to prevent fish from cooling too much.

Note: Have all accompanying vegetables and sauces ready and hot. Properly poached fish should not be held under warm cover, but served immediately.

Serves 2 to 4

Basic Steamed Fish

Every season our commercial fishermen bring home a number of odd and uncommon fish which they have netted as an incidental catch. There is no commercial market for this fish, so it's given to friends or relatives. Most of this fish is so fresh it's still flopping, making it a prime candidate for steaming. Be sure to serve fish cheeks to your favorite person—they're the best part. Sinclair Philip of Sooke also likes to eat the steamed eyes: they're flavorless and tough like chewing gum.

Small white-meated fish, firm-fleshed*   1 to 1½ pounds, cleaned
Coarse salt   2 teaspoons
Dry sherry (or rice wine)   2 tablespoons
Thin soy sauce**   3 tablespoons
Sesame oil   1 tablespoon
Scallions   2, shredded lengthwise
Fresh ginger   4 thin slices, shredded
Water   2 cups (or more, as needed)

1. Clean and scale fish. Do not remove head and tail. Score fish at 1½- to 2-inch intervals. Cut to, but not through, center bone.
2. Place fish on a platter. Sprinkle with salt and sherry. Let stand 10 minutes.
3. Sprinkle with soy sauce and sesame oil; then place shredded scallions and ginger on top of fish.
4. Place 2 inches of water in a large roasting pan. Place 2 soup bowls upside down (or clean bricks) in the water. Bring water to boil and carefully lower platter with fish onto top of bowls. Cover roasting pan and steam fish for 10 minutes over high heat.
5. Remove cover carefully, taking care to avoid hot steam. Use a plate lifter or 2 potholders to remove platter from steamer. Place platter on top of another platter of equal or larger size. Serve fish immediately.
6. Remove fish in sections, working from tail to head. Lift up backbone and break near head. Serve bottom half.

 * We never use an oily fish for this recipe.
** Koon Chun is a good brand of thin soy sauce. Whatever brand you buy, you should try to find one that says "thin" on the label.

Serves 4

Poached Salmon with Mustard and Cream Sauce

Here is one of the simple, tasty ways in which fresh salmon is prepared at Ray's Boathouse, Seattle's number one fish house. The recipe comes in two steps: first poach your salmon, then make your sauce. This is one of Chef Wayne Ludvigsen's favorites.

Water ½ gallon
Fish stock ½ gallon
Dry white wine 2 cups
Bay leaves 6
Peppercorns 6
Parsley 1 bunch
Thyme pinch
Fresh lemon juice 1 tablespoon
Salmon fillets six, 8 ounces each
Mustard and Cream Sauce
Parsley garnish

1. Bring first 8 ingredients to a rolling boil for 15 minutes, strain, and reduce temperature to just under a boil.
2. Place a rack or screen in the bottom of pot (so fillets don't touch bottom of pot) and place fillets on the screen (completely submerged).
3. Poach salmon for about 10 minutes per inch of thickness at the thickest part.
4. Remove poached fillets to warm platter and cover with foil, reserving stock for sauce. Prepare sauce. Pour sauce over fillets and garnish with chopped parsley. Serve.

Serves 6

Mustard and Cream Sauce

Fish stock 2¼ cups
Dry white wine ¾ cup
Shallots 1 tablespoon chopped
Cream 1 cup
Stone-ground, Dijon, and tarragon mustards to taste
Unsalted butter 3 tablespoons, chilled

1. In a large pan reduce fish stock, wine, and shallots to about ¼ original volume.
2. When golden brown and large bubbles are forming, add cream and reduce by about ½. Mixture should have a thick enough consistency to coat a wooden spoon.
3. Strain mixture.
4. Add equal parts stone-ground, Dijon, and tarragon mustards to taste.
5. Heat mixture to simmer and swirl in cold butter.

Makes 1½ to 2 cups

Salmon in White Wine John Rauner

Here is an interesting salmon recipe from John Rauner, wine maker at the Yakima River Winery in Prosser and a fisherman par excellence. The fish for this dish should, of course, be very fresh. Serve with new potatoes, Yakima Valley asparagus, and Yakima River Winery riesling.

Silver or chinook salmon   four 1-inch thick slices
Riesling   ½ cup
Salt   1 teaspoon
Freshly ground pepper   ½ teaspoon
Fresh chives   1½ tablespoons chopped
Celery seeds   ½ teaspoon
Bread crumbs   ¼ cup
Swiss cheese   ¼ cup grated

1. Place salmon steaks and wine in well-buttered 2-inch deep pan; salt and pepper to taste, then sprinkle with chives, celery seeds, and top with bread crumbs and Swiss cheese.
2. Bake uncovered at 350° for 20 minutes or until fish flakes easily.

Serves 4

Sooke Harbour House Poached Salmon with Alaria and Rhubarb Sauce

The seaweed used in this sauce will not add a strong flavor to the sauce itself, but it adds a nice texture, releases its flavor upon chewing, and makes the addition of salt to the dish unnecessary. Serve with mashed potatoes, crisp cooked vegetables, and a dry, fruity riesling.

Garlic clove   1, halved
Dry northwest riesling   ½ cup
Small shallot   1, chopped
Fish fumet   1 cup
Unsalted butter   1 tablespoon
White wine vinegar   1 tablespoon
Sockeye salmon*   two 8-ounce fillets from a 2-pound salmon
Fresh alaria seaweed**   2 tablespoons diced
Crème Fraîche (see Index)   4 tablespoons
Rhubarb   1 stalk, peeled, cut into ½-inch sections, blanched, and pureed in blender
Edible blue borage flowers   garnish

1. Rub poaching pan with garlic. Add wine, shallot, fumet, butter, and vinegar. Bring to a boil, boil for about 5 minutes, and add fish.
2. Poach fillets for a maximum of 3 minutes. (Do not overcook!) Remove salmon from

poaching liquid (reserving liquid), cover with foil, and keep warm.

3. Sieve poaching juices into an enamel or stainless steel pan. Add alaria and Crème Fraîche and reduce.
4. To finish the sauce, incorporate 1 tablespoon of rhubarb per person to thicken.
5. Pour sauce onto a warmed plate, place salmon over sauce.
6. Decorate with flowers.

* Fillets cut from a large salmon have a different texture and larger flakes than those cut from a small salmon. If you buy the suggested 2-pound salmon, you can use the remaining pieces to make the fumet.

** Clean the alaria and soak it in fresh water for less than 1 minute (it loses flavor and will not be as crisp if soaked longer). Japanese nori seaweed can serve as a substitute. You may also buy the local dried seaweed available in Chinese food markets. This seaweed comes in two varieties: #1 (early picked) and #2 (picked late). Ask for the #1.

Serves 2

Chardonnay Salmon Medallions Sokol Blosser

Bill and Susan Blosser not only run a very successful winery in Oregon's Willamette Valley, but they really care about the way their wines match up with food. The following recipe should, of course, be accompanied by a Sokol Blosser chardonnay, and perhaps by fresh asparagus and boiled new potatoes.

Salmon steaks   4, boned and skinned
Bay leaf   ½
Ground thyme   ⅛ teaspoon
Lemon   ¼ slice
Black peppercorns   3
Unsalted butter   1 tablespoon
Chardonnay   1 cup

1. Skewer salmon steaks in pairs, with the smaller end of one slightly overlapping the smaller end of the other. Run the skewer through the thick end of one fillet first, then through its smaller end, through the smaller end of the second fillet, and finally through its larger end.
2. Place bay leaf, thyme, lemon, peppercorns, butter, and wine in small lidded saucepan. Heat until boiling. Reduce heat to simmer and add salmon medallions.
3. Cover and poach approximately 10 minutes.
4. Remove to serving plates and serve.

Serves 4

Ray's Boathouse Summer Salmon Barbecue

Ray's Boathouse consistently serves the freshest fish of any restaurant in Seattle. Here's one of their favorite ways of barbecuing fresh salmon.

Soy sauce   1 quart
Brown sugar   1 pound
Dry mustard   1 tablespoon
Whole cloves   2, freshly crushed
Fresh ginger   1 tablespoon finely chopped
White wine   ½ cup
Salmon fillets   six, 8 ounces each
Toasted sesame seeds

1. Prepare marinade by combining all ingredients except salmon and sesame seeds.
2. Place fillets in the marinade and allow to marinate 4 to 6 hours.
3. Broil salmon on a barbecue grill until done, about 7 to 10 minutes.
4. Top with toasted sesame seeds and serve.

Serves 6

Klamath River Half-Dried Salmon

First time I had this delicious salmon was during an art class I taught ten years ago when Barbara Risling, the wife of Dave Risling, a well-known leader of the Hupa/Yurok/Karok, brought some to class.

Salmon   1 (or more)
Salt   as needed
Alder wood   enough for cool, long-lasting smoke fire

1. Prepare fresh, cleaned salmon by splitting down back; then cut fish lengthwise into strips, about 2 to 2½ inches wide. Split each strip up center, leaving 2 inches or so joined at larger end, so strips will hang evenly over poles in smokehouse.
2. Fish may be left unsalted, or dry salted, or brined lightly. Some people like to use other flavors, like pepper, garlic, or brown sugar, but that's not "traditional," i.e., unsalted. (Look out for yellow jackets while fixing fish!)
3. Smoke over low fire about 24 hours, more or less, till firm but not really dry (it may not take that long, depending on how dry and smoky you want it).
4. After smoking, cut salmon into convenient serving lengths (3 to 8 inches), wrap <u>well</u>, and freeze. Or process 180 minutes in jars in hot water bath. Salt may be added to jars before

sealing. No water is necessary in jars.

5. To serve frozen fish, place fish in shallow pan, cover with foil, and bake for about 15 or 20 minutes in 400° oven. Don't overcook, or it will turn tough and dry.

Note: The canned smoked salmon can be used in many ways: steamed with potatoes and onions, creamed, with or without eggs, or with vegetables. The flavor goes a long way! Watch for bones!

Salmon Bisque Captain Whidbey

This is a great summertime backyard party or beach party dish. Make ahead of time and reheat just before serving. Serve with chilled chenin blanc or lager beer.

Salmon   4 pounds, skinned and cut into chunks
Large onions   3, medium diced
Unsalted butter   2 cups
Mushrooms   1 gallon sliced
Chicken stock   1½ gallons
Half-and-half   2 quarts
Flour   ½ cup
Diced pimentos   1 pound
Cocktail sherry   1 cup
Worcestershire sauce   8 tablespoons
Salt and freshly ground pepper   to taste

1. Boil salmon in water to cover until just done (test for flakiness).
2. Sauté onions in ½ cup butter.
3. In separate pan, sauté mushrooms in 1 cup butter.
4. Combine mushrooms and onions. Add heated chicken broth, half-and-half, and Worcestershire sauce.
5. In separate pan make a roux with remaining butter and with flour. Thicken onion-mushroom mixture with roux.
6. Add first salmon and pimentos, then sherry. Season with salt and pepper to taste.

Serves 8 to 16

Rita Schlotterback's Seafood Stew

This recipe is an old Bellingham favorite. The fish, crabs, and clams are very much inter-changeable with different species. Use whatever is available locally. Serve with freshly baked garlic bread (or Indian fried bread) and with a full-bodied Kiona lemberger.

Marjoram 1 tablespoon
Rosemary 1½ teaspoons
Sage 1½ teaspoons
Thyme 1½ teaspoons
Sweet basil 1 tablespoon
Parsley ½ cup chopped
Garlic cloves 4, chopped
Small red peppers 4, diced
Swiss chard or spinach 4 cups chopped
Littleneck clams 40
Large fresh local shrimp 36 (or 2 to 3 times as many small)
Large crabs 4 (or 12 or more small)
Firm whitefish (sculpin, greenling, rockfish, or whatever) 2 pounds, cut into chunks
Stewed tomatoes 7 cups (including juices)
Tomato paste 6-ounce can
Olive oil ¾ cup
Pepper 2 teaspoons
Dry red wine 2 cups

1. Mix herbs, garlic, red peppers, and chard. Set aside.
2. Layer clams, shrimp, crabs, and fish with herb mixture.
3. Combine stewed tomatoes, tomato paste, olive oil, and pepper. Pour over seafood. Cook for 20 minutes. Then add wine and cook for 15 minutes more.

Serves 6 to 8 generously

Crabs

L anny always got excited when the time came for pulling one of his crab traps. Leaning over the gunwale, he would grab the line just below the marker buoy, and as I held the tiny, seven-foot pram steady with the oars, he would give a strong jerk to snap the star trap shut. Then, making sure to keep tension on the line, he would haul in the contraption, hand over hand, shouting as he pulled: "Oh, it's heavy! Ooooh, it's really heavy!! There's something in it! I'm sure there is! It's heavy!" Fortunately, crabs cannot hear, for he waxed louder as the trap came into sight: "I've got one! No, I've got two. I've got three! Three, four..."—the resemblance to an auctioneer was startling— "I've got five!...There's one hanging on the outside....eeeech! Don't fall off! Don't you dare fall off! Don't you know there's crab-eating octopus down there? You don't want to fall off! Come on, Daddy wants you! Stay, boy!! Sit! Don't you dare fall off! Why you little...I'll get you next time....Down boy!!"

As he swung the eelgrass-bedecked trap from the water into the boat, one or two, and sometimes more, large and small crabs would commonly fall off, and we could see them descend the clear water of the bay, frantically balancing and moving their legs to stay level as they slowly sank back to the sandy bottom amid Lanny's cries of anguish. He would suffer acute pain when the trap came up empty, especially when it had given a false impression of fullness because of its yield of eelgrass, or if the haul brought in nothing but female and undersized crabs, illegal to keep.

My friend truly loved Dungeness crab, and failing to attract any of legal size to his trap meant that he would have no fresh crab for dinner that night. He rightly considered crab that had been out of the water a dozen hours or crab that had been cooked and put up for sale at a fish shop or supermarket unworthy of a gourmet. Dungeness crab, to do justice to its superb flavor, must be cooked and eaten shortly after it is taken from the water, or it loses its exquisiteness. And, as far as Lanny was concerned, commercially caught and frozen Dungeness crab were things you just didn't mention in polite company.

As a youngster, Lanny and his friends had raided the eelgrass flats of Samish Bay at low tide. Walking slowly in the shallow water, they would probe the clumps of grass with their bare feet—a Dungeness is surprisingly hard to detect from above, blending very well into the multicolored background of the sea floor—and, whenever a crab tried to scurry away, they would pounce upon it, grab it, and stick it into a waiting bucket. Few crabs are quick enough to escape from the grabby little fingers of experienced boys, and Lanny early acquired his taste for fresh crab, lots of it, sometimes cooked in the driftwood shelter of a nearby beach.

When I met Lanny, he had returned to the Sound and, having become a bit older and more sedate, had just learned to catch crabs with a trap. He had once tried using crab rings on the Oregon coast, but he thought little of them: they were nice for keeping tourists occupied and gave visiting children something to do, but were not worthy of a serious crabber's attention. He spurned big crab pots, because even the unskilled could use them to catch crabs, if they just waited long enough. The crabs would be entrapped in the pot, with no way of escape, until the crabber returned to check up on them, be it within hours or days. I like these enclosed traps, because they help me catch crabs, but Lanny preferred star traps. He considered them more sporting.

These contraptions, made of a square piece of wire mesh with hinged, triangular side flaps, look like four-pointed stars when spread open on the ground, but close into pyramidical cages when the crabber pulls them up. Crabs are attracted to bait preferred in the center of the trap (firmly tied down with wire, or the crabs will walk off with it) and are free to feed and come and go, until the crabber pulls in his lines and snares them while retrieving his trap. The trap must stay closed until it is safely brought inboard, or the catch will go tumbling into the water. The trick in using star traps lies in giving the crabs enough time to be attracted to the bait, but not enough leisure to eat it all and walk off. We had good luck with checking our traps every twenty minutes or so. This type of crabbing can keep you fairly busy, especially if you set out too many traps.

The crabs brought up in the traps were spilled unceremoniously into the bottom of our boat, while the traps were rebaited and sent back to the bottom of the bay. In this operation the line was paid out very carefully and the trap allowed to settle gently onto the ground to make sure it would land right side up and open properly (with experience we had learned to recognize the little tug on the line as the springs folded back the triangular sides of the trap). Only after the traps were safely reset, did we chase down our shipboard captives as we drifted with the tide. (Crabs like to hide in dark places, and pant legs are mighty handy.) Legal-sized male crabs, checked with a plywood caliper, went into the bucket, as did all rock crabs and odd crustaceans for which no legal size limits were set. Females and undersized Dungeness crabs went overboard, but well away from the traps—there was no sense in encouraging freeloaders. (Male and female crabs can be easily told apart: the males have a narrow, triangular flap under their bellies, the females a broadly scalloped flap.)

Trying to catch half a dozen or more angry Dungeness crabs as they scuttle for safety in the limited space of a seven-foot pram adds a touch of excitement to a crabbing expedition. Crabs are very fast, and their serrated claws can impart a painful pinch, often drawing blood. The only way to handle a live crab safely is to grab it from behind, making sure to stay out of reach of those snapping claws—once a claw locks on to an object, it cannot let go (this is one way crabs secure their prey before they tear it apart), and it is impossible to shake off the crab without breaking its claw.

Lanny and I had worked out an effective system of dividing the chores involved in crabbing. He provided the truck that took us to our crabbing spot, the dinghy, and the traps. I brought the bait. This was a bit more complicated than it sounds. We tried every conceivable bait: hole-punched cans of different brands of cat and dog food, old sausages, stale meat, and anything handy and/or recommended. But nothing worked as well as fish heads. And, strange as it may seem, fish heads are a rare commodity, especially during crabbing season (which lasts eleven months out of the year in our inland waters). I had managed, by sheer luck, to get myself onto a local fishmonger's "head list." If you aren't on such a list, you might as well not try to get fish heads—the fishmongers gladly pass on the heads to their regular customers, but they don't permit interlopers.

Lanny loved tying the bait to the traps, and the older and raunchier the heads were, the better he liked it. He positively chuckled when they had reached a state of advanced putrefaction and semiliquefaction—he thought they were at their best when they had lain in the sun to ripen for about three days. The messier the bait, the better it worked, and we commonly caught our limit within a few hours. I never thought that crabbing could be that much fun. We went out regularly, rain or shine. If the weather was too wet, we brought along some hot mulled wine, sheltered under an overhanging rock, and took to the water only when the traps needed checking. During the warm weather, on calm days, we were often surrounded by other small boats and by lots of bobbing crab floats—the poor crustaceans never stood a chance—but let a cloud show in the sky, and we had the bay to ourselves again.

We never left our traps out of sight, for no code of ethics seemed to apply among amateur crabbers. An unguarded trap often became an appropriated one. Things were even touchier among commercial crab catchers. Competition was fierce. One family (I have forgotten their name) claimed proprietary rights over certain favored sections of the public waters. An interloper who set pots in their "territory" would find, on returning to check his traps, that the bait and any captured crabs had been taken from the pots and a red plastic rose left in their place. If he was foolhardy enough to refuse the warning, destruction of his equipment, a beating, and even a bullet would be the next step. (I still remember the mysterious abandoned boat, with no sign of a skipper, found drifting in Bellingham Bay during the early years of my residence.)

But these things belong to the past, for now the big crab boats from the outer coast come to the inland waters in the fall of each year, trap all of the legal-sized male Dungeness crabs within a period of two or three days, and leave nothing behind for the few remaining local commercial crabbers to catch. So little Dungeness is caught in the Northwest at this time that most of the crab for sale in our seafood markets is flown in, fresh or frozen, from Alaska.

We were fortunate to catch as many crabs as we did, for Dungeness crabs undergo cyclical fluctuations in population (somewhat like rabbits and lemmings). Our crabbing expeditions coincided with a high point in the regional crab population, but ever since the number of crabs in Oregon and Washington waters has declined severely. An upturn is expected soon. The cyclical slump may last until the mid-1980s, but afterwards Dungeness crabs should increase dramatically. None of this concerned us at the time of our weekly exploits, for we were blessed with a surfeit of fresh crab.

Our favorite way of eating these delectable crustaceans was, and still is, to do as little to them as possible and eat them shortly after they have been caught (they're great for beach picnics). The directions are simple: bring a large pot of salted water (one tablespoon salt to each quart of water) to a boil—the crabs can be cooked in freshwater, but the salt will firm the meat and improve the flavor—and drop the <u>live</u> crab quickly into the boiling water. Cover the pot, boil the crabs for about ten to fifteen minutes, take them from the water, and cool them quickly in ice water. When the crabs have cooled enough to be handled, lift the top shell from the rear (a bottle opener will be helpful) and pull it off. Break the carcass in half. It is customary to wash out the intestines, gills, and other internal organs, but many of these can be eaten and are quite tasty. The gut should be discarded, but just about everything else can be eaten—even the gills can be sucked. (I would be careful with eating any of these internal organs during a red tide—crabs eat clams.)

Cleaning out the halves of the crab's body will leave you with the body meat and the leg meat. The body meat can be loosened by hitting the body halves with the palm of your hand, and it can then be shaken out. The legs and claws can be cracked with pliers or with a nutcracker and the long pieces of meat shaken, pulled, or sucked from the cavities. Crab may also be cleaned before it is cooked, but then you will not be able to eat the internal morsels. There are two ways of doing this. (1) Lay the crab on its back and place the cutting edge of a sharp knife along the center of the narrow triangular flap on the crab's belly. Strike the back of the knife blade with a mallet, a piece of wood, or your fist. The blow should be heavy enough to cut through the abdomen, but not strong enough to break through the top shell. As you hold the shell down with the knife, grasp first one set of legs and then the other, twisting away the body meat with them. Rinse off the remaining bits of intestine. (2) Prop up a spade or other sharp-edged object. Grasp the crab firmly by the legs (watch those claws!) and hold it facing away from you. Strike the narrow triangular belly flap against the edge of the sharp object. This will break the crab into three parts. The carapace with the intestines will fall away, and you will hold the legs with the attached body meat. Rinse off the few bits of entrails and gills clinging to the meat. You are now ready to cook the crab (just follow the directions for cooking whole crab).

I like to eat crab meat fresh, as it comes from the shell, and see no reason to disguise its exquisite flavor beneath spices and sauces. I may dip the meat into some melted butter for added richness, or sprinkle it with a little lemon, or maybe even use a more elaborate seafood sauce—for dipping, but never for cooking. Crab meat dipped in a sauce will retain its flavor, and the sauce will merely provide a stimulating contrast. Crab meat cooked in a sauce and in a blend of strong spices will take on the flavor of the condiment and lose its own. Fortunately, some of the things done to delicate crab meat elsewhere in the country seem to be foreign to northwest cuisine. Yet this crab may be prepared in a number of interesting ways. Dungeness is low in calories, only ninety-one per three-and-one-half-ounce serving, low in fat, only 1 percent, and very high in protein, about 19.5 percent of the meat.

There appear to be five kinds of regional crab cookery in North America. The Northeast likes its crab served with cream sauces or as crab patties, and often eats it with tartar sauce, that culinary abomination which masks the taste of seafoods (but what can you expect from this wicked mixture of mayonnaise, ball-park mustard, and coarse pickle relish). The South steams its crab in vinegar vapors (a good way to hide an inferior taste) and spices it with nutmeg or pimentos, or serves it in soups—that is, when it does not deep-fry molting soft-shell crabs (in the Northwest it is illegal to collect Dungeness crabs in the soft-shell/molting stage). The Gulf Coast boils its crabs in a blend of flavor-killing crab boil spices (mustard seed, coriander seed, cayenne, bay leaves, dill seed, allspice, and cloves—there's nothing wrong with some of these, except for the large quantities used), then tops this off with hot peppers and tomato sauce. California does much the same—its cuisine is derived from the same Spanish sources—and adds even hotter peppers and Mexican salsas, unless it fixes its crab San Francisco style—with steak sauce and vermouth. Only the Northwest seems to like the pure, unadulterated taste of its crab, because, perhaps, only the Northwest has crab flavorful enough to warrant a simple treatment.

Until the blissful days of weekly crabbing expeditions to the waters of the northern Sound, I had rarely had the opportunity to enjoy really fresh crab, spiced or not. My first taste came in the small Mexican fishing village of San Felipe, when one of the natives treated me to a dish of freshly caught Gulf (of California) blue crab (in exchange for a drawing of his *rancheria*). But I'm afraid I really didn't taste a thing but chili—the delicate meat had been slathered with hot sauce. I encountered my first fresh Dungeness crab in San Francisco some twenty years ago. I had just finished up my initial semester of college work and I took off for San Francisco to get away from the Los Angeles smog and to escape the finals blues. Driving all night, with only two interruptions—horrible coffee at Gaviota and a two-hour nap in the Castroville artichoke fields—I arrived in the early morning hours when the crab boilers on Fisherman's Wharf were heating up for the day's cooking. The morning catch had just gone into the pots, and the delicious scent of Dungeness crab steam wafted past the piers. I could hardly wait to get a taste of freshly cooked crab. Avoiding the crabmongers who used "crab boil" in their stew (they thought it gave San Francisco a "southern" air), I ordered some crab to go, planning to eat it for breakfast in a quiet corner of the port. Settling myself on a breakwater wall, I opened the container and found...crab soaked in hot sauce. I had failed to order carefully enough. I was hungry and ate it anyway. It had a nice taste of chili, tomato, onion, and comino. Later in the day, I succeeded in getting my way. I returned to the boat harbor with a loaf of sourdough bread and a bottle of white wine and bought a whole, hot, uncracked crab. Finding a quiet spot on the rocky shore of Fort Mason, I set to with gusto. The crab was delicious, and I have been addicted to fresh Dungeness ever since.

But there can be a wide gap twixt the yearning for a certain food and its availability. I soon learned that truly fresh crab was the exception in San Francisco. Local supplies had become increasingly scarce (and polluted), and much of the crab sold in the Bay City came from the north—from areas as yet unknown to me—and it was often of uncertain age and frozen. Commonly it was thawed and quickly heated in a crab cooker before it was sold as "fresh." Tourists couldn't tell the difference, but everyone else complained—to no avail. The local crab stocks were and have stayed depleted.

As I extended my journeys to the north, I encountered even less fresh crab. Eureka and the small ports along the Coast did land and process a lot of crab, but it was all shipped south. I missed the large crab cooker and soon discovered, to my chagrin, that the cooked crab sold in seaside fish markets was not up to the culinary standards I had come to expect. I soon learned why. San Franciscans relied on the large commercial crab cookers because they liked to come to Fisherman's Wharf and buy freshly cooked crab for the day's lunch or dinner. Oregonians, on the other hand, caught their own in the shallow water of coastal bays and inlets and took it home to cook. In Washington and British Columbia, crabbers who were lucky and caught a lot shared their catch with friends and neighbors, and there was thus little demand for commercially processed crab. Stale fish market crabs were left for tourists who had come to the Coast to try the famed Dungeness and who had not learned to tell good from bad.

Later, when I moved to the Puget Sound area with its large urban population, I expected to find fresh, locally caught Dungeness crab in the seafood shops, but I suffered some awful disappointments. I learned that here also much of the crab sold as "fresh" had actually been frozen and thawed. Dungeness does not freeze well, and after it is defrosted, it spoils very rapidly. Rotten crab has a horrid, lingering taste and, to spare myself further frustrations, I stopped eating crab—until I could catch my own. Even now, I never buy frozen or precooked "fresh" crab.

In recent years, storage of live crabs in saltwater tanks has become more common in the Pacific Northwest, and even crab cookers have made their long overdue appearance. This may be an indication that fewer people take the time to catch their own, but it also shows a rising interest in the quality of the crab bought from seafood markets. Just a word of caution: when buying fresh crab, make sure you get to select the crab you want from the tank and watch it being cooked while you wait (take a close look at the mouth of your crab: if it is covered with foam or bubbles, the crab has started to die and you don't want it). Otherwise you have no guarantee of freshness. It is difficult to tell how long ago a cold crab was cooked—unless it has developed a putrid smell—or, if it is hot, if it was merely reheated. Besides, it is much more fun to select your own live crab and wait till it is freshly cooked.

You can look at the other seafoods displayed in the market, and you may have a great time asking the fishmonger all sorts of questions. You might even discover something interesting you have never tried before. But don't be talked into buying something you don't want, and always insist on smelling seafood before you buy it—if it doesn't have a fresh smell, turn it down (i.e., if it smells fishy, muddy, or stale, it is too old). It is up to you, not your fishmonger, to test the freshness of their products. After all, you'll be the one to get indigestion—or worse—from a tarnished crab, not your fishmonger.

As the quality of the Dungeness crab sold commercially has increased in recent years, so has the demand for it, especially on the East Coast. The Dungeness is perhaps the best of all American crabs and has the greatest percentage of meat per body weight (24 percent versus a typical 20 percent). It is now airfreighted regularly to eastern markets, where it is sold still very much alive. Sad to say, it is sometimes possible to buy fresher Dungeness crab in Denver or New York than in the Pacific Northwest port cities.

Bright orange crabs, cooked who knows when, their legs tidily folded underneath their bodies, look nice when displayed on sparkling mountains of crushed ice, but they taste awful. Here, however, the consumer is to blame. If Northwesterners were to refuse these tarnished specimens and demand fresh crabs instead, fishmongers would comply quickly. But as long as enough people are willing to buy an inferior product, merchants will have little reason to change. Fortunately, for those who care, fresh, live crab is commonly for sale in the Chinese and Japanese markets of our larger cities. Portland gourmets regularly can buy live crab (flown in from Alaska) at Peter Troy's seafood stores, Seattleites are occasionally able to buy it at the Pike Place Market, and in British Columbia, Vancouverites can find a ready supply of fresh Dungeness, graded according to size, in the live tanks at the Lobsterman on Granville Island. But those of us who live in small coastal towns with lots of fresh seafood in nearby waters, but without reliable seafood markets within driving distance, are still better off catching our own. Gourmets living in the inland areas of the Pacific Northwest must travel to the Coast to taste really fresh crab—and hope for luck in finding it.

The increased demand for Dungeness crab on the East Coast, steady overharvesting of the resource, and the cyclical slump in supply have put a greater strain than ever on the crab supply available to local gourmet crabbers. But we are fortunate in having several other crabs in our waters which are at least as tasty (perhaps tastier) as the Dungeness.

Our crabs may be roughly divided into three groups, based on their outward appearance. Representatives of the *cancer* group look more or less like the Dungeness, though most of our other species are generally smaller and have harder and/or spinier shells. Spider crabs, with long legs and compact bodies that are small in relation to their size, look like, but aren't, marine spiders. Hermit crabs have large claws and shrimpy bodies with soft abdomens, which they prefer to hide in the abandoned shells of gastropods. Small ones can withdraw completely into those shells and look like snails. They have even fooled the experts. The West Coast people of Vancouver Island once thought that marine gastropods came in two incarnations: edible snail and inedible crab (thought of as a snail that had temporarily grown legs). They were wrong. Hermit crabs are not only edible, but also delicious. And so are all of our other crabs, even though some of them take on quite bizarre shapes to discourage the gourmet.

The red rock crab (*Cancer productus*) looks very much like a Dungeness crab, but has a deep reddish-brown coloration and smaller, black-tipped claws. Like its larger cousin, it is very common both on the outer coast and in the inland waters, and it is the only large crab in Puget Sound south of Tacoma (no one quite knows why the Dungeness shuns the lower Sound, but it becomes plentiful only north of Seattle). The red crab reaches the respectable size of eight to nine inches, to the Dungeness's potential size of ten to twelve inches, but our Dungeness have been trapped so efficiently that large specimens are quite rare now. The red crab has a heavier shell and less meat than the Dungeness, but its flavor is exquisite and crab fanciers regularly argue about their preference for one or the other of these two large crabs. The red crab occupies much the same habitat—eelgrass beds and sandy bottoms—but it can often be found on rocky shores among cobbles and boulders or partly buried in sand. It is often taken with the Dungeness crab in pots or traps. This crab, like our other large crabs, is prepared like the Dungeness.

The red crab's much smaller cousin, the dull-red rock crab (*Cancer oregonensis*), is found only on rocky shores. It likes to hide in holes, where it defends itself with its large, powerful claws, but it can sometimes be taken in tidepools. The rock crab yields only a few morsels of meat from its little body, but it more than makes up for this with the copious amount of meat contained in its claws.

Several small crabs are found along our rocky, sandy, and gravelly shores. All are edible. They range in size from the two-inch purple shore crab, which is found in large numbers under almost every boulder or rock, down to tiny kelp crabs clinging to eelgrass stalks. Their flavors vary quite a bit, but all add interesting tastes to seafood stews. Boiling Dungeness or red crabs in a cioppino or other stew has always seemed a waste of good crab meat to me. But the small shore and seaweed crabs are ideally suited for this purpose. (Crabs with plant or animal growth on their carapaces should be scrubbed clean before cooking—not all of these hitchhikers are palatable.) Too small to give much meat, these lesser crabs can be boiled and sucked clean, and their shells may be ground to thicken the bisque. The shore crabs may be broken in half and cleaned before they are thrown into the stew pot. The body meat should fall out during the cooking, and the legs can be picked clean with toothpicks. Prolonged cooking will just about dissolve the crab meat, however, but the flavor will linger in the stew. When cleaning a female crab (other than a Dungeness which must be thrown back), never throw out the yellow pâté, the gonads, clinging to the inside of the carapace—I think they are the most delicious part of these crustaceans. If you are lucky enough to find a (legal) female crab with roe clapped under its broad tail, carefully remove it and serve it on sushi, topped with either a raw quail egg or a dab of Japanese horseradish (*wasabi*).

Bizarre looks are not reserved for our small crabs. Several large crabs, much larger than even a Dungeness, live in the deep inland channels and offshore waters of the Pacific Northwest. A large spider crab (*Chionoecetes opilio*), one of two species caught commercially in Alaska and sold as "snow" crab (formerly "tanner" crab), occurs as far south as Puget Sound and is sometimes caught in large crab pots set in deep water. It looks like a small king crab and is prepared like king crab: the thick legs can be split lengthwise down the middle, broiled, and served with lemon butter.

The large, chunky, and very spiny box crabs (*Lopholithodes foraminatus*) and the Puget Sound king crabs (*Lopholithodes Mandtii*), not to be confused with the spidery Alaskan king crab, are sometimes taken by divers. These crabs grow to be very large; the Puget Sound king crab grows to be more than a foot across, up to six inches thick, and the large legs, which can fold up to the body, making the crabs look like spiny boxes, can reach a length of eleven inches or more. Crabs weighing nine pounds are fairly common; larger ones may reach a weight of thirteen to fourteen pounds. These crabs should be killed and cleaned before they are cooked. Their meat is so thick that the outside will be overcooked, while the inside may remain raw. It is excellent broiled. The meat can be treated like lobster or like Dungeness crab meat, and it can be used in all dishes calling for crab. Its taste is richer and more satisfying, however, and a little may go a long way.

It is a curious gastronomic fact that the French, those inveterate lovers of lobsters and crawfish, have little use and few recipes for the crab. Yet the Bretons, the gaelic-speaking inhabitants of the Armorican peninsula, love to eat crab. They may have inherited this culinary preference from their crab-eating forebears who migrated to Brittany from Cornwall and Wales at the end of the Roman era. And the Bretons rightly prefer one kind of crab to all others—*Bernard l'eremite*, the lowly hermit crab. The Pacific Northwest has a great variety of tasty hermit crabs, from small species living under the rocks of the upper littoral fringe to large ones living in deep water. All are delicious to eat, but they are now eaten primarily by the few descendants of Breton fishermen living in our area and by the Chinese. Hermit crabs are a gourmet treat and are well worth gathering. They are easy to clean: if you cannot pull them from the shell—beware of their pincers—break the shell with a hammer and remove the crab from its hiding place. Small hermit crabs can be treated like shore crabs and added to stews; larger ones may be boiled, steamed, or stir-fried and cracked, sucked, or picked. The large claws are especially rewarding; the abdomen and the yellow coral are the tastiest tidbits.

Pea crabs are tiny, soft-bodied, half-inch crustaceans found in the mantle cavities of oysters, clams, and sometimes mussels. They can be eaten whole. The females of these commensal crabs, which live on diatoms and other microorganisms, lead the sluggish life-style of filter feeders, and they are commonly taken with the bivalve they inhabit. The much smaller males are more agile, often moving from clam to clam to fertilize female pea crabs, and they are sometimes mistaken for large ticks, to which they are not related. Like the females, they are perfectly edible and quite delicious, but you'll need a lot of crabs to make a meal. You're in luck if you know a commercial oyster or clam shucker who will save them for you (they must be eaten fresh) or you can watch for them when you shuck oysters and clams yourself.

Pea crabs begin life as larvae which settle in the shells of small steamer clams and oysters. As they grow in size, they move to larger cockles, soft-shell, or butter clams, and they reach their maximum development in horse clam (gaper) shells. These tiny guests do not harm their hosts, but they may cause an irritation of the bivalve's mantle. (Pea crabs living in tropical oysters often end up inside pearls for this reason.) The largest pea crabs, living in the largest clams, can reach a diameter of about one inch, but they rarely do.

Pea crabs can be eaten steamed, sautéed, or stir-fried, and they add a nice touch to seafood stews and appetizer trays. If you steam your clams open and discover pea crabs inside, you can just pop them into your mouth—they should be cooked to perfection. I like dipping them into a lemon butter or a Japanese (rice vinegar) sweet and sour sauce. They are excellent served on sushi in small clusters.

Crabs are among the most delicious of seafoods, but we have not taken full advantage of their variety and plentitude. Concentrating almost exclusively on the large Dungeness, we have ignored the great numbers of tasty little crabs crowding our beaches. Sure, you'll have to gather your own, and there isn't much meat on them; but the same is true for snails and shrimp. Our little crabs are well worth the effort it takes to catch and cook them. Besides, they look very pretty in a seafood stew or as garnishes for a seafood or vegetable platter. And, unlike the large Dungeness, they are plentiful.

Basic Cooked Crab

First method:
(Cleaning crab before cooking)

1. Remove back of crab by forcing front edge of shell against solid object (bucket rim, oar blade, gunwale, shovel blade, etc.) and pulling down.
2. Break crab in two by folding shell up and down.
3. Remove viscera, but save for crab bisque or stock.
4. Pull off gill filaments. Discard.
5. Cook as soon as possible after cleaning: use 3 to 5 ounces of salt per gallon of fresh water (or use clean seawater). Bring to a boil, add crab, and boil for 15 minutes after water returns to boil. Remove crabs from kettle and immediately chill in ice or iced water.

Second method:
(Cooking crab before cleaning)

1. Bring saltwater to boil, add crab backside down (the legs will fold over the belly as the crab dies instantly in the hot water). Cook for about 20 minutes after water returns to boil.
2. Place crab in iced water as soon as it is removed from pot.
3. When thoroughly chilled, raise and break off tail (triangular flap beneath belly). Break off back; wash out and discard insides, leaving clean white meat.
4. Break crab body in half and separate legs from body. Crack legs. Eat directly from shell or reserve meat for later use.

Stir-Fried Dungeness Crab

Leftover crab meat may be used for this recipe. Accompany with a good local ale or lager beer.

Vegetable oil   2 tablespoons
Celery   8 stalks, diced
Green pepper   1, diced
Medium onions   2, diced
Crab meat   from 4 crabs or 1 pint assorted chunks
Bean sprouts or mixed sprouts   1 pound
Cooked rice

1. Heat wok or skillet until it smokes. Add oil. When oil is hot, add celery, pepper, and onions. Cook until tender.
2. Add crab meat and bean sprouts. Cook for 3 minutes more. Serve hot over rice.

Serves 4 to 6

Jerilyn Brusseau's Crab Vermouth

This dish should be made with only the freshest Dungeness or rock crab. Serve with freshly baked bread and Blackhook Porter.

Unsalted butter   ¼ pound
Garlic   2 tablespoons minced
Shallots   2 tablespoons finely chopped
Parsley   2 tablespoons chopped
Dry vermouth   1 cup
Rich chicken stock   2 cups
Soy sauce   1 tablespoon
Lemon juice   1 tablespoon
Medium-sized crab   2 (about 2 pounds each)
Dry vermouth   ¼ cup

1. Melt butter in large stock pot. Add garlic, shallots, and parsley. Cook gently 2 minutes over medium heat. Add 1 cup vermouth, chicken stock, soy sauce, and lemon juice. Bring to a boil. Reduce heat, cover, and simmer for 10 minutes.
2. Clean and crack crab. Add to above broth and simmer an additional 10 to 15 minutes.
3. Just before serving, add an additional ¼ cup vermouth to stock pot.
4. Ladle into individual shallow bowls.

Serves 4 to 6

Sooke Harbour House Crab Bisque

This is a very good recipe which has met with resounding acclaim from the patrons of the Sooke Harbour House, that lonely outpost of good dining on Juan de Fuca Strait. It is best put together in three stages: velouté, crab stock, and the finishing of the bisque.

Velouté:

Unsalted butter   6 tablespoons
Flour   4 tablespoons
Hot milk   3 cups
Freshly ground pepper   to taste
Freshly ground nutmeg   pinch

1. In heavy bottomed saucepan, melt butter over low heat.
2. Blend in flour and stir slowly until roux bubbles, about 2 minutes.
3. Remove from heat, pour in hot milk, and blend using a wire whip.
4. Return saucepan to stove and over high heat bring to boil for 1 minute, stirring carefully to avoid scorching.
5. Remove from heat and season lightly with pepper and nutmeg. (Do not add salt as crab is high in iodine.)

Crab Stock:

Live crabs (Dungeness, rock, Puget Sound king or box crab)   3, all parts except gills
    (size should be about 6 inches across the back)
Olive oil   ½ cup
Onion   ½ cup finely chopped
Lovage   ½ cup finely chopped
Carrot   ½ cup finely chopped
Garlic cloves   2, minced
Paprika   1 teaspoon
Fresh tarragon   1 tablespoon chopped
Cayenne   ½ teaspoon
Bay leaf   1
Dried thyme   pinch
Reduced stewed tomatoes (or canned tomato paste)   3 tablespoons
Brandy   ½ cup
Fish stock   4 cups
White wine   1 cup

1. Plunge live crabs upside down into a bowl of very hot water and when bubbles cease, crabs will be limp and ready to work with.
2. Over a bowl, remove shells, reserving juices, and cut up shells into smaller pieces.
3. Discard gills which are attached to the chest on either side (save all other internal parts).
4. Pull off all legs and break in half.
5. Cut body in half and then into smaller pieces.
6. Place all crab and shell into a roasting pan with olive oil, onion, lovage, carrot, garlic, paprika, tarragon, cayenne, bay leaf, thyme, tomatoes, and brandy.
7. Mix together and place in a hot oven (375°) for 20 minutes.
8. Remove from oven and scrape ingredients into a large saucepan.
9. Add fish stock, white wine, and reserved crab juices and bring to a boil.
10. Simmer for ½ hour.
11. Carefully correct seasoning to taste with salt and pepper.
12. Strain, reserving stock.
13. When crab has cooled, remove meat and set aside for garnish.
14. Pour Crab Stock into Velouté using a wire whip to blend the two together.
15. Bring to a simmer. If too thick, thin with additional fish stock.

Finishing:

Whipping cream   1 cup
Crab meat   reserved from Crab Stock
Bisque   prepared in first two stages
Paprika   garnish (optional)
Parsley   garnish (optional)

1. Mix whipping cream and crab meat together and pour into bisque.
2. Serve in a hot tureen or in soup bowls and sprinkle with paprika and/or finely chopped parsley on top for color.

Serves 6

Betty Freeberg's Crab Casserole

Both Betty and her husband Hjalmar just love fresh crab. Here is one of their favorite recipes for surplus crab meat. Serve with asparagus, tossed salad, and a dry white wine. Indian fried bread goes well with this dish.

Crab meat   2 cups
Evaporated milk   ¾ cup
Mayonnaise   1 cup
Eggs   6, hard-cooked and chopped
Parsley   1 tablespoon finely chopped
Onion   1 tablespoon chopped
Salt   ½ teaspoon
Freshly ground pepper   dash
Unsalted butter   3 tablespoons, melted
Bread crumbs   ¾ cup

1. Mix crab meat, milk, mayonnaise, eggs, parsley, onion, salt, and pepper. Place in oven-proof casserole and top with melted butter and bread crumbs. Bake at 350° for 45 minutes.

Note: Mixture will be "soupy" looking when mixed, but it firms up and makes a moist dish with perfect texture. Rich, of course. Shrimp or chicken may also be used. This can be prepared ahead, but the topping should be put on just before baking.

Makes 6 hearty servings

Shrimp, Crawfish, and Other Crustaceans

One chill, foggy March morning, I was happily ensconced on the *Lady Rose,* the Alberni Canal mail boat, one of two survivors from a once-numerous fleet of steamers that plied the west coast of Vancouver Island. I was glad we had radar aboard, because there was a pea soup fog outside, and we had a large Canadian Coast Guard vessel just off our port bow, traveling in the same direction. Gathered around the hot coffeepot in the ship's tiny galley, we discussed local events. There was no breakfast (just about all of us had indulged in the plain, but tasty fare at the Blue Door in Port Alberni), and the galley did not look as though it could turn out gourmet fare. How wrong we were.

Halfway down the canal, the fog lifted and, as we approached Barkley Sound, the sun began to warm us. After unloading passengers, groceries, and logging equipment at Kildonan and other small villages and logging camps hugging the steep rock walls of Uchucklesit Inlet, we steamed down the fjord into a dimpled reach of blue and silver. Fifteen minutes later, in midchannel, the *Lady Rose* slowed again. The mate tapped me on the shoulder: "Why don't you come along for a minute? I'd like to show you something." I followed him down the companionway, through the narrow passage leading past the heads to the lounge, through the lounge, the galley, the crew's mess to the cargo hold in the fo'c'sle. The hatch cover was down, and the hold lay in darkness, except for a narrow streak of light emanating from a narrow slit beside the partially closed cargo door in the starboard bow. The mate opened and secured the door. Bits of spume from the bow wave blew in through the opening, but now the skipper cut the engine and the vessel lost headway. The mate clipped a large snatch block into an eyebolt in the overhead doorframe, picked up a boathook, and stepped out the door onto the rubbing strake. Grasping the doorframe with one hand, he leaned out over the water, holding the gaff ready.

Just then we drifted up to a small, white marker buoy. The mate snagged the line with his hook, stepped back, and flipped it over the sheave in the snatch block. Turning toward me, he yelled, "Heave!" We both pulled away, as fathom after fathom of wet line coiled at our feet. The load was quite heavy, and I wondered what in the world we were bringing up from this deep fjord in the middle of nowhere. The mate said, "Shrimp pots." A few minutes later, after we had gathered several hundred feet of line, the first shrimp pot, a large, sturdy wire cage, splashed into sight and was swung into the hold. The mate reached through the door and pulled up two more pots, smaller hobby traps, attached to the commercial pot with short lines. He opened the traps and poured a mess of pastel-colored side-stripe shrimp, each between four and six inches long, onto the deck. He quickly broke them in half, dropping the tails into a bucket, and shucking the heads overboard. When he had finished, he rebaited the traps and lowered them back into the hundred-odd fathoms of water which separated us from the bottom. The buoy was flung out last.

Having disposed of the traps, the mate grabbed the bucket of shrimp, slammed the door shut, and headed for the galley, chuckling, "A shrimper accused us of raiding his pots— so he decided to let us have some of our own. He claims it stopped the poaching." In the galley another crew member had brought a pot of water to a rolling boil. The mate dropped in the shrimp tails—cooking them for about three minutes only. He claimed there was nothing worse you could do to these delicate crustaceans than to overcook them. He quickly drained the tails and presented them on a platter with hot sauce.

In the meantime, the other passengers (all two of them) had joined us, and we dug in. No one used the hot sauce. The shrimp were tender, flavorful, slightly crisp, with a subtle saltwater undertaste. I had never before eaten any shrimp that even approached the taste of these Uchucklesit Inlet shrimp. Their flavor was sublime, and they have affected my attitude toward other shrimp ever since. Don't look for sidestripe shrimp in your seafood market's sales bin: they are among the most delicate and quick-to-spoil crustaceans. None are processed commercially, because they will not keep. Yet I cannot help continually comparing any other shrimp I eat to those I enjoyed on this chill March morning in this most improbable location: on a tiny mail ship, drifting in a backwoods inlet along Vancouver Island's sparsely inhabited west coast. Who would have thought the *Lady Rose's* inadequate galley could produce such a meal, much less establish a new standard of culinary excellence.

The Pacific Northwest is blessed with a number of delectable saltwater shrimp, but trying to procure these from a fish market is quite a chore. The Pike Place Market fishmongers in Seattle sometimes sell local shrimp, and they can be found—much too infrequently (and frozen)—in other urban seafood shops. Little wonder the owner of one of my favorite restaurants argued with me when I complained about the Gulf (of Mexico) shrimp she was serving that night: "But there are no northwest shrimp!" Of course, there are. Yet this same protest was echoed a few weeks later when I asked for local shrimp in a small-town fish market. The problem lies with our wholesalers, who want to deal only with those products that are available in bulk, preferably all year long. This is one reason they like to freeze seafood for lengthy storage and dole it out a bit at a time. It also helps keep prices high at the height of the season.

Very few people have experienced the delightful taste of fresh shrimp. Much of the shrimp sold in the Pacific Northwest, including some that passes as "local," is tropical shrimp, caught in the Gulf of Mexico and farther south. Beheaded and iced aboard trawlers, these large shrimp (that is, their tails) are delivered to processors onshore who wash them, grade them by size, and re-ice them (or freeze them) before they ship these crustaceans across the country as "fresh" shrimp or "prawns." There is nothing wrong with these packaged tails, except that a large percentage of the Gulf shrimp or "prawns" sold in our seafood markets or served in our restaurants are quite stale, a fault even the best of sauces cannot hide—yet so few people can tell! It is surprisingly easy to forget the good taste of fresh shrimp, particularly if you have become accustomed to a diet of frozen or highly spiced shrimp (flavor-killers both). A Chinese acquaintance, Umon Ewart, uses the only method I know that seems to succeed in removing some of the staleness: he commonly soaks frozen "prawns" in straight vodka before stir-frying them. The strong liquor refreshes the meat and leaches out some of the processed taste and mustiness. I must confess that I myself, though I had eaten "fresh" shrimp on the North Sea Coast, in southern California, and on the coast of Oregon, had failed to establish a taste standard (or a taste memory, for that matter) until the flavor of truly fresh shrimp was brought home to me on that early March morning aboard the *Lady Rose*.

Most of the local shrimp you can buy are the tiny pink shrimplets, two hundred to four hundred tails per pound, that are caught off our outer coast, from Oregon to Alaska. Many of these, sold as "fresh," have been frozen. Our most delicious shrimp, besides the fragile sidestripe, are the large (to six inches or more) coonstripe and spotted shrimp, often called "prawns." We have no prawns—a type of large freshwater shrimp—in our region. Nor do we have "scampi"—saltwater crustaceans that look somewhat like small spiny lobsters. Yet our large shrimp are commonly marketed as "prawns" and these are called "scampi" by restaurateurs whenever they are cooked in butter and garlic. According to Waverly Root, this is even done in Italy, where cooks and gourmets should know better.

In the inland waters, Hood Canal produces a fair number of shrimp, from tiny, trawl-caught cocktail shrimp to several-inch-long coonstripes. But you may have to go to the canal during the season to get these delicacies fresh (check your local newspaper: these shrimp have been overharvested, like almost everything else). You may be able to buy some really fresh shrimp at the few shrimp shacks on the canal, but it is more likely that you will have to catch your own.

Shrimp are carnivorous and are attracted to decaying animal matter. This makes it fairly easy to catch them in shrimp traps (smaller-meshed versions of crab traps)—if they are around. Shrimp are strange creatures when seen in their native habitat. They may walk across the sea floor on their long, insectlike legs, as their bulging mobile-stalked eyes and their whiplike antennae probe the water, looking for something good to eat. Or they may swim, flipping their powerful, muscular tails to escape from danger. Live shrimp have translucent, almost gelatinous flesh (it turns white on cooking), and their see-through shells are marked with colorful lines, streaks, and dots (most of which disappear on cooking). Gray, that is, clear-colored, shrimp taste better than pink ones, for the pinkness comes from iodine stored in their bodies—very pink shrimp can have an almost medicinal taste, good for goiter, though not for your palate. The shells of shrimp, like those of other crustaceans, turn reddish/orange/pink when boiled.

Shrimp are very delicate and, no matter what the species, they should be eaten quickly after they are captured, because they lose their taste rapidly once they are removed from the sea. This culinary fact is known to many shrimp fanciers in the Pacific Northwest. Hordes of amateur shrimpers descend upon Hood Canal each year during the shrimping season with their kith and kin and shrimp traps, filling the woodsy campgrounds and seedy motels with their boisterous numbers in a ritual somewhat reminiscent of the annual pilgrimage to the razor clam beds of the ocean beaches. Yet there often is quite a gap twixt theory and practice. Some of these visitors do catch shrimp, and sometimes these shrimp are even eaten while they are still fresh. But more often than not, they are simply dumped into ice chests (newly emptied of beer), taken home, and consumed days later or, worst of all, thrown into the freezer, to be eaten after the rest of their flavor has evanesced. This is a shame, for the inimitable taste of fresh shrimp should never be traded for insipid frozen staleness.

You might be lucky and be in the right place on the Oregon coast at the right time, when you can buy fresh shrimp direct from the boat. But how fresh is fresh? Ocean-caught shrimp are commonly laid on ice, head and all, until the trawler comes into port, and it may have been out there for quite a number of days, since it does not pay to come in with a partial load. Storing these shrimp on ice retards spoilage, but it doesn't do much to improve the flavor. The head—actually the cephalothorax, fused from the head and thorax—rots much more quickly than the tail. If attached for too long, it will affect the taste of the tail, the part we commonly eat. In other words, you'll never know for how many days the shrimp you buy have been "fresh" already until you taste them.

The best way to assure yourself of a fresh supply of shrimp in the Pacific Northwest is still to go out and catch your own. But you need shrimp traps and a boat to catch any of our sidestripe and coonstripe shrimps or their relatives. It is sometimes possible to catch shrimp close to shore, and without a trap—if you are willing to get your feet wet. Small "broken-back" shrimp (they look that way, because they have a sharp kink in their tail at the third joint) are common on kelp and in tidepools; other shrimp cling to subtidal algae and eel-grass and surf grass. All are good to eat and they are easy to catch—if you can see them. These inch-long crustaceans can be so transparent they hardly throw a shadow, even in bright sunlight. They look somewhat like glass models of shrimp, and you can watch their hearts beat beneath their see-through carapaces. These shrimp can sometimes be shaken from bunches of kelp (it is possible to trap them on bundles of kelp suspended in the water), and seining with a fine-meshed fish net or with a butterfly net can bring good results. Sub-tidal species often take on the coloration of the seaweeds to which they cling. They are cooked like other shrimp—boiled very quickly—or they may be eaten raw (when collected from unpolluted waters).

There is a trick to eating shrimp raw. I like doing it in the Japanese fashion: rinse bunches of shrimp-bearing seaweeds off their crustacean tenants by swirling them around in a bucket of seawater (you may use trap- or net-caught shrimp or "prawns" instead) and carry them home. Stir some toasted sesame seeds into a (rice vinegar) sweet and sour sauce, or prepare a lemon-butter sauce. Wash the shrimp in clean salted water (¼ tablespoon per quart) or in freshwater. Grab the animal firmly by the tail and break off the head with a quick, twisting motion (don't throw away the head!). Break the shell by running the finger-nail of your free thumb along the underside of the tail, between the rows of leglike appen-dages, and twist off the shell in one quick motion (you'll get better with practice). You may remove the "sand-vein," the dark line running along the dorsal ridge, or leave it for extra flavor. Dip the tail into one of the sauces, or sprinkle it with a few drops of lemon, lime, or (yes!) rhubarb juice before eating it.

The bodies of shrimp, like those of other primitive animals, sometimes continue to move for short periods of time after death, and your fresh, raw shrimp tail may twitch a bit when you dip it into an acidic sauce. Don't let that disconcert you. You killed the animal quickly and painlessly when you took off its head (cephalothorax)—the twitching does not mean that the shrimp is still alive and suffering pain as you eat it.

The shrimp heads can be added to seafood stews to give them flavor, and they may be ground up and used to thicken bisques. Just inside the carapace, you can often find a pâtélike mass, the coral (gonads), which is very good to eat spread on crackers, toast, or sushi. I prefer it on sushi, because the taste and texture of the pâté go better with the acidulated rice than with the crunch of crackers or the baked flavor of bread. Large raw shrimp may be butterflied and served as appetizers, again preferably on sushi. You may prepare the sushi patties ahead of time. I wrap mine in seaweed, because they keep their shape better. There are few ways to dramatize a meal more than by serving sushi for appetizers: the host sits at the head of his table, preparing raw and cooked seafood which he hands to his guests as he completes them—and what could be more histrionic than serving wiggly-fresh shrimp? Besides, the taste is excellent; the meat will be sweet and slightly crunchy.

If you don't like the idea of eating your shrimp raw, drop the tails into rapidly boiling salted water for about a minute. If you must eat them well-done, wait till they float to the top, about three to five minutes. You may sauté them in butter or stir-fry them in a hot wok, using a neutral oil (apricot kernel oil works best), for about five minutes. Fresh shrimp may be used in soups, grilled over charcoal, baked and, yes, covered with batter and deep-fried.

If you buy "fresh" or frozen shrimp from a seafood market, make sure the shrimp are translucent, have a clean fresh smell, and show no black spots, a sign of spoilage. These spots may only affect the shells, or they may penetrate the meat: in either case, the shrimp have become inedible. Frozen shrimp should have no fuzzy white patches which indicate dehydration. But why not buy fresh local shrimp in season instead? Or catch your own? Why settle for less than the best?

Two large, shrimplike crustaceans are occasionally dug up by clammers searching for bivalves on sandy, muddy beaches. Both the ghost shrimp and the mud shrimp make extensive burrows, marked on the outside by small, conical mounds. The ghost shrimp grows to an average length of about four inches, but may reach six, and is a pale pink and orange pastel color. It burrows at the midtide level in areas where the sand is heavily intermixed with mud. The somewhat smaller blue mud shrimp often occurs in the same habitat, but it sometimes lives in quite muddy tideflats and likes it deeper down in the littoral zone.

These shrimp are filter feeders, and they have been poisoned with insecticides by Oregon shellfish growers, because they may compete for food with cultivated oysters. What a ridiculous thing to do! Both of these shrimp are very delectable when collected from unpolluted tideflats, and I simply do not understand why anyone would wish to poison them when they are so good to eat. They can be prepared like other crustaceans.

Cautious digging is advisable when searching for mud or ghost shrimp, for their fragile tunnels may cave in before the animals are found. A stealthy approach and a quick stroke with a long shovel blade a foot or so beneath the surface often spells success. These crustaceans are quite flabby and helpless once they lie exposed on the beach—but beware of the ghost shrimp's large claws! If you accidentally bisect a shrimp with your shovel, just dig out the rest of the body, wash it in the surf, and cook it as soon as you get home. Mud shrimp look a little like a saltwater crawfish, without the claws, on first glance; but a quick check under the abdomen will show a series of modified legs which help this shrimp pump water through its burrow. Crawfish are something else! They are not, of course, fish but freshwater crustaceans.

Among the many arguments presented in nominating our region's tastiest crustacean, the crawfish always scores highly. Many gourmets claim it is the tastiest. But this may have more to do with the fact that this small freshwater lobster rates highly on the list of French gourmet foods (it really made a comeback with *nouvelle cuisine*), than with its excellent taste alone. I have always been very partial to crawfish, yet it would be hard to champion its flavor against the different, though equally exquisite, savors of fresh Dungeness crab, sidestripe shrimp, or gooseneck barnacles, because all of these delectable crustaceans make unique taste statements. But the meat of fresh Pacific Northwest crawfish is far superior to that of the lobsters flown in from Maine or the Canadian maritime provinces. Lobsters, like other crustaceans, begin to die as soon as they are removed from their native habitat and, while they may still be somewhat alive when you buy them from your fishmonger, they will have lost much of their tastiness. Crawfish on the other hand, are available fresh from our lakes and rivers, and they keep well in freshwater tanks.

In recent years, numerous attempts have been made on the West Coast to come up with a successful method of aquaculture for growing lobster. I wish the experimenters would concentrate on crawfish instead. These not only taste better and have a better meat texture, but they are small enough to make cooking and serving fairly easy. I have eaten fresh crawfish for at least a couple of decades now, but I have never yet bought any. I have always caught my own. In recent years, I have had good luck on Lake Whatcom, using shrimp traps baited with fish heads, but I have most often caught crawfish with my bare hands. I still fondly remember one of my greatest crawdad hauls—and it happened some fifteen years ago.

I had stopped at a small meadow on the banks of southern Oregon's meandering Applegate River. The place looked as though it had once been a homestead or ranch. The buildings were gone, but here and there a crumbling foundation or a hewn stone poked through the brambles, and blooming fruit trees mingled with the buckbrush and oaks of the abutting hillside. I had spent the night in the shelter of several large weeping willows which grew near the shore, watching their long branches trail in the sluggish stream. The morning fog rose from the upstream cataracts and veiled the Siskiyous, reminding me of a painting by the emperor Kao-tsung. Walking to my car for my sketchbook, I repeated several lines from a Su Shih poem:

> The fisherman wakes.
> At noon on the spring river;
> Fallen blossoms, flying catkins intrude into his dream.
> Sobered up from wine and still drunk, drunk and yet sober—
> He laughs at the human world, both past and present.
>   Translated by Irving Y. Lo

I felt entrapped in an enchantment. Returning to the river, I noticed a slight commotion in the foliage of a Hind's willow and saw something I had not expected to see this side of the tropics. Several feet off the ground, a slender green snake was gliding through the branches of gray willows and brown dogwoods. I tried to follow, but the snake (it turned out to be a yellow-bellied racer when I looked it up later in my reptile guide) easily outdistanced me. Reaching the end of the thicket at the weeping willow grove, the snake dropped onto the trunk of an old red willow and vanished. I searched the surrounding grasses and sedges to get another look at it, but to no avail. The racer had flushed a small aquatic garter snake from its hiding place under the bank, and I watched this snake for a while as it stemmed the current with its writhing body, head erect like a periscope. After it had reached the further shore, I looked into the water and beheld—breakfast.

A large grandfather crawdad sat on the bottom of the stream, only a foot and a half beneath me. I stepped back carefully, trying not to alarm him, got a bucket from my car, and filled it a quarter full of river water. Then I stretched out on the bank and carefully put my hand into the water above the unsuspecting crawfish. Snatch! I had him! His large claws bent backwards, trying to nip me, but I held him firmly at the junction of tail and carapace, just out of reach of his pincers, and dropped him into the bucket. This crawfish must have occupied a favored spot under the bank (with little birds and other food dropping down from the willow?) for, no sooner was I back in place than another crawfish walked out of the weeds to occupy the newly abandoned gravel patch. Grab! Then two more, fighting each other. They didn't even disengage as I put them in the pail. This was too good to be true, I thought, as crawfish after crawfish joined his buddies in my bucket. I seemed to be going right down the pecking order among local crawdads, but the crustaceans weren't getting any smaller. My arm numbed from the cold water, and I did not even notice I was bleeding until I saw little curls of red flow downstream. Had a crawdad pinched me? My arm was too numb to tell. The blood really seemed to bring out the critters and numb or not, I kept snatching them until my bucket was overflowing. Here was not just breakfast, but lunch and dinner as well.

I killed about two dozen of the crawfish by twisting off their tails (this separates the spinal cord), then dropped the tails and the large claws into a bowl of white wine and left them to marinate as I built a small fire in a ring of fieldstones. While the coffee water heated up on the fire, I cut myself a few slices of french bread, scooped the coral from the carapaces, and spread it onto the slices. It was delicious. When the coffee was done and the wood had burned down into white coals, I set my small portable grill onto the rocks, pulled the crawfish tails and claws from the marinade, and arranged them on the barbecue. After they had warmed up, I threw a handful of Oregon myrtle and cut-leaved sage leaves onto the fire. The short flare-up sealed in the juices and the myrtle and sage flavored the crawfish nicely. A touch of salt and pepper and the crawfish were done.

I ate about half of the claws and tails hot for breakfast and the others cold for lunch. I changed the water in the bucket a couple of times to make sure the live crawfish would have enough oxygen and wedged the pail behind my seat before I drove off. Later that day, I had crawfish and mussel stew for dinner as I camped on a protected beach near Bandon.

I have always made sure to have a ready supply of crawfish on hand, but not until several years after the Applegate bounty did I once again encounter that many crawfish in one place (outside a trap, that is). Crawfish are common in lakes and streams in Oregon, Washington, and north into British Columbia, but they seem to do best in moderately warm waters. I have consistently caught more crawfish in Oregon than in Washington, and I have found the crawfish south of the Columbia River larger and tastier. But I may be splitting hairs: all Pacific Northwest crawfish are delicious, wherever they are found, and, best of all, they can be prepared in a variety of ways.

Some of the crustaceans inhabiting the waters of the Pacific Northwest—spider crabs, box crabs, hermit crabs, crawfish, and shrimp—attract a lot of attention because of their grotesque shapes. But, no matter how extraordinary they seem to the human eye, they at least maintain the basic structure of decapod crustaceans, and all of their weirdness lies in their external appearance. The most strange-looking crustacean we encounter in our region is, however, the common barnacle. Most visitors to our beaches ignore barnacles, merely viewing them as lumpy encrustations on seaside pilings and rocks—as some kind of pointy shellfish that isn't good for anything, but that cuts your bare feet if you walk across their beds. Mariners hate barnacles because they settle on ships' hulls, below the waterline, and can noticeably slow a vessel's speed. They fight barnacles with poison paints or scrape them off by force. Yet these sailors would be much better off carrying the barnacles to their galleys, because these strange crustaceans are uncommonly good to eat.

Just imagine a boat's hull covered with tiny shrimp instead of barnacles. The vessel's owner would consider himself fortunate and, several times a year, he would careen the hull and descend upon the exposed crustaceans with hungry glee. After all, the lowly barnacle is, for all practical purposes, much like a shrimp that has enclosed itself inside a thick, calcareous shell and spends its life "fixed by its head and kicking the food into its mouth with its legs" (as Thomas Huxley said so aptly), instead of swimming or walking about.

We have two types of barnacles on our coast: the short, squat acorn barnacle, with its white chalky shell, and the brownish-black stalked gooseneck barnacle. Large acorn barnacles of at least an inch or more across may be collected; the smaller ones aren't worth the labor. The giant barnacle, *Balanus nubilus*, the largest of the West Coast barnacles, often reaches a diameter of as much as two to three inches and a height of four to six inches. When crowded, its shell grows into a long, somewhat fragile tube which may stretch to a length of six inches. The giant barnacle prefers deep water, below the low-tide level, and is best collected by divers. Where these barnacles assume a squat form, they are almost impossible to remove from rocks, and they should be collected from a soft support, such as wooden pilings or the holdfasts of kelp. Where they grow close together, their tubes can often be broken off in large chunks (new barnacles will quickly colonize the bared spot).

Large acorn barnacles have a sizable lump of meat inside their shells (crack them with a hammer) and can be fixed in many different ways, boiled or steamed. The meat can be cleaned and cooked, or the whole animal can be steamed. In the latter case, the meat can be pushed out with a skewer or toothpick after it is done.

The gooseneck barnacle lacks the hard external shell of the acorn barnacle. It is sheathed in a tough, leathery skin, which is studded with white, tightly fitted calcareous plates at the pointed crown of its body. This barnacle protects itself from aggression by living in such tight clusters on exposed rocks that only the armed crowns rise above the communal mass. Gooseneck barnacles living on the margins of these colonies are very short; those in the middle may have stalks up to half a foot long. These barnacles are easy to collect—just separate them from their support by inserting a sharp knife between the stalk and the rock they sit on. They should be cooked as soon as possible after they are collected.

Gooseneck barnacles are an easily prepared gourmet treat. Wash them carefully in fresh water (you may have to scrub the base of the stalk with a small brush), bring the water to a boil in a steamer, and place the barnacles on a rack and steam them for about twenty minutes (or less). Peel off the skins after they are cooked. Discard the plate-covered crown and eat the pink-fleshed stalk. The meat looks like crab or shrimp meat, but it is more flavorful. It can be dipped into the usual sauces, or it may be used in crab or shrimp dishes.

Americans eat lots of shrimp each year, often paying exorbitant prices for crustaceans that have traveled from distant ports and have lost the pleasing taste of freshness during processing. Yet we crunch down on the barnacles which line our intertidal rocks with our heavy-soled shoes, rarely considering that the small pink crustaceans inside those craggy shells are at least as tasty as their free-swimming shrimpy cousins.

Yet we haven't done our shrimp the justice they deserve either. Eaten straight from the water, they are exceptionally delicious. But so are our crawfish, those small, lobsterlike crustaceans which inhabit our rivers and lakes. Unfortunately, both shrimp and crawfish suffer quickly from overharvesting, but here perhaps aquaculture may hold the key to a future bounteous supply. Let us hope for the success of programs established to raise these tasty crustaceans in ponds—we will eat the better for it.

Fresh Boiled Shrimp

Shrimp dishes are among the few I rarely, if ever, order in a restaurant. Shrimp must be impeccably fresh to be good, and I would much prefer eating them only once or twice a year, when I can have them fresh from the water, rather than suffer through a meal of the overcooked, iodine-flavored shrimp (an off-taste few sauces can successfully hide) served at our restaurants. Shrimp may be eaten raw, so there's no reason to overcook them. Cook them only until they have just turned opaque, no longer. If you're not quite sure how shrimp should taste, go to a sushi bar of your choice and try the shrimp both raw and cooked.

Fresh uncooked shrimp in the shell   3 or 4 pounds (or however many you can catch)
Water   to cover
Salt   to taste
Lemon Butter

1. Kill shrimp quickly by breaking in half (with a twisting motion) where the tail and main body join.
2. Drop both heads and tails into boiling salted water (clean seawater may be used).
3. Cook until they turn opaque. Immediately remove from water. Serve hot with Lemon Butter and cold, dry semillon or sauvignon blanc.

Note: The tails can be peeled and eaten in the conventional fashion. The heads may be sucked clean. It is quite permissible to slurp loudly when sucking shrimp heads. This recipe may also be used for crawfish.

Serves 6 to 8

Lemon Butter

Unsalted butter   ½ cup
Fresh lemon juice   from ½ lemon
Worcestershire sauce   1 teaspoon
Salt and freshly ground pepper   to taste
Garlic clove   1, crushed but not peeled

1. Heat butter until quite hot and almost bubbling.
2. Add remaining ingredients and stir, blending well.

Note: Serve with freshly cooked shrimp, either as a dip or poured over individual servings of shrimp.

Makes ½ cup

Crawfish in Cream Sauce

You'll probably have to catch your own crawfish for this dish, but the little morsels are so delectable it's well worth it. Serve over toast, accompanied with a crisp chardonnay or a good lager beer.

Unsalted butter   2 tablespoons
Cooked crawfish tails   1½ pounds shelled
Salt and freshly ground pepper   to taste
Paprika   1 tablespoon
Shallots   1 tablespoon finely chopped
Dry sherry   ⅓ cup
Heavy cream   1½ cups
Crawfish coral (from thorax, if available. Can be omitted)   as available
Egg yolks   2

1. Melt butter in a large, heavy skillet and add crawfish tails. Cook briefly—just long enough to heat through—and sprinkle with salt, pepper, and paprika.
2. Sprinkle with shallots and stir. Sprinkle with wine and stir.
3. As soon as crawfish tails are warmed through (check by eating a large one, since cooking time will vary with size of tail), transfer to another skillet and cover to keep warm.
4. Reduce pan liquid by half and add 1¼ cups of cream. Add coral or other flavorful substances retrieved from cephalothorax. Cook about 5 minutes over high heat. Stir to keep from burning.
5. Beat the yolks with remaining ¼ cup cream and add to cream sauce, stirring rapidly. Bring almost, but not quite, to boil. Add crawfish tails and reheat.

Serves 4 to 6

Crawfish in Apple Cider

This recipe calls for a dry cider made from tart apples. You may have trouble using the sweet ciders sold in our stores, unless you have a sweet tooth, but you should have no difficulty finding a nice, tart cider at a roadside stand or at a farmers' market. Serve with mashed potatoes, crisp-cooked vegetables, and a chilled dry sauvignon blanc or semillon or, if you have used sweet cider, with a sweet riesling.

Cooked, peeled crawfish tails   1½ pounds, preferably same size
Unsalted butter   3 tablespoons
Shallots   2 tablespoons finely chopped
Concentrated dry cider*   2 tablespoons
Heavy cream   ¾ cup
Salt and freshly ground pepper   to taste

1. Rinse crawfish tails under cold running water, remove vein running down the back, and pat dry.
2. Melt butter in a heavy skillet and add tails and shallots.
3. Add cider and stir.
4. Remove tails with slotted spoon. Keep warm.
5. Add cream to skillet and cook over high heat for 1 minute. Add salt and pepper to taste. Return crawfish tails to skillet and cook just to heat through.

* Boil down 1 cup of dry cider until you have 2 tablespoons of concentrate. If you like a stronger flavor, boil down 2 cups.

Serves 2 to 4

Gooseneck Barnacles: Basic Preparation

Cooked gooseneck barnacles taste very much like shrimp, though they have a bit more flavor. Only the pink meat of the elongated stalk is eaten. (It tends to be longer in gooseneck barnacles taken from dense clusters.) Accompany with Indian fried bread and a dry white wine or a good, well-chilled lager beer.

Gooseneck barnacles   48
Butter   ½ cup, melted (optional)
Fresh lemon juice   from 1 lemon (optional)

1. Collect barnacles by cutting through stalk at the bottom, avoiding grit and rock at base.
2. Cook immediately after collecting: place barnacles on steamer rack in steamer and steam

over a small amount of water for 20 minutes.

3. Remove from steamer, pull off shells with fingers, then pull off feathery legs. Peel away tough, rindlike skin of stalk with sharp knife. The pink, delicate meat may be used in recipes calling for shrimp. Or the morsels may be dipped in lemon juice, melted butter, or both.

Serves 4 to 6

Marinated Gooseneck Barnacles and Cheese

Accompany with Indian fried bread and a well-chilled dry sauvignon blanc, semillon, or lager beer.

Pleasant Valley gouda (or other mild cheese)   1 pound
Gooseneck barnacle (pink stalk) meat*   1 pound, cooked
Olive oil   1 cup
Red wine vinegar   ¼ cup
Sweet basil   ½ teaspoon
Dry mustard   ¼ teaspoon
Oregano   ¼ teaspoon
Salt   ¼ teaspoon
Garlic   1 teaspoon minced
Pepper   pinch
Japanese kyūri cucumber   1, thinly sliced

1. Cut cheese into slices about 2 inches square. Arrange a simple layer of overlapping slices in a shallow serving dish. Spread barnacle meat over top.
2. In jar combine remaining ingredients, except cucumber. Shake to blend. Pour over barnacle and cheese.
3. Cover and refrigerate at least four hours or overnight.
4. Garnish with cucumber rounds before serving from dish with a slotted spoon.

* Prepare gooseneck barnacles as in Basic Recipe (see Index).

Serves 6

Oysters

*"Oysters are healthful and nourishing, . . . They keep you fit, do oysters, with vita-
mins and such, for energy and what is lightly called "fuel value." They prevent
goiter. They build up your teeth. They keep your children's legs straight, and when
Junior reaches puberty they make his skin clear and beautiful as a soap-opera an-
nouncer's dream. They add years to your life. . ."*

M.F.K. Fisher,
"Consider the Oyster,"
in The Art of Eating

By midnight the temperature has dropped to several degrees below freezing. A steady
drizzle of rain, leaking from a black January sky, has soaked into wood and stone,
spreading a glaze of ice over pilings and over the tops of rocks exposed by the reced-
ing tide. A wind cold enough to chill the maples to their sapless heartwood beats the
waters of Quilcene Bay into a froth and drives sleeting clouds across the ridges of the wooded
hills. At two in the morning, Ray Canterbury leaves the warmth and comfort of his beachfront home and ventures out onto the tideflats to collect oysters for the gourmet restaurants
of the Pacific Northwest. He drives his small truck across the slippery foreshore, stops in a
promising spot, lights a Coleman lantern, and begins to work. Shining his light onto clumps
of small oysters attached to rocks and to old oyster shells spread over the hard ground, he
breaks the frozen clusters from the substrate with stiff fingers and loads the oysters into
baskets. Because these oysters grow close to the ground and fatten best in the lower tidal
zones, Ray has to collect them during the lowest tides of the day, and in Quilcene in winter
the lowest tides are in the middle of the night.

Ray runs the family oyster farm—owned by Canterburys for three generations—as a
one-man operation, selling the limited number of oysters he harvests to a small number of
restaurants and to oyster fanciers who call their orders ahead (see Appendix). His oysters
are much smaller than the average oyster marketed in the Pacific Northwest, but they bring
a good price for their high quality. The annual spawn has been very generous in recent years—
small oysters abound on the beds—and Ray can afford to harvest yearlings and two-year-
olds because of this plentiful supply of replacement stock. Canterbury oysters are firm-
fleshed and mildly flavored, with a pleasant taste of oyster and fresh ocean. They are
delicious to eat raw and are best eaten as fresh as possible. Try not to buy Canterbury
oysters anywhere but at the Canterbury Oyster Farm. Some dealers have taken advantage of
the fame of these oysters and are selling inferior oysters as "Canterburys." If you see an offering of these oysters in a restaurant or market and are in doubt about their origin, just call
Ray Canterbury (at 206-765-3959); he will gladly tell you whom he supplies.

Canterbury oysters, like most oysters produced in the Pacific Northwest today, belong to a species called the Pacific oyster (it was known as the Japanese oyster, until political expediency brought about a name change during World War II). This oyster was first introduced into the Northwest in the early 1900s to replace the native oyster stocks, which had been depleted almost to the point of extinction by ruthless overharvesting. The immigrant Pacific oyster readily took to its new home, quickly growing fat in the nutrient-rich estuaries and bays of the Northwest, yet it refused to reproduce. Other than that, it showed few problems of adaptation.

The Pacific oyster is hardy and can withstand repeated exposures to climatic extremes. In its tightly closed shell, it can survive the hot rays of the midsummer sun—something it is exposed to for several hours each day during the summer low tide (this is one reason why an oyster baked in the shell can tough it out in a hot oven for such an incredibly long time), and it can take the frigidity of midwinter nights when the rain- or snow-covered shells may actually freeze shut while the tide is out. But the Pacific oyster has a finicky sex life. Like other oysters, it starts life as a male, becomes female as it grows older, and then switches back and forth between sexes at its pleasure. Further, it will reproduce only in areas where the salinity and water temperatures are to its liking. Even then it will spawn in only a few areas of the Pacific Northwest where these conditions are met every year.

In the past, Pacific Northwest oystermen could only stay in business if they annually imported large quantities of oyster spawn attached to *cultch* (old oyster shells) from Japan. But this importation became too costly a few years ago. The French, who almost overharvested their native oyster to the point of commercial extinction, also began to import Japanese oysters and drove up the price of the spawn. Fortunately for our oyster growers, the Pacific oyster had begun to adapt to northwest waters after half a century of sojourn and started to produce copious quantities of spawn in a few select locations.

One place where Pacific oysters spawn regularly is Pendrell Sound, a warm, rock-bound inlet on East Redonda Island, at the northern end of the Strait of Georgia. This narrow fjord is situated somewhat like a natural solar heat collector. It faces south and is flanked by concave mountain faces which reflect the heat of the sun toward the water. Every summer, British Columbia oyster growers gather here in their boats and wait for the oysters to spawn and for the spawn to settle on cultch that is strung together and enticingly suspended in the water from portable floats.

The tiny oyster larvae go through a free-swimming "veliger" stage, when they float around in the water for some two or three weeks. After this short period of freedom and mobility, they become "spat" and are ready to "set"; that is, they will attach themselves to a firm object of their liking, preferably something familiar, such as an old oyster shell, where they will spend the rest of their lives eating, drinking, procreating, and growing fat. Settling down is a momentous decision for a small oysterling to make—at this stage they are somewhat smaller than a grain of sand—because a Pacific oyster can live for some twenty years or more in the wild and grow to the size of a foot or more, reaching a weight of several pounds.

Those spat who make the wrong decision for oysters, but the right one for gourmets, by settling on the tempting cultch provided by the thoughtful oystermen, are carried off to the oyster farms where the seeded cultch is spread out to let the oysterlings grow and fatten. They will be left to mature for a period ranging from one to three years—depending upon their rate of growth and the market demand—before they are plucked and shucked. Mortality is high among the spat. It seems as if everyone likes to feast on tender young oysterlings, and from 50 to 90 percent of all oyster larvae die before they get ready to settle down; but those that survive often ride the tidal currents for considerable distances before they set, eating and growing as they go.

The Pacific oyster spawns regularly in Ladysmith Harbour, in Hood Canal, Dabob Bay, a mountain-ringed inlet near the northern end of Hood Canal, and in Quilcene Bay. Commercial growers from Oregon and Washington regularly bring their cultch to Dabob Bay to trap oyster seed. Pacific oysters have also spawned occasionally in Willapa Bay (they reproduced well during World War II, when Japanese spawn was unobtainable). Today more than 90 percent of all West Coast oysters are grown in Washington State, and more than half of this state's production comes from Willapa Bay. Willapa oysters are mild, often bland, but they can have a coarse side taste, especially in late spring, summer, and early fall, and they quickly become insipid once they have been shucked. The best have a nice, tangy undertaste when fresh. Most of the Willapa Bay oysters are harvested mechanically— a traumatic, shell-cracking experience for oysters—shucked, canned, and sent to out-of-state markets. The Willapa Bay oyster is the oyster which M. F. K. Fisher (taking a little liberty with geography) called the "tinned steamed Japanese bastard from the coast of Oregon."

With a few exceptions, I prefer the oysters grown in our inland waters to their brethren from the outer coast. Hood Canal oysters are among the tastiest produced in our region. My favorites come from the Hamma Hamma River, about halfway up the canal. These oysters have a pronounced clean marine flavor, with a rich butteriness and a complex aftertaste. The Hama Hama Oyster Company relies on naturally spawned oysters, but once every three to five years the local spawn fails, and the oyster growers have to go north to Dabob Bay to catch spat. This is a risky undertaking, however, since Dabob Bay is much warmer than Hood Canal and, unless the water temperature is just right when the cultch is set out, the transplanted oysterlings will take a chill, fail to acclimatize, and die. Those oysters that survive the rigors of the transplant often weaken and, growing up in a strange habitat, never reach the taste and plumpness of the locally spawned molluscs.

I have fond memories of Hamma Hamma, for it was here, some years ago, that I mustered the courage to eat my first raw Pacific oyster. I had, of course, eaten raw European oysters and raw bluepoints (the generic name under which East Coast oysters are sold in the West), but eating a raw Pacific oyster took courage, for I had heard strange tales from respectable gourmets about its palatability. I had dined on Pacific oysters before, but they had been cooked, stewed, sautéed, baked, and fried. These had come from the muddy estuaries of the northern California and southern Oregon shores, a stretch of coast not known as the West's best oyster country. Some tasted of oozy mud on the tangled roots of marsh willows and of cattle pastures; others had been in storage too long. Most were prepared in innovative ways, designed to hide the ambiguously flavored molluscs' taste. Whether the oysters were hidden beneath a blanket of toasted chilies and melted cheese, under boiled spinach, thyme, and Worcestershire sauce, below a thick and greasy crust of deep-fried egged-on crumbs, drowned in catsup, or wrapped in fat bacon and baked until the lard streamed freely through shriveled gills, the cooks' elaborate efforts were insufficient to hide a suspicion of spreading putrefaction.

But this had been California cuisine. Oyster lovers in the Pacific Northwest prefer to eat their molluscs in a simpler, more direct fashion. And I agree, having been raised on fresh, raw oysters, where even the notion of a cooked oyster, much less a fried one, appalled. Though I had frequently been offered raw Pacific oysters by hosts eager to introduce me to new northwestern taste treats, I could never quite partake of this dubious culinary pleasure, advertised by a potent smell of iodine and lemon wafting from the half shells. I had calmed my nagging culinary conscience by reassuring myself that only those eaters who had been raised on Pacific oysters and had swallowed them since childhood possessed constitutions strong enough to face these molluscs in the raw. Yet my inner voice continued to prod, making me feel uneasy, even unwilling to accept dinner invitations when I knew raw Pacific oysters would be served, because my reputation as a gourmet would be on the line. In the end, it forced me into the step I was about to take.

The moment of truth had come. I was ready to suffer unknown agonies of distaste, but I was not prepared to die from eating an inferior raw oyster that had spoiled through bad storage. Besides, having never tasted a raw Pacific oyster, how would I know if my first one would be spoiled or not? Thus, only the liveliest oyster, plucked fresh from the cold northwest waters, would do. Having decided that if I had to go, I might as well go in a beautiful natural setting, I traveled to Hood Canal on a perfectly clear spring morning. I came prepared for all contingencies, carrying a sleeping bag in my car (to keep myself warm, should I suffer from unexpected shock), a freshly baked loaf of rye bread, sweet butter, a couple of scallions, several lemons, a good bottle of crisp white wine (again hoping that if the worst scenario materialized, I would at least pass on in style), and a brand-new, never-before-used oyster knife.

Keeping one eye on the winding road and the other on the lookout for oyster farms, I slowly drove northwards, stopping the car every few miles to scan the edge of the water for encouraging signs of oyster beds and to sniff the light breeze blowing shoreward from the tideflats. An oyster fancier once told me that you can often predict the taste of a raw oyster from the smell given by the beds at low tide. The tide was ebbing, and I was searching for a clean scent.

Unexpectedly, I came upon the perfect place as I rounded a curve near the mouth of the Hamma Hamma River. The Hama Hama Oyster Company looked the way a first-rate northwest oyster company should look. Weather-worn shucking sheds, half-hidden behind piles of discarded oyster shells, were tucked into the shelter of a small grove of maples, madronas, and firs. A small, herby alluvial flat, covered with rocks, grasses, and beach peas, stretched from the precipitous edge of the mountainside to the deep water of Hood Canal. But more important, it bore a large sign which boldly proclaimed: FRESH oysters! I walked around the place for a while, sniffing the air, the tideflats, the piles of cultch, and the early flowers. No doubt, this was the right place. Everything had a clean smell. And for once, an advertisement had told the truth. The oysters were fresh. Entering the small sales shack, I found a battery of saltwater tanks which held live oysters, graded according to the size of their shells. I bought two dozen of the smallest ones, clean-shelled yearlings, and set out to look for a likely spot where I might attack them in privacy.

I found a hidden place for a picnic a little farther up the road, a quiet retreat beneath the spreading branches of a huge maple. I made myself comfortable on a fallen branch from which I could overlook the waters of Hood Canal to the northeast, the spring grasses of the Hamma Hamma estuary beneath my perch, and Olympic peaks rising above alders to the west. The birds sang with abandon. Setting my picnic basket upon a carpet of last year's leaves, I spread out the accoutrements, sliced a lemon, chopped the scallions, and reached for an oyster.

The oyster was beautiful. Its whitish-gray, grotesquely scalloped shell had a surface marked by bumps and ridges and deeply fluted rays spreading and widening from the hinge end to the lip, interrupted by irregular concentric circles of fragile chalk. These were also sharp-edged and made holding the shell firmly somewhat painful. I had often seen these molluscs opened, almost effortlessly, by crows and gulls who soared high into the air and dropped the shells onto a convenient rock, road, or car top where they were shattered by the impact; however, this approach was too messy for me. Oysters can also be opened by steaming or barbecuing, but these methods were taboo today, because the heat cooks the tender little oyster bodies. There was only one thing to do.

Remembering the instructions that came with my oyster knife, I placed the heavy round handle of the knife firmly in my right hand, blade facing outward, and firmly grabbed an oyster with my left hand, shell hinge toward me. Ouch! Wrap napkin around oyster, proceed as above. Insert oyster knife between the shells (making sure the deeper of the two shells is on the bottom so the liquor does not spill), cut upper adductor muscle, remove top shell, cut the lower adductor muscle, squeeze a few drops of lemon juice onto the oyster, smell again, lift the shell to your mouth, sip the liquor and suck the oyster from its cup. Chew slowly, savor the different parts of the oyster, and swallow. Open next oyster.

I had braved my first raw Pacific oyster and found it simply delicious. But how do you describe the taste of a fresh oyster? Every authority I have consulted on the subject agrees—after the usual learned obfuscation—that an oyster tastes like. . . well, an oyster. Yet there is no question that different species of oysters taste different, and even oysters of the same species, fattened in different locations, all have a distinct, local taste, a flavor which appears to depend on the minerals and nutrients suspended in the water and on the type of substrate on which the beds rest. Yet all of these individual flavors can be described as degrees of refinement and variation on the basic oyster taste.

The smell and taste of a good oyster, no matter what species, will always remind me of the scents rising from a pristine estuary on a foggy morning, a delicate blend of salty marine flavors and a tender, fresh earthiness (there is more of the earth in Pacific oysters, and more of the sea in our tiny native oyster and in the European oyster). On the other hand, the smell and taste of an inferior oyster remind me of the penetrating stench of harbors and slimy waterway bottoms on hot summer noons. An inferior Pacific oyster is a caricature: it will taste musty and muddy rather than earthy, of iodine instead of seawater, and its marine smell will be the reek of decaying seaweed.

Oysters growing in sand or mud have a flavor inferior to that of those raised on hard ground or rock. They can often be spotted, because their shells are smoother, with lower ridges than on those growing on a hard substrate. Oysters that grow too close together—they can be lean from a lack of nutrients—tend to have long, narrow, snaky shells. But then again, large oysters that show no fluting could be examples of the Atlantic oyster, which was introduced into our region earlier in the century. The Atlantic oyster can easily be told from the Pacific oyster, however: it is light brown, not gray, and the adductor muscles leave highly visible black or dark blue scars inside each shell.

Since the taste of oysters varies from one growing region to the next—there can even be a distinct difference between oysters grown in the same inlet—and since it varies with the seasons, depending on the type of waterborne nutrients and the changes in salinity brought about by rainfall and run-off, oyster lovers in our region should regularly try to taste the full range of oysters available locally and regionally. Oysters can be eaten during the summer months, when the warm weather causes food microorganisms to multiply (contrary to the traditional belief that they should only be eaten during months that have an r in the name), but they don't taste good at that time. As oysters get ready to spawn during warm weather, they turn flabby and translucent, and most oyster growers will not sell them during this stage (it may not occur in cold summers).

I find that I do not like the taste of oysters that were grown on a muddy bottom, though I can tolerate the flavor of oysters from Boundary Bay and from the northern fringe of Samish Bay (Rock Point), and I dislike the muddy, tincture of iodine taste of the oysters raised in Drayton Harbor, on Samish Island, in Similk Bay, Grays Harbor, and Gig Harbor, Washington. All of these oysters, if eaten at all, should only be used in recipes that call for very strong spicing.

An oyster should always be smelled before it is eaten, for oysters have complex bouquets, just like wines, and unless you savor this harmony of scents, you lose much of the pleasure of eating a fresh oyster. An oyster should not be swallowed in one gulp, a much too precipitous method of ingestion. Finally, its flavor can be enhanced by the juice of a freshly squeezed lemon, but the oyster should be of a quality to be appreciated on its own.

Pleased with my first taste of raw Pacific oysters, I reflected on all the opportunities for tasting these savory molluscs I had missed in the past and decided right there and then to make up for the lost opportunities with extra fervor. I began to taste all the commercially produced northwest oysters I could find in the raw (including many I had once rejected for cooking purposes). But I was in for another surprise. My original opinion of their quality still held true. Most of them were fit only to be eaten in cooked and spiced incarnations: eating them fresh on the shell was no pleasure. I quickly learned that Hama Hama oysters ranked close to the top of my culinary scale. Only a few others, including Ray Canterbury's Quilcene oysters, the delectable Mats Mats oysters from Port Ludlow, the Pacific oysters raised in the sheltered inlets of southern Puget Sound, and the oysters grown in Penn Cove, Sooke Harbour, on the islands in the Strait of Georgia, and the Hayes oysters from Tillamook Bay matched or surpassed the taste of the Hama Hamas.

Our local oysters should never be bought at a supermarket, especially when they come packed in little plastic or glass jars (never buy a canned oyster!!). I once had an interesting conversation with a shellfish specialist from the Washington State Department of Social and Health Services. She told me that there are no industry-wide standards to guarantee the freshness of shucked oysters sold on supermarket shelves throughout our region and pointed out that the commonly marketed containers of shucked oysters have no easily decipherable pull date. Aside from the question of taste, this can be dangerous to the health of anyone consuming these oysters. Questioning her assertion—because, if this were true, people would die from eating oysters that had stayed in a supermarket cooler for too long—I received a quick reply: "But they do!" She suggested that consumers lobby their respective legislatures to have strict legal rules of conduct imposed on oyster shippers. Oysters should be bought directly from a grower, wherever this is possible, or from a reliable fish market (see Appendix). The only time they should be bought shucked is when they are obtained directly from the grower and even then only right after they have been shucked. Oysters should, of course, be consumed within twenty-four hours of shucking (and they should be refrigerated at all times) to assure the best and freshest taste.

Smoked Pacific oysters are also delicious. They can be prepared by anyone who has a home smoker, but they can sometimes be bought already smoked. Here a reliable supplier is an absolute must. The Hama Hama Oyster Company does an excellent job with their smoked oysters. Unfortunately, most of the commercially smoked oysters sold throughout the

Pacific Northwest today are imported from Korea and other East Asian countries. The quality of these oysters—they taste as though they had been dried and then soaked in liquid smoke for an excessive period of time—is just not up to that of our native product, fat little Pacific oysters smoked slowly over fires of alder wood.

Oysters, incidentally, are much fatter than other shellfish. This is one reason for their rich flavor. They have a fat content of about 3 percent, compared to about 2 percent for clams and mussels, and a meager .5 percent for scallops. They are, however, somewhat lower in protein than other molluscs, with about 10 percent, compared to 12 percent for mussels, 14 for clams, and 16 for scallops.

One of the best Pacific oysters for eating raw is grown on quite soft ground in Tillamook Bay, Oregon, by the Hayes Oyster Company. (Tillamook oystermen have been known to spray their oyster beds with Sevin to kill off sand shrimp, but this does not appear to have affected the taste of their oysters.) The mild Tillamook oysters have a rich, buttery flavor followed by a pleasant array of marine savors. Like Quilcenes, they are best eaten *in situ*. They go surprisingly well with the fat little smoked rainbow trout sold in Tillamook. One of the stranger breakfasts I have ever eaten was consumed in Tillamook on a crisp fall morning when I was too rushed to eat at a restaurant. I had stopped at the Blue Heron Cheese Company and bought several of their soft-ripened cheeses, a loaf of french bread, and some smoked trout. I then purchased some buttermilk and well-aged Cheddar at the Tillamook cheese plant and dropped in at the Hayes farm to talk about oysters. Eating a few freshly shucked oysters awakened my appetite, and I decided to have a breakfast picnic, composed of the medley of oysters, cheese, bread, smoked fish, and buttermilk I had assembled that morning. This impromptu meal was surprisingly good—though I still prefer wine instead of buttermilk with my oysters.

Oregon has only a few inlets suited to the commercial cultivation of oysters. Most of the state's estuaries are either too turbulent, too small, too low in salinity, or too muddy for successful oyster culture. Coos Bay once produced considerable quantities of oysters, but the lumber industry and pollution have so affected the beds that the few remnant molluscs are not worth tasting. Pacific oysters from Yaquina Bay (Newport, Oregon) are also not of gourmet quality. Yet Yaquina Bay supported a thriving oyster industry in the nineteenth century, based on the exploitation of a native "oyster."

The Yaquina oyster was not a true oyster, but a rock oyster, or jingle. This delicious mollusc, considered by many gourmets to be the finest tasting shellfish on the West Coast, is nowhere common. Only Yaquina Bay provided an environment in which the rock oyster thrived. By the early 1860s, the California oyster companies, whose thoughtless harvesting techniques had already driven the native oyster population of San Francisco Bay to the brink of extinction and who were engaged in the process of doing the same to the seemingly unlimited supply of oysters in Willapa Bay, started the rush to harvest the Yaquina Bay oysters. The rock oyster beds were quickly depleted. By the late 1860s, the harvests had dwindled to a trickle, and the native oyster business ceased altogether by 1893. East Coast oysters were first introduced to Yaquina Bay in 1893, but neither they, nor the Pacific oyster, which was imported later, have ever reached the culinary quality of the native rock oyster, and oyster farming in Yaquina Bay has remained marginal ever since.

The Pacific oyster was first introduced into British Columbia, at Ladysmith and Boundary Bay, in 1912, seven years after it made its first appearance in Washington State. But its presence has not always led to successful commercial cultivation. Until quite recently,

British Columbia, the Pacific oyster country par excellence, regularly imported a large number of the oysters consumed in the province from Washington State. Only in the last decade, after the British Columbian government began to help oyster growers develop more efficient methods of raising oysters, has production increased. Several new approaches have brought better yields than the traditional bottom culture (in which the cultch was simply spread out across the foreshore).

Stake and *umbrella* culture permit the growing of tastier oysters on muddy tideflats: in the first, the oyster cultch is nailed to the top of a low stake, about a foot off the ground; in the second, it is attached to ropes radiating downward from stakes. In *tray* culture the spat is placed in perforated trays, which are suspended from floats or mounted on low stakes. Oysters grown in these ways are less silty than they would be if they were grown right on the mud (and their shells are deeply fluted), and they do not have the muddy taste commonly associated with oysters grown on mucky ground. The stake and umbrella culture oysters are covered by water at high tide, but are completely exposed at low tide, just like ground culture oysters. Tray culture oysters placed on stakes are sometimes raised in shallow water where they may be uncovered at ebb. However, the trays are more frequently placed in deep water, since growers have discovered that oysters which are always covered by water do not suffer from climatic extremes and thus undergo little stress. They can feed for twenty-four hours a day, grow fat more quickly, and often have a better taste than their littoral neighbors. *Raft* and *longline* culture are similar to tray culture. The cultch is threaded onto long ropes which are either suspended from rafts (raft culture) or styrofoam floats (longline culture).

The success of these oyster growing experiments and the improved taste of the oysters have led to an increase in demand, and British Columbia oysters are now regularly exported, primarily to gourmet restaurants in San Francisco. Yet not all British Columbia oyster growers have adapted to the new times. Several have given up production, and even the tasty oysters from Sooke Harbour on southern Vancouver Island have recently become commercially extinct, though wild stocks can still be harvested. The delectable oysters from Tofino and Ladysmith harbours, and from Denman, Lasqueti, and Kuper islands, however, more than make up for the loss. But the tastiest Pacific oysters in British Columbia come from the wild beds on the east coast of Vancouver Island. Numerous public beaches allow access to these beds, and all that a gourmandizing traveler needs for happiness are an oyster knife, a lemon, a bottle of wine, and a loaf of bread.

The success of the British Columbia oyster growers has inspired several Washington State oystermen to improve their production methods. Pete Jefferds raises oysters on rafts in Penn Cove, several growers in the southern Puget Sound grow oysters in enclosed trays, and Randy Shuman, a Willapa Bay oysterman, grows oysters by a new method called *rack* culture (the oysters are placed in bags of sturdy plastic mesh and held on racks, about a foot off the ground, for several years). And, finally, we have the crème de la crème, the artificially spawned oysters from the Webb Camp oyster farm on San Juan Island.

Webb Camp, tucked into the trees on the sheltered eastern shore of Westcott Bay near the northern end of the island, is the most innovative oyster farm in the Puget Sound region. It was once a summer camp for children run by two capable counselors, Bill and Doree Webb. The Webbs have given up on entertaining truculent kids, and they are now running what appears to be a permanent camp for promising young marine biologists. In the process, they are managing to produce some of the best oysters in the Pacific Northwest.

Several decades ago, when the shellfish growers of our region searched for a commercially responsive oyster to replace the depleted stocks of our native Olympia oysters, they settled on the common Japanese oyster, but neglected a much better tasting Japanese oyster, the Kumamoto. The Kumamoto, a tasty sport of the Pacific oyster, has a more deeply cupped shell than its close relative and a more delicate and complex flavor. But it grows very slowly, making it difficult for the grower to obtain a quick profit. The Kumamoto adapts well to northwest waters, but today it is grown by only two producers, the Hayes Oyster Company at Tillamook, Oregon, and the Calm Cove Oyster Company in Shelton, Washington. The Webbs have succeeded in crossing the Kumamoto with the common Pacific oyster, getting a hybrid which has the growth rate of the Pacific, but the deep cup (to contain the precious liquor) and much of the flavor of the Kumamoto. It also has the most fluted, almost feathery shell of any of our oysters, buff with whitish and brownish marks, and can be told from other oysters by its shell alone.

The entire oyster-growing operation is tightly controlled, down to the last calorie. Only the final fattening of the oysters is left to nature. The oyster spat is obtained not from wild oysters, but from selected oysters which are held in the controlled environment of specially designed saltwater tanks, where they are fed on a diet of artificially grown algae. When the spat are released, they are kept in a battery of similar tanks (of increasing size) until the tiny oysterlings reach a diameter of about five millimeters. They are then transferred to fine-meshed trays which are stacked and suspended in the nutrient-rich waters of Westcott Bay. After the oysterlings have grown to a size of approximately thirty-five millimeters, they are moved to Japanese lantern nets. These are long, tubular nylon nets, divided into a series of horizontal compartments. Each net has ten compartments, and each compartment holds about fifty growing oysters. The nets are suspended in deep water from floats which rise and sink with the tide. These oysters grow fat surprisingly quickly, reaching a marketable size of 2.5 to 4 inches in only ten months. The Webb Camp oysters, sold under the trade name "Westcott Bay," are only sold wholesale (see Appendix for retail sources). Visitors to the oyster farm should not expect to be able to buy oysters, though Bill Webb will gladly explain the operation.

Pacific and Kumamoto oysters are not the only oysters introduced to the Pacific Northwest. The Atlantic oyster, long a favorite with American cooks from the East Coast (where the oysters were eaten fresh) to the Midwest (where the oysters arrived in dubious condition, packed in barrels), was the first to be introduced. But it failed to reproduce in profitable quantities and was soon abandoned. The Atlantic oyster has survived in the feral state in a few spots in the Puget Sound region and it can still be found in a few estuaries, in particular near Boundary Bay, just north of the British Columbia border. One tasty newcomer, the European flat oyster (a close relative of our native Olympia oyster), is beginning to show promise. It has succeeded very well in southern Puget Sound, where Peter Becker at Little Skookum Shellfish Company is growing moderate quantities, and even better at Webb Camp on San Juan Island.

The Little Skookum oysters are grown in enclosed trays, raised a foot above the ground, to protect them from predators and to assure a free flow of nutrients. The Webb Camp flat oysters are grown in lantern nets, just like the Pacific/Kumamoto hybrids. The European flat oysters must always stay at least a few inches below the water surface, for they are tender and will freeze to death in winter if they are exposed. They are adapting well to the different growing conditions prevailing in the inlets and, just like their European ancestors, they are beginning to show a great variation in taste. These oysters—sometimes incorrectly called "belons" after the name of their most famous French beds (though Bill Webb prefers to call them "Whitstables" after his favorite British oysters)—are superb. They should always be shucked just before eating, and they must be eaten raw, on the half shell, with perhaps an accent of lemon. They should never be cooked. Their taste is truly memorable and well worth the steep price they command. Their exceptional flavor is eclipsed only by that of one other oyster: our native Western or Olympia oyster, which is finally making a comeback from the brink of extinction.

Our native oyster, a much smaller and more delicate mollusc than any of the oysters introduced to the Pacific Northwest, rarely exceeds two inches in length. It is not much to look at, having none of the baroque flutings and knobs of the Pacific oyster, but its superb taste more than makes up for the drab exterior. The Olympia oyster is widely distributed throughout our region, but it is nowhere common. Its exquisite flavor can be directly blamed for its rarity. Immense beds of Olympia oysters once covered tidal flats in the estuaries and bays of the Pacific Northwest. The appeal of the Olympia oyster was discovered soon after the first American settlers arrived on the West Coast. By 1851 these oysters were carried from Willapa Bay, then the center of their abundance, to California, where gold miners payed high prices for them. One wonders why. These oysters are delicious when fresh, but, like other shellfish, they do not profit from extended storage and putrefaction.

Collection and transportation methods in the middle of the nineteenth century were primitive, to say the least. The oysters were gathered from the beds by rake, piled into large baskets, and stowed in the holds of small sailing schooners. I doubt that the slow, bouncy sea voyage down the coast to the Golden Gate improved the oysters' quality (the bottom layer of oysters commonly died *en voyage*), and I wonder how many miners died from eating spoiled oysters for which they had paid a king's ransom? We know that the Olympias were eaten in pies and stews whose spices hid any flavors (and warning signs of spoilage), and that those oysters that survived the voyage in passable shape were served in omelets and Hangtown fries (but many of the eggs used for these omelets were the wild, strong-flavored eggs of seabirds gathered from cliffs and offshore islands).

I don't think any of the miners would have eaten these oysters raw. But, for an unknown reason, neither did anyone else, even when fresh oysters were available. It is strange that, until quite recently, when continental European food habits conquered the Northwest, not many people—not even the native Indians—ate them raw. The Ahousat on Vancouver Island's west coast, one of the few native tribes who still have access to native oysters, prefer to steam and boil theirs. They also believe that the juice from boiled oysters enhances a man's virility, which puts them on a par with European libertines like Casanova, who downed about fifty oysters a day to sustain his strength. (The European oyster is, of course, a close relative of our native oyster. Bill Webb is thinking of crossing the two to get a new commercial "super-oyster.") Casanova ate his oysters raw, in the approved fashion, and our Olympias are also at their best if they are eaten as fresh as possible, raw, from the half shell.

The flavor of the Olympia oyster has been variously described as "coppery" or as "strongly marine." This description can be traced back to Washington pioneer, trader, libertine, and ethnographer James Swan, who harvested oysters in Willapa Bay during the early 1850s. He is the first to mention the "coppery taste" of the native Willapa (i.e., Olympia) oyster; but in the same sentence, he immediately denies its existence, describing it instead as "a strong, fishy, saltwater flavor." Swan assures us that this undesirable taste is "driven off by cooking."

The Olympia oyster was not a hit with early visitors to the Northwest. Thirty years before Swan, East Coast journalist Thomas Franham (who had been sent west by Horace Greeley) had described our native as "an inferior kind of oyster." But he had been raised on bland eastern oysters and had no experience with gourmet fare. And he does not state where he picked his oysters. Having tasted Olympia oysters, wild and raw, from different parts of the Coast, I can only state emphatically that there is no such thing as *one* Olympia (or western) oyster. The little mollusc tastes so different in different parts of the Pacific Northwest, that one might be tempted to split it into several species on the basis of flavor alone. But no matter where I gathered it, I always found it to be delicious. Swan's oysters may have taken on a "fishy" taste from the muddy Willapa Bay bottoms, or it may all have been in the taster's mind, but the native oysters I have tasted had a clean taste of oyster, very much like the European oyster, but crisper and with a pleasing tartness. New Yorker Raymond Sokolov has described the Olympia oyster's taste as "sharply marine but also refined," and Pierre Franey, during a visit to Seattle in the spring of 1983, admitted that they were among the best oysters he had ever tasted.

Taste proved to be the Olympia oyster's bane because the virgin stocks were raped by harvesters subscribing to the ruggedly individualistic, free-enterprising methods of the nineteenth century. The vast beds were quickly depleted, scraped clean to squeeze out a final dollar of fast profit. Only in southern Puget Sound, in the narrow maze of intricate channels reaching west into the Olympic Peninsula from Harstene Island, did our native oyster make a last commercial stand. The Olympia oyster did not take to cultivation everywhere. It is surprisingly tender for a native mollusc (it prefers to grow on the underside of rocks, unless the bottom is muddy, when it will set on top), and it cannot take exposure to extremes of cold or heat. James Swan reported heavy frost damage to wild oysters in 1853-54, and we can assume that cold winters periodically cut back the size of our native oyster beds. This posed no problems to the oysters' survival as long as they could replenish their numbers during the mild winter intervals. But the Olympia oysters could not withstand sustained pressure from both the elements and from overharvesting.

The oystermen in southern Puget Sound found an effective solution to this dilemma. By the 1890s they succeeded in increasing their oyster production by creating shallow, diked saltwater ponds in which a sufficient water level could be maintained at low tide to keep the oysters covered with a protective layer of water (the southern Sound has a tidal range of about fourteen feet). After they learned to construct their dikes in such a way that they would not block the free flow of nutrients (and avoid starving their oysters), the commercial cultivation of the Olympia oyster increased quickly, and the oysters were soon shipped throughout the West.

A major change had taken place in the transport of oysters from grower to market. The delicate little oysters were cooked and canned before they were sent to the hinterland. While this may have prevented spoilage, it did destroy the taste. But it did not decrease the oyster's popularity. Just as they had once penetrated the deep defiles of the Sierra Nevada, the Olympia oysters began to travel to the remote valleys of the Pacific Northwest's mountain ranges. Olympia oysters made their appearance, for example, on the menu of a Canadian Pacific steamer in the Kootenay country in 1899, but as "Fried Olympia Oysters." Why fry them, after they had already been cooked and canned?

While we can forgive the cook of a remote backwoods steamboat for frying canned oysters, we must question a traditional dish served today at a "historic" oyster house in Olympia. Why would a restaurant with ready access to fresh Olympia oysters willingly spoil their exquisite taste by breading and deep-frying them? Why would anyone want to treat an Olympia oyster this way? I can only surmise that the settlers of the Olympia area, many of whom came from the farmlands of the Midwest, were not accustomed to the taste of fresh oysters and simply did not know what to do with them. They treated the local dainties in the same fashion as they had the Atlantic oysters which arrived by slow boat on the Erie Canal—making them palatable by hiding them under a thick crust of deep-fried batter. I find it amusing to contemplate that generations of Puget Sound families have faithfully trekked to Olympia to eat big, greasy chunks of batter with little deflavored oysters inside, when they could have feasted on the real thing, fresh and on the half shell, by driving to the other end of town.

The dike-generated bounty of Olympia oysters fell victim to a new culprit, however: sulfite paper mills. Daniel Jack Chasan related (in *The Water Link*) how the noxious chemicals released by the mills killed the oyster spawn and cut severely into breeding stocks (though regional booster Bill Speidel claims, somewhat unconvincingly, that hungry ducks and tiny snails did in the oysters). The waterborne wastes also poisoned the Pacific oysters, especially in Padilla and Samish bays and in Port Susan, but the Pacific oyster showed a great tolerance for a variety of growing conditions. They were not, like the Olympias, limited to a narrowly restricted habitat, and new oyster farms could be easily started in toxin-free environments throughout the inland waters. Besides, at this time their spawn, the stage at which the oyster is most susceptible to poisoning, was still imported from Japan. But the Olympia oyster growers could not move their beds because there were no other favorable locations available to them, and they had to sit and watch as their worst enemy, the Shelton pulp mill, almost single-handedly destroyed the Olympia oyster beds.

Fortunately for Northwesterners, this mill proved to be unprofitable and now, several decades after its closure, the Olympia oyster is making a strong comeback. In the meantime, most of the oyster growers in the southern Sound had given up on growing the Olympia and concentrated on the tougher Pacific oyster instead. By the late 1970s, only two growers kept up an intermittent production of Olympia oysters, yet by the end of 1982, when the positive effects of the pulp mill closure had become noticeable, eight growers had begun to restock their Olympia oyster beds.

Several years ago, when Olympia oysters were all but unavailable anywhere, I scouted the southern Puget Sound country for a supplier. After having followed up several leads without much success, I accidentally ended up in the mill town of Shelton. Making a virtue out of a mistake—I had taken a wrong exit on the freeway—I stopped at the local Chamber of Commerce, just a few blocks from the notorious pulp mill, on a wild hunch. Here a very cooperative gentleman directed me to the Skookum Bay Oyster Company, a small family operation on Skookum Inlet. His directions were easy to follow, until I came to the part where I had been told to drive all the way to the end of a dirt road. I couldn't miss it. The road led to a steep bluff where it branched into three directions. After a moment's reflection, I took the central road, because it showed traces of oyster shells. Arriving at the bottom of the incline, I found a plain concrete block shucking shed, several heaps of old shells, and a tiny parking lot squeezed onto the shore of the narrow inlet. It was a very unromantic place, looking more like a small factory than a northwest oyster farm. But, in one way, it was just like an Olympia oyster. Once I got inside the drab shell, a delicious surprise awaited me. Owner John Blanton had just begun to pack freshly shucked Olympias into jars, and he offered me a generous taste.

I have often bought oysters from the Blantons since that first day, usually making a special trip from Bellingham to Shelton the day before I put on a special dinner party (but only between October and April, when the Olympias are in season). I have watched the production of these oysters increase steadily during this period of rising hope. Since early 1983, Olympia oysters have once again become available in Seattle, and when I don't have the time to drive all the way to Shelton, I can make arrangements to pick up Olympia oysters in Seattle (see Appendix). They are not inexpensive (their price is close to that of caviar and may rise further), but they are well worth the price. I hope these delicious oysters will increase their production so that they may once again be available to discriminating consumers throughout the Pacific Northwest. A time may come when oyster fanciers will make pilgrimages to Puget Sound to taste these inimitable oysters fresh and on location.

Captain Whidbey Inn Poached Oysters

This recipe, when made with fresh Penn Cove oysters, is very tasty. You may substitute mussels for the oysters. Serve with a crisp white sauvignon blanc or semillon.

Dry white wine   2 cups
Dried sweet basil   1 tablespoon
Paprika   1 teaspoon
Unsalted butter   1 cup
Shucked oysters   6 pints
Toasted french bread rounds

1. Combine wine, basil, paprika, and butter in large, heavy skillet and heat until it just boils.
2. Add oysters all at once.
3. Poach until oysters become firm and opaque. Immediately remove from liquid (do not overcook).
4. Serve oysters on rounds of toasted french bread.
5. Carefully skim butter off top of poaching liquid and pour over oysters.

Serves 8 to 12 generously

Marinated Oysters I

This is a very good appetizer recipe. Make it in the evening before a dinner or party, keep it in the refrigerator, and serve it well chilled with crackers, toast wedges, and Blackhook porter.

Extra small oysters   2 pints, shucked
White wine vinegar   1 cup
Fresh French tarragon   2 teaspoons
Pickling spice   3 tablespoons
Amontillado sherry   ¼ cup

1. In a large saucepan, simmer oysters in their liquor until curled at the edges (about 3 to 5 minutes).
2. Combine remaining ingredients in a small saucepan and cook over medium heat for 10 minutes.
3. Drain oysters thoroughly and transfer to a bowl.
4. Strain sauce and pour liquid over oysters.
5. Cover and refrigerate for at least 3 hours (preferably overnight).

Serves 6 to 8

Marinated Oysters II

This dish makes a great hors d'oeuvre. It's perfect for stilling the first pangs of hunger and for stimulating the appetite for the good things to come in the main dish. Serve with freshly baked bread and a very dry white wine or sparkling wine.

Dry white wine   ½ cup
White wine vinegar   1 tablespoon
Water   ½ cup
Salt   ½ teaspoon
Peppercorns   8
Vegetable oil   1 teaspoon
Small onion   1, sliced
Small carrot   1, sliced
Celery   1 stalk, sliced
Parsley   1 sprig
Thyme   pinch
Capers   1 teaspoon
Shucked oysters   1 to 2 pints, drained
Parsley   1 tablespoon chopped
Chives   1 tablespoon chopped
Lemon wedges   garnish

1. In saucepan combine all ingredients except oysters, chopped parsley, and chives. Bring to a boil and simmer for 20 minutes.
2. Add oysters and simmer 5 minutes longer.
3. Remove pan from heat, cover, and refrigerate oysters in marinade for at least 3 hours (preferably overnight).
4. To serve, put oysters in a serving dish and pour enough marinade over them to keep them moist. Sprinkle with chopped parsley and chives. Garnish with lemon wedges.

Serves 6 to 8

Grilled Oysters

The weather in the Puget Sound region is often quite sunny and balmy during the month of February—a great time for beach picnics. Here's a simple but tasty dish to serve as an appetizer. It can be cooked on any barbecue grill.

Medium oysters in the shell 36
Unsalted butter 8 tablespoons, melted

1. Wash oyster shells thoroughly.
2. Place oysters on grill at least 4 inches from hot coals.
3. Roast for 10 to 15 minutes or until shells begin to open (a barbecue with a hood works even better—just close hood).
4. Serve in shells with melted butter.

Note: You'll get too cold if you serve these oysters with a well-chilled dry white wine (unless you cook them in summer), so try a hot tea instead into which you have blended a sweet white wine. It'll go well with the oysters and it'll warm you at the same time.

Serves 6 to 8

Oysters O'Reilly

The ingredients for this dish are pretty much standard supermarket shelf condiments, but the result is surprisingly delicious. Everything depends, of course, on the quality and freshness of the oysters. Serve with a dry sauvignon blanc or a hearty Blackhook Porter.

Catsup ½ cup
Cocktail sauce ½ cup
Green pepper ¼ cup diced
Worcestershire sauce 1 teaspoon
Horseradish 1 teaspoon
Medium oysters in shell 18
Bacon 18 pieces, partly crisped
Parmesan cheese 6 tablespoons grated
Rock salt

1. Blend catsup, cocktail sauce, green pepper, Worcestershire sauce, and horseradish into a sauce.
2. Shuck oysters. Discard top shell. Leave oysters in bottom shell.
3. Place 1 tablespoon of sauce over each oyster in shell.
4. Add a piece of bacon to each oyster.
5. Sprinkle oysters with parmesan cheese.
6. Place oysters in an oven-proof dish on a bed of rock salt (make sure shells are level and pressed down firmly, or the contents may spill).
7. Bake for 10 minutes at 375°.

Serves 4 to 6

Shellfish

The storm-blasted outer coast of Washington State is as rough a winter shore as any in the northern world. Yet here, on the unquiet sandy beaches stretching from the mouth of the Columbia north to the Olympic Peninsula, the cold and blustery days of late winter and early spring witness a strange ritual when thousands of inland dwellers come to the Coast for weekends of frantic activity. Neither rain, nor sleet, nor wind can keep the hordes of visitors away from the surf-beaten, hard-packed sand flats of the Long Beach peninsula, the Grayland beaches, and the Olympic shores. These are clam diggers, gathered here from all over, from Seattle, Tacoma, Portland, and as far away as Spokane. They come equipped with determination, shovels, clam guns, and lots of beer. And they come in such numbers (on one weekend in late February 1983, more than forty thousand came at once) that each clam digger often has only a few feet of ground, usually not enough space to swing a shovel in. These scores of enthusiasts are the prey of seaside merchants and they, in turn, prey on the elusive razor clam.

The razor clam is a tasty, cream-colored mollusc, a flavorful, elongated clam that is too large for its narrow, fragile shell, but that makes up for its lack of defensive armor by digging an escape from danger quickly and efficiently with its flexible muscular foot. When undisturbed, razor clams lie below the surface, their siphon tips flush with the sand, sucking nourishment from the water when the tide is in. But, unlike clumsy hard-shell clams and cockles, which lie in the ground just waiting to be picked up, the razor clam is not easy to catch. A clam digger who misses his prey on the first effort is better off pursuing another clam, for the one missed will have dug itself down so deep that it can be extracted only with a major effort (fishing regulations do not permit the use of the tool most useful at this point: a backhoe). Digging up a razor clam with a mere shovel takes uncanny skill and speed. But a clam gun, a long tube with a plunger which can be forced down into the sand surrounding the clam and which sucks the mollusc from its burrow when the plunger is raised, commonly puts success within reach of even the most inexperienced novice clam digger. Aiming for a clam with either shovel or clam gun is notoriously difficult—sand is not a very transparent medium—and many clams are killed or maimed during the harvest. Many more die from neglect and unskilled handling before they reach the clam digger's kitchen.

Razor clams should be cleaned as soon as possible after they are taken from the beach. If you would like to keep the tasty molluscs alive until you cook them, keep them cool and moist and put a heavy rubber band around their shells. Clams are not very bright animals; the pressure of the rubber band creates the illusion that they are back in their burrows, and the lack of water makes them think the tide is out. This keeps the clams happy and expectant —and in prime condition for a gourmet's feast.

The razor clam's popularity, combined with continual overharvesting, has led to an inevitable decline in the number of clams harvested and to a decrease in the size of the average clam dug by recreational clammers. There is little question that the party atmosphere of the razor clam digging ritual has led to an unnecessary waste of this delicious natural resource. The Washington Department of Fisheries has halfheartedly imposed restrictions on digging seasons, size limits, and license fees, but so far the government has had little success in limiting the appalling amount of waste. One of the worst abuses, which causes an inane wholesale destruction of clams, is the custom of driving heavy automobiles and pickup trucks over the clam beaches. Several thousand pounds of vehicle weight compresses the burrows and suffocates the clams, or presses them to death. The concussion caused by an automobile traveling at high speed has a particularly devastating effect. One enthusiastic beach racer once told me that the thing he liked the best was to drive his heavy station wagon along the edge of the water and "just watch the clams pop from the sand." I can see nothing wrong with making clam diggers park their cars on paved roads and walk a few hundred feet to the water.

The coastal Indians have been more successful in preserving their razor clam stocks. The same type of abuse that still hurts the clams along the southwest Washington coast, exacerbated by the rude behavior of campers and the unsightly heaps of trash and empty beer cans left behind by weekend clammers, forced the Quinault tribe to close the beaches of its reservation to all outsiders several years ago. The result once again was predictable. South of Moclips the razor clams are in decline; north of the reservation boundary they flourish. The Quinault have an abundant supply of razor clams for the use of tribal members, with a sufficient number of clams left over to support a small commercial harvest. Chances are, if you see fresh razor clams for sale in Pacific Northwest fish markets, they will have come from the Quinault beaches.

I like the taste of razor clams very much. There is a crisp tang to their flavor which makes them unique, and these clams should always be cooked as delicately as possible to preserve this flavor. They should never be breaded and deep-fried (one of the worst meals I was ever offered was a curious dish called a razor clam "Swiss steak"). I have long ago given up on participating in the annual hullaballoo on the ocean beaches. Unless I can get away for some quiet midweek clamming—and only if I can get the tasty molluscs to a stove shortly after—I prefer to rely on commercially harvested razor clams (always making sure to buy only clams that are still alive; razor clams spoil quickly once they have died).

Oregon also has razor clam beaches, but they are smaller than the sandy expanses north of the Columbia, and pressure from diggers can be even greater, especially on beaches within easy access of roads leading to the Coast from Portland or Eugene. Beaches south of Coos Bay, remote from the population centers to the north and south, are least disturbed by hordes of amateur diggers and thus offer some of the best clam digging on the Oregon coast. But the most productive razor clam beaches in the Pacific Northwest, long sandy stretches of surf-beaten shore, where the clams are packed close together and where they are dug up mostly by the undertow and by the odd scoter or raven, are on the west coast of Vancouver Island. There is a simple reason, however, for their continued abundance: it is illegal to harvest them.

Razor clams, like mussels, oysters, scallops, butter clams, and other bivalves, are filter feeders; that is, they gather their nourishment by sifting microorganisms from the seawater. One of these food organisms, the minute dinoflagellate *Gonyaulax catenella*, contains a small amount of toxin. Molluscs are unaffected by this poison, but they cannot digest it and it can temporarily accumulate in their bodies, before it is eliminated through regular physiological processes. But this toxin is quite venomous to warm-blooded animals. *Gonyaulax* is always present in the seawater of the Pacific Northwest, but in very small quantities, allowing the ingesting bivalves to rid themselves of the residues before a buildup occurs. But at certain times of the year, when a combination of environmental conditions favor *Gonyaulax*, the microorganisms "bloom"; they become so numerous that they may change the color of the water into the infamous "red tide."

This sudden multiplication of dinoflagellates is a boon to the filter-feeding molluscs, for it means a suddenly expanded food supply, but a bane to man and other warm-blooded predators who eat shellfish, because at these times the toxin carried by *Gonyaulax* builds to a dangerous level in the shellfish bodies. Any bird or mammal eating these suddenly toxic bivalves will be affected by PSP, Paralytic Shellfish Poisoning. This toxin is a complicated, and as yet little understood, chemical compound which affects the transmission of nerve impulses. Symptoms in humans, depending on how much toxic shellfish has been eaten, include numbness, difficulty of speaking and swallowing, and lack of muscular control. In severe cases, breathing will be affected and, unless artificial respiration keeps the victim alive, death may result. There is no known antidote.

It is, however, quite easy to analyze the quantity of *Gonyaulax* toxin in shellfish, and commercially grown or collected bivalves are always thoroughly checked before they can be sold. Environmental health agencies in Oregon, Washington, and British Columbia conduct regular tests to make sure these shellfish are safe to eat. *Gonyaulax* infestations have increased in the inland waters in recent years (perhaps in response to a more widespread pollution of our once-pristine waterways), but conditions favoring the blooming of *Gonyaulax* occur much more often on the outer coast, especially during the summer months. This is the reason behind the closure of beaches in Washington State from Dungeness Spit west, including the ocean beaches, to the harvesting of all clams, oysters, scallops, and mussels from April 1 to October 31 each year. Outbreaks can happen so quickly during this time and they can be limited to such a specific locality, that it is impossible for health departments to monitor all potentially toxic areas.

Pacific Northwest natives, who have regularly eaten local shellfish since childhood, seem to have a slight advantage in immunity over newcomers. Their tolerance to *Gonyaulax* toxin appears to be much higher, and a negative reaction may set in much later than for shellfish fanciers who have been raised on bivalves from other regions. But tolerances vary by individual, and I would advise no one to count on conditioned immunity: you might be in for a paralyzing surprise.

The Province of British Columbia, which claims to have very limited funds and manpower to monitor the shellfish-growing areas, has restricted its PSP surveillance to the inland waters from Bonilla Point east through Juan de Fuca Strait and north through Georgia

Strait, and has closed all of the beaches on the outer coast (north to the Alaska border) permanently to the harvesting of bivalves, because of the unpredictable presence of *Gonyaulax* in offshore waters.

Ergo, we have a situation where we can find thriving colonies of razor clams on the long beaches of Vancouver Island's west coast, but we cannot legally harvest them. In Washington State, on the other hand, shellfish closures do not apply to razor clams, because this bivalve concentrates the *Gonyaulax* toxin in the digestive gland which is eliminated when the clam is gutted. So, there really is no reason for the razor clam closure on the Canadian beaches. Yet the fisheries' bureaucracy remains immobile in the face of reality. In the meantime, the razor clams on British Columbia's outer coast continue to thrive and grow fat in relative peace. The fishermen, beach bums, squatters, loggers, and Indians who make up the human population of Vancouver Island's western fjords regularly consume the local razor clams (and other shellfish) with impunity, despite the ban. These molluscs are, after all, very good to eat.

The razor clam has little molluscan company in its milieu of shifting sands. The jack-knife clam, a close relative which plays even harder to catch, is an occasional neighbor, and small, colorful tellins and purple olives plow through the upper crust of the beach in search of food. The unstable habitat of pure sand, even where it is not constantly gnawed and pounded by heavy surf, offers few nutrients and thus supports very little plant and animal life. The sand clam, a hard-shelled *Macoma*, also lives in clean sand, but it prefers the shelter of quiet bays to the rigors of the open coast.

Protected sandy beaches and quiet bays, where the sand is mixed with gravel, silt, and organic matter, provide a rich feast of microscopic plants and animals for filter-feeding bivalves. Often these bights are lined with weathering driftwood logs along the shore which protect small littoral meadows from the scouring of the spring tides. Here beach pea, hard-hack, and wild roses grow, and trees, protected from saltspray by headlands, islets, and rocks, come down to the edge of the water, providing a fragrant retreat from rain or sun. Little matter that it may be wet and windy out on the squishy tideflats. Clamming is a pleasure on even the wettest days, when the prospect of a warming fire in the shelter of a spreading maple or cedar and a feast of freshly gathered steamed clams compensates the hardy clammer.

Bays and marshes where fine silt has settled into cozy mud are a great habitat for sea blite, saltwort, sedges, and waterfowl, but they are not favored by either clams or men. They provide insufficient oxygen and support for bivalves, and they keep men at bay with knee-deep muck and a reek which can offend the most inured nostrils, especially on hot summer days. The few clams that survive in such an environment have an uncouth, muddy taste if the tideflats are made up largely of putrified organic matter. Pollution from industrial operations and sewage—the latter can be a problem not only near cities, but also near clusters of beachfront homes with inadequate septic tanks—may settle on these flats and, in the absence of strong flushing currents, remain behind for decades.

These residues not only spoil the taste of even the most flavorsome molluscs, but they can make anyone who eats these contaminated shellfish quite ill. This is another reason I like to rely on commercially produced shellfish: the professional growers have a knack for preempting the best clam beaches. Yet even these producers are in trouble in parts of our region, in particular in those areas where greed and ignorance hamper the implementation of strict sewage and industrial waste standards. Coos Bay, Oregon, Grays Harbor and some inlets in Mason and Kitsap counties, Pierce County, and Bellingham Bay, Washington, and inlets in the populated east coast of Vancouver Island are most affected. It may be time for outraged shellfish connoisseurs to descend upon their seats of government and pressure legislators to set stricter standards of cleanliness in our precious waters.

Despite all of the current impediments, some surprising delicacies can be discovered by the gourmet foraging on the mud flats if he uses caution, a knowledge of local geography (in particular a knowledge of tidal flows which may carry pollutants—avoid the neighborhood of harbors, smelters, and refineries), and his infallible nose when he goes prospecting in the ooze. Clams and other shellfish collected in muddy areas should be kept in clean salt water for several days, either suspended from a boat or dock or in tanks where the water circulates or is frequently changed, to allow the bivalves to clean themselves of mud or debris. The addition of a little cornmeal to the water improves both the purification and the flavor of the shellfish.

Several clams live in this habitat. The name of one, the "Polluted *Macoma*" (*Macoma irus),* speaks for itself. Another *Macoma,* the small (to one inch) inconspicuous *Macoma,* which prefers bays that open onto the outer coast, can be quite tasty, however, when cleansed properly. The soft-shell or mud clam, a nineteenth-century immigrant which has prospered in northwest waters, likes tideflats and estuaries composed of mud and sand or mud and gravel where the salinity is reduced by a considerable inflow of fresh water. Like the razor clam, this bivalve is too large for its fragile shell. It can have a nice flavor, especially when it hybridizes with our native blunt soft-shell clam, which it often does in our inland waters.

The soft-shell clam is identical to the steamer clam of East Coast clambake fame. It is not much used for food in the Pacific Northwest, since we have so many clams available to us which are tastier, though it is quite common and may well be worth digging in clean, unpolluted estuaries. The soft-shell looks superficially like a razor clam, though its shell is round, rather than elongated. Because it grows in a muddy habitat, it should never be eaten raw, but always steamed or cooked.

The best-tasting hard-shell clams of the Pacific Northwest grow in a substrate of sand or silt with a large admixture of gravel. In this type of ground, a plentiful amount of organic matter and proper aeration combine to create an abundant food supply for bivalves. Tideflats and bay shores of inland waters, where glacial sand and gravel deposits are mixed with fertile silt carried to the Coast by creeks and rivers, provide the ideal habitat for littleneck, butter, gaper, and geoduck clams, but these bivalves are also locally abundant in sheltered bays and inlets of the outer coast.

Our littleneck clams belong to several species of flavorful bivalves, in contrast to the East Coast littleneck clam which is a young Quahog (after it becomes too large to remain a cherrystone). We have two species, the native littleneck clam, and the thin-shelled littleneck clam. Both taste very good. The native littleneck was harvested extensively by commercial harvesters, until it was replaced in the fancy of gourmet clam eaters by an upstart which hitchhiked a ride into the country on imported Japanese seed oysters sometime during the 1930s and rapidly spread throughout the hospitable Pacific Northwest waters after its arrival.

The Japanese littleneck clam is the kind of animal that outrages ecological purists. Not only was it introduced inadvertently, but, in its rapid adaptation to our region, it did not compete with our native species for living space. The Japanese littleneck can sometimes be found growing together with the native littleneck, but it prefers a higher tide level on the beach, filling a previously underutilized ecological niche. This immigrant clam, known in the trade as the "Manila clam," also tastes better than the native littleneck and has more meat per total weight of clam. Its meat tastes sweeter because of its higher glycogen content, and the clam survives handling and transportation much better.

When Manila clams are handled properly by being kept cool and moist, about 100 percent of the clams will open when they are steamed, in sharp contrast to the native littlenecks which have a high mortality rate in transit. Hardly any commercial growers bother with the native littleneck anymore, but concentrate on farming the Manila clam instead. As a result, the introduced Japanese clam has reduced the harvesting pressure on our native littlenecks, allowing them to multiply.

Most shellfish growers content themselves with preparing a suitable beach for the clams and hope that Manila clam spawn will find it attractive and settle down. Beaches that are too muddy may be conditioned with pea gravel. Some growers go further, though, to achieve better harvests. Bill Webb of Westcott Bay once again seems to be in the forefront of development here. His shellfish farm grows large numbers of Manila clams without damage to the environment: a clam beach, above the tide level at which native littlenecks and other hard-shell clams thrive, is cleaned and a fine meshed fishnet is spread out across the ground and tightened down. Spawn from the company's hatchery, which have grown in trays suspended in Westcott Bay for a year, are transferred to this beach. They quickly dig through the mesh of the net and settle down. The net protects the small clams from predators like fish and crabs. The Webbs' chowder pot takes care of molluscan enemies of the littlenecks, such as moon snails. The survival rate of these cultured Manila clams is an astonishing 70 percent, compared to only 9 percent for unprotected littlenecks (the netted beach provides such an ideal, protected habitat that some native clams, which commonly prefer to live at lower tide levels, move into the Manila clam colony). They grow to a marketable size in as little as two years from spawn, instead of the usual three to four years. After the harvestable clams have been dug from the beach, the ground is reseeded with further transplants from the culture trays.

Clam growers in Puget Sound and in British Columbia produce most of the West Coast supply. But all of these littlenecks can also be harvested as wild stock on public beaches. None of the speed and skill demanded for catching the wily razor clam are needed here. The littlenecks derive their name from their short siphons, and they live just below the surface of the beach at the half-tide level. They can be brought out into the open with the flick of a shovel.

Littleneck clams are commonly steamed before they are eaten, though very young littlenecks, collected from clean, unpolluted beaches, are delicious to eat raw. The Manila and the native littleneck clams grow to a size of about two and a half inches across. The thin-shelled littleneck tops out at about four inches. This clam, as well as the sand clam, is often confused by dilettante clam diggers with the butter clam, a thick-shelled bivalve that reaches a diameter of about five inches.

The butter clam, known as the Washington clam south of our region, is somewhat misnamed. There is nothing buttery about its tough flesh. But it is tasty; butter clams make a delectable chowder. Puget Sound and the Strait of Georgia are the center of abundance of this bivalve, but it also occurs in other areas of the Coast. It is the most important commercial clam in British Columbia where, unfortunately, most of the catch is canned.

Amateur clam diggers should be very careful when digging butter clams, because these tasty bivalves are not only periodically affected by the *Gonyaulax* toxin, but they store this toxin in their bodies for a long time, sometimes for years after a heavy outbreak of red tide. About 80 percent of the poison is stored in the siphon and gills of the butter clam. As a precaution, these clams should be opened by steaming and their necks and gills removed before the meat is eaten. Whenever there is a doubt about the safe edibility of these molluscs, the liquid released by the steaming should also be discarded—difficult as this may be for clam fanciers to do.

Sexual cycles have a different effect on the palatability of clams than they have on the taste of oysters during the spawning season. The stimulated gonads of littleneck and butter clams positively affect these bivalves' flavor. They are thus most savory during the early summer months when the clams prepare to spawn. Immediately after spawning, they are tough, darker in color, and insipid.

Butter clams prefer to live close to the surface of a beach, but, even though they are filter feeders with relatively short siphons, they can be found as much as a foot below ground. A little deeper than the butter clam (and somewhat more difficult to dig up) lives the largest bivalve that a clammer can hope to dig from the tideflats. The gaper, or horse clam, lives intertidally where the ground is primarily composed of mud with ample quantities of gravel and bits of broken shell mixed in. But it also can be found in a variety of other substrata, ranging from sand to heavy clay. The gaper is another clam that grows too big and fat for its shell (it can almost, but not quite, withdraw its siphon into its shell). However, unlike the razor clam, it is not agile enough to pull itself deeper into the ground to escape a clam digger's shovel.

The gaper is not a pretty clam, as its alternate name, horse clam, denotes. "Horse" neither signifies a relation between this clam and horses, nor implies that the gaper infests equines, but retains its colloquial meaning of "large, strong, coarse." The horse clam is indeed a coarse clam with a less refined flavor than other clams and a crude appearance; nevertheless it makes a refined chowder. The gaper's thick, black, wrinkled siphon can protrude from its white shell, blotched with mangy-looking pieces of brown periostracum, for about a foot. This neck has two leatherlike flaps at the tip (often colonized by tiny algae, barnacles, sea anemones, and hydroids), and the inner edge of the siphon opening is lined with small tentacles.

Our area has two subspecies of gapers. One (*Tresus nuttalli*) prefers the outer coast; the other (*T.n. capax*) likes the inland waters better; but the subspecies intermingle to some extent in the Puget Sound and Strait of Georgia regions. This poses a problem for gourmets. The Pacific gaper, from the outer coast, spawns in summer; the inland horse clam does so in winter. Since the spawning affects the taste and tenderness of the clams, the clammer should be able to tell them apart. But this is easier said than done, because the subspecies are not easy to separate (some scientists even claim that we have only one subspecies in our region, but this is disputed by marine biologists from British Columbia who have studied these molluscs in excruciating detail). So, if you have gotten a tough, flavorless gaper in either summer or winter, you will at least know that you have dug up a member of the wrong subspecies for the season, and you will not have to be afraid that, all of a sudden, all gapers in your area have gone bad. Clammers do not have to worry about this in the spring and fall when both kinds of horse clams should be tender and tasty. They can vigorously dig away— unless a red tide warning closes all the beaches.

I have always found it interesting that the name horse clam was bestowed on the gaper and not on the much larger geoduck clam, but this is perhaps due to the geoduck's more refined taste. The geoduck is an enormous clam, by far the largest found on the continent. The shell, which is quite small in proportion to the clam's body, can reach a length of nine inches. The siphon may stretch to a length of three feet. This allows the geoduck to live deeper in the substrate (it also likes deeper water), where it is almost beyond the reach of any but the most energetic clam diggers. But this clam is a prize well worth seeking out. With the geoduck, the standard rule of bivalve flavor, that large molluscs have an inferior or coarser taste, does not apply. Of course, the geoducks I have obtained from seafood markets have weighed out at an average of three to four pounds. That is quite small for this clam, and perhaps the ones I have sampled still possessed a juvenile flavor. Full-grown geoducks in the Puget Sound region reach average weights of eight to twelve pounds; clams weighing more than twenty pounds are found occasionally, and specimens weighing up to forty pounds have been recorded.

Geoducks have a rather silly scientific name, *Panope generosa*, which translates into something like "fat sea nymph." I have often been amused by biologists who have felt the need to debunk the highly unscientific spirits of classical mythology by bestowing their ethereal names on sea slugs and other odd marine creatures. But with the geoduck they have outdone themselves. There is nothing nymphlike about this clam. It is, instead, very phallic looking, the subject of many Northwesterners' jests.

Geoducks, like other clams, should always be bought when still alive, preferably a short time after they have been dug from the ground. Lively geoducks, kept in salt water until they are sold, can be found regularly at the Hama Hama oyster farm in Shelton, Washington, and in the fish markets of Vancouver's Chinatown. When clams have been removed from the water and are displayed on chunks of ice, they can still be fresh. Make sure they are alive by poking their siphons with a finger. The clam should twitch and straighten out its neck. (Never buy one that is dead, or you may be in for a quick trip to the hospital to have your stomach pumped out.) Always make sure the water has been removed from the clam, first, because you don't want to pay for the extra deadweight and, second, because you might be in for a wet surprise.

I watched a surprise of this kind a little while back, after I had just bought a geoduck from a saltwater tank. Both the fishmonger and I were in a hurry and, after a few perfunctory squeezes, she carried my purchase, upright, toward the cash register. Geoducks are capable of a powerful squirt (their hiding places on the tideflats can often be spotted by these geysers), and this clam, annoyed by being carried, put its heart into the squirt. Its water hit the fishmonger right between the eyes, wetted her hair, and began to run down her face in rivulets. This proved too much for the monger's composure. She angrily grabbed the clam by the neck, held it over the basin, and began to squeeze with a vengeance. I don't think I paid for a single drop of water. It may have been my imagination, but the neck of this geoduck seemed uncommonly tender when I cooked it later that day.

Geoducks (and gapers) have tough outer skins and need to be skinned before they can be prepared. This is a simple process if done properly. Bring a pot of water to a rolling boil and immerse the clam, shell and all. Remove after a few seconds and chill immediately under cold, running water. The skin, shell, and guts should have loosened and be easy to remove. Geoducks have two kinds of meat, the somewhat tough meat of the siphon, which can be beaten into tenderness and fried as a "steak" or ground for chowder, and the tender belly meat, which includes the mantle and foot muscles. This can be cubed and sautéed lightly in butter, or it can be served raw as sashimi—though I prefer mine cooked. It can also be added to stir-fried vegetables.

Surprisingly few Northwesterners, both natives and newcomers, have actually eaten fresh geoduck. I can understand why. It's difficult to get past this clam's outlandish appearance. A few years back, several commercial processors decided to start the wholesale marketing of geoducks, but they ran into an image problem—not with the way the clam looked, but with its name. After all, what squeamish cook would like to have a "gooey duck" in the kitchen? So the geoduck was renamed the "king clam." And why not? Willapa Bay oyster sales had jumped after the Japanese oysters were sold as "king" oysters. And demand for the northern spider crab, one of the ugliest creatures in the Pacific seas, a thin, anemic-looking beast with a tiny body and long, spindly legs skyrocketed (to a point where this crustacean is now becoming scarce) after it was renamed "king crab." The clam processors were smart enough to disguise the shape of the geoduck by selling its meat chopped up or flattened into fillets (I sometimes think you can sell anything to the American consumer, as long as it is ground up like hamburger or sliced and sold as "steak").

Today, if you look hard enough, you can find processed geoduck in many supermarket freezer bins. On the other extreme, you can find sliced, raw geoduck sold as sashimi in Japanese markets. I still prefer to buy my geoduck live and fresh, do the cleaning myself, and thus enjoy its flavor at its best. There are several delectable ways of fixing this clam. And don't worry about taking this odd-looking creature home: fishmongers will wrap it in newspaper, and you should be able to get it to the privacy of your kitchen without exposing yourself to the stares and giggles of less enlightened gastronomes.

The geoduck often lives so far below the lowest tide level that it is most easily harvested by divers using a suction dredge, but another tasty northwest clam, the basket or heart cockle, lives in very shallow ground (it has only a stumpy siphon) and can sometimes be picked off the beach gravel or clay at low tide. The cockle is quite small, only two or three inches in diameter, but it is very motile for a clam. It moves along the surface of the substrate by the vigorous action of its long, muscular foot, often digging a shallow trench on the surface. Cockles are capable of jumping several inches off the ground when touched by a starfish or other predator.

Cockles are a bit tough, and they have a strong, though delicious, marine flavor. Most people find them too strong tasting and don't like to eat them steamed or sautéed, but they add a superb taste to clam chowders. I like to eat small cockles raw on the half shell, served with a little lemon or hot chili sauce, or Chinese vinegar and ginger sauce. Cockles used in chowders should be added to the stew raw, chopped coarsely, a few minutes before the chowder is done. They can be opened like oysters, with the oyster knife inserted carefully at the front of the shell.

Cockles are not the only clams that add interesting flavors to chowders. The beaches and tideflats of the Pacific Northwest have a number of assorted clams, none of which are common enough in one locality to be harvested by themselves, and some of which may be too small to eat from the shell. They can be added to seafood stews whole (make sure they are still alive and have been cleaned of sand and mud). They will open during cooking, and their shells can be pulled out later. These clams have different tastes and demand different cooking times. Most will become tough if overcooked. A good rule of thumb is to add the larger ones first—unless you prefer to open and chop them like cockles—and the smallest ones last.

Cockles may be able to leap from danger, but another bivalve, the scallop, regularly swims through the water. This is an odd thing for a clam to do, but it has provided gourmets with a special delicacy. Most bivalves have two small adductor muscles with which they open or close their shells. They tend to be tough, stringy, and too small to bother with. The scallop's adductors, on the other hand, have been fused into one large, tender, juicy, and very savory muscle. The rest of the scallop's body is a bit of an enigma. Like other bivalves, scallops have no head. But they have eyes, lots of them, up to a hundred in some species. In the absence of a head, these eyes are arranged like little beads along the outer edge of the scallop's mantle, in both shells. Scallops are brightly colored, but the flashy pigmentation blends in surprisingly well with the colors of the underwater eelgrass meadows and kelp forests where scallops live. Divers searching for scallops can often spot them by the even brighter colors—shiny blue, green, and orange—of the rows of beady little eyes which peer out from under the edge of the half-opened shells.

The large, delicious adductor muscle is the only part of the scallop that is commonly sold in our fish markets, and this is a shame, for the rest of this mollusc is just as tasty, and very tender. It is very good to eat, eyeballs and all. The scallop has not been harvested as extensively on our coasts as it could be. Scallops are gregarious, and large quantities of these tasty shellfish inhabit the waters of the Pacific Northwest, but they are harvested only intermittently because their presence cannot be predicted accurately—scallops may migrate in "herds" for short distances—making dredging a risky proposition. The industry also suffers from a lack of motivated shuckers. But why shuck scallops at all? Why not sell them in the shell? They are certainly prettier presented in this way than in their more common commercial incarnation, as ambiguous white lumps of translucent meat. I know of only one restaurant which serves our small local inland water scallops in the shell, the Sooke Harbour House on southern Vancouver Island, and here they are at their best—tender, flavorful, and cooked to perfection.

Scallops, whether whole or as a stripped muscle, should never be overcooked, for they toughen quickly. There are several simple ways of fixing them, but the best way of enjoying a scallop is to make sure it is fresh and has never been frozen.

The scallops of our inland waters are quite small, only growing to some two inches in diameter, but the giant weathervane scallop, which is fished commercially off the Oregon coast, can reach a size of nine inches. The best of our free-swimming scallops are the ones that have been collected by divers in the Gulf and San Juan islands, the Strait of Juan de Fuca, and the bays and sounds of Vancouver Island's west coast. My first taste came on a beautiful, limpid summer evening on a Sucia Island beach. We had anchored in Fox Cove to spend the night and had rowed the dinghy ashore to stretch our legs. Sucia is a low island of soft sandstone, carved into a maze of rocky fingers by glaciers; of rocks cut into strange, surreal shapes by erosion; and of fossil-bearing, cave-riddled cliffs rising above scraggly forests and sandy beaches. We had planned to have chowder for dinner that night and were debating if we should take a short walk through the woods to Mud Bay and collect some cockles from the tideflats, or if the occasion demanded that we row the dinghy along the shore to pick sea cucumbers along the way. At this point, a band of scuba divers arrived in the bay, landed near our group, and pulled their shallow-drafted boats high onto the beach. They had returned from a diving trip to several nearby islets and reefs, and they were quick to invite us to dine with them and share the marine delicacies they had just collected.

I rowed the dinghy back to the boat for some chilled beer, and on my return I was handed a paper plate of perfectly prepared pink scallops. They were much tastier than any commercially processed scallops (which I have found to be dull ever since), and I ate perhaps more than my share. These scallops went beautifully with fresh sea urchin roe spread on french bread, barbecued silver salmon, and chilled beer. Needless to say, these scallops are not sold in any of our fish markets. Gourmets who wish to savor them must either dive for these elusive bivalves or make the acquaintance of a diver who is willing to share his catch.

Free-swimming scallops often flutter through the eelgrass meadows like colorful underwater butterflies, and I know several divers who pursue them with hand-held nets; but scallops show their affinity with other nonburrowing bivalves by anchoring their fragile shells, at least temporarily, to a resting place, preferably eelgrass blades, while they feed. To do so, they extrude a threadlike byssus, which helps them resist the pull of tidal currents, but which is sufficiently brittle to break when the scallops take flight. One species of scallop, the purple-hinged rock scallop, swims about freely only in its youth. It permanently attaches itself to rocks as it grows older. After the rock scallop loses the power of flight, its pretty shell becomes thick and coarse (the animal opts for armor instead of speed) and quite lumpy; it may grow to be ten inches across. It can still be recognized as a scallop, however, because its original, finely fluted juvenile shell remains embedded near the hinge of the adult shell.

The rock scallop is the most sweetly flavored of our shellfish—its flesh has the highest glycogen content of any bivalve—and many gourmets claim it is also the tastiest. Young rock scallops should be eaten raw; older ones may be prepared like other scallops or like mussels and oysters. The rock scallop can sometimes be found attached to beach rocks in the lower tidal zones, but it is encountered more commonly in deeper water. Rock scallops are not currently sold by our fishmongers (their desirability has led to overharvesting and a decline in population) but Bill Webb, at Westcott Bay on San Juan Island, is experimenting with their commercial production.

Scallops are very flavorful shellfish, but I would leave open to disputation whether they or the cultured mussel of the Puget Sound region are our tastiest bivalve. Our mussels, perhaps more than any other seafood produced in the Pacific Northwest, may serve as a paradigm to show that the quirks and vagaries of regional eating may not so much depend on the quality of a locally produced food, but on the mental attitude of a region's gourmets. And on fads. I was astounded to discover that the fishmongers in Seattle's Pike Place Market now make a special effort to sell East Coast seafood on a regular basis, offering (besides several "standard" exotic fish varieties) such "delicacies" as cherrystone clams, which are not as tasty as our young Manila clams, and East Coast sea scallops, coarser and inferior in flavor to our own scallops. This new development does not show that Northwesterners have finally become so sophisticated that they have awakened to the superior flavors of East Coast shellfish, but rather harkens back to an odd, yet existing prejudice against the superb foods produced in our region. Such an attitude is galling, but it becomes ridiculous when we consider the blue mussel.

I must digress here for a moment and go back in time. Traveling along the channel coast of France, I have always encountered numerous quantities of fresh mussels offered for sale and have savored them in a variety of delicious ways: with shallots and butter, with wine, garlic, cream, or in soups. Buying mussels from roadside stands, I always made sure they were fresh, smelling them and touching their shells to see if they would close. They are usually fresh, except during the height of the summer tourist season, when it is better not to buy them. I could also ascertain the mussels' place of origin. Wild mussels, gathered on surf-beaten rocks, may carry the romantic appeal of the open coast, but tend to be tough and leathery. On the other hand, mussels that have been cultivated in protected bays (the French use brushwood hurdles for support) are plump, meltingly tender, and have a rich, buttery flavor.

Imagine my dismay, when I first came to the West Coast of North America in the early 1960s and found there were no local mussels to be had. One fishmonger dissolved in mirth when I tried to convince him that "those ugly, weedy things, messing up pilings" were not only edible, but delicious, and should be harvested. Mussels grew wild all along the West Coast, and I soon gathered my own (avoiding them during outbreaks of red tide). But neither the brown California mussels nor the blue mussels growing on the rocks and pilings of the southern coast had the exquisite flavor to which I had become accustomed on the coast of Picardie. During my peregrinations to the north, in search of the best foods of the Coast, I discovered the tastier wild mussels of the Oregon coast; but still, these did not compare to the cultivated mussels of the French coast. Nowhere in Oregon could I find a cultivated mussel. Farther north to Willapa Bay, Grays Harbor, Puget Sound, and the inlets of British Columbia, I continued to gather and taste wild mussels, but found none cultivated. The natives, apart from the Indians, consumed large quantities of local shellfish, oysters, razor clams, littlenecks, and butter clams. But not mussels.

Finally, sometime in the mid-1970s, I discovered cultivated mussels on a restaurant menu. Victoria and I were spending a relaxing weekend at the Captain Whidbey Inn near Coupeville. A local shellfish grower, Pete Jefferds, had asked the chef to try serving some of the mussels he grew in Penn Cove using a novel approach, long-line culture (the mussels are suspended on ropes from log booms, and stay submerged at all times, so they can grow fat and plump quickly). These mussels were an instant hit. But the supply was still very limited —Pete was the first grower to start long-line culture on the West Coast, and he was still working the bugs out of his system. Late diners were commonly out of luck and had to forego mussels until the next day's delivery. We struck out on our first night, but reserved some mussels for the following day's dinner.

These mussels were well worth waiting for. If my taste memory did not fail me, these were tastier than any I had ever eaten on the coast of France. They were tender, luscious, and, presented in a delicate wine and shallot sauce, they were a feast. Buy my quest was not yet over. I tried to buy some of these mussels to fix at home, but there were none to spare.

Mussels grew more popular during the next several years and I was delighted when I saw some for sale at my local fish shop. I bought out the whole supply, took the mussels home, and steamed them right away. Only three opened. The rest were dead. I couldn't believe it. In my eagerness I had failed to check them properly for freshness. I returned to the fishmonger and asked him where his mussels came from. New England. I was aghast. Here I was, in the Puget Sound region, where local growers were producing some of the best mussels in the world, and our wholesalers brought in inferior mussels from New England. After several weeks of haggling, my fishmonger finally agreed to order some Penn Cove mussels. But he warned me that he would have to charge me a higher price, because the local distributors did not handle them and he had to make a special effort to get some. On the day the Penn Cove mussels finally arrived in Bellingham (by this time they were often available in Seattle) I had received an invitation to dine with a locally renowned gourmet. I had considered bringing him some of these fresh Penn Cove mussels, but I was afraid I might insult him, assuming he had discovered their availability earlier in the day and not passed up such an opportunity. Sure enough, we had mussels for appetizers. I took a bite and was dismayed. I knew the horrid taste that affronted me quite well.

Earlier in the year, before Victoria and I set out on a camping trip through Europe, my well-meaning mother had added several cans of Portuguese mussels to our food chest. One evening, in a godforsaken, sandy campground on the Flemish coast, we had parked our camper in the lee of an intact World War II coastal defense bunker to get out of the chill wind that blew across the sea from the English fens. We decided to drive away the gloomy atmosphere of the place by having an elaborate candlelight dinner. We had not yet reached the mussel country, so, for appetizers, we opened a can of Portuguese mussels. Victoria took one sniff and decided to forego her share. I took one bite—I'll try everything once— set down my fork, wiped it carefully, washed out my mouth with wine, then dumped the bowl of canned mussels into the trash. I next searched out the rest of our supply (no easy task in the crowded camper) took them outside and, braving the blowing sand and frigid wind, carried them to the public washroom, where I set them down in a conspicuous place. They were gone the next day, and I pity the poor soul who took them. The next day we began to feast on fresh Picardie mussels. I had all but forgotten this incident until I was once again confronted by canned Portuguese mussels—but this time in the Pacific Northwest. Although fresh Penn Cove mussels were available, they had been ignored by my host for the exotic appeal of a "genuine imported" product.

Even now, Puget Sound mussels, especially those from Penn Cove, are often difficult to find. But New England mussels—most of which are not cultivated, but wild mussels bought from collectors by the seafood processors—can be bought almost daily at our fish markets. I have heard many excuses for this absurd situation. I have even heard it said that New England mussels have a better taste than our own, "because they wouldn't fly them out all the way from the East Coast if they weren't better." Notwithstanding such sophistry, I have continued to maintain that our mussels are tastier, and I buy them whenever possible.

As part of a recent fish exposition, a mussel-tasting competition, comparing fresh mussels fixed in identical ways from a dozen different locations, was held in Boston with a panel of food experts as judges. Pete Jefferds's Penn Cove mussels won the tasting by a wide margin. Some bottom-cultured mussels from Maine came in a distant second, and, right behind, in third place, mussels from Race Lagoon, just around the corner from Penn Cove. This victory, one in a long string of tasting successes for Puget Sound mussels, was of interest not only because it told us once again what we already knew, but for the way it was reported in the press. The media in western Washington hardly considered this to be a newsworthy event. The *National Fisherman*, reporting on the tasting, brushed over the clear victory of the Puget Sound mussels and concentrated on the losers instead, bemoaning the fact that Irish mussels entered in the contest were frozen solid (making it difficult to experience their superior taste) and that the California mussels were still too highly laced with PSP to be servable. But there was a glimmer of hope for the frustrated East Coast establishment gourmets: green mussels from New Zealand may yet prove to be a match for Puget Sound's best. And the Kiwi molluscs would, of course, possess those two magic words: "Genuine imported."

This whole episode illustrates—aside from repeating the old saw that the East Coast does not like the Northwest because we are blessed with better harbors, a milder climate, higher mountains, and tastier seafood—that promotion, not quality of product, may be the most important factor in consumer awareness of a particular food. The national food establishment has seemed loath to accept anything as "good" that deviates from the Northeast/Southwest axis of supply and marketing power. California wholesalers have long affected the supply and distribution of food in the Pacific Northwest, buying up the best produce from our area and in return dumping its surpluses in our region. This is strongly reflected in recipes published on the West Coast—just count how large a percentage of the cookery directions you find in books and magazines demand some raw or processed materials produced in California, from avocado to ziziphus. There is no question in my mind that a continual push by the California publishing media has led many of us into a colonial dependence, making us believe we can eat well only when we rely on California produce, and I have no doubt that a proliferation of East Coast (primarily New York) cookbooks calling for East Coast ingredients has led to a rising demand for East Coast seafood.

The Pacific Northwest offers an incredible variety of tasty bivalves. Many of these have been eaten as emergency food in the past, because they were so plentiful, or used to supplement the larder in times of economic stress. They deserve better. I prefer them over the shellfish from other regions and feel sure that I will be joined by many Pacific Northwest natives in this appreciation. These shellfish *are* good sport, fun to catch or dig, but they are also great eating.

Clams Tarragon O'Reilly

This dish, made from impeccably fresh clams, makes a very tasty appetizer. Serve with freshly baked french bread and a chilled semillon.

Fresh clams   2 to 3 pounds
Water   ¼ cup
White wine   ¼ cup
Thyme   pinch
Dill   pinch
Herb Butter
Bread crumbs   as needed

1. Barely steam clams in water, wine, and herbs until they pop open.
2. Snap off ½ shell of clam, place other ½ shell with clam in oven-proof dish.
3. Place a dab of herb butter on each clam. Sprinkle with bread crumbs.
4. Bake for 5 to 7 minutes at 375° till bubbling. Serve.

Serves 4 to 6

Herb Butter

Unsalted butter   ½ cup
Shallots   ¼ cup chopped
Fresh tarragon   1 tablespoon (or tarragon preserved in vinegar)
Salt and freshly ground pepper   to taste
Fresh parsley   1 tablespoon chopped

1. Mix ingredients well until blended.

Makes ¾ cup

Stuffed Clams

Here is another one of the tasty shellfish dishes prepared by Rick O'Reilly at La Petite Maison in Olympia. Rick uses only the freshest local clams—and you can certainly tell the difference. Serve with a dry chardonnay or with a well-chilled Hinzerling or Château Benoit sparkling wine.

Steamer clams   24
Unsalted butter   ½ cup
Garlic cloves   2, peeled
Parsley   1 tablespoon chopped
Tarragon   1 tablespoon chopped
Salt and freshly ground pepper   to taste
Ground nutmeg   to taste
Bread crumbs   2 tablespoons

1. Steam clams in large pot with ½-inch water just until they pop open. Remove clams and set aside. (Save broth for other recipes.)
2. Blend remaining ingredients, place a teaspoon of mixture in each clam and sprinkle with bread crumbs.
3. Bake at 375° for 5 minutes. Serve at once.

Serves 2 to 4

Oregon Mussels and Clams with Linguini

This delicious recipe was given to me by Virginia Fuller, wife of Tualatin Vineyards' wine maker Bill Fuller. It is, of course, best with freshly gathered mussels and clams, and it is simple enough to cook on the beach. All you need is a goodly pot (or two) and a few basic ingredients. Serve with chardonnay and crusty french bread.

Linguini (or other pasta) *   16-ounce package
Butter   2 tablespoons
Medium onion   1, cut into rings
Unsalted butter   1 tablespoon
Crème Fraîche (see Index)   1 cup
Chardonnay   1 cup
Thyme   1 tablespoon fresh (or 1 teaspoon dried)
Mussels and clams, mixed   2 pounds, soaked and rinsed well

1. Prepare linguini to package instructions, toss in butter, and set aside in warm place.
2. Sauté onion in butter until tender. Add Crème Fraîche, wine, and thyme. Bring to a boil and add shellfish. Cook 2 to 3 minutes or until shells open.
3. Pour shellfish and sauce through cheesecloth (you can't do this one on the beach unless

you have a second pot with you).
4. Arrange shellfish on serving platter with linguini.
5. Return sauce to saucepan and reduce over high heat by half or until quite thick. (Allow time to reduce liquid, for it will take quite a while.)
6. Pour over shellfish and linguini and serve immediately.

* Fresh pasta is also good to use. Just be sure to cook it 30 to 60 seconds only.

Serves 6

Marty McLean's Oregon Mussels

We ran into a little problem the first time Marty fixed these mussels for us. Between the two steps of preparation (steaming and broiling), Marty had to run an errand. Well, he was run right into the Coupeville jail on a minor traffic infraction (they're very tough on the island), and we had to finish preparing the mussels ourselves. Marty was bailed out just in time to help us eat them. Serve with a dry riesling, chardonnay, sauvignon blanc, semillon, pinot noir blanc, chilled lager, or Blackhook Porter—we've tried them all and they work—and freshly baked french bread.

Fresh scrubbed and debearded mussels   72 (more or less)
Unsalted butter   1 pound
Parsley   ½ cup chopped
Garlic   ½ cup chopped or to taste
Salt and freshly ground pepper   to taste (optional)

1. Steam mussels until they are <u>barely</u> open. (Keep an eye on them and do not overcook.) They can be done ahead up to here and kept cool.
2. Squeeze a dab of butter, parsley, and garlic into each shell. (You may add salt and pepper here if you must.)
3. Place mussels under broiler (or on barbecue), as close to the source of heat as possible. When butter sizzles, they are done.

Serves 6

Rick O'Reilly's Seafood Salad

This salad is best when made with fresh mussels, but when these are not available, use scallops, clams, squid, or some other shellfish. Serve on top of potato salad arranged on spinach or lettuce leaves. Accompany with a good chilled lager beer.

Ripe tomatoes   2 cups chopped, cleaned, and seeded
Onion   1 cup chopped
Celery   1 cup chopped
Lemon   1, zest and juice
Orange   1, zest and juice
Fresh fennel   ½ teaspoon chopped
Fresh thyme   1 teaspoon chopped
Salt and freshly ground pepper   to taste
Steamed mussels   48
Parsley   garnish
Lemon slices   garnish

1. Sauté tomatoes, onion, celery, lemon, orange, herbs, salt, and pepper until cooked through.
2. Add mussels and cook just until all are heated through. (Don't overcook.)
3. Garnish with parsley sprigs and lemon slices.

Serves 6 to 8

Pacific Pink Swimming Scallops in a Sabayon Sauce

At certain times of the year, Sooke Harbour seems to be just filled with pink scallops. Sinclair Philip makes full use of them at the Sooke Harbour House. Serve with a dry gewürztraminer.

Fresh swimming scallops   16
Cream   1 cup
Green peppercorns (bottled in water)   1 level teaspoon (taste to make sure they don't have too strong a flavor)
Parsley   4 teaspoons finely chopped
Egg yolks   2
Gewürztraminer   4 tablespoons
Nasturtium flowers   garnish

1. In a medium-sized pot, place scallops (in shell), whipping cream, and peppercorns, plus 3 teaspoons of parsley.
2. Cover, bring to a boil, and steam open scallops in mixture. Remove scallops from pan

(leave in shell) and keep warm.

3. Continue to boil cream mixture; reduce until thick.
4. Beat yolks with a wire whisk until foamy, add wine, and whip mixture into cream, blending well.
5. Discard upper part of scallop shells; arrange open scallops on serving plate and pour sauce over scallops.
6. Garnish each with remaining parsley and a nasturtium flower.

Variation: This recipe also works well with mussels.

Serves 4

Mark's Favorite Clam Chowder

Both Ragnhild Costello's husband Tripo and her son Mark have worked as commercial fishermen. Mark gave up fishing after a purse seiner sank under him in southeast Alaska. But he still likes seafood. Here's his mother's way of spoiling him.

Potatoes   3 to 4 cups cubed
Salt   to taste
Horse clams   2 cups chopped (plus reserved nectar)
Large onion   1, chopped
Bacon   ½ pound, cut in pieces
Flour   ¼ cup (approximately)
Milk   4 cups
Unsalted butter   2 tablespoons (optional)
Flour   2 tablespoons (optional)
Salt and freshly ground pepper   to taste
Parsley   2 teaspoons chopped

1. Cover potatoes with water, bring to a boil, and add salt.
2. Add clams with their nectar and boil gently until potatoes are done.
3. Sauté onion and bacon in heavy skillet until bacon is crisp and onion soft.
4. To make roux (thickening), add about ¼ cup flour to bacon-onion mixture, stirring gently so no lumps form. (Skim excess fat.) Mix together until well blended.
5. Scald milk in double boiler. (Do not boil.)
6. Add potatoes, clams, and broth.
7. Add bacon-onion roux a little at a time; stir well until slightly thickened.
8. If you like thicker chowder, soften a couple of tablespoons butter, add a little flour, and blend, dropping little bits into the hot milk mixture.
9. Salt and pepper to taste.
10. Garnish with a little chopped parsley as you serve.

Serves 6 to 8 generously

Creamed Mussel Soup Captain Whidbey

This dish is best when made with the superb mussels raised on rafts in Penn Cove, the inlet next to the inn. Serve with freshly baked bread and a well-chilled Oregon chardonnay.

Unsalted butter ⅓ pound
All-purpose flour 3 tablespoons
Milk 1½ quarts
Cream 1 cup
Mussel meat ¾ pound, lightly chopped
Mussel nectar 1⅓ cups
Salt ½ teaspoon
Ground nutmeg dash
Dry white wine 3 tablespoons

1. In soup kettle, melt butter and stir in flour to make a roux. Cook for 2 minutes.
2. While stirring, add milk and cream; continue cooking and stirring until slightly thickened.
3. Add mussel meat and nectar, salt, nutmeg, and wine; continue to heat until completely warm. Serve.

Serves 8

Snails and
Odd Marine Creatures

Ed and his cousin Gary, two amiable drifters, happened upon us at the wrong time. They ran away from California in their midtwenties and, slowly moving up the Coast from one harbor to the next, lived in Gary's van as they looked for longshore work and odd-jobs along the way. The allure and expense of Portland's nightlife made a major dent in their exchequer, jobs promised in Astoria did not materialize, and Grays Harbor proved to be its usual gray and unemployed self. When the two wanderers reached Tacoma, they had run out of beer and were down to one tank of gas for their van—just enough to get them to Bellingham.

Victoria and I lived in a tiny, two-room tree house at the time, with a dog and a family of chickarees for company. We had planned to withdraw for a while into the woods in this "perfect hideaway" to paint and write without disturbance, but things just didn't work out, and the going proved tougher than we anticipated. Fortunately, there were large quantities of wild apples and blackberries, and the neighbors shared their vegetables with us. We also ate large quantities of free or inexpensive seafood, salmon, crabs, and clams.

Ed and Gary, hungry and disheartened, put an immediate strain on our limited resources, depleting our inadequately filled larder within a few days. Overcome by hunger and claustrophobia, our visitors raised some money from their families and rented a small apartment in town. Next, they had to make the difficult decision of whether they wanted to eat regular meals or spend their remaining funds on beer. Here we were able to help them out. Our supplies needed replenishing, but Bellingham Bay was closed to clamming because of red tide alerts. In this hour of need, we discovered some of the Pacific Northwest's greatest delicacies: marine snails.

Most marine snails (with the exception of a few filter feeders and predators) browse on algae and thus stay free of the harmful accumulations of PSP toxin which affects bivalves. All of these vegetarian gastropods, whether large or small, are edible, and they soon became our fair game. Victoria and I explored slowly, tasting carefully as we proceeded, but Ed and Gary waded in with a vengeance. They ate everything they could find on tideflats and rocky shores, tasty or not. They ate limpets raw and sucked tiny littorines, margarites, and olives from their spindle shells. But these two rapacious gourmands quickly learned to clean these molluscs first, for some have a bitter gall which waits for the unsuspecting eater at the end of a sweet morsel of head and mantle. Ed and Gary soon graduated to cooking these snails and even mastered the art of spicing them, but they never learned to appreciate their delicate taste and, once they found jobs, gladly returned to their regular fare of pizza, steak, and beer. Though they have petulantly foresworn marine snails, they still eat *escargots* from time to time.

This is scarcely odd, for *escargots*, or at least their flavorless canned incarnations, have no taste at all. They have become the favorite appetizers of pretentious diners, because, once the diner has overcome the initial resistance to eating a snail, he finds the actual process painless, since it is free from any exotic or challenging flavors. Even the texture is quite familiar—for who has not eaten bubble gum before? The demand for these bland molluscs imported from France is as high as it is only because dilettante gourmets can think of no easier way to show as readily (and safely) that they have mastered the initial steps of culinary refinement. Sinclair Philip of Sooke calls these imported snails the "loggers' delight," because *escargots*, followed by steak, have become the favorite dish of the fallers, the highest paid of the timber cutters: snails to show sophistication and steak for the food value.

Now, a true French *escargot* (*Helix pomatia*, the vineyard snail), is a gourmet's delight. It is coddled, allowed to clean itself (it may have eaten plants whose residues are harmless to snails, but toxic to humans), and—depending on the culinary outlook—it may either be starved in the Burgundian fashion or fed dainties like lettuce or wheat flour in the Roman fashion to improve its flavor. These fat, tasty gastropods bear little resemblance to the black, shriveled objects canned in a suspicious broth, labeled "*escargot*," and sold as a delicacy throughout the civilized world. Demand for true *escargots* among French gourmets alone has long exceeded the supply of prime snails, and the few that are available are quickly snatched up by the better restaurants. The French now import large quantities of snails from all of the western European countries and from eastern Europe as well. These snails belong to several (often undesirable) species and are frequently of dubious origin. You can't fool a true French gourmet with these fakes, but a provincial or foreign barbarian—oh well! Snails are astonishingly difficult to speciate once they're removed from their shells, and an honest identification becomes even more difficult once they're cooked. And snails without a tail look much like slugs. Besides, who can tell the difference after a gastropod has been spiced and sauced. As one budding gourmet once exclaimed: "Ooh, I think I could like *escargots*, if they just didn't have such an awfully strong garlic taste!"

Several of the land snails commonly encountered in the Pacific Northwest have a natural garlic taste. The little black *Oxychilus alliarius,* with a glossy ochre shell, is quite common (though it has no common name as yet) in greenhouses and under backyard trash heaps. It isn't worth bothering with, since it only grows to be a quarter of an inch across. Another snail, *Monadenia fidelis*, though also going about without a common name, is quite common in late spring throughout our region. It is a beautiful gastropod, with a bluntly conical shell marked by broad black and yellow-brown bands, and a mottled reddish body. It grows to be almost an inch and a half across. We have a few more snails in our region, not quite an inch in diameter and probably edible. The rule of thumb with snails seems to be that land snails able to lock themselves into their shells with the aid of an operculum, a horny plate attached to the foot, which fits tightly over the shell orifice when the snail withdraws into its shell, are edible. Once the snails have been chased into their shells, they can be properly starved and detoxified. (Snails without an operculum will dry out and die.) This rule does not apply to marine snails, which are much cleaner animals—a quick soak in a bucket of fresh water for snails collected on sand or mud suffices; rock snails can be eaten as they are.

But why pick on our pretty native land snails? The *petit-gris* (*Helix aspersa*), the snail you think you are getting when you buy canned "*escargot*," is slowly spreading as a gardener's pest north from California, where it was successfully introduced by misguided gourmets. It, too, is a yellowish-black snail, but the bands are broad and interrupted, and it does not supply its own garlic. Because it ravishes flowers and vegetables, most gardeners poison it with slug and snail bait. Eating these snails instead will reduce their populations much more effectively. (Just make sure not to gather them where poison has been put down.) The *petit-gris* is quite easy to prepare, once you've gotten the knack of it. The directions work well for large numbers of snails—it takes as much time to clean one as it takes to purify ten thousand. (Don't worry about an oversupply. A proper gourmet can easily eat a gross at one sitting—just for appetizers.) Pen the captured gastropods in an escape-proof, ventilated holding box. (Make sure the box is duck-proof, too. I once had a pet mallard who liked snails very much. I quickly learned that *Quack-Quack* could eat even more snails at one sitting than the most voracious gourmand.)

Once your snails have been starved and/or fattened for at least a week, you may remove them from their prison box and soak them in cold water for about ten minutes. Any snails still alive after the prolonged fast will emerge from their shells and try to crawl out of the water. These you eat—just pick them off as they reach the edge of the container—the dead ones you discard. Toss the live snails in coarse salt (a cup or a bucket, depending on how many snails you are cooking at one time) to draw out their sticky juices and kill them. After a last rinse, simmer the snails in a pot of boiling water which you can flavor with a variety of herbs and spices. Thyme, bay leaves (Oregon myrtle), salt, peppercorns, and wine— white, red, or vermouth—are commonly used. One gourmet who likes his snails "meaty" stews them in a beef or chicken broth. After they are cooked, the snails must be removed from their shells and gutted. They can then be served with a standard "snail butter" or in a variety of meat sauces. Or they can be dipped in a very garlicky mayonnaise. If you want to serve these snails in their shells, thoroughly rinse the shells and put the cleaned gastropods back inside. Serve with a butter or sauce topping. Take great care in preparing your snail sauces, because they'll be the only flavor you'll get.

A few people on the West Coast are now laboriously raising the *petit-gris* and its nobler cousin, the vineyard snail. But I wonder if this is really worth the effort. The Pacific Northwest has a large number of marine snails that look like *escargot,* but are much tastier. I suspect they are not more widely served in restaurants only because they lack the snob appeal of the *escargot.* Besides tasting better than land snails, our marine snails have the added advantage that they can be eaten the day they are collected—fresh from the rocks if need be—for they do not have to undergo the elaborate purification ritual of their terrestrial cousins.

The tastiest of these saltwater gastropods is the black turban (or top-shell) snail, which is quite common on the rocks of the outer coast. This mollusc grows to about the size of a walnut. It is delicious in all recipes that call for *escargot,* but it can also be eaten raw, on the full shell, if the intestines and gall are removed as the snail is pulled from the orifice. It can be dipped in garlic butter, lemon butter, *nuoc mam,* or Chinese hot sauces. Its close relative, the blue top-shell, is commonly found in deeper waters where it can be collected by divers.

From the margins of the littoral zones down into deeper waters, and within the reach of beachcombers during the lowest clam tides, live several other tasty sea snails. The red turban is quite startling in appearance: a large brownish snail carrying an inverted spinning top on its back. Another gastropod, the Oregon triton, has a shell so hairy it could be mistaken for a small mammal by a casual observer looking at the animal from a distance, but the spindle shape, whorls, and prominent ridges quickly identify it as a marine snail. The red turban feeds exclusively on films of algae; the triton is an aggressive predator, attacking even such well-protected creatures as sea urchins. We have several other snails in our waters that prey on a variety of other marine animals. Some drill holes through the shells of oysters and clams and feed on these tasty bivalves. The largest of these shellfish fanciers, the moon snail, inserts a long proboscis equipped with small rasping teeth into the pierced shells of its victims.

The moon snail can grow to the size of an apple and is a rapacious feeder for its size, often eating several clams a day. This hungry gastropod can multiply rapidly on large clam beds, where the bivalves are packed close together, and it can be quite destructive, often wiping out most of the clams in a particular locality. Fortunately, the moon snail itself is very good to eat. You can help both the cause of conservation and improve the variety of your dinners if you occasionally concentrate on the moon snail instead of clams.

Moon snails dig themselves into the ground, like marine moles, to attack clams in their burrows, but they can be easily spotted on sandy or gravelly beaches by the low, smooth humps they leave on the surface of tideflats. When you find a moon snail, quickly grab its body and pull it from its shell, cut off the large foot, the only part eaten, and discard the rest. This large slice of meat may be tenderized by breaking down the tough muscle fibers through lengthy pounding with a meat hammer. I prefer to place it between two pieces of muslin and beat it with my fish club, a foot-long mallet that is heavily weighted with lead at the tip. The moon snail "steak" should not be cooked for more than a minute on each side, over high heat, or it will really toughen. Some people claim that the meat will be tastier and more tender if it is refrigerated overnight, or even frozen for a short while; others recommend a commercial tenderizer (I have never been able to justify using chemicals to soften my meats, but if you feel a tenderizer is necessary, an infusion of dry wine and crushed papaya seeds is sometimes as effective as the best commercial tenderizers). The moon snail's foot can also be ground up in a food processor and used in stews or fried as meat patties. Moon snail has a very delicate flavor. When caught fresh and cooked right away, this snail can be sweet and savory and can match clams in flavor.

Several other gastropods which prey on bivalves and may cause a severe depletion of clam and oyster beds are also best controlled by biological means; that is, gathered at low tide and served, steaming hot, on shellfish lovers' dinner tables. The largest, and one of the tastiest, of these snails is the leafy hornmouth, a much-flanged mollusc which grows to a length of about three inches. The equally voracious oyster drills, purples, and dog whelks are smaller, reaching a size of only one to two inches at the most. Other Pacific Northwest marine snails, both predators and vegetarians, are quite tiny—wendletraps, littorines, margarites, olives, et al. Some reach less than half an inch in size. Just collect a bucketful, put them into fresh water for a couple of hours so they can clean themselves of sand or mud, and simmer them gently for twenty minutes in water (or oil). Peel off the operculum and pick the morsel from its shell with a toothpick. The intestines usually stay behind in the twisted part of the tiny shells. If they don't, brush them off on the orifice. These snails are good dipped in melted butter or other condiments, can be added to seafood stews, or can be ground—if you must. None of the predatory snails should be eaten when the beaches are closed due to an outbreak of red tide because they may acquire concentrations of *Gonyaulax* toxin from their filter-feeding prey.

Few marine snails are filter feeders. Most of these sessile gastropods are not very common, except for one introduced snail that does not look like a snail at all, but like a tiny French liberty cap—the common Atlantic slipper shell. These tasty one-and-a-half-inch snails are very strange animals. They settle on the shells of oysters, clams, and mussels, and on other slipper shells—one on top of the other, in piggyback fashion, up to a dozen snails high. These gastropods start out in life as males, but, as the animals grow older, settle down, and after other slipper shells attach themselves more or less permanently to their calcified backs, they change sex and become females. Of the slipper snails' bizarre group-sex life, only two things are of concern to the gourmet: these gastropods are very prolific, and the females—the ones on the bottom of the pile—are larger, fatter, and have a more interesting taste because of their larger gonads. Slipper shells can do some damage to oyster beds as they weigh down the oysters' shells with the sheer numbers of their spired colonies and they compete with the oysters for food.

In Europe, where the Atlantic slipper shell multiplied rapidly after its introduction, these gastropods have done considerable damage to oyster beds. In France, where they have become even more common, they are eaten as a delicacy. The latter seems to be the best way of controlling these tasty snails. They are excellent eating and can be served like bivalves. Their flesh is quite tender, because these snails' soft muscles are not used for gallivanting about the tidal rocks. The only wandering slipper shells will do after they settle down is via the free ride they receive if they have attached to the shell of a more active animal—though here they must limit their colonies' height or get knocked off. We also have several native, less common, species of slipper shells. Some of these affix themselves to rocks or dead shells (including those inhabited by hermit crabs). Others attach to living gastropods, such as top-shells, turbans, abalones, or even to the back of the predacious moon snail—well out of reach of this snail's wicked little rasping teeth.

Abalones are everyone's favorite marine snail, maybe because they don't look much like snails at all, especially after their feet have been sliced off, tenderized, cooked, and covered with a delicate sauce. The tasty abalones can be eaten year-round, because they browse on marine algae and do not filter nutrients from the sometimes toxic plankton of ocean waters. These slow-growing snails have become scarce in recent years because of overharvesting, and the few still commercially available are thus quite expensive (there is, unfortunately, a flourishing black market for undersize abalones which threatens to deplete the stocks even further). But even where these gastropods are still fairly common, catching your own is not easy. Abalones are very muscular and, unless a collector can dislodge them from their rocky perch with a crowbar before they take alarm, it may be impossible to pry them loose. (Don't ever get your fingers between an abalone and a rock!) Abalones are sometimes found in the lower littoral zone, but they prefer deeper waters where only divers can reach them. They are very hard to see under water, especially when their shells are camouflaged by an overgrowth of algae. Make sure to check local fishing regulations and license requirements before setting out on a hunt for this uncommon mollusc.

Abalones may have become scarce in Pacific Northwest waters, but their close relatives, limpets and keyhole limpets, are thriving along our shores. Limpets are much smaller than abalones, but just as tasty—just think of them as penny and two-bit abalones. A few, including the rough keyhole limpet, grow to the respectable size of two to two and a half inches. This is almost as large as a small abalone. Limpets share some of the abalones' traits, and they also have the power of clamping down tightly onto a rock when disturbed. Large limpets can be prepared like abalone. Small ones can be eaten raw, steamed, boiled, or added to seafood stews.

Squid are one of the most plentiful and underused of Pacific Northwest seafoods. Unless these molluscs gather to spawn, they are difficult to catch. Squid are the speedsters among invertebrates; they literally fly through the water, and some species can propel themselves through the air for short distances when pursued by voracious predators. More commonly, however, the squid do the pursuing. They are able to move so rapidly because their streamlined cylindrical bodies are equipped with the original jet drive: powerful muscles allow these cephalopods to suck water into their mantle cavities and squirt it out through a flexible siphon which works like a jet nozzle. By varying the size of the siphon orifice, the squid can increase its speed or slow down. By moving the nozzle and the direction of the squirt, the squid can change direction in midflight. The squid's stubby arms trail behind when the animal travels at full speed (its bulgy eyes can look forward and backward), but the two long tentacle arms, thin and flexible and equipped with powerful suction disks at their tips, stay poised, feeling the water, ready to snatch hapless fish and other prey in passing. Squid attack aggressively and hang on tightly once they have made contact with a food object. This is one reason they can be caught on jigging rigs that simulate prey.

Squid have been eaten by humans for thousands of years, but we know surprisingly little about them, except that they are good to eat. They hunt in packs, which means you'll either catch a lot of them in a short time or none at all. Squid live a pelagic life in offshore waters where they have space to roam, but they come inshore to spawn. Like most animals, they become careless during the breeding season and are easily caught. Pacific Northwest squid have changed their breeding habits during the last several years and have begun to spawn in larger numbers than ever before in our inland waters.

Squid live a life of only eighteen hectic months and both sexes die after spawning. Our common edible species, the Pacific long-finned squid, *Loligo opalescens,* grows to an average length of about ten to twelve inches (smaller squid, about four or five inches long, sold frozen, are commonly imported from California and New England), but larger or smaller squid are sometimes encountered in local waters. *Loligo* has short arms and a long body. Another northwest squid, *Gonatus fabricii,* grows to about the same size, but has longer arms and a shorter mantle. Its fins are also longer than those of the "long-finned" squid. *Gonatus* is just as edible as *Loligo.* The large offshore squid, which regularly reach a length of eight to nine feet (a twenty-four-foot squid has been documented, and encounters with even larger cephalopods are rumored), have too high a concentration of iodine in their bodies to be palatable.

Squid have a highly developed nervous system with large nerve fibers and three hearts to rapidly pump their blue blood, so you don't have to worry much about killing squid after you've caught them: they are so high-strung, they will die from either fright or rage by the time you're ready for them with your knife. (Squid are regularly for sale in our better fish markets.) Despite their odd appearance, squid are molluscs, and they are quite tasty when prepared properly. Their translucent bodies are very tender and should be cooked lightly, because they quickly toughen when overcooked. Some connoisseurs claim that squid freeze well and that their flesh has a better texture after it has been frozen, but I like the taste of fresh squid better. Squid at its best will have a delicate molluscan taste with a pleasant, underlying nuttiness.

Squid are very easy to clean: wash the animal in cold water to remove the natural lubricant which allows it to slide through the water so easily, hold the mantle down with one hand (the fins make a nice handle), and pull the head and tentacles away from the body. The intestines are attached to the head and should come away with it. Cut the tentacles off just below the eyes—remove the parrotlike beak—and discard the head, gills, and guts (save the ink sac if you want to use the ink in a sauce). Pull the "quill," the long, clear plasticlike pen (the last vestige of a molluscan shell the squid possesses) from its sheath and clean the mantle by thoroughly washing the insides (large squid can be turned inside out like a glove). Scrape or rub off the thin skin. The squid is now ready to be cooked. It can be boiled, sautéed, baked, fried, or smoked. The tentacles may be ground or chopped—short tentacle sections connected at the mouth will open up and radiate like flower petals when sautéed briefly in butter. The mantle can be stuffed and baked, or sliced into rings, or cut open and flattened and pounded into "steaks."

Squid has finally attracted the attention it deserves among our seafood processors, and Pacific Northwest diners may be in for some interesting new tastes at our region's restaurants. I hope that our chefs, experienced as they are in handling fresh seafoods, will do a better job with squid than the greasy-spoon cook managed to do at the Monterey fisherman's wharf restaurant where I ate my first squid. It was a horrible, pathetic experience. I had steeled myself to buy this exotic new food (it was "new" twenty years ago, even on the California coast) and I brashly ordered some squid (festooned with a spurious Italo-Graeco-Mexican name that I did my best to forget right afterward). I received a platter filled with large, golden-yellow (from the grease), oleaginous chewing gum—or perhaps thinly sliced sections of old rubber tires. It was an awful dish. But the *padrone* was intently watching me eat, and I had heard rumors of hidden trapdoors in restaurant floors (the tide was running out), and I tugged and tore and gnawed away, washing down the horrid little pieces I could detach with cheap red wine. Unfortunately this incident gave me a wrong impression of the culinary merits of this delightful cephalopod, and I avoided squid for at least a dozen years. It was only after I moved to the Pacific Northwest that I accidentally ordered some squid again at the Black Swan in La Conner, where Martin Hahn knows what to do with fresh seafood, and realized what I had missed. I have been an avid squid eater ever since.

My introduction to octopus was quite different. I met my first octopus in a tidepool. It was small, and it had backed into a dark corner, among some pale sea anemones. Its long, sinuous arms delicately probed the water. The six-inch kraken changed color when it saw me —whether for fear or rage I could not tell—rose on its undulant arms and, though I know perfectly well that octopi cannot make sounds, I imagined it hissing at me. The miniature sea monster hid beneath a cloud of ink when I touched the water. It looked more like a ragged piece of animated seaweed than a delectable mollusc. I had not yet learned to prepare octopus, and I made no attempt to capture it. I withdrew to let the animal relax and the water clear, and when I returned a short while later to observe its behavior, I watched it murder a small tidepool crab. This octopus was a very dainty eater. It picked the crab apart with grace and poise.

Octopi are very intelligent animals—perhaps the most intelligent sea creatures I ever had the pleasure to eat. Their nervous system is as highly developed as the squid's, but octopi do not waste their powers on speed-jetting and water-skiing. They sit back and think, and brood, and skulk. And, though they also have a built-in jet drive, they prefer to outthink their prey, to stalk it rather than outswim it, and to sneak up on it suddenly. Squid have many enemies, mostly large and fast fish, but few marine predators will grapple with an octopus. They are very strong for their size, quick to react to attacks (the entire animal consists primarily of brain and brawn) and, in a pinch, they can jet from danger, leaving an inky cloud behind to confound the aggressor.

Yet octopi are frequently entrapped in crab pots, and they can be readily caught in a simple, time-proven trap. A dark, deep container, be it an old milk can, clay jar, or wooden box, is attached to a rope and lowered into the water near a rocky shore frequented by octopi. Left overnight, it will attract an octopus looking for a better hiding place (octopi are always looking for better hiding places). Octopi can also be caught on squid jigs or with the aid of crab lures that have been studded with bait hooks, and they are easily taken by divers. Octopi, like squid, can die from sheer frustration and rage, but they will do so only after they have explored every conceivable route of escape. They have not a bone or even the vestige of a shell in their flexible bodies, and they can squeeze themselves through the tiniest of cracks. Their progress is limited only by the size of their parrotlike beaks. Octopi can survive out of the water for short periods of time (they have been known to tiptoe across beaches in pursuit of crabs), but their flavor is affected by excess stress. They should be killed quickly after capture by pinching a nerve between the eyes with pliers.

Our octopi grow to be quite large. The Puget Sound octopus (*Octopus dofleini*) may be the largest in the world. It regularly reaches an arm spread of more than ten feet and a weight of one hundred pounds (four-hundred-pound octopi have been found). Octopi this large do not taste as good and are not as tender as smaller ones that weigh out at a maximum of twenty to twenty-five pounds. Unless I can get octopus really fresh—preferably from a fisherman or from a Chinese fish market—I prefer to buy them already cooked.

Fresh octopus should be washed in cold water and then skinned (the rough outer membrane can be removed with a stiff brush or with coarse salt—wear gloves). The octopus is then cleaned in the same way as a squid (there is no quill to remove), but on large animals you may have to cut open the mantle to remove the head and intestines. The octopus is then boiled for about five to ten minutes (depending on size). Small octopi are cooked whole; the mantles and tentacles of larger animals can be cut into more manageable pieces first. Octopus tentacles can be sliced thin or cubed and served in seafood salads, or they can be pounded into "steaks" and fried or sautéed, or ground up in a food processor and added to chowders. Overcooking will toughen octopus and endow it with the consistency of prime shoe leather.

My second encounter with an octopus took place in a Chinese fish market. A large, fresh octopus was hanging down from a ceiling hook and a fishmonger, trying to satisfy a critical customer, held up its still-quivering tentacles in succession. When a desirable arm had been agreed upon, he reached for a cleaver, sliced off the tentacle, and chop, chop, chop, cut it into wok-sized pieces on his cutting board. None of this looked very appetizing. I did not need to work up my courage to buy an octopus, however, for this cephalopod quite frequently made its surreptitious appearance in dishes served to us by friends, mainly in the form of appetizers. Its flavor is most commonly described—like most white, firm seafood meats—as tasting like "shrimp," but this catch-all description does not do justice to the octopus's unique taste. I find it sweeter (though tougher) than shrimp, more complex, and with a pleasant, underlying marine flavor.

Chitons are segmented marine molluscs whose flesh has a taste similar to that of octopus, but it can be quite tough. The largest of our chitons, aptly named "gum shoe" (*Cryptochiton* or *Amicula stelleri*), is the largest chiton in the world, growing to a length of eight to ten inches. The more common, and tastier, Black Katy chiton (*Katharina tunicata*), only grows to a size of about three inches. Chitons graze on algae-covered rocks in limpet fashion. There is no reason to describe the various species in detail—as long as you know what the basic chiton looks like—because all are edible and taste more or less alike. They should be cleaned immediately and cooked as quickly as possible, within two hours after capture, because their meat spoils rapidly and takes on a strong fish-pond odor. For this reason it is best to cook chitons on the beach right after they are gathered. Only the foot is eaten (some Indian tribes also cherish the strong-flavored gonads) and it is easily sliced off. The thin slice of meat needs to be tenderized by thorough beating before it can be eaten. This is good exercise for kitchen-softened gourmets: place the chiton "steak" between two pieces of clean muslin and beat it as hard as you can for as long as you can; then, when your arm is about to fall off, pound it some more, take a rest, and hit it with renewed vigor. Try switching sides to give the muscles in both arms a good workout. The longer you beat the chiton, the more tender it will be, but even so, it may still remind you of well-worn rubber. Fry the steak <u>very</u> quickly, for overcooking will toughen it beyond repair. Very few people eat chiton, despite its excellent taste—they just can't handle the exercise.

I like to eat sea urchins, a non-molluscan "shellfish," but not many people do. They just don't know what they are missing. I am always surprised by the squeamishness shown by otherwise adventuresome gourmets when they are suddenly confronted with this exquisite shellfish. Perhaps this has nothing to do with the taste of urchins, but with their formidable appearance: they look unapproachable, with their many mobile spines reaching out from their hard tests, warning predators to stay away. But, as sea otters have known for a long time, sea urchins are exceptionally good to eat. Most of our cookery book compilers have ignored this prickly creature in their discussion of American cuisine, conveying the impression that sea urchins are not a part of our national cookery.

That may be true for other parts of the country, but in the Pacific Northwest sea urchins have been eaten with gusto for centuries. The native tribes have always considered them delicacies and readily distinguish between the different tastes of sea urchins from different species and habitats. The gonads of these echinoderms are the favored morsels (but then there isn't much else in a sea urchin shell) along with the roe. Depending on the time of year, these gonads are surrounded by a milky fluid. The men of the Kelsomat tribe (near Tofino, B.C.) avidly search them out at this stage—though they have a stronger, less delicate taste—because they believe that milky gonads will enhance a man's virility. Gourmets prefer to eat the gonads when they are clear and orange-colored because the taste is better. They should always be eaten raw; six urchins per person at one sitting.

Sea urchins were also popular with French Canadian fur trappers in the past, and today they are regularly eaten by Americans and Canadians of Mediterranean and Japanese descent. But the demand for sea urchins is increasing among WASPs and other ethnic groups, at least in the Puget Sound region. The fishmongers of Seattle's Pike Place Market regularly sell sea urchins, but most connoisseurs prefer to gather their own from docks and rocky shores.

Sea urchins are plentiful in our region. They can be collected in both the inland waters and on the outer coast. The green sea urchin (considered the tastiest of the group by many connoisseurs) is often found on floats, but it generally lives in the lower tidal reaches of rocky shores in company with the red sea urchin. The latter is our largest urchin, reaching a diameter of more than five inches. A third species, the purple sea urchin, prefers the surf-swept rocks of the outer coast and those parts of the Strait of Juan de Fuca which are exposed to oxygen and nutrient-rich wave splash. This fragile echinoderm often anchors itself in exposed rocks by digging hollows into soft strata. It is best extracted with a stick, for the spines make for a painful handhold. Sea urchins feed on detritus and on marine vegetation, and I have found that the ones gathered by divers in deep water have a better taste than the ones which I have collected in littoral seaweed gardens. Sea urchins are not affected by red tides and can be eaten throughout the year. They are at their best from August through April.

Sea urchins should be eaten as fresh as possible, though they can survive (after a fashion) for about two days after they have been removed from the water (when the weather is cool). They are very easy to clean and prepare. I usually pick up an urchin with my left (gloved) hand, turn it upside down (the mouth opening is on the concave side), and cut off the bottom of the shell with a sharp pair of scissors. The urchin's simple gut is attached to the mouthpiece (an elaborate structure known as an "Aristotle's lantern") and comes off with the cut-away section of the test. The gonads and the roe stay behind, clinging to the walls of the shell. They are now ready to eat in several different ways. I like to dip a chunk of bread into the shell, or shake out the gonads, rinse them in salt water—for a milder flavor—and spread them on buttered toast. Sometimes, when I'm in a hurry, I just crack the sea urchin like an egg and shake out the gonads.

Sea urchin roe can be eaten as is, or it can be pressed through a sieve to remove the membranes holding the eggs together. The roe is also good spread on toast, can be pureed and used as a tasty filling for tarts, or can be eaten chilled like caviar. I like it spread on sushi. Sinclair Philip, of the Sooke Harbour House on Vancouver Island, commonly takes the roe and gonads from several sea urchins, fills an empty urchin shell to the top, and serves it as a dip or side dish. He catches his sea urchins by diving for them in the small bay below his inn and often serves these echinoderms so fresh that the spines still move in a slow, probing rhythm. Fresh sea urchin roe has a subtle, nutlike flavor.

Sea urchins may also be lightly cooked whole, like soft-boiled eggs—thus their alternate name, sea eggs—and they are delicious when eaten on toast or combined with chicken eggs in omelets and in scrambled duck eggs. When cooked, their flavor becomes very delicate, somewhat like fresh crayfish, but with a pronounced salty tang.

Sea cucumbers are another misunderstood seafood of the Pacific Northwest, though more gourmets I know have eaten them than have tasted sea urchins. A casual observer, unfamiliar with these saclike creatures, would hardly suspect that they are closely related to starfish, sand dollars, and to the delectable sea urchin. The relationship shows in the radial symmetry of the cucumber and in the five tasty muscles which run the length of the animal's body (things come in fives for echinoderms). The sea cucumber is even easier to clean than a sea urchin. When properly agitated, the animal will eviscerate itself. This is thought to detract predators (the evacuated parts are eventually regenerated), but this does not work in the case of human gourmets. It merely eases the job of cleaning the cucumber. Once the sea cucumber has eviscerated itself, the rest is easy. Slice the body open lengthwise. Five long, whitish muscles run along the inside of the body cavity. Remove these by running a sharp knife between the body wall and the strips. After a quick rinse in cold water, they can be fried or used in chowders or in stir-fried dishes. The native Indians and the Chinese boil and dry the body walls and use them in a variety of preparations (they are commonly sold in Chinese stores as *bêche de mer* or *trepang*), but I prefer to stick to the muscles alone. They taste like mild, white seafood, the flavor commonly described as "clam," "shrimp," or "lobster," but their meat has a more interesting, somewhat gelatinous texture.

Our sea cucumbers range in size from as little as four inches to as much as eighteen inches or more, depending on the species. All are edible. I have found sea cucumbers, especially the bright orange *Cucumaria miniata,* in shaded rock crevices during minus tides, but they are more easily gathered by divers in deeper water. They should, of course, be cleaned right after capture and eaten as quickly as possible to preserve the flavor.

Gourmets who enjoy eating sea cucumbers must gather their own, for our holothurians are not commonly sold in seafood markets. They are gathered commercially in the inland waters of the Pacific Northwest, but almost the entire population is exported to Japan. Sea cucumbers are sometimes—but very spottily—available in Chinese markets in Vancouver, B.C., and some of our restaurants specializing in northwest cuisine serve them occasionally. Like sea urchins, they are unaffected by red tides and can be safely eaten all year.

One more edible marine creature must be mentioned here, because it is edible and, supposedly, tastes good. I have not yet mustered the courage to taste it and thus cannot vouch for its flavor: the sea anemone. The native Indians of the west coast of Vancouver Island have regularly eaten sea anemones, preferring the brownish ones to the whitish ones, which are said not to taste as good, but making little reference to the probable toxicity of some species or to the painful stings inflicted by their tentacles. (I will check with a knowledgeable marine biologist first, if I ever decide to eat an anemone.) The West Coast people collect anemones growing on rocks, because a sandy bottom makes them gritty and hard to clean. They were formerly steamed in pit ovens, but today they are baked in bread pans in a regular kitchen oven.

Some day, I know, I will have to eat a sea anemone, but every time I see the beautiful animals at high tide, their luminous tentacles spread out in floral arrays, I don't have the heart to vandalize this beauty by pulling it off the rocks. And, quite frankly, every time I try to collect them at low tide, when the anemones are collapsed into their slimy selves or hang down from the dank rocks like limp, wet rags, I haven't had the appetite.

Fresh Squid with Bean Sprouts

Some people don't like to eat squid, just because they look a bit strange. Well, they don't know what they're missing! Here's a simple recipe that works well as an appetizer. Try serving it with a well-chilled, crisp sauvignon blanc.

Squid 1½ pounds
Fresh ginger 1 teaspoon minced
Bean sprouts 3 cups
Light soy sauce 1 tablespoon
Salt ¼ teaspoon
Sugar ¼ teaspoon
White pepper dash
Cornstarch 1½ teaspoons
Vegetable oil 3 tablespoons
Fresh ginger 3 slices
Garlic 1 teaspoon minced
Dry sherry 1 tablespoon

1. Clean squid (see Index). Cut head and tentacles into narrow strips, bodies into 1 by 2-inch pieces.
2. Mix squid with 1 teaspoon minced ginger and set aside.
3. Wash bean sprouts in cold water, drain, and set aside.
4. In small mixing bowl combine soy sauce, salt, sugar, white pepper, and cornstarch. Set aside.
5. Set frying pan over high heat. When hot, add 1 tablespoon oil, ginger slices, and bean sprouts. Stir-fry for 1 minute, and transfer to a plate.
6. Clean frying pan. Return to high heat. When very hot, add remaining oil, garlic, and squid. Stir, and add sherry. Stir constantly for about 1 minute. Add soy sauce mixture; when thick, add bean sprouts. (Do not overcook, or squid will be tough.)
7. Transfer entire contents of pan to a plate and serve.

Serves 4

Barbecued Limpets

This recipe was invented one August afternoon when Don McManman and a press party from the Bellingham Herald *went to Chuckanut Island just before a staff barbecue. They returned with a bucketful of limpets (kept alive in wet eelgrass). These limpets turned out to be very delicious, and even finicky eaters ate their share. These are excellent with dry white wine—even better when accompanied by Redhook Ale or Porter.*

Assorted limpets   24 to 36
Fresh lemon juice   to taste

1. Wash limpets in seawater and place upside down on barbecue grill (about 4 to 6 inches above a bed of white coals).
2. Cook limpets until they curl away from side of shell.
3. Sprinkle limpets with lemon juice and serve in shell.

Serves 4 to 6

Limpet Fritters

Limpets are exceedingly common on our rocky shores, but they are among our most misunderstood shellfish. André Simon, the renowned midcentury food writer, described them quite succinctly in his Encyclopedia of Gastronomy: *"Unattractive rockfish of real gastronomic merit; in many dishes in which cooked oysters appear they could easily and advantageously be replaced by limpets." So, here's an old oyster recipe I have adapted to limpets.*

Large limpets   24 or more
Coarse salt   as needed
Salt and freshly ground pepper   to taste
Eggs   2, preferably duck
All-purpose flour   ⅔ cup (approximately)
Milk   1 cup
Vegetable oil   for deep frying as needed
Lemon wedges   garnish

1. Wash limpets and place upside down on a bed of coarse salt in a flat oven-proof dish.
2. Broil until limpets curl and pull away from side of shell. Remove from oven; season with salt and pepper.
3. Break eggs in a bowl, mix in flour, then gradually add milk. If batter is too thin to coat a spoon, add a little more flour.
4. Dip limpets in batter and fry in deep, boiling oil at 375° until brown and crisp.
5. Remove with slotted spoon and serve immediately with lemon wedges.

Serves 4 to 6

Chiton Soup

Serve with Indian fried bread and dry white wine.

Live, unshelled chitons (all species are edible)   2 quarts (the number of chitons will vary
    with size and species)
Water   1 cup
Unsalted butter   2 tablespoons
Onion   1, finely chopped
Medium potato   1, diced
Carrot   1, diced
Garlic clove   1, diced
Green pepper   ¼ cup chopped
Celery or lovage   ¼ cup chopped
Salt and freshly ground pepper   to taste
Dry white wine   ½ cup
Salmon caviar or chiton roe   1 tablespoon (or more)
Parsley   1 tablespoon chopped

1. Drop chitons into kettle with water. Steam for 10 minutes after water begins to boil.
   Strain broth and set aside. Remove chiton meat (the "foot"); discard viscera and shell.
   Roughly chop large chitons. Pound to tenderize.
2. Melt butter in heavy skillet. Add chiton meat and vegetables. Sauté, covered, over low
   heat until onion is transparent. Add enough water to broth to make 1 quart. Add to
   chiton/vegetable mixture. Season with salt and pepper to taste.
3. Simmer gently for 30 minutes, add wine, and simmer until potatoes are soft. Pour into
   serving bowls. Garnish with caviar and parsley.

Serves 4 to 6

Periwinkle Appetizers

Accompany with a good, chilled lager beer or a semillon blanc.

Freshly gathered periwinkles or other small marine snails   48 (or more)
Water   1 gallon
Salt   1 tablespoon
Unsalted butter   ½ cup, melted

1. Scrub periwinkles with an old toothbrush to remove any foreign matter.
2. Discard any snails not tightly closed, with the operculum—the snail's horny "door"
   plate—in place.
3. Bring water to a boil.
4. Drop snails into rapidly boiling water and remove as soon as operculum falls open (about

20 minutes).
5. Serve snails in small bowls; pick out meat with a toothpick and dip in melted butter (do not eat the operculum).

Variation: Instead of plain melted butter, use a parsley butter with a chopped clove of garlic added.

Serves 6 to 8

Fried Sea Cucumbers

Serve as an appetizer with dry white wine.

Sea cucumbers   12, cleaned
Unsalted butter   4 tablespoons (or more, as needed)
Bread crumbs   1 cup
Salt and pepper   to taste

1. Rinse muscles well.
2. Quickly blanch meat in boiling salted water for 5 seconds to remove the slime and firm the meat. Do not cook it.
3. Remove meat and roll in bread crumbs seasoned with salt and pepper.
4. Fry quickly in hot butter. The cooking should be fast and to a golden-brown color. (Slow frying or overcooking makes sea cucumber tough and gummy.) Serve.

Note: Sea cucumbers are easiest to clean right after they have been removed from the water because their muscles are firmer. They have not had a chance to relax and stretch out into a thin strip. To clean, cut off both ends, split animal from end to end, and shake out internal organs (unless the sea cucumber has done that part of your work for you by eviscerating itself). You will see the edible muscle as a thin layer of strips (5) on the inside. Cut these loose at one end and strip out carefully. Too sharp a knife will cut the muscle instead of stripping it loose. When removed, the muscles will be white to salmon color and will roll up to a finger-sized piece of meat. Wear gloves when cleaning sea cucumbers or they may turn your hands reddish-brown. This color will not wash off, but will fade away in several days.

Serves 6 to 12

Meats

For the last several years, I have visited most of the county fairs in the Pacific Northwest to take good stock of the best beef on the hoof our region can produce. The show animals are an impressive sight: magnificently bulky, fat steers, their powerful muscles rippling under sleek, well-groomed coats of shining hair, contentedly chew their cud as they wait to be auctioned off. But looks, though they are important for both beasts and men, can be deceptive. The taste of meat depends as much (or more) on the feed as on the breed. And it is hard to tell how an animal was raised and what it was fed until you cut it up and eat a piece of its meat. That is pretty difficult to do when the animal is still alive—judging meat on the hoof is notoriously inaccurate, and even experienced professional buyers have only about a 50 percent accuracy rate in predicting a steer's dressing-out quality and tenderness (sheep and hogs are a bit easier to judge, but not much).

As I tasted my way across the Northwest, I found that the prejudices I had developed over the past years were constantly reinforced by the quality of the beef I sampled. I have eaten lots of meat in my career, mainly pork, but ample quantities of lamb, and a great variety of beef, from Burgundian Charolais to the best grain-fed steers the Midwest can produce, from California Brangus to Dutch dairy cows. Without doubt, northwest lamb and the grain-fed beef from Idaho, eastern Oregon, and the dry ranges and feedlots of eastern Washington are among the best I have eaten. I can still remember, for instance, how much I enjoyed the superb, meltingly tender charbroiled sirloin tips I ate in a small Yakima Valley restaurant, the Selah Mining Company, last summer; or the prime roast of Idaho's best—an exquisite chunk of pure round—selected for me by Warren Dimmick of Burlington for a special dinner.

But what about western Washington beef? I not only had doubts about its quality, but I had also had some unfortunate experiences with its rank taste. Most of the beef produced west of the Cascades (as is true for all of our dairy regions) comes from surplus Holstein steers—the ones that are not turned into milk-fed veal—barren heifers and milked-out dairy cows. I have been familiar with the watery, flavorless, stringy meat of these animals for a long time, for I grew up next door to a butcher's shop which specialized in processing dried-up dairy cows for the table. I should have gotten used to the taste of this meat from habit alone, but I developed a permanent dislike for its peculiar flavor instead. I must admit that I have been disappointed as well by the quality of the beef steers raised on the wet grasses of the west side. So, to learn more about the local beef and to see what kind of creatures enter the market besides the sleek county fair animals I admired so much, I headed for one of our region's prime stockyards, the renowned Marysville Livestock Auction, to talk to the professionals.

The Marysville Livestock Auction attracts sellers and buyers from all over western Washington, and the auction itself is dramatic:

Bare lightbulbs throw a stark, glaring light onto the damp sawdust of the stage. Wooden benches rise in tiers almost to the high roof of the hall. The two front rows have upholstered theater seats. Prettily engraved wooden nameplates hang from the back railing, which separates these reserved places from the rows of public benches above. This is where the regular buyers sit, the professionals. The chairs are filled mostly with big men dressed in dusty western clothes: jeans, embroidered shirts, designer broadbrims, and high-heeled riding boots. In the back benches are a few families with small children, several groups of Southeast Asian immigrants, and a couple of men in prim business suits. They have come here with the hope of buying fresh meat at wholesale prices.

The stage set is simple and utilitarian. A tall rostrum occupied by two officials covers most of the backdrop. One of these men sits next to a microphone, waiting; the other one writes. A large electronic scoreboard hangs behind his desk and a thin wire moving on pulleys runs from his side across the stage pit and auditorium to a slit in the back wall. Two large gates to either side of the rostrum complete the scene.

A lanky, sawdust-covered cowboy, armed with a blunt stick, enters the proscenium. Crash! The stage gate to the right of the rostrum flies open and a large whiteface steer trots across the sawdust. The man at the microphone comes to life in a high nasal whine: "Forty-fourennahalffortyfiveennahalfennfortyfiveennahaveforyfivendthreequattafortaseven-who'llgimmefortaight?Fortynineennfortaninennahaff?Ennafortyninennthreequarter? Commongimmefotteeninennthreequarter!—forty-nine-and-three-quarter?—forty-nine-and-a-half?—forty-nine-and-a-half!Sold!" The cowboy goads the steer with the blunt stick. Crash! The beef exits through the door to the left of the rostrum.

You've got to talk fast if you want to sell all of the slaughter cattle brought to the Marysville Livestock Auction every Tuesday and get done at a reasonable time. The professional buyers who have been bantering and laughing in shoulder-slapping style have become quiet, their eyes glued to the pit. They have only some twenty to twenty-five seconds to judge each animal's high points. They quickly look at eyes, nostrils, stomach, feet, check the brisket for signs of unnatural breathing, scan the skin for lumps, spots, swellings, or roughed hair, and estimate the weight before they signal the auctioneer. You've got to be fast, for the steers keep coming and you might miss a good buy. And you have to know what you want and why: steers for steaks, bulls for bologna, and old dairy cows for hamburger meat. There is even a market for day-old calves (Washington is only one of seven states that permits the butchering of calves).

The Marysville Auction is popular with professional buyers, because here many of the pampered pets of the livestock trade are sold, steers that were raised by farm families on the side to bring in a little extra cash. They have been fed only the best grass, hay, and grain and they are as sleek and fat as they can be, their well-developed muscles bulging under smooth shiny skins. They come from a variety of breeds: Aberdeen Angus, white-faced Herefords,

Maine/Anjou, Limousin, Charolais, Simmental, Shorthorn Durhams, and now and then a shaggy Scottish Highland steer. Most of the parade of steak on the hoof are hybrid cattle, crossbred to combine the most desirable qualities of different breeds.

All of these are eagerly sought by cattle buyers, but occasionally a family, intent on a year's supply of beef, outbids the professionals on a particularly fat steer. The buyers wish them good luck. It is hard to tell how the meat really looks under the skin—at least until the steer is slaughtered. Even the most experienced cattlemen have an accuracy rate of only 50 percent in their predictions. A professional buyer can always bury his mistakes in hamburger or salami, but a family can only rid itself of a tough steer by eating it. It is always better to listen to the advice of a professional.

I am sitting next to Norman Dalrymple, who helped start the Marysville Auction back in 1961 after the old Seattle stockyards were closed down by progress and industrial development. He has been telling me about how to judge beef cattle: I am quite surprised by the high quality of the steers passing through the arena—they look like the spitting images of those perfect county fair animals.

Now the dairy culls are arriving: Holsteins, Guernseys, and Jerseys who don't pay for their feed in milk anymore. (These dairy cows are destined for the soup pot, the sausage machine, and the hamburger grinder. A buyer has just told me how supermarket hamburger is made: you take a cut-up dairy cow, mix it with the surplus fat from a grain-fed steer, and grind it up.) Some of the Holstein steers and dry heifers look pretty good, however, and sometimes one of the amateur buyers puts in a bid; but only the professional hamburger scouts buy the old cows.

But why, you ask, does prime beef have all that excess fat to spare?

There are three main reasons: tenderness, taste, and aging. In the most commonly raised breeds of beef cattle, it is the fat, whether it drips down onto your barbecue coals or penetrates your roast, that flavors what might otherwise be a bland chunk of muscle. That's why Europeans like organ meats so much: they cannot afford to fatten their cattle properly (and breeds which do not need fat for flavor are rare or expensive to raise), and the kidneys, for example, added to a steak and kidney pie are the ingredient that give the dish some taste.

Meat from Angus, Hereford, and Shorthorn cattle, the primary beef breeds of the Northwest, also needs to be marbled with fat to be tender. But, as the desirable fat builds up in the animal's muscle tissues, extra fat forms a thick layer of tallow beneath the animal's hide. This latter thick layer is of paramount importance when the meat is aged, as all good beef should be.

There is, perhaps, more misunderstanding about the processes involved in the proper aging of beef than about any other aspect of meat production. And some of this misinformation is spread by butchers who do not want to be bothered with the labor and cost of properly aging the beef they sell. A hunk of beef can lose a lot of moisture through evaporation as it ages (as much as 12 to 15 percent of its weight). This means that the butcher has to charge a higher price per pound to make up for the lost weight, and that may make him uncompetitive in a tight market. So, it's much easier to tell your customers that aged meat isn't all it's made out to be. (This also saves him storage costs.)

Apart from the cost of storage and the loss in volume, there is nothing difficult about aging beef in the cool climate of the Pacific Northwest—if it is done properly (and not with the aid of chemical additives). It calls for a large cellar or cooler in which a carcass or a side of beef may be hung for at least two, but preferably several more weeks at a temperature of between thirty-four and thirty-eight degrees Fahrenheit. Only the top grades of beef, prime and choice, can be aged effectively, because the carcass must be encased by a heavy layer of fat to protect it from spoilage by harmful aerobic bacteria during the aging process.

The aging of beef is an anaerobic process, a form of mild fermentation in which the lactic acid present in the meat right after slaughtering is broken down by soluble ferments in the carcass, which also soften the tough muscle fibers through autolysis (a form of spontaneous decomposition), a process not to be confused with putrefaction by aerobic bacteria. The latter can happen when meat is enclosed in plastic wrap and stored for lengthy periods of time in the sales cooler of a supermarket where it slowly turns dark and putrid because it lacks a protective layer of fat (a change in meat color indicates oxidation—properly aged meat will be red).

I know of several pseudogourmets who search out heavily oxidized meat, commonly sold by the markets at bargain prices, because they erroneously believe its color indicates proper aging. I am afraid, however, that all they are buying is putrefaction. There is quite a bit of difference between the superb taste of a well-aged steak and the decayed flavor of a flaccid slice of beef that has been on a sales counter for too long. But, *chacun à son goût.*

The aging of beef—even the eating of beef on a regular basis—is a luxury among many people, and as little as a hundred and fifty years ago not only were proper cooling facilities a rarity in the Northwest, but beef for eating was hard to come by as well. The only beef cattle native to the Northwest, the bison, became extinct in its westernmost ranges, the grasslands of eastern Washington and Oregon, before the arrival of the first white explorers. The few herds remaining west of the Rocky Mountains were restricted to the upper Snake River plateau by the time the first of the brigade trappers arrived in our region during the early nineteenth century.

The interior plateau tribes of the Northwest, the Nez Perce, the Cayuse, Umatilla, et al., who were among the first Native Americans to tame the horse, had begun annual treks to the buffalo country (some traveling as far as eastern Montana) when the bison became scarce west of the mountains.

Early in the 1800s, missionaries, fur traders, and immigrant farmers introduced several native tribes, in particular the Nez Perce, Cayuse, Yakima, and Kittitas, to animal husbandry, and by 1850 the Indians owned large herds of cattle. Some of these native herdsmen traveled regularly to the Willamette Valley to exchange horses for blooded cows; a few rode all the way to Sutter's Fort in California to buy cattle.

But the dream of an Indian cattle empire was short-lived. Driven from their native rangelands by a series of fierce wars with encroaching white settlers and cattlemen, the Indians lost most of their stock and had to abandon their dream of becoming successful ranchers in a world increasingly dominated by whites. From British Columbia south to Oregon, many native cattlemen were forced to become mere cowboys instead.

The arrival of the railroads in the Pacific Northwest revolutionized the cattle business (as it had done earlier elsewhere in the country). Ever since beef cattle were first introduced into the Pacific Northwest, conscientious breeders have tried their best to improve the quality of their herds. This has not always been true for other areas of the western cattle country. The European breeds of beef cattle which provide the most tender and tasty meat have adapted well to the climate of the Pacific Northwest, on both sides of the Cascades, but they failed to adapt to the humid weather and annoying mosquitoes plaguing the southern and midwestern rangelands (they often dropped dead from overheating in the exhausting summer heat of the dry Southwest). Only the toughest could survive. Thus the steers of the legendary cattle drives from the Texan ranges to the rail terminals in Kansas were wiry, gaunt, tough-meated Spanish longhorns, closely related to the equally stringy California mission cattle.

It is one of the great ironies of American culinary history that the gourmets of New York City were paying high prices for tough, stringy steaks from Texas longhorns at a time when the everyday meats sold in the butcher shops of the Pacific Northwest were tender, flavorful cuts from some of the world's best beef breeds, raised on some of the continent's best pastures. It was only after the ranchers of the Southwest thought of crossing the European beef breeds with hardy Zebu cattle from India ("Brahma" bulls) that they were able to produce beef that fattened well in the torrid ranges. These new, exotic crossbreeds such as Brangus (Brahma crossed with Angus) or Santa Gertrudis (Brahma crossed with Durham) were more resistant to the heat and bugs but, while their meat could be tender, it still did not have the exquisite taste of the improved British breeds raised on the cattle pastures of the Pacific Northwest.

Cattlemen in the Pacific Northwest have ever been more fortunate than their southwestern brethren. The Northwest's amenable climate and the quality of the available feed was particularly well suited to the requirements of the meaty English Durham and Hereford breeds and to the heavy Scottish Aberdeen Angus. The lanky crosses between Durhams and Herefords were once popular as range cattle when the steers had to walk for long distances between ranges, be it from summer pastures in the high mountains to winter meadows in the bottomlands bordering the region's rivers and lakes, or merely from their fattening grounds to the railheads or markets. As the railroads began to penetrate even the remotest rangelands, however, the chunkier crosses between Aberdeen Angus and Hereford (or even pure Whitefaces or Black Angus) gained favor because they grew fat more quickly.

But the open ranges of the Pacific Northwest were overgrazed within the space of only a few decades, and the free-roaming style of cattle herding gave way to the raising of cattle in fenced pastures and feedlots. Even though the interior grasslands of the Northwest have shrunk to where they can support only a fraction of the cattle raised in the region, there are still a few areas where steers can roam freely and graze primarily on the flavorful native vegetation.

Patches of native grasslands survive throughout the region, but only in British Columbia do extensive ranges of bunchgrass survive. Today these nutritious grasses are holding their own in the Nicola Valley, on the Kamloops plateaus, in the Cariboo, and in the Chilcotin. Here large numbers of grass-fed beef may still be raised. Without question, the Pacific Northwest's best beef still comes from these natural pastures, from Durham Shorthorn cattle which grow obscenely fat on protein-rich inland grasses alone, or from some of the newly introduced continental European breeds such as Simmental, Charolais, or Tarentais, or from Aberdeen Angus and Hereford which do, however, need to be finished on grain.

One recent development has profoundly affected cattle husbandry. A change in consumer preference has forced breeders to develop new crossbreeds which have less fat in their meat (but which must still be tender) because of nutritionists' concern about the high cholesterol content of beef fat.

Well, we all know that the meat from the traditional breeds which have thrived in the Northwest for more than a century needs the marbling of fat for flavor and tenderness. Without marbling, this meat might just be plain and insipid, for most of its taste comes from its seared fat. Cattlemen have tried to solve this vexatious problem by introducing several continental European breeds of beef cattle (Charolais, Limousin, Maine-Anjou, Simmental, Tarentais, Chianina, et al.) whose meat has all of the desired qualities of taste and tenderness without a heavily fatty marbling (though the Charolais, which is a cross between the French Manceau and the English Durham Shorthorn, has some light marbling). But here new problems have arisen.

Steers pastured in the dry interior uplands of the Northwest must possess a foraging instinct to survive: that is, they must willingly wander over the ranges to look for feed. The continental European breeds, whose ancestors never had space to roam but were confined in small, fenced or hedged pastures, never developed this vital foraging instinct. Northwest ranchers quickly learned that their new prize cattle refused to stray more than a mile or so from a water source and would starve to death rather than forage.

This is a bit unfortunate for northwest gourmets, for it has restricted the spread of these breeds in the prime rangelands and limits their crossbreeding with the more traditional varieties of cattle. It also makes our most exquisite beef quite scarce: the tender, flavorful meat from Charolais steers raised in the cool mountain regions of the northern interior of the Pacific Northwest, where needle- and wheatgrasses, bromes, fescues, and inland bluegrasses provide a rich feed, high in vitamins, minerals, and concentrated proteins.

Today, after a century of changes in the cattle industry, one pattern persists. Calves are still raised west of the Cascades—in the lush spring meadows of the coastal valleys and plains—and shipped east of the mountains to fatten up and grow into steers. However, they are no longer put out to pasture, but rather are placed in feedlots where they feed on the grains produced in the vast Transcascadian corn, wheat, and barley fields.

Sometimes the beef cattle are interbred with Holstein dairy cows to get fast-growing, but not necessarily tasty, steers, and they may be fed on a wide variety of fodder, ranging from good hay and grain to potatoes, cannery wastes, or even wood fiber (topped with processed blood from slaughtered cattle).

The best of this feedlot beef comes from the Snake River Plateau of Idaho and from eastern Washington's Kittitas Valley, where the cattle are not generally interbred with Holsteins and where the feedlot steers are fattened on dry hay and finished on a protein-rich grain mixture of wheat, corn, and barley, producing meat of superior flavor and texture. Some excellent feedlot beef also comes from the Yakima Valley (the tastiest beef I have ever eaten was raised here), but the meat buyer really has to know his supplier well, for even experienced butchers ordering sides of beef from Yakima have had some unfortunate surprises from one shipment to the next.

The quality of the feed can affect the taste of beef almost as much as the quality of the breed. West-side grass (excluding that from a few dry areas in Oregon's Rogue and Willamette valleys), alfalfa, and pea hay with their high moisture content are excellent for inducing a high milk production in dairy cows; but, in contrast to the dryland grasses of the interior pastures, they make beef taste watery and bland. A heavy feeding of potatoes makes the meat of cattle soft but, if fed with a good grain supplement, may still produce good beef. Excess amounts of corn (maize) makes the meat greasy, and too high a percentage of wheat in the fodder can make the meat "doughy." Barley seems to be the best overall grain for finishing cattle; it has none of the drawbacks of the other cereals, and it makes the meat firm yet tender, causing it to shrink very little during cooking. (There are, incidentally, no legal standards for the terms "grain-fed" or "grain-finished." It depends on the integrity of the feeder and may range from a handful to several pounds a day. Nor are there any standards for the feeding period. Beef that has been fed a handful of grain for a period of only a couple of days may still be legally called "grain-finished.")

Much of the beef cattle in the Pacific Northwest today is raised on feed mixtures put together by computers, which work out the total digestible nutrients, proteins, vitamins, minerals, and roughage needed to fatten the animals quickly. So far, however, no computer has succeeded in blending the motley of available feeds into a fodder which can give feedlot cattle the superb taste of beef raised on a combination of dryland grasses and grain.

Age is also a consideration in the quality of beef. Today's steers are commonly slaughtered at an age of about two years. Grass-fed beef achieves its best taste at an age of about five years (this is mentioned as a sign of superior quality in Homer's *Odyssey*), since the amount of water in the flesh decreases and that of fat increases as the animals mature. At the age of five, a perfect harmony between natural fat, flavor, and tenderness is achieved. But it has simply become uneconomical for ranchers to hold over cattle for that long. Instead the steers are fattened up quickly on grain and patent feeds. Thus the grain fed to these steers is a means of overcoming the lack of age through an artificial acceleration of the fattening process.

Some gourmets like their meat very young, in the form of veal. Much milk-fed veal is raised in Washington State today in conjunction with dairy operations. The tiny meat calves are raised (strictly confined) on scientifically determined baby formulas (provimi—i.e., protein, vitamins, minerals) and slaughtered as soon as they reach a weight of about two hundred pounds. Grass, hay, or grain are never fed to these calves, because this would add iron to their diet and turn their meat red—a bane to lovers of milk-fed veal, who prefer their meat white and watery.

I have eaten lots of veal over the years, prepared in a number of different (often excellent) ways, but I have never become fond of this bland meat. It is one of those indifferent foods which are popular in European cuisines precisely because they have no flavor and thus cannot interfere with the most perfect creations of *haute cuisine* chefs—their sauces. Northwesterners have traditionally preferred tastier meats, and almost all of the veal produced in our region is shipped to East Coast markets. Provimi veal is nearly impossible to obtain locally, unless one contacts a producer directly (and is willing to do some home-butchering).

But, after all this talk of beef, back to the Marysville Livestock Auction. Beef cattle were not the only animals to pass through the arena. Three ponies and several sheep were sold while we discussed the cattle. The ponies were lucky. There is a brisk market for horseflesh in the Northwest (most of it is exported to France), but today's offerings were spared: they were bought by the parents of three wide-eyed girls. The sheep also fared well. They have lovely fleeces and will be sent out to pasture to produce more wool.

Several goats were bought by Southeast Asian immigrants. Now the pigs have arrived. They are smaller and pinker than the ones we raised at home (most of my experiences have been—apart from a few visits to county fairs—with tough, half-wild farmstead hogs, left to roam in acorn-strewn woodlands for much of the year, and with the wild razorback, the squint-eyed boar out of the tangled wood, the desperado who once ravaged the fields of Calydon, the changeling who slew Adonis and Diarmuid, the great Parnassian boar who gashed Odysseus's thigh).

The soft little grain-mash-fed piglets before us are very unmythical, white, red, and pinto black swine with wiggly tails, not even knee-high, weighing only from two hundred to two hundred and fifty pounds. They are a modern crossbreed, long and lean: tender pork chops, roasts, streaked bacon, picnic shoulder, breakfast sausage, and family-sized hams. These represent the best in modern husbandry and are designed to satisfy a diet-conscious market: red Durocs, white, lop-eared Landraces, belted Hampshires, and a few long-snouted, golden Tamworths. But the round, fat butterballs, Chester Whites and Spotted Poland Chinas, are not represented. Raised mainly for their lard, they have little appeal for weight-watching consumers. Yet they were very popular with the pioneers, whose primary cooking fats were lard and butter; and these pigs fattened well in the remote backwoods of the Pacific Northwest (and the lard tasted much better than bear grease, the only native shortening available east of the Cascades).

Hogs do best where there is a plentiful supply of natural feed, preferably acorns, pine nuts, tubers, or roots. Some early settlers reported good, though temporary, results from turning their hogs loose in camas prairies and Indian potato patches (incidentally destroying the staples of the native population). Pigs can be raised on a surprisingly large variety of feed and, unlike beef cattle, still produce palatable meat. Only an extensive diet of spawned-out salmon or rotting fruit spoils the flavor. Clams, however, do not. Early Puget Sound settlers who preferred the taste of pork to that of clams sometimes let their pigs root in the Sound's extensive clam beds. Today most pigs raised in the Northwest are fed on potatoes and finished on a grain formula. They are slaughtered at the unripe age of six months, at a time when their meat is tender and mild, since old pork, especially boar's meat, can take on a strong, gamy taste.

Until now, the pigs at the Marysville Auction had entered the arena in small groups of equal age and size, but presently a solitary old boar limped into the limelight, a big, black Finn MacCool who had become gaunt and bent-backed in the prolonged and constant pursuit of gallantries. I wondered if there would be any interest in the old beau, but he sold for a fair price, and my cicerone told me that he would most likely be sent to Chicago, where they know how to market old rogues properly. I suspect he will soon perform his final act in a fancy New York restaurant, his star appearance billed as *"sanglier solitaire."*

At present, there are more than four hundred distinct breeds of domestic pigs but, curiously, after escaping to the woods, the domestic pig will revert to the wild, furry, bristly razorback type within only a couple of generations. Feral hogs once found plentiful feed in the camas prairies, wapatoo fens, and Garry oak coppices of the Northwest; but this natural habitat has been largely plowed and planted to grain, vegetables, and orchards—and there is little feed for wild hogs in the adjacent conifer forests. A belated attempt to introduce wild pigs to the rugged foothills of the northern Cascades was made a few years back by Skagit County Tarheels longing for the wild pork of their native Smoky Mountains. But the Washington State Game Department, an agency which refused to share the yearning, soon rounded up most of the illegal porkers, and the rest have probably perished from lack of feed.

The black boar, squinting in the strong light of the Marysville sales rink, reminds me of another black boar, of the errant Hudson's Bay Company hog which was the cause of the "Pig War" (which never quite broke out) between the British colonial government in Victoria and the rambunctious American settlers on San Juan Island. That erring boar became a *cause celebre* when it was dropped by Ohio sharpshooter Lyman Cutler back in 1859 with a single shot from his long Kentucky rifle. But, when all's said and done, it must be admitted that this historical fray really had less to do with hogs than with sheep: the British, those enthusiastic eaters of lamb and mutton, had learned that the dryland pastures of the Pacific Northwest—whether in the rain shadow of the Olympic Mountains or east of the Cascades—produced sheep whose meat was of superb taste and texture. They just made the mistake of pasturing some of their sheep on land which the American settlers claimed for their own.

Nor was the further history of sheep raising in the Northwest free from other struggles: sheep were seen as interlopers on the vast cattle ranges of Transcascadia and, in the late 1800s and early 1900s, cattlemen fought an extensive and vicious antisheep campaign. An unfortunate outgrowth of this antisheep campaign was a regional antipathy to sheep. Northwesterners ceased to look upon sheep as food and considered them as "unclean" animals instead, as furry brutes who polluted the ranges and watercourses and thus were somehow not very nice to eat. This is why for so many years the Northwest's best-tasting meat animal was raised primarily for its wool and hides, not for its delectable legs and chops. A small ethnic and specialty market for mutton survived, but it has not been until quite recently that the high quality and superb taste of Pacific Northwest lamb was rediscovered by our region's gourmets.

Today, sheep are still raised in the San Juan Islands, though mostly for their wool, and the herds are down to about three thousand ewes from a peak of about eight thousand head earlier in the century. But a lamb revival is in progress now. Connoisseurs of fine lamb vie with each other in their search for the tastiest meat and the most reliable producer.

I have been very fond of northwest lamb ever since I had my first taste some ten years ago. No matter where the sheep are raised, whether on the dry ranges of southern Idaho and southeastern Oregon (by Basque shepherds), on the bunchgrass lands of eastern Washington, or on the grain stubble of the Willamette Valley, it is exceptionally delicious. But I consistently heard that the lamb raised on the gravelly pastures of the San Juan Islands was the tastiest of all. My only problem was that this lamb was not exactly easy to find. After a bit of research, I did, however, discover a source.

Marti Clark and Bobbi Sumberg, two women who have had extensive experience not only with sheep but with other aspects of farming as well, raise a superior strain of sheep on the dry pastures and gravelly meadows of southern Lopez Island. Each summer and fall, they harvest a crop of about one hundred to one hundred and forty lambs—they have made arrangements with a local butcher to slaughter the lambs and cut and wrap the meat. But I wanted to have the first lamb I ordered from them left whole, for a spit barbecue. This called for special arrangements.

Thus it came about that I learned about the San Juan Island delivery service: early one morning, on what promised to be an unusually cold August day, I waited at the Anacortes ferry landing for my butchered lamb. It was supposed to arrive on the *Klickitat*, the morning's first boat, but I did not know who would bring it. We had agreed, in typical island fashion, that Marti would send the lamb to the mainland with any friend who happened to be traveling there ("to the U.S.," as the islanders say). The transaction was quick and easy: shortly after the ferry docked, a green van pulled up next to my car. The lamb had arrived in style, riding on the front seat with Russell Borneman, Lopez Island's dentist.

I took the lamb to Warren Dimmick's butcher shop in Burlington to have Warren check out the quality of the meat. Warren looked over the carcass and pronounced it to be of the highest quality. It was firm-fleshed, had excellent meat coloration and marbling, but no excess fat (big globs of fat, common when lambs are fed on grain instead of grass, give lamb a "strong" taste, hiding the delicate flavor of the meat). Warren removed the musk glands from the lamb's shoulders and hind legs. Some butchers feel this is unnecessary, but Warren maintains—and I agree with him—that the glands can cause an unpleasant odor and "strong" flavor when the meat is cooked. Besides, the cavity left behind provides a nice place to put a clove of garlic. I suspect that the reason many butchers don't bother with removing the glands is the inferior meat they work with. Lamb that already has an off-taste because it was raised improperly (like the frozen, imported New Zealand lamb, for example) does not benefit from the removal of the glands; the delicate, flavorful lamb grown in the Pacific Northwest, however, warrants such special treatment.

We hung our lamb in Warren's cooler for twenty-four hours (lamb, unlike beef and mutton, does not benefit from lengthy aging), and the next day Warren came up to Bellingham to help us cook and eat the lamb. It was superb, a true gourmet's delight, with a delicate yet rich lamb flavor, and it was tender. Even guests who loudly proclaimed that they "didn't really care for lamb" loved this. It was unlike any they had ever tasted before.

Lamb barbecues are becoming increasingly popular in the Northwest as more people are becoming aware of the exceptional quality of the lamb produced in our region. Marti and Bobbi, incidentally, raise special meat sheep; they do not merely sell the culls from wool sheep herds. Their sheep are meaty Suffolk-Finn crosses, a crossbreed that is just made for doing well on island pastures.

In the fall of 1982, we found the Northwest's best meat and fish together. We traveled to Sooke Harbour House for a special dinner to celebrate the unveiling of a mermaid mosaic. On our arrival, we were captivated by the scent of lamb and salmon cooking over smoldering alder fires. Victor Newman, a Kwakiutl printmaker and carver, was in charge of the barbecue. He had planked several large Chinook salmon (provided by the Sechelt Indian Band) in Northwest Indian fashion and set them up next to an open fire; three lambs were turning slowly on spits set above beds of alder coals.

The roasted lamb was delicious. It came from Metchosin, a perfect lamb country in the rain shadow of the coastal mountains, where the weanlings feed on bromegrass, wild rye, and aromatic herbs exposed to the salt-laden shore breezes that blow across the strand from the Strait of Juan de Fuca. Metchosin lamb ranks with Lopez Island lamb among the three best in the Pacific Northwest. The third comes from Saltspring Island.

Saltspring, the largest of the Canadian Gulf Islands, is a fractured land of steep hills and sparse soils, rugged terrain which grows the kind of grasses and herbs sheep favor. On Saltspring, as on several nearby Canadian islands, sheep have been raised since the nineteenth century and, over the years, many have escaped to the wild hills and established feral populations. It is difficult to tell the difference between wild and domestic stock (since sheep, unlike hogs, do not revert to a wild prototype), and it is quite understandable that the islands' sheep farmers frown upon hunters searching for a taste of wild mutton.

The biggest lamb barbecue of them all is held each Labor Day weekend near the Saturna Island ferry dock. It started out as an annual celebration of the island folk, a time for getting reacquainted with each other, drinking, and eating up part of the island's surplus lambs. But as the fame of the fête spread, it grew in size—though not in style—and is now attended by throngs of visitors who come to the island just to eat lamb. The Saturna Island method of barbecuing lamb is unique in our region: it was adapted from the method used by the sheepherders of the Argentinian Pampas. The lamb is skinned, split open, and stretched (crucified) on an X made of steel fenceposts. It is then barbecued upright, like Indian salmon, in front of an open campfire. It is well worth a pilgrimage to Saturna.

Sheep have always appealed to herdsmen living on marginal lands, whether these be islands or desert ridges, because they can do very well on land not suited for other domestic animals (with the exception of goats). They just thrive on sparse forage and the lambs produce their tastiest meat on nothing but mother's milk, sear grasses, and fragrant herbs. Lamb is bound to become more popular in our region in the immediate future, because sheep can produce tasty prime or choice, that is well-marbled, meat on a diet of grass alone, without any supplemental feeding of grain. This is an increasingly important competitive advantage, since the price of feed grain and processed fodder has skyrocketed in recent years. A few growers insist on feeding grain to their lambs, but this is a waste, for it produces nothing but excess weight and, unfortunately, those globs of fat which spoil the clean taste of grass-fed lamb.

I always make sure to buy my lamb (preferably at an age of only three to six months) directly from a grower, and I insist on lamb that has been fed on grass (or milk) alone. For my own table, I also prefer lamb raised on the gravelly (unfertilized) pastures bordering the inland waters—it reminds me of the renowned pré-salé lamb of France—but the lamb raised in other parts of the Northwest is also excellent. Lamb from the cool, arid hills of the southern Okanogan Valley, from the volcanic ridges of the Yakima country, from the dry downs of Idaho, from the woodlands of southeastern Oregon, or lamb finished on the stubblefields of the Columbia Basin wheatlands or on the dry upland fields of the Willamette Valley, are all delicious to eat and much better tasting than lamb which has been raised on the Great Plains or in the arid Southwest, where the delicate animals suffer through exceedingly torrid summers.

Goats, which are closely related to sheep, can survive better in hot weather than their woolly cousins and on even sparser forage. For this reason, goats are very popular as food animals in such regions as the deserts of northern Mexico and the southwestern United States. Surprisingly, goats do exceptionally well in the moist, cool climes of the Pacific Northwest, too. Most of the goats in our region are dairy goats—the lush pastures of the Puget Trough lowlands are particularly conducive to the production of excellent goat's milk. But wherever there are dairy goats, there is also a surplus of kids, since goats bear an average of two to three (and often as many as four) young per year. Goat farmers in the Northwest have experienced problems marketing these kids in the past (many were simply killed at birth), but in the last several years a market for young goat flesh—sold as "chevon"—has developed.

I first became aware of the abundance of young goats during my annual visits to the county fair goat pens. Here just about every goat farmer advertised—a few did so almost desperately—the various pleasures of eating kid. I had never eaten kid before, but I decided that it was about time for me to do so. Besides the farmer's alluring advertisements, I frequently ran across assertions that good kid tasted much better than lamb. From the fourteenth-century French work Le Ménagier de Paris to the recent writings of Elizabeth David and Waverly Root, this claim is made with an almost haughty assurance.

The problem was that I could not find anyone who had actually eaten both lamb and kid and might thus have substantiated the claim. So we had to do the test ourselves. We obtained a lamb and a kid of equal age—three months—from Lopez Island, and roasted both slowly over beds of white alder coals.

We never settled the question of which of these meats is tastier, the lamb or the kid, since both turned out to be delicious. They were so different in flavor, that a comparison would have been meaningless. The lamb was exquisite, as was to be expected of Lopez Island lamb, but the kid proved to be the real surprise of the tasting: its meat had a lovely, delicate flavor (no trace of the billy goat here) and, as several hunters present averred, it tasted more like an excellent pheasant than like a four-legged farm animal.

During my childhood in Europe, another meat figured significantly. Venison. Poached venison. Its taste was not up to that of the excellent venison of the Northwest, but there was more of it than lamb or other domestic animals, because it was not subject to seasons. Once I was old enough to learn that poaching was not a proper way of procuring meat, I really felt guilty about having eaten innocent animals. I stopped eating meat for several years. In the end, however, my taste buds triumphed over my scruples and I have never again had qualms about eating meat—as long as it is procured legally.

It may, at times, be difficult to tell whether a meat you are eating in the backwoods of the Pacific Northwest was procured by legal or illegal means. Supplementing the family larder with game was quite common in the valleys of the Cascades and the Okanogan Highlands until but a generation ago, and even today large numbers of hunters still head to the woods and fields during the hunting seasons. But how do you tell whether the elk stew you have just enjoyed was indeed canned during the last hunting season or if it came from a recently poached animal. (It is definitely unwise to question your host's honor in such matters.)

Unfortunately, poaching is a way of life in many of our region's remote woods, especially during times of economic depression. There is an abundance of game in the Northwest—deer, elk, bear, grouse, quail, pheasant, ducks, and geese—but this is now hunted by our largely urban population for sport, not for subsistence. While hunters add wild meat to their fare in season, this has become a luxury for most Northwesterners. The game diet of the rural population has become a culinary oddity, a curious survival from a more primitive period in our history.

I have eaten my share, or perhaps more than my share, of northwest game, even though I do not hunt regularly. Some of this game has been given to me by friends who like to share their bounty, some of it by hunters who like the excitement of the chase and the kill but do not enjoy the taste of game. I enjoy the taste of game, but as a rule, I prefer the delicacy of a domestic squab to the coarseness of a band-tailed pigeon, the fatness of a farm pond duck (especially a muscovy) to the stringiness of its wild cousins, and the flavor of goat and lamb to that of venison. Yet game can add interest to meals, it can provide a welcome change, or it can be a highlight in an otherwise undistinguished dinner. But only when it is prepared properly and when it is served in moderation.

Pheasants—the wild kind, not the farm-raised birds that are exposed to the wild only a day before they are gunned down by eager hunters—and grouse, especially blue grouse and ruffed grouse fattened on wild huckleberries, can be a gourmet's delight. But they are very hard to come by.

Fortunately, the chickens raised in the Northwest are also exceptionally tasty. Our best chickens do, of course, come from farms where they are allowed to roam and obtain part of their food from scratching in the farmyard and probing the weeds. There seems to be a magic diet for chickens which brings out their best taste. But it is a diet that can not be reduced to easy scientific feeding formulas: it calls for a certain amount of grain, a quantity of grubs, and a variable percentage of weeds and wild seeds and whatever else strikes a chicken's fancy. Chickens should be allowed to look for some of their food on their own—it is a natural impulse. Even caged county fair chickens will spill grain from their feeders, scratch the bottom of their cage, and only then commence to eat; but they should not be allowed to roam too far and run too fast or fly too much, or they will become muscular and tough and stringy. It almost seems as if the weedier the farm, the less the chickens need to roam, the more they have to eat, and the better they will taste. A clean-swept farmyard provides little forage for a hungry fowl.

Northwest chicken fanciers not only have access to tasty chickens, but to a great variety of chickens as well. Some of these are tiny, some are huge, all are good to eat—with one possible exception: the fighting cocks raised in appreciable numbers from the Fraser to the Willamette. These are lean-bodied, strong-legged; all tough drumstick and no tender meat. Besides, fighting cocks are too valuable to eat and once they lose a battle they are not fit for anyone's table anymore.

Among the multitude of fowl available to northwest chicken fanciers, there are Jersey Giants, Plymouth Rocks, and Rhode Island Reds; Araucanas, Wyandottes, and Cochins; Chanteclers, Barnvelders, and Orpingtons; Dorkings, Leghorns (for stewing), and Polish; Sebrights, Mille Fleurs, rose-combs, and silkies. And, for more exotic tastes, there are guinea fowl, partridges, francolins, quail, grouse, and ruffed, Chinese ring-necked, silver, impeyan, and long-tailed pheasants—or peafowl—for pampered palates. The Northwest's farm ponds are inhabited by Blue Swedish, Cayuga, runner, Pekin, Muscovy, mallard, and rouen ducks, and by African, Chinese, Toulouse, Embden, and Canada geese. It's a true embarrassment of culinary riches. Most of these fowl are easy to find: the display cages at the county fairs list the owner's name and address, and farm produce ads in our major daily newspapers always offer a few odd fowl for sale. In Bellingham, for instance, one farm ran an advertisement for catch-your-own turkeys which were guaranteed to be farmyard raised—and probably very wild (and tasty!).

Many of these uncommon and exotic fowl can be expensive, but we can authoritatively (and safely) maintain that even the commercially raised chickens in the Pacific Northwest are tastier than the chickens raised elsewhere in the country. The quality of our chickens is related directly to the quality of the feed: northwest chickens are raised on a diet of primarily wheat and barley, instead of the more common corn fed elsewhere. This diet also turns the chickens' skins white and improves the quality of the fat. Additionally, we are able to buy our chickens very fresh; quite often a chicken that is displayed whole or cut into pieces in a supermarket cooler may have been killed earlier on the same day. The processing plants kill and clean the chickens at night and deliver them to the markets before 9:00 A.M. to make sure that the consumer receives only the best and freshest meat. Large markets with a high turnover are at an advantage here; smaller markets may display chickens that were delivered several days ago. These are, of course, still perfectly edible.

The meat of battery-raised chickens is quite mild, pleasant, and indistinctive. Still, it possesses a very pleasant delicacy: a fresh, tender chicken breast, quickly sautéed in sweet butter and sprinkled with salt, pepper, and fresh herbs, is a delight, no matter how the chicken was raised. The only problem with battery-raised chickens lies in the excess fat produced by the high-energy feed. This fat lies mostly under the skin. I usually just pull it off with the skin and use both for chicken stock (I can afford to do this since I never bread and deep fry my chicken—if you believe in cooking your chicken in grease, you don't have to worry about the fat under the skin).

Not all of the meats in the Pacific Northwest are inexpensive—it takes a lot more money, invested in both labor and feed, to raise a superb steer in the Northwest on quality feed, than it takes to raise a corn-fed Midwestern steer, for example—and the best may be quite expensive and hard to find. But their exceptional quality makes both the extra effort and the extra cost worthwhile. Long ago I reduced the amount of meat I eat to be able to enjoy the highest quality. Anyone can produce an acceptable ground beef patty, but it takes a special talent to produce, say, a superb Lopez Island leg of lamb, an Idaho roast, or a fat Rouen duck. Anyone, with the right amount of money, can serve a good prime rib, but it takes special dedication to serve a goose that has been roasted to perfection, a plump, stuffed farmyard chicken, a suckling pig, or a tender, succulent milk-fed kid.

Meat has been taken too much for granted in the Northwest—as in the rest of the country. It should be considered primarily for special dishes, as a food of special quality which is to be served on special occasions. Thus, perhaps, we will once again learn to appreciate the quality of the meats produced in our region, instead of settling for mere quantity.

Northwest Duck

This delectable recipe comes from John Rauner, wine maker at the Yakima River Winery in Prosser and an avid hunter of Columbia Basin wildfowl. Serve with carrots and Yakima River chardonnay.

Wild (or domestic) ducks   2
Chardonnay   1½ cups
Salt and freshly ground pepper   to taste
Wild rice   6 tablespoons
Tart apple (Granny Smith)   1, diced
Small (Walla Walla sweet) onion   1, chopped
Bread crumbs   ¾ cup
Unsalted butter   as needed

1. Marinate ducks overnight in chardonnay with salt and pepper to taste. (Reserve marinade on following day.)
2. The next day, cook wild rice.
3. Drain rice and mix with apple, onion, and bread crumbs. This is the stuffing for the ducks.
4. Rub ducks with unsalted butter and bake slowly at 275° for 2½ to 3 hours, basting with remaining marinade every 15 minutes.

Serves 4

Simply Grouse (or Pheasant)

We had to prepare this recipe with pheasant, for the elusive grouse eluded us, despite the hard work we put in slogging through wet blueberry thickets and windfalls. This dish is best when the birds are wild (not farm-raised) and fresh. Serve with roast potatoes, crisp cooked vegetables, and a good merlot.

Grouse or pheasant   1, cut up and skinned
Merlot   1 cup
All-purpose flour   1 cup
Salt   ⅛ teaspoon
Freshly ground pepper   ¼ teaspoon
Unsalted butter   2 tablespoons
Homemade cream of mushroom soup   2 cups (preferably made with chanterelles or boletes)
Green onions or shallots   ¼ cup chopped
Fresh chanterelles (or boletes)   ½ cup sliced
Small garlic clove   1

1. Moisten cut-up bird by marinating in wine for 30 minutes; turn often.
2. Dredge pieces in flour seasoned with salt and pepper.
3. Brown pieces in butter over medium heat. (Brown carefully; don't scorch!)
4. Add soup, onions, chanterelles, and some pulp of crushed garlic clove.
5. Turn heat to low and pan-fry for 30 minutes, turning and stirring occasionally.

Note: The secret of this recipe lies in seasoning and cooking the bird very lightly, letting the bird's flavor dominate.

Serves 2

Northwest Chicken Sokol Blosser

Fresh spinach   2 bunches
Chicken breasts   4, skinned, boned, and lightly pounded
Garlic clove   1, bruised
Unsalted butter   1 tablespoon
Gewürztraminer   ½ cup
Cream   ½ cup
Capers   7 to 8

1. Rinse spinach well and pat or spin dry.
2. Finely shred spinach and divide among 4 serving plates.
3. Sauté chicken breasts and garlic in butter until lightly browned. Remove and place on

heated platter.

4. Deglaze pan with wine; add cream and capers.
5. Reduce mixture until thickened and light brown, over medium heat.
6. Top spinach with chicken and sauce. Serve immediately.

Serves 4

Chicken Piquant with Oregon Pinot Noir

It seems as if the Oregon wine country just spawns excellent cooks. It must be because these wines go so well with food! Here's a great chicken recipe from Mary Benoit of the Château Benoit Winery in Carlton. Enjoy this dish with a glass of Oregon pinot noir.

Large chicken breast halves   4 (about 2 pounds)
Oregon pinot noir   ⅔ cup
Olive oil   1 tablespoon
Unsalted butter   1 tablespoon
Garlic cloves   30 (yes, 30!), peeled
Sugar   2 tablespoons
Oregon pinot noir   ½ cup
Raspberry vinegar   ½ cup plus 1 tablespoon
Unsalted butter   4 tablespoons
Salt   ½ teaspoon
Freshly ground black pepper   to taste
Red seedless grapes or fresh raspberries (depending on season)   ½ cup

1. Bone, but do not skin, chicken breast halves, and cut crosswise into 3 or 4 pieces. Marinate in ⅔ cup wine 1 hour. Wipe dry.
2. Heat oil and 1 tablespoon butter in heavy skillet until sizzling. Sauté chicken pieces until well-browned, about 4 minutes on each side. Set aside chicken and pour off fat in pan.
3. While chicken is marinating, combine garlic, sugar, ½ cup pinot noir, and 1 tablespoon vinegar in saucepan. Bring to a boil over high heat, stirring to dissolve sugar. Lower heat to medium, cover, and cook until garlic is fork-tender, about 12 minutes. Uncover, increase heat to high and cook until liquid is reduced to a thick syrup and garlic is glazed, about 10 to 15 minutes. Stir in remaining ½ cup of vinegar.
4. Pour garlic and sauce into skillet in which chicken was cooked. Cook over high heat until syrupy, scraping up any chicken residue left in the skillet.
5. Quickly stir in remaining 4 tablespoons butter, salt, and pepper.
6. Return chicken and any residual juices to skillet, tossing gently with sauce. Garnish with grapes and toss very gently again.

Serves 4

Lamb Chops in Wine Sauce Henry

Lest you think that red meats always demand a red wine, here's a recipe for lamb chops from the Henry Estate Winery in Umpqua, Oregon, that calls for chardonnay. But then Scott Henry's chardonnay is a very big wine, big enough to stand up to the delicate lamb produced in the Pacific Northwest. These chops can be enjoyed with either a bottle of Henry Estate 1979 pinot noir, or with the 1979 chardonnay.

Shoulder lamb chops 6
Garlic clove 1, finely minced (or more, to taste)
Salt and freshly ground pepper to taste
Unsalted butter 4 tablespoons
Medium onion 1, chopped
Parsley 1 tablespoon chopped
Flour 1½ tablespoons
Chardonnay 1 cup

1. Rub chops with garlic, salt, and pepper.
2. Brown chops in heavy skillet on both sides in 3 tablespoons butter. Transfer chops to casserole and keep warm.
3. Sauté onion and parsley in 1 tablespoon butter. When these are soft, stir in flour, blending well.
4. Gradually add wine, stirring constantly, and cook until sauce is thickened.
5. Pour sauce over chops.
6. Cover casserole with buttered parchment paper and bake at 350° 20 minutes or until tender. Remove paper and bake 10 minutes longer.

Serves 6

Medallions of Fresh Kid with Plums and Chanterelles

Fresh kid is one of the best meats produced in the Northwest. Sinclair Philip makes full use of it in the kitchen at Sooke Harbour House. Serve with a Yakima River Winery merlot, or an Adelsheim merlot, or a Kiona lemberger.

Kid loin   2 pounds
Buttermilk   1½ cups
Fresh rosemary   2 sprigs
Fresh lemon thyme   2 sprigs
Olive oil   2 teaspoons
Fresh medium chanterelles   16 (slice if too large)
Italian or Chinese plums   12, pitted and quartered
Brandy   2 tablespoons
Lamb or beef stock   2 cups
Dijon mustard   1 tablespoon
Fresh lemon thyme   1½ teaspoons chopped

1. Marinate loin in buttermilk with rosemary and lemon thyme sprigs. Cover and refrigerate overnight.
2. The next day, discard marinade, pat loin dry with paper towels.
3. Cut loin into 18 slices (3 per person). Place medallions (slices) between sheets of waxed paper and carefully flatten each with a mallet.
4. Heat olive oil over high heat. Sauté medallions, browning meat lightly on both sides (about 2 to 3 minutes). Keep warm without cooking further.
5. Leave burner on high. To pan juices add chanterelles and plums. Sauté mixture until chanterelles are cooked (about 2 to 3 minutes).
6. Add brandy and flambé (light brandy with match), shaking pan back and forth.
7. Add lamb stock, mustard, lemon thyme, and reduce until thick. Arrange medallions for serving and cover with sauce.

Serves 6

Steak Sokol Blosser

This is an excellent way to fix some of the well-marbled steaks coming from the fat cattle raised in the dry foothills bordering the Willamette Valley.

Top round of beef 1½ pounds
Garlic cloves 3
Olive oil 1 tablespoon
Rosemary 1 teaspoon crushed
Unsalted butter 2 tablespoons
Pinot noir ¾ cup
Worcestershire sauce ½ teaspoon
Green peppercorn mustard (or Dijon) ½ teaspoon

1. Rub beef with garlic, olive oil, and rosemary. Let sit out at room temperature for 10 minutes.
2. Wipe garlic and rosemary from steak.
3. Heat butter in medium-hot skillet until melted and bubbly.
4. Add steak and quickly sauté 2½ to 3 minutes on each side, or until done to your taste. Remove to heated serving platter.
5. Deglaze pan with wine, Worcestershire sauce, and mustard over high heat. Reduce by half.
6. Pour over steak and slice diagonally to serve.

Serves 4

Milk, Cheese, and Butter

The click-clack-swish of the apple orchard sprinklers give way to the chirp of roadside crickets. Irrigated creek bottoms are still green, but the hillsides looming above the worn ranch houses and barns are dry, covered with sagebrush, rabbit brush and, every so often, patches of prickly pear. Pale clumps of bunchgrass rise at first between, then above the sage. We have passed the old Indian racetrack on Antoine Creek and the grass becomes denser, lusher, as the road climbs higher into the hills. Havillah, the "land of gold," is swathed in green; the hamlet's ancient white church, manse, and schoolhouse rise from mountain meadows as unexpected specters in an increasingly wild landscape.

This is a rough cattle country, where vicious battles between ranchers and sheepmen were fought less than a hundred years ago. Today, the land lies undisturbed; only here and there a chalky sheep's skull or bleached bone lying in a dry gully mark a site of violence past. Now, several thousand feet above sea level, we approach the edge of the wild, the bear and eagle country of the Okanogan Highlands, a remote region of stark fells and spongy moors rising above the Okanogan and Columbia river valleys, where the wheatgrasses, oats, and wild ryes of the lower slopes give way to bluegrasses, sunflowers, and columbines.

Here, tucked beneath the rocky humps of Bimetalic Mountain and Knob Hill, in the shelter of a scraggly aspen grove, two wilderness dairy farmers, Roger and Sally Jackson, make raw milk cheeses in a thoroughly old-fashioned way. Their herd is small, a dozen goats and three cows, because feed is limited; the thin soil supports just one sparse crop of dryland alfalfa each year. The Jacksons prefer making straight goat or cow cheeses, but the quantity of milk available in their harsh environment is limited and often forces them to make cheese from a blend of goat's and cow's milk in the old Hudson's Bay Company tradition.

The Jacksons are the only commercial cheese makers in the Northwest who still make cheese in a time-honored hit-or-miss fashion, but they do so from choice, not from necessity. They have few modern amenities in their highland cottage, no electricity (all their heat comes from wood, all their light from kerosene lanterns), and no telephone.

Every day, Sally Jackson milks her goats and cows by hand and carries the milk to her small cheese house, where she heats the curds on an ancient kitchen range over a fire of tamarack wood. After the whey is drained, the curds are ladled into a wooden cheese press and pressed for several hours. The cheeses are kept in the cheese house for two weeks, brushed with brine to form a natural crust, turned daily, and inspected for flaws. They are finally stored in a most unusual storing room: a small hollow inside a giant straw pile.

Aging cheese in this fashion was once quite popular on small farms. Nineteenth-century cookbook author Eliza Leslie advised the cheese maker to "Place the cheese in the haystack, and keep them there among the hay for five or six weeks. This is said to greatly improve their consistence and flavor." The straw maintains the cheese at a steady temperature of forty-five degrees for the sixty days of aging required by law for raw milk cheeses (this allows the beneficial anaerobic bacteria in the slowly fermenting cheese to destroy any pathogens present in raw milk). The finished products of the Jacksons' cheese-making operation are firm, with a mild taste. The goat cheeses have a very pleasant, delicate tang. Further aging will improve the flavor even more and make the cheeses quite creamy, but the Jacksons usually sell them after sixty days (they need the cash). Both cheeses can be ordered by mail (see Appendix).

The Jacksons' weathered farm buildings and cheese house remind me strongly of the centuries-old mountain dairies of the European Alps, yet the art of dairying is very young in the Pacific Northwest—it arrived less than two centuries ago. Milk (other than mother's milk), butter, and cheese were not known to the native people of the Pacific Northwest until the first white explorers and fur traders arrived on the Coast in the latter part of the eighteenth century. The very first European visitors, accustomed to their regular allowance of fresh milk, butter, and cheese, brought dairy goats and cows to our region.

Because of the lack of native fats in the Northwest (other than bear grease or eulachon oil), the family cow(s) became a necessity in remote agricultural settlements and in mining or logging camps on both sides of the Cascades. Some logging camps even ran their own dairies. In a curious development, dairy cows increased in the camps after the introduction of steam donkeys and locomotives, taking up the stable space left vacant by the departed oxen and draft horses.

On small homesteads out in the sticks, reached only by snaggled waterways and boggy roads on the west side of the Cascades, and isolated from towns by sagebrush steppe and barren coulees on the east side, many a family owed its survival to the ever-present cow. Homemade butter and cheese supplemented a vegetable, venison, and fish or grouse diet, and surplus butter could be exchanged at the nearest general store for flour, sugar, and other necessities of civilized life. A family which lost its cow lost its prime means of livelihood and, on the sagebrush plateaus of eastern Oregon and Washington where only precious beef and sheep were available as alternate sources of protein, a family without cows had to move on and try to make a living elsewhere.

The flow of milk began to increase late in the nineteenth century as ever more productive strains of dairy cattle were introduced: improved Holsteins (the first of these supermilk cows reached the Pacific Northwest shortly after completion of the transcontinental railroad), Ayrshires, Guernseys, Jerseys, and Brown Swiss. But in the early decades of the twentieth century, even these improved breeds were seen as inadequate. Suddenly the breeding of cattle which could deliver an ever higher volume of milk became every dairy farmer's overriding ambition.

At the turn of the century, the average American dairy cow gave about 3,500 pounds of milk a year; today she produces about 7,500 pounds a year, with cows in western Washington regularly giving from 12,500 to more than 20,000 pounds. During most of the nineteenth century, the quantity of milk a cow produced (beyond a necessary minimum) had been of less concern to the farmer than the percentage of butterfat the milk contained. Because of the difficulty of transporting the raw milk from the farm to the markets, the quantity could, in some cases, even become a burden.

Raw milk, which is neither pasteurized nor homogenized, contains free cream which will rise to the top sooner or later. The rough jolts of even a short trip over unpaved, rutted country roads can set up a churning action which will quickly convert the cream to butter. So, most farmers simply avoided the problem and made butter from their cream in the first place. Butter could be protected from spoilage by salting and could be packed into barrels and stored for reasonable periods of time. Sometimes it was cached in the volcanic ice caves of southern Washington and eastern Oregon.

Pasteurization and homogenization improved the keeping qualities of milk. But the most important change came after the turn of the century. Transportation by refrigerated truck, more than anything else, revolutionized the distribution of fresh milk. Dairy farms could now locate wherever the grass was sufficiently tasty and the pastures green, without concern for proximity to railroads and waterways.

Milk, under the pressure of consumer demand and modern processing techniques, has changed its nature—and incurred the collective wrath of the nation's food writers. During the second half of the twentieth century, complaints about the declining taste qualities of our milk have become one of the rites of passage for budding gourmets, but much of this zealous criticism is not based on a careful study of the facts (I don't know anyone who really remembers what milk tasted like in, say, 1901). Most important for the Northwest, it does not apply to our milk for it is based on the taste of the milk produced in the Midwest (wild garlic and other noxious weeds do interesting things to the flavor of milk), the Northeast (as does pollution), and the South (or hot, muggy weather).

Other factors must be considered. The French, with their tendency to classify everything, have long maintained (with justification) that the quality of the soil, the nature of a given terrain, and the type of climate affect the taste of the foods produced in a particular region. In the Pacific Northwest, rich bottom soils, lush meadows moistened by a reliable rainfall, and pleasantly cool summer temperatures have made it little wonder the region has always produced some of the best milk on the continent. Several breeds of dairy cattle do very well in our area: Jerseys and Guernseys, originally from the British Channel Islands, give a very rich milk (5 percent butterfat); Scottish Ayrshires and Dutch Holsteins produce high volumes of milk with a lower fat content (3.8 to 4 percent); and here and there one encounters Milking Shorthorns and Brown Swiss cows.

Because the fat content of milk is of high concern to diet- and cholesterol-conscious consumers, much of our milk is sold as a skimmed and de-fatted beverage. But with thin milk, flavor becomes very important. Many of our dairies are currently experimenting with the blending of milk from different breeds of cows to get a more flavorful and satisfying milk. Nevertheless, per capita milk consumption has dropped, as the sales of colas and other carbonated soft drinks, especially low-calorie sodas, have increased.

The consumption of goat's milk, on the other hand, has risen in recent years. The Northwest produces some of the best dairy goats in the country (the breeders have numerous blue ribbons to prove it). Goats are amazing animals: gentle, intelligent, and inquisitive.

And, contrary to popular belief, they are finicky eaters. In a pinch, when properly hungry, they will eat almost anything, even climbing into trees to forage. If given a fair choice, however, they will nibble on only the most succulent grasses and the tastiest herbs. The Pacific Northwest, with its luscious meadows, has become a veritable paradise of delectable fodder for dairy goats, and the goats have gratefully responded to this bounty by giving their best milk.

Goats raised on abundant feed can give a surprisingly large amount of milk for their size. The average dairy goat can deliver some 3,500 pounds a year west of the mountains (the U.S. record is about 4,900 pounds). Goat's milk is pure white in color (it lacks carotene) and is more easily digested than cow's milk. It has a slightly higher fat content (an average of 4.3 percent versus 3.9 percent), but the fat globules are smaller, more soluble, and do not stick to each other as they do in cow's milk. Thus no cream is formed which could rise to the top; this makes homogenization unnecessary. Goat's milk tastes "skinnier" than cow's milk because of this. It is an excellent food for infants and invalids, and even people who are allergic to cow's milk may safely consume it.

Good, thick cream is still around, though much of the cream now sold in supermarkets is nondairy or has been so denatured with stabilizers, nonfat milk solids, and preservatives that it has lost its taste. Fortunately for Northwesterners, several of our region's large dairy co-ops—Dairyland in British Columbia, Darigold in Washington, and Tillamook in Oregon—still produce excellent cream which, best of all, sits on the supermarket shelves right next to the denatured products. The label on the carton gives the clue: real, fresh cream lists "Grade-A Pasteurized Whipping Cream" as its only ingredient and it always lists a pull date; the imitations list a number of chemical ingredients and are not inclined to go sour— they are pickled and preserved to last indefinitely.

But the best and freshest cream of our region is commonly found at the numerous small dairies of the countryside, family farms and co-ops whose distribution system may not extend beyond a small town or county (newspaper advertisements and telephone yellow pages are very helpful in the quest for the best local cream, and so are restaurant staff). If you like the cream served with your dinner, ask where it came from, and you may have discovered a secret source of fattening pleasures. While everyone living in the Northwest has easy access to luscious sweet cream, sour cream is quite another story. Most commercially produced sour cream is adulterated beyond recognition and flavor (Tillamook is one exception). Here it is simply not worthwhile to search for a local source, since it is so easy to make your own from fresh cream.

The best-known dairy product made from cream is butter. It can be made from either fresh or sour cream, though I prefer the fresh cream butter. Butter has been around since men first milked cattle, and it was, for several millennia, the primary cooking fat of many Eurasian tribes. Introduced to the Americas as soon as the first European settlers were able to raise cows, it spread across the continent with the migrations of white farmers. But butter has now lost some of its standing in our cookery, ever since margarine and cholesterol-free cooking oils have gained in popularity. Margarine has a less venerable history. It was conceived in the nineteenth century when Napoleon began looking for a butter substitute to lower the cost of feeding his troops—and margarine has tried to copy the flavor of butter ever since. It has been made from a number of obscure, and sometimes odd, fats and oils, and though some promoters claim that it is healthier than butter (at least by its low-cholesterol atavars), the taste of even the most successful margarine has never approached the flavor of fresh butter. In the past, Northwesterners used a diverse number of native oils and fats besides butter, from whale blubber to eulachon oil and lard; but at the present time, butter is the only native cooking fat in regular use. It is heartening that many of our small restaurants which specialize in northwest cuisine use copious amounts of fresh northwest butter in their cookery.

Butter should never be bought presalted. Salting was once necessary to prevent the butter from turning rancid in hot weather, but modern refrigeration techniques make it superfluous. Our commercially produced butter keeps its freshness because it does not have to travel far. Most of it is made in regional creameries by our large dairy co-ops. Butter benefits if it is made from cream with a high percentage of Jersey and Guernsey cream, because of the richer taste these breeds give, and this is precisely what happens in our area. The milk from which this fresh cream is obtained is refrigerated on the dairy farm right after the milking, taken to the creamery in special tank trucks, checked for quality, pasteurized, run through a separator, and homogenized. The cream is aged for about eight hours before churning. To assure the freshness of the unsalted butter, it is frozen as soon as it has been packaged and should be kept in the freezer until just before it is used.

This butter is always excellent for cooking and for eating fresh, but on those special occasions which call for freshly made butter served on oven-fresh bread, crispy garden vegetables, or steaming crab, butter can easily be made at home. Butter making was a major chore back in the days of the old dash churn, when large quantities of cream were needed to make a batch. But the modern food processor has eliminated the labor, and it allows us to make butter from as little as a pint of cream at a time. Whichever method is used, the principle involved is the same. The churning action violently agitates the cream and eventually causes the butterfat to separate from the emulsion and to form big, easily removable clumps of butter. A liquid milk residue containing the milk sugars and casein remains. In the old days, letting the cream age to allow the lactic acid bacteria to go to work and begin the breakdown made the final churning easier (but it also encouraged unwanted microorganisms). The churning left a pleasantly sour, partly fermented liquid behind: buttermilk. Today, using fresh cream in our continuous churns or food processors, we get only de-fatted milk, perfectly fresh and drinkable, but without the pleasant tang of real buttermilk. But not all is lost.

Our modern "cultured" buttermilk is a different, though perhaps even more wholesome, product. It is closely linked to yogurt, another fermented milk product, which has only become popular in the West during the last two decades. Buttermilk and yogurt are basically the same product, though their fat content and the temperature at which they are fermented and length of fermentation may differ and create slight variations in texture and acidity. The process is simple: the microorganisms of the culture change the structure of the milk by converting the lactose (milk sugar) into lactic acid; the milk's casein and fat become destabilized and a soft, custardlike curd is formed. To make buttermilk, the curds are stirred to make the milk fluid again. The mixture is then chilled to stop further fermentation, packaged, and marketed. Cultured buttermilk is thus much like Miss Muffet's curds and whey, though it has a different taste because it is made with different cultures.

Considering that cultured buttermilk is a fermented product made from skimmed milk and has never been close to a butter churn, it is somewhat ridiculous that some of our dairies insist on adding freeze-dried butter flakes to the concoction, as though bits of butter had remained behind after churning. This is merely a silly affectation if done in moderation; if done to excess, it can make the buttermilk greasy. The quality of a cultured buttermilk depends on the quality of the milk used in the production. In our region, numerous small and large dairies make excellent buttermilk. Darigold, Tillamook, Edaleen, Palm, Dutchman, Dairyland, and many others all do an excellent job. I like buttermilk very much and have made it a habit always to stop and buy some local buttermilk while traveling throughout the Northwest. There is a lot of variety among buttermilks, and all are different yet excellent as energizing refreshments. Tasting as many of them as possible is a practice I can highly recommend.

In the making of yogurt, though the same cultures are used as with buttermilk, the milk is fortified with extra milk solids (casein, et al.) and the solidified curds are not broken up after fermentation. They are often strengthened with such stabilizers as gelatin or pectin. Natural yogurt has a delicate, delightfully sourish taste, yet yogurt did not become popular in the United States until sugar and fruit were added to the packaged product. Like a good sweet wine, this mixture is best when the ingredients are natural, and when a good sugar/acid balance, with the proper amount of fruit, is maintained. In the Northwest, (low-fat) yogurt is also used extensively in cooking, often as a substitute for fattening sour cream, but more often because its fine sourish flavor contributes a unique tang. In our region, Darigold has consistently made excellent low-fat yogurts, experimenting from time to time with a completely natural product where no additives but a small amount of pectin for stabilizing are used. But the best yogurt in the Northwest, a truly sumptuous gourmet's delight—without any pretensions toward a low calorie count—is made by Alamar Farms in Delta, British Columbia, from only whole, rich Jersey milk. It is completely natural (only milk and culture) and contains the full 5 percent milk fat of fresh Jersey milk. This yogurt is buttery, silky, delicate, and addictively fattening. But it is superb. It is, unfortunately, marketed only in a small area of southern British Columbia, but may perhaps be distributed throughout our region in the future.

Both yogurt and buttermilk, as fermented milk, are a form of simple cheese, a kind of protocheese in which the curds have not been separated from the whey. Both, when drained in cheesecloth, will give a delicate, soft cheese. Proper cheese making, however, involves a few more steps such as heating the curds to firm them, further fermentation, pressing, etc. But fresh cheeses and cream cheeses can easily be made at home. They are tender, mutable creations. Cream cheeses in particular have a very short life-span. If they are sold commercially, they have to be stabilized and laced with preservatives to have any shelf life at all. The natural, unadulterated product will change in a period of only a few days and begin either a soft ripening fermentation, like a Brie or Coulommiers, or attract undesirable bacteria and molds, and spoil.

There appears a consensus among northwest cheese makers that you cannot use the ambiguous white cakes sold as "cream cheese" in our markets. These professionals maintain that cream cheese is easy to make and, following their instructions, I have found this to be true. I always make my own cream cheese now. This cream cheese also makes the best cheesecake. It does not have the gum arabic taste of the commercial product and stays light and fluffy in baking. Several small dairies in the Northwest make fresh cream cheese; The Pike Place Market Creamery in Seattle's Pike Place Market often has some for sale—just remember, it is for immediate consumption and will not keep long.

Cream cheeses can be made from milk ripened with buttermilk cultures, but the milk is best curdled with an animal (or vegetable) enzyme called rennet. The use of rennet in cheese making gives a firmer curd and a higher yield (i.e., more solids are precipitated from the milk). Cream cheeses made with rennet have more body and can be easily molded. Fresh cheeses with a firmer curd, such as cottage cheese, require the use of a rennet. Cottage cheese, a simple cheese made from unpressed curds bound with a dressing of milk or cream, can also be made at home, but acceptable commercial products are available. Darigold in Issaquah, Washington, makes an excellent natural cottage cheese. The company has experimented with preservatives to increase the shelf life of this cheese, but cheese maker Sam Culmback objected to the chemical taste of the additives, so now the cheeses are natural again and will remain so. These cottage cheeses have a shelf life of only about two weeks and should be consumed as fresh as possible (each container has a pull date).

A less common fresh cheese is made by the Scardillo family in Burnaby, British Columbia: a fresh ricotta. It is very light and should be consumed fresh with antipasti or fruit. This is the best commercially available cheese for cheesecake in the Northwest. It stays fresh for only seven to ten days and, to assure perfect quality control, the Scardillos sell this cheese only through two family-owned delicatessens in Vancouver. Cognoscenti come from as far away as Seattle and Portland to buy this uncommon delicacy.

Most of the cheeses made in the Pacific Northwest are firm or hard cheeses, that is, cheeses in which the curds have been drained, firmed up through heating, pressed to extract a high percentage of the free whey, further fermented to raise the lactic acid content as a natural barrier to spoilage by undesirable bacteria and molds, and aged to achieve maximum flavor. Among the simplest of these firm cheeses are the so-called farmer's cheeses, which are really nothing more than cottage or cream cheese curds that have been drained thoroughly and pressed in a cheese press. This does not mean that they are simple in taste and cannot be aged for some time to improve their flavor. Many simple cheeses are "washed-curd" cheeses: the curd is washed (more or less, depending on the type of cheese) after curdling to lower the acid level, and the milk sugar, or lactose, is washed from the curds at the same time to avoid souring the cheese. Such a cheese can be eaten almost immediately, but it will improve in flavor if it is stored in a cool, dark place for a year or more.

One of the most famous of these "simple" cheeses is Dutch Gouda, a firm cheese with excellent keeping qualities that was developed in the thirteenth century. It has been much copied throughout the world, with little success. But two Ferndale, Washington, farmers now successfully produce a Gouda-style cheese that may actually be better than the original. The secret of their success lies not so much in a magic cheese-making formula, but in the milk produced by their dairy cows from the lush grass grown in a very special miniclimate.

Verdant pastures throughout our region provide succulent, mineral-rich, and exceptionally nutritious forage for dairy cows. But there seems to be something unique about the meadows north of the Nooksack River where the fat soils (a highly productive amalgam of glacial and alluvial deposits and organic matter) grow—under the benign influence of our mild, moist climate—the kind of lush, savory grasses cows dote on. And those contented, well-fed cows do their best to turn the tasty greens into large volumes of superb milk.

In Ferndale, George and Delores Train have taken advantage of the quality of this milk to create several exquisite raw milk cheeses on their small Pleasant Valley Dairy farm. Raw milk cheeses, which depend on natural, milk, or airborne bacteria for their development, can be influenced by atmospheric conditions and, since the local climate reminded the Trains of the climate of southern Holland, where Gouda cheese is made, they decided to experiment with Gouda-style cheeses (instead of the Cheddars more commonly produced in the Northwest), when they began to make cheese for their own use some six years ago. The results of their experiments were so gratifying that the Trains decided to go public with their product; they have made cheese commercially since December of 1980.

The Trains have about thirty-five dairy cows, and they do not plan to increase their herd, no matter how much demand for their cheese rises (right now, there's a two-month waiting list). They sell the milk from the evening's milking as fresh raw milk (it is packed into half-gallon cartons like homogenized and pasteurized milk), and they make cheese from the morning's milk—a maximum of about two hundred seventy pounds of cheese per week (it comes in two- to six-pound wheels).

To most consumers (unless they have spent much time on farms, or even helped milk cows, the way I did in my younger days—and what ornery beasts those cows were; they did not like being milked by hand, and more likely than not, you risked being kicked across the room for an inept stroke), milk is an ambiguous white liquid that sprouts up on supermarket cooler shelves in convenient cardboard cartons or plastic bottles. But whole milk is more than that. It is a complex mixture of water, protein, minerals, milk sugar, milk fat, and trace elements. Raw milk gives a firmer curd and tastier cheese than processed milk, but exceptional care must be taken to make sure that the cows are healthy and that the milk is free of pathogens. Raw milk also contains a beneficial natural flora, a number of active microorganisms which aid the cheese making (these have to be reintroduced when cheese is made from pasteurized milk). It is the action of these bacteria which causes raw milk to curdle if it is left to age. The cheese maker speeds up and controls the curdling process by adding rennet, an enzyme derived from a calf's stomach, to the milk. George Train prefers using a natural calf rennet for making his cheeses, because cheese made in this fashion will age better and have a nicer flavor; but he also makes a small number of cheeses with a microbial enzyme to meet the requirements of vegetarian customers.

George Train mixes the fresh milk from the morning's milking with the rennet and a special "Gouda" culture, which will give the cheese its special character. The milk is then heated to a temperature of eighty-seven degrees Fahrenheit and allowed to sit for a while to age. As the rennet curdles the protein part of the milk solids, the casein, the milk solidifies into a soft gel. Assistant cheese maker Ray Schultz checks on the progress of the curd by pressing down onto the custardlike mass with the back of his hand. When the curd comes away cleanly from the sides of the vat, it is ready to be cut.

Ray Schultz cuts the curd gently, with special instruments called cheese harps (he first uses one with horizontal wires, then one with vertical wires), into small pieces of fairly homogeneous size. As the curd is cut, the solids separate from the whey, a thin greenish liquid which contains most of the milk's sugar and water (the fat stays with the casein). The curds must be of a fairly uniform size because they will be firmed up through heating, and they will not achieve proper texture and consistency if "cooked" unevenly. But first the bulk of the whey is drained. As the liquid runs out, the curds are restrained with the aid of a curd dam, a perforated sheet of stainless steel which is inserted into the vat, and with a sieve at the end of the drain pipe. Then hot water (one hundred degrees Fahrenheit) is gradually added to the curds, and the cheese is allowed to heat and solidify gently for a couple of hours. This water/whey mixture is drained off when the curds are sufficiently firm—of about the consistency of a fresh cream cheese (at this point any spices, herbs, or seasonings are added for the flavored cheeses).

The fresh curds are carefully scooped from the vat into individual cheese molds (these had to be specially ordered from Holland) and pressed. The solid balls of cheese are next soaked in a heavy brine (strong enough to float a fresh egg). This is the only salting they will receive. Pleasant Valley cheeses are, fortunately, not as oversalted as most commercial cheeses. After the cheeses have been brined sufficiently—some twenty-four hours for small cheeses, two days for larger ones—they are transferred to aging shelves. For the first thirty days, they are turned almost daily to assure an even distribution of moisture as they dry. They are then covered with red wax and aged for an additional thirty days. By law, raw milk cheeses must be aged for a minimum time of sixty days before they may be sold (this assures that the fermentation process of the cheese has killed off any pathogens which might have been present in the raw milk), but most Pleasant Valley cheeses are much older when they are sold. Pleasant Valley "Goudas" are true "vintage" cheeses: each is inscribed with the date of its manufacture.

Because these cheeses are completely natural, their taste will vary with the season. The best cheeses are made in May and in June when the new spring grasses have achieved their most luxurious growth, and then again in September, when the pastures which were seared by the summer's heat have been rejuvenated by fall rains and cool weather. But by October the grass loses its vigor, the days become short, and the weather turns cold. It is difficult to make natural cheeses in winter, when the weather is too chilly for the best development of beneficial bacteria and when the cows are fed on grass silage. Winter cheeses are gassier and have larger, more numerous eyes (this is when George Train makes a lot of "Swiss" cheese), but they are still delicious to eat. However, the Trains make most of their cheeses during the prime months and age them. I like the fresh, nutty taste of the sixty-day-old cheeses as well as the old, pleasantly sharp wheels which may have grown to perfection for a year or more.

Despite the great variety of cheese made in our region, the most popular cheeses made in the Northwest, as in the rest of the country, are the hard Cheddars, and their somewhat softer cousins, Colby and Monterey Jack. These cheeses are made from similar bacterial cultures; the main difference between the Cheddars and the Jacks and Colbies lies in the way they are handled after they have been heated. Jack and Colby, produced by modern factory methods, are basically identical cheeses. The Colby curds are commonly dyed to an orange shade with annatto, a tasteless and harmless South American vegetable dye (this supposedly gives the impression that the cheese is high in butterfat); the Jack curds are left white. In the making of both of these cheeses, the curds are washed to reduce the residual acidity after the whey has been drained off and then are salted and pressed. These mild, low-acid cheeses will not keep for very long. They are marketed at ten days to two weeks of age and should be eaten young.

With Cheddar, the whey is drained; but then the curds, whey still clinging to them, are left on tables to mat under their own weight and age ("cheddar") for several hours. This raises the lactic acid content of the curds and creates a favorable habitat for beneficial ripening bacteria. When the desired level of acidity is reached, the curd mats are broken up in a curd mill, salted, and pressed. Cheddars can age for a long time because of their higher acid content; the beneficial bacteria living in the cheese prevent spoilage and improve flavor by fostering a slow fermentation during the aging process. Mild Cheddars are usually sold at an age of about two months, medium Cheddars at four months, sharp Cheddars at six months or more, and extrasharp Cheddars are aged for at least one year. The best Cheddars of our region can age for two and a half to five years—and at that stage they can compare with the best in the country—though ours have a structure and taste that is uniquely northwestern, setting them apart from the Cheddars of other areas, such as New York or Vermont.

The first large-scale commercial Cheddar producer in the Northwest, the Tillamook County Creamery Association, invented a new type of this cheese, a Cheddar which becomes soft and smooth as it ages rather than dry and crumbly, a style which has influenced other cheese makers in our region ever since.

The lush meadows of Tillamook County are nearly free from frosts, but almost continuously soaked with moisture by the frequent coastal fogs and rains. They allow year-round feeding on fresh grass, making for happy dairy cows—and happy cows give large quantities of excellent milk. Some of this surplus was once turned into butter, some into cheese (as yet lacking in distinction, perhaps no different from the other farmer's cheeses and Cheddars produced in our region).

Only in 1894, after Peter McIntosh, an itinerant and very knowledgeable Canadian cheese maker, introduced the Tillamook farmers to the fine and complex art of making Cheddar, did the now-renowned Tillamook Cheddar cheese come into being. The farmers may not have known initially how to make cheese, but they sure knew when they had a good thing. They recognized that they had come up with something special, and by 1909 they had begun to standardize their cheese—to make sure its quality did not vary (which did in turn, of course, enhance their reputation with the American consumer)—and market it under the brand name Tillamook. A strange-sounding name doesn't exactly hurt either, especially in this country, and sales of the smooth Cheddar reached meteoric proportions throughout the West. The cheese has changed very little in the intervening years. Today's Tillamook Cheddar is still made from the raw milk (though some detractors claim the milk is actually pasteurized) of Holstein, Jersey, and Guernsey cows.

Unfortunately, modern cash flow demands make it difficult to age Tillamook Cheddar properly at the factory. And young Tillamook is really rather ordinary. The youngest Tillamook is aged for about three months—barely longer than your average Gouda—sharper Cheddar for six. You almost have to age your own extrasharp Cheddar; recently (due to a number of consumer complaints) extrasharp Cheddars which have aged for several years have sometimes been available at the cheese plant in Tillamook. These are luscious, creamy, flavorful, and well worth searching out. Cheeses show great individuality as they age (the season and sometimes even the weather can have an impact on the quality of a particular cheese batch) and not all Cheddars are destined for a great age. This is why well-aged Cheddars are so expensive: the cheese makers have culled all of the lesser cheeses, and only the best have survived to a ripe and flavorful old age.

Other commercial cheese plants in the Northwest have not been around as long as Tillamook, but several make excellent Cheddars in the Tillamook tradition. The Darigold plant in Chehalis and Olympia Cheese in Lacey participate with Tillamook in a cheese culture program sponsored by Oregon State University in Corvallis. Their cheeses differ somewhat because Darigold and Olympia pasteurize their milk.

Darigold once operated "the largest cheese plant in the world under one roof" in Lynden, Washington, but the company felt that cheese making did not pay, converted the Lynden plant to a milk dehydrator, and began to buy cheese from the mountain states and the Midwest. It did not work. Darigold quickly learned that cheese from other regions does not have the superb flavor of the cheese made from northwest milk—and the customers could tell the difference. So, Darigold built a new cheese plant in Chehalis and the quality is back to where it should be. No further changes are anticipated. Darigold is now Washington

State's largest cheese maker, but the company has proved that large size does not necessarily lead to a decline in quality. Darigold currently makes Jack, Colby, and Cheddar at Chehalis from milk obtained from dairies in Thurston, Lewis, and Pacific counties. The Darigold extrasharp Cheddar is a very well-made cheese that can age for years (one block at the plant is now seven years old and still improving) and acquire the fine flavor and texture demanded of the best aged cheeses.

The dry oak and ponderosa pine woodland of Hawk's Prairie is a strange setting for a northwestern cheese plant, but the Olympia Cheese Company does not depend on it for pasturage. It buys milk from all over the Northwest. Plant manager Gunnard Pylkki is one of the oldest and most respected cheese makers in the region and has made major contributions to the Oregon State University cheese program (the same program that has contributed so much to the quality of Tillamook and Darigold cheeses). Because of Olympia Cheese's good reputation, most of it is sold in other states.

The Washington Cheese Company in Mount Vernon is a newcomer among northwest cheese plants. It has been in operation for a few years only, and was founded by a group of dairy farmers who left the Darigold cooperative. Washington Cheese makes a number of raw milk and pasteurized washed curd Jacks and Colbies and white and yellow Cheddar from the rich milk, mostly Jersey and Guernsey, produced on the Nooksack and Skagit river floodplains. These cheeses are so mild as to be almost bland in flavor, very salty, low in acid, and should be consumed young, for they do not keep well. The Mount Vernon plant sells fresh, squeaky curds, both salted and unsalted, at its cheese store—these are very tasty and always an excellent buy.

Armstrong Cheddar, made in the small town of Armstrong in the asparagus fields of the Spallumcheen Valley by the Dairyland cooperative, is British Columbia's equivalent of Darigold cheese. It is a solid, somewhat coarse, salty yellow cheese which never quite reaches the quality of Oregon or Washington Cheddar.

At first glance, the small backwater of Sicamous, British Columbia, hidden in the tall forests at the southern shore of Shuswap Lake, seems an unlikely home for British Columbia's finest Cheddar. But this remote lake country, about halfway between Vancouver and Calgary, grows a rich, nutritious grass on its bottomlands. Lush grass on which cows love to feast, clean juicy grass which they convert into sweet delicious milk. The Dewitts' Dutchman Dairy is turning this creamy bounty into a tyrophile's dream. The Dewitts set out in the spring of 1982 to make the "best Cheddar cheese available," and they may be succeeding. Their product is a flavorful, very "cheesy" white Cheddar, a cheese with a taste and texture encountered only among the most noble of its kind. At this time, no really old Sicamous Cheddar can be sold since the cheese has been made for such a short time. But the Dewitts have laid down ample amounts in storage, and well-aged Cheddars should be available on a regular basis.

A truly unique Cheddar is made at Washington State University in Pullman, Washington. Cougar Gold is a firm, white cheese manufactured from surplus milk produced by the collegiate milch cows. It is superb, especially when aged for a year or longer, and possesses a delicious sharpness, fruitiness, and complexity. Washington State University alumni sometimes confuse their school's best product with a plain Cheddar which is also made by the academic dairies. Both cheeses are shipped in flattish, dated tin cans. Cougar Gold is expensive, but well worth the price. It is traditionally served at televised college football games.

Tillamook has dominated our consciousness of Oregon cheeses so much that we sometimes forget that southern Oregon has a tradition of cheese making of its own. Cheese has been made on the banks of the Coquille River for almost as long as it has been made at Tillamook, but Bandon, the region's small commercial center, has been even more isolated than Tillamook. The Coquille River is a quiet, pastoral river, lined by meadows which abut the weathered pilings of abandoned docks and rush and willow tangles along its banks. These lowlands are uncommonly tranquil. Herds of doe-eyed, fawn-colored Jersey cows and angular, black-and-white-checkered Holsteins graze in these pastures, and only the cries of seabirds penetrate the silence.

The village of Bandon started out as a river port and later transformed itself into a resort. Today Bandon would be merely another refueling stop on the coastal highway (U.S. 101), if it were not for its renowned cheese. It is the Cheddar, a rich, full-flavored cheese made primarily from Jersey milk (in both white and yellow versions) which brings visitors to Bandon, for the superb, extrasharp Cheddar, aged for several years, is only available at the cheese plant's small store. The other cheeses, even the fine, alder-smoked Cheddar (this is a true smoked cheese, without a trace of that modern abomination, liquid smoke), can be bought by mail; but the extrasharp can only be obtained here and is well worth this special trip. Bandon Cheddar was once carried by schooner to San Francisco, where gourmets appreciated the fine flavor of the well-aged cheese; today gourmets have to trek to Bandon to get a taste of the best.

A similar Cheddar is made in a most unlikely area. At first glance, southern Oregon's Rogue River and Bear Creek valleys do not look like prime dairy country. Heavyset beef steers graze in the dry oak woodland of the hillsides and vast pear orchards cover much of the valley floors and the lower slopes of the Siskiyous. But this first impression is deceptive. Shaded bottomlands and moist, hidden glens grow the kind of dense, sweet grass beloved by milch cows. Milk, cream, and cheese have been produced in these valleys since the early 1850s, when the Jacksonville gold rush attracted settlers; natural caves and the numerous abandoned mine shafts in the area provided convenient cold storage before refrigeration was widely available. Now only the Rogue River Valley Creamery at Central Point, just outside Medford, still makes cheese. Its excellent Cheddar is a dense yellow or white cheese which ages superbly. It is best consumed at several years of age, when it has become very crumbly, sharp, and nutty. If it seems strange that a Cheddar of such a high quality should be produced in Oregon's pear valley, it is stranger still that the creamery also makes one of the continent's best blue cheeses.

Blue cheeses are semifirm, internal-mold cheeses which have been purposely infected with a blue penicillin mold. The mold penetrates the cheeses as they age in caves, and gives them a special flavor and texture. Most blue cheeses on the market today are copies of Roquefort, a noble French sheep's milk blue cheese, of Gorgonzola, an equally select Italian cow's milk blue, and of Stilton, an English cow's milk blue. The American blue cheeses, popular primarily for use in indistinct salad dressings, are often quite coarse in flavor. Though well made enough for their intended primary purpose and for use in cooking, they are inadequate for being eaten alone or for accompanying some of the superbly luscious fruits grown in the Pacific Northwest.

But we are indeed fortunate, for our region produces one of the world's great blue cheeses. It is generally agreed among gourmets that the Oregon blue is a cheese of the highest quality—and one of the few truly singular blue cheeses made today. This outstanding cheese is silky when properly aged, with a strong blue marbling. Its taste is rich and creamy, with a perhaps imagined whisper of pear blossoms, a delicate tanginess, and a remote smoky undertaste. It is a very complex cheese, one of the most complex blues made, and it changes a great deal at different stages of its aging process. There is absolutely nothing simple, direct, and commercial about it. It is thus very hard to describe with any precision—it must be tasted! Fortunately, it, as well as the Cheddar (even the extrasharp), can be ordered from the creamery by mail.

Not all "blue" cheeses are made by design. The famous, rare English blue Cheshire and the even rarer blue Cheddar are but two examples of accidentally created culinary delights. I have only tasted a blue Cheddar once, and it was a very uncommon cheese, a blue goat's milk Cheddar. This cheese's "imperfection," its fortuitous infection with blue mold, was totally accidental—the cheese maker fervently wished he could reproduce the effect in a more reliable manner—but the taste which resulted from this accident was sublime.

This cheese was served at breakfast by Michael and Carmen Estes, Skagit County goat dairy farmers and makers of our region's only true goat's milk Cheddar. I had traveled to their cheese factory (in Marblemount, Washington, on the North Cascades Highway) in the company of Martin Waidelich, a *Bellingham Herald* photographer. Martin grew up as a dairy farmer's son in the upper Skagit Valley, and he was quite curious about tasting a locally produced goat cheese. Goats were not very popular during his childhood in the valley, and here was a farmer who not only had a hundred and two of the frisky creatures, but one who also made Cheddar, that standby filler of American cookery, from their milk. Martin's interest was considerably roused.

I had tasted the Marblemount cheese before, but I had never met the goats. Before the morning was over, I had become very close to them. Too close. They tried to eat me (or at least my clothes): we had worked our way across a large, slippery pasture so Martin could take photos of Michael and Carmen Estes with some of their cheese, all of their goats, and the glaciers of several North Cascades peaks behind the farm. I was idly watching, when Saturn, the head goat, decided to investigate me.

I could hear her coming; she was the only goat with a bell around her neck. Saturn brought several of her eager followers, about a dozen or so hungry young goats, along. This capricious court surrounded me, hemmed me in, stared, advanced, and nibble-nibbled, chomp-chomped. (Taking notes is quite difficult when a dozen goats nip at your shoes and pull your coattails.) I shooed them and shoved them away. Saturn was insulted. Her eyes glazed over, turned into narrow, yellow dragon's eyes; she snorted and lowered her head, ready to butt me. I made peace by leaving the pasture.

We had arrived at the Estes farm at daybreak to watch Carmen milk her goats. Her milking parlor is highly mechanized, very much like a milking parlor for cows, only all the equipment is reduced to a goat scale. Prior to milking, the milkers are separated from the other does and driven into a holding barn. From here they can walk up wooden ramps leading to the milking stations. Carmen lets four goats into the milking parlor at a time. They enter through a small door at one end and stand on a narrow, elevated shelf, nibbling grain from cribs while they are milked.

Carmen locks the goats' heads into the feeding station grid, washes the does' udders, dries the teats with paper towels, presqueezes a few drops of milk by hand from each teat—the initial spurt might be contaminated—and attaches the inflations (the suction units). The milk is sucked from the teats by a machine which emits a cacaphony of low moans and horrid gasping noises when the udder is dry. Carmen then removes the inflations and drops them into a washing solution; the teats are dipped into a blue teat dip which closes the orifice and fights bacteria; the goats' heads are freed from the crib grids; and the does exit by a small door opposite the entrance. Carmen washes and sterilizes the inflations, opens the entrance door, then repeats the performance. She milks some sixty-four goats each morning—in an hour and a half.

The milk flows from the milking stations through stainless steel pipes into a clean cooling and holding vat (the milk is not pasteurized). From here it can be pumped into the long, heated cheese-making vat. Each of these stages takes place in a separate room. The entire operation is sparklingly clean (special care must be taken with goat milk to make sure no "goaty" taste creeps in) and highly efficient. Little wonder, for Michael Estes is a consulting engineer who has designed and built the cheese house and equipment himself.

The cheese making itself differs little from the standard Cheddar making process. After the curds have been drained, cheddared, and pressed, the cheeses are held in a series of special cheese rooms which are cooled with well water that is pumped through special heat exchange units (there is no mechanical refrigeration anywhere in this plant). Michael Estes makes his Cheddar in twenty-pound wheels—he feels that a smaller size will not allow the cheese to age properly—and he makes only some six or seven wheels a week. The cheeses are finished in two ways: cheeses that are meant to be sold young (these are made with a lower acidity than cheeses designed to be aged) stay in the conditioning room for only two or three days—long enough to dry out and form a rind—during which time they develop a plain, mottled finish; cheeses that will be aged are kept in the conditioning room for one or two weeks, to develop a black mold finish before they are stored in an aging room. They will then age for a year or more. Michael Estes also makes a superb, creamy white feta from goat's milk (this cheese is sold in buckets and glass jars, not in plastic wrap), and he is considering the production of soft-ripened goat cheeses (these will be pasteurized to allow for better control of the white mold cultures).

Currently, ever since the Kapowsin goat cheese plant in Graham ceased its operation, there is only one cheese plant in the Northwest that makes soft-ripened cheeses. The Blue Heron Cheese Company in Tillamook (just down the road from the famous creamery, but unrelated) makes two soft-ripened cheeses from cow's milk in the French tradition. These are sold as "Camembert" and "Brie," but they are quite different in taste and texture, quite unlike the French originals, and are really unique creations. The Brie can be ordered by mail; the Camembert can only be bought at the cheese plant.

Cooking and cheese making in the Northwest have not only been influenced by the traditions of England, France, and the Scandinavian countries, but also by attitudes introduced by the great multitude of immigrants from the countries of southern Europe: Italian truck farmers, Croatian fishermen, Greek restaurateurs, and Sephardic shopkeepers all contributed their share. But Mediterranean cooking calls for special cheeses, and it is little wonder that several specialty cheese factories have prospered in the Northwest.

The Castrilli family has made cheese in Washington for several generations, first in a small dairy near Hamilton and now in a modern plant in Kent (though much of their milk still comes from the northern counties). Currently they make only mozzarella, a *pasta filata* (spun or stretched curd) cheese. Some of it is sold fresh under the company's Green River label, but most of it goes to restaurants and pizza houses.

The Mazza family runs a more complex operation, and they have found the perfect location for their plant, a habitat which provides conditions similar to those found in parts of Italy. Some six hundred years ago, a minor eruption melted part of the western glaciers of Mount Rainier. An immense flood rushed down from the Puyallup Glacier, covering the valley of the Puyallup River with volcanic mud. Today these fertile, mineral-rich deposits support a thriving dairy industry. The Mazzas located in Orting, in the shadow of Mount Rainier in the 1920s, and they have been making excellent cheeses from the local milk ever since. The cheese plant makes three cheeses, all from well-guarded secret family recipes: a provolone, a mozzarella, and a feta. They are sold under the Mazzas' Seal Brand label.

The Greek-style feta, the only cheese of this type made in the Northwest, is the Mazza family's best cheese. It is a chalky, crumbly cheese with a zesty sourish flavor and is traditionally stored in brine. The Mazza version contains only cow's milk, and is thus not as exciting as the superb feta made by Michael Estes at Marblemount, yet it develops nicely and can be stored for at least three or four years if it is kept in its bath of brine. With age, Mazza feta becomes creamy, quite sharp, and develops a uniquely rich flavor. The high quality of this cheese is appreciated by the crews of Greek ships visiting Puget Sound: they always stock up on large quantities of Mazza feta.

While neither of the Mediterranean cheeses made by the Mazza or Castrilli families are made with goat's milk, several other cheeses made in the southern European tradition are, and they are all made by one tiny cheese plant.

In the summer of 1982, as I enjoyed a delicious lunch at La Petite Maison in Olympia, Chef Rick O'Reilly told me about several exciting goat cheeses he had discovered, excellent for eating fresh and for cooking. These cheeses from Briar Hills Dairies in Chehalis have been made in an old, ivy-covered creamery since 1946, but they have only recently become available to the gourmet market. Briar Hills has kept a low profile for most of its corporate existence, refusing to advertise its cheeses (not even the company's phone number was listed), and sales were by word of mouth alone, until the old plant was acquired in 1981 by three Lewis County dairy goat farmers, William Moomau and Don and Marilyn Wells. Fortunately, the new owners have begun to distribute their products more widely throughout the Northwest.

Briar Hills buys the milk for its cheeses from five Lewis County goat dairies (with a combined herd of about four hundred prime milkers). The plant currently produces four raw milk goat cheeses. Chehalis Natural, a firm white cheese, is made from a Greek formula. It becomes moderately sharp and crumbly with age and is good for eating with fruit and excellent for cooking, especially in Greek or other Mediterranean dishes. Chehalis Caraway is a cheese I like, in spite of my long-standing prejudice against flavored cheeses. I prefer natural cheeses because in the flavored ones the seasoning is too often used to disguise an inferior taste. But the addition of caraway to Chehalis Natural has created a delightful blend of cheese and herb, perfect for desserts. My favorite, Cascadian, is a very firm, mild white goat cheese of superb flavor and texture, tasting of fresh curds and hazelnuts and keeping its mildness even after several years of aging; yet it is more complex than many Cheddars. This is without doubt one of the best firm goat cheeses made in this country, much better than the insipid goat "Cheddars" from California or Wisconsin commonly sold in our health food boutiques. Briar Hills' last cheese is truly unique, and perhaps a bit of an oddity. Viking is an almost impossibly rich, deep-brown whey cheese, full-flavored, with a taste of caramel-chocolate and licorice—a kind of hyperconcentrated gjetost. (Briar Hills also makes the Northwest's best butter, a delicately flavored goat butter.)

Cheese making in the Northwest is a continuous and flexible art that has its ups and downs. Sometimes old, well-established cheeses vanish from the market, usually without forewarning, or new cheeses appear, bide for a while, and go away. Some cheeses have only a very limited market, like the excellent mozzarella and the three different types of ricotta made by the Scardillo family in Burnaby, British Columbia, for the Italian community of greater Vancouver. Milk and cheese production in British Columbia is subjected much more to rules and restrictions than in Oregon and Washington. And small operations are frowned upon.

The Grisnich family once made a pleasant, sharp raw milk "Gouda" on their Chilliwack farm in the Fraser Valley, but they soon ran into trouble with provincial authorities, since it is illegal in British Columbia to make cheeses from raw milk (in the U.S. it is, of course, legal to make raw milk cheeses, provided they are aged for a minimum of sixty days; but it is illegal to import them). The Grisnichs have been forced to install a pasteurizer and now make a slightly different cheese. It is closer in texture and taste to a German Tilsit than to a Dutch Gouda. This cheese can only be bought at the farm.

There are no true cottage cheeseries in British Columbia. I was informed of this fact by one minister of agriculture who proudly implied that the province did not care about such a riffraff of small manufacturers. Canada, a small country in terms of population, likes to think big. We are much better off on our side of the border, for there are a multitude of exciting cheeses made in cottage operations throughout the Northwest. Most limit themselves to the milk from the family cow or from a handful of dairy goats and thus make cheese on a very small scale. But these "homemade" cheeses can be very well made and have an exquisite flavor.

It is always well worth exploring your own neighborhood—you may find many pleasant surprises. Most of these cottage and backyard cheese makers are not licensed to sell their products, but they are always willing to share or barter. I, for example, make a lot of cream cheese from both goat's and cow's milk and regularly share these cheeses with friends. One word of warning here: if you make cream cheese from raw milk and cream, make sure the cows or goats from whom the milk came were healthy and had no diseases of any kind. In the summer of 1983, several people became seriously ill and two died when they ate queso blanco made from the raw milk of a cow whose udder was infected with *Streptococcus zooepidemicus*. These cheeses would have been fine and safe to eat if they had been aged for the requisite sixty days—an impossibility with a cream cheese. So, if you must use raw milk for cream cheeses (I do), make sure the cows are healthy. If you're unsure, pasteurize the milk.

We will see many exciting new developments in cheese making in the Northwest in the near future. It seems that just about every valley west of the Cascades has someone who is thinking of making commercial cheese on a small scale, but a number of dairymen in the Yakima Valley are thinking big: they are planning a large-scale production of Dutch-style cheeses.

In recent years, Northwesterners have become very aware of the distinct qualities of goat's and cow's milk from different breeds and from different areas, and they are more conscious than ever before of the many varieties of excellent cheese that can be made in our region. Consumer awareness is the cheese maker's best friend, and the key to his economic survival. It is significant that northwest cheese eaters are beginning to appreciate our cheeses for what they are, not because they may be cast in the mold of a European original. I am particularly pleased that our most successful cheeses (from both artistic and commercial standpoints) have transcended their stylistic origins and are on their way to becoming true northwest originals.

But strange novelties may also be in store for us. Llamas are becoming quite popular as pack animals in our mountains, and I often wonder if anyone has yet tried to milk a llama or if their milk makes good cheese. Can you milk a llama? How fat is it? I am certain we will find out, sooner or later. And just wait till someone starts importing yaks!

Basic Cream Cheese

Whole milk or half milk/half cream   2 quarts
Buttermilk (preferably Darigold or Tillamook)   4 tablespoons
Rennet   ¼-ounce packet
Water   1 tablespoon

1. Heat milk to 100°, add buttermilk, stir thoroughly, and cover pot. (The longer you leave it to culture, the stronger the final cheese will be.)
2. Dissolve rennet (available from health food and gourmet shops throughout the Northwest) with water in a cup.
3. Reheat "started" milk to 100°, stir in dissolved rennet, cover pot, and let rest for another 2 to 3 hours. After that time, a soft curd will have "set," or separated from the whey.
4. Line a colander or cheese mold with washed cheesecloth, gently spoon curds into mold, and let whey drain off for 8 to 10 hours in a cool room.
5. Scrape down curds clinging to sides of cheesecloth and fold down cheesecloth. If you use a mold, you may press down curds with a heavy jar that fits inside (gradually fill with water to slowly increase weight). If you use a colander, tie cheesecloth into a bag after most of the whey has drained and suspend cheese above a container to drain off more whey and to let it compact under its own weight.
6. The higher the cream content of milk mixture, the richer cheese will be—and the softer and more difficult to handle curd will be.

Makes 6 to 8 ounces

Crème Fraîche

Crème Fraîche is the kind of thing culinary snobs like to veil in a cloud of mystery. There's really nothing to it, yet it is very essential in a number of tasty dishes. Here is Virginia Fuller's recipe.

Whipping cream   1 cup
Buttermilk (preferably Darigold or Tillamook)   1 cup

1. Mix cream and buttermilk.
2. Let stand and culture at room temperature for at least 8 hours.
3. Stir and refrigerate until needed.

Note: The longer you let it culture, the thicker it will be. If you make more than you can or want to use, pour the rest into your food processor and beat it with the steel blade until it turns into butter.

Makes 6 servings

Small Curd Cottage Cheese

Here is a quick cottage cheese recipe that makes very good cheese despite its simplicity. This is a rennetless cheese that will have a softer texture and smaller curd than a rennet-curdled cheese, but it has a pleasant sourish taste and will keep in the refrigerator for about 1 week. It is delicious when eaten alone, excellent with fresh fruit, and it may be used in any recipe calling for cottage cheese.

Skim milk 1 gallon
Buttermilk 4 tablespoons

1. Warm milk to 72°. Stir in buttermilk. Cover pot to set for 16 to 24 hours at 72°. (This is quite easy to do if you have heated your milk in a heavy clay pot. I like to use a large Chinese sandy pot which retains heat exceptionally well.)
2. After curd has coagulated, cut it into ¼-inch cubes and let it set for 15 minutes.
3. Raise temperature of curd 1 degree a minute until it reaches 100°. Stir every several minutes to keep curds from matting.
4. After keeping curds at 100° for 10 minutes and stirring regularly, raise temperature to 112° over a 15-minute period (again at a rate of about 1 degree a minute).
5. Hold temperature at 112° for 30 minutes or until curds are firm. (The test for firmness is very "scientific"; squeeze a curd particle between thumb and forefinger. If the curd has a custard consistency inside, it is not ready and should be cooked longer.)
6. When curds are cooked sufficiently, let them settle to bottom of pot for 5 minutes.
7. Carefully pour off the whey, making sure not to lose any curds.
8. Line a colander with cheesecloth and pour curds into it. Let them drain for several minutes. If a less sour cottage cheese is desired, curds can be washed by dipping the bag of cheesecloth into a bowl of cool water: dip curds several times and allow to drain for several minutes. Next, rinse curds in a bowl of ice water to cool, and return bag to colander to drain for 5 minutes.
9. To salt and cream curds, place them in a bowl and break up any pieces that are matted together. Add several tablespoons of heavy cream to produce a creamier texture. Add salt to taste and blend well.

Variations: You may make a goat's milk cottage cheese in a similar fashion: follow the same steps as above, but add a small amount of rennet to the culture after the temperature has been raised to 72°, and do not raise the temperature over 102° when cooking the curds.

You may also press the curd to get a hard farmer's cheese. But it is better to make a hard cheese from a hard cheese recipe that calls for rennet—especially if you plan on aging the cheese.

Makes about 1½ pounds cottage cheese

Sour Cream

Whipping cream   1 pint
Yogurt   1 teaspoon

1. Stir yogurt into whipping cream.
2. Let sit for a couple of days in a warm (but not hot) place.

Note: The best sour cream is made by letting unpasteurized cream (from a certified dairy) sour naturally at room temperature for a few days.

Variations: You may produce a quick sour cream by stirring a teaspoon of lemon juice into a pint of pasteurized whipping cream and letting it stand in a warm place for an hour or so.

Or blend a tablespoon of soured raw milk into a pint of pasteurized sour cream and let stand overnight.

Or substitute Crème Fraîche (see Index) for sour cream.

Makes about 1 pint

Salmon Caviar Yogurt Dip

Good with unsalted crackers or crisp raw vegetables. Serve with a chilled, dry sauvignon blanc or semillon, or with a good lager beer.

Plain yogurt   ⅔ cup
Salmon caviar   ¼ cup
Parsley   1 tablespoon minced
Onion (and juice)   2 tablespoons grated
Dijon mustard   1 teaspoon

1. Combine all ingredients in bowl and mix thoroughly.
2. Serve at once or cover and chill.

Serves 6 to 8 (Makes about 1 cup)

Eggs—Fish and Fowl

At the precociously mature age of six, I made a strategic mistake which would affect my appreciation of eggs for half a dozen years: I took an intimate look at a chicken. I had, of course, looked at chickens before, but only in a cursory fashion. I couldn't help it, actually, I grew up with the feathery beasts ranging about my backyard. But never before, until that fateful day, had I beheld the true nature of a chicken or contemplated its chickenness.

An awful truth struck me: our hens and roosters were ugly, strange-looking birds. Big-thighed with long, scaly shanks and grubby claws, they had chunky bodies, raggedy tails, and tiny heads with large beaks and—curious to behold—red combs and wattles. Worst of all, their beady little eyes were incapable of expressing any emotion, except a greedy, ceaseless desire for food. The ugliness of our fowl exceeded that of any other chickens I have known.

A hen's egg is such a lovely, smooth, clean, white or brown *objet d'art* that I had never really considered where <u>exactly</u> it came from. A hen squatted, cackled, rose again, and there, o miracle, was an egg. Finally, after much stealth, I managed to come close enough to see exactly where the egg came from. I was shocked! I kept the awful secret to myself for years; it seemed too terrible to share, even with close friends. And I did not eat another egg for half a dozen years (it was, of course, the delicious, tempting scent of cooked eggs that lured me back to the feast).

Accident must have achieved just the right balance of breeding traits in our motley hens, which allowed them to create a perfection of yolk and white, of taste and texture, in their eggs. Or perhaps our hens were accidentally fed the right mix of grain, weeds, worms, and bugs to flavor their eggs properly. Or maybe the cool climate helped—chicken eggs produced in hot or muggy climes do not have the exquisite taste of eggs from cooler regions. Then again, it may have been a combination of all of these factors, for not until I moved to the Pacific Northwest, where the climate is pleasantly temperate and where chickens are fed on barley and wheat, did I once again encounter such good eggs.

Luckily, I never got around to watching how fish rid themselves of their eggs, though, strangely enough, it never bothered me when my mother seasoned herring salads by squirting the milt from a "ripe" male herring over a mixture of marinated herring chunks, roe, beets, pickles, and onions.

I learned early that a herring—or other fish—that still contains milt or roe is quite good to eat. The eggs and sperm add a delicious tang to sauces, garnishes, or stuffings for the fish. Yet once fish have spawned naturally, their flesh softens and becomes unfit for gourmet palates. Their eggs and sperm are lost into the water (as a general rule, though there is some internal fertilization among fish, the female releases her eggs into the water and a male squirts his milt over the eggs to fertilize them). Except for the herring: this fish comes inshore to spawn and the large masses of its adhesive ova attach themselves to seaweeds, eelgrasses, submerged rocks or branches, and other suitable objects. The roe, which by now has been fertilized, remains perfectly edible and is delicious to eat.

The herring roe fishery along our coasts is a multimillion-dollar industry. Both the unspawned females and the egg-bearing seaweed fronds are harvested. Almost the entire production is shipped to Japan, where these delicacies are properly appreciated. Herring spawn during a short period of several weeks in late winter and early spring. Their eggs may often be so abundant that they are tossed onto beaches in undulating windrows. Predators like herring roe even better than the fish itself, and a mad feeding frenzy accompanies the spawning. Seabirds and mammals and fish gather in large flocks to feast on the aggregates of silvery blue herring and their pale eggs.

Gulls, cormorants, murres, and ducks attack the herring schools from above; seals, porpoises, and fishermen charge them from the water; and salmon, squid, and crab pounce upon the eggs as soon as they are released from the oviducts. It is a mad submarine carousal of birth and instant destruction, where every animal preys and is in turn preyed upon while the herring frantically spawn. Waters opaque with ova and sperm and blood and cephalopod ink veil the frenetic conflict. It is surprising that any herring or eggs survive at all to reproduce and to be harvested by men.

On the outer coast, the herring spawning season often coincides with rough weather, but the fishermen cannot afford to wait. The herring might sneak into the coves and, escaping the idle nets, might spawn and be gone before the weather clears and with them much of the year's profits. Little surprise that a frenzy possesses the fishermen, a frenzy born of the storms and roiling waves, and a reflection of the underwater turmoil of the spawning fish and hungry predators. Herring season on the outer coast, in the deep, narrow inlets of Vancouver Island's western shores, and especially in the small fishing villages of Bamfield, Ucluelet, and Tofino, is something else. It is the equivalent of the Klondike gold rush coming back to life again once a year.

Throngs of eager fishermen looking for quick riches (a single catch may net as many as twelve million fish) flood the coast in boats, often dilapidated, ranging from wooden skiffs to modern factory ships (in an early 1983 check by the Canadian Coast Guard, some 90 percent of the vessels failed the voluntary inspection), fishing as long as the fish run, crowding bars and brothels and boarding houses between laps or living it up on the rafted vessels of the impromptu boat towns which spring up in every protected cove. No one ever sleeps until the runs are over.

The ripe herring are scooped up in trawls or trapped in purse seines and gill nets. They must be fresh to assure a good quality of roe; their still-writhing bodies are torn open, the sacs of ova carefully removed and iced or frozen immediately. The empty herring shells are sent to reduction plants to be turned into fish meal. This is a rather outrageous waste of such a tasty fish, but the fishermen are paid according to the percentage of oviferous females their catch contains; they receive a high price for egg-rich fish and but a pittance for the fish-meal bunch.

Once the herring have completed the spawning cycle (their played-out schools chased back to sea by seals and salmon) but before their eggs begin their rapid embryogeny, fishermen collect the edible seaweeds which have become heavy with adherent eggs. Roe attached to kelp has long been a delicacy in the Orient, but the white fishermen learned about this delicacy from the native tribes of West Coast people for whom the annual herring spawn meant a delectable and nutritious addition to the larder. The West Coast people suspended hemlock branches in the water to trap the sticky spawn and later dried and/or smoked the egg clusters for consumption during the lean winter days, when storms made fishing too hazardous (even now, large, modern herring boats are lost to the winds and waves each season).

Today, the egg-laden kelp is cleaned and then pickled in a heavy brine. It is often packed into small jars and is readily available in this form in Japanese and other oriental markets. This roe can be eaten right from the jar—after a quick rinse to remove excess salt—kelp and all. The small, firm, almost rubbery clusters of roe which were removed from unspawned female herrings are very delicious. The Japanese prize them as a traditional dish of the (lunar) New Year, and their high cost has earned them the nickname "yellow diamonds." Herring roe can be eaten straight from the fish, it may be salted like caviar, poached, or used in croquettes and pâtés, or it may be marinated in sweet sake and soy sauce and served on sushi.

Herring is the only fish in our region that is pursued primarily for its roe and it is the only one whose roe is collected even after it has been ejected from the fish. The edible roe of other fish are collected incidentally when the fish are processed for their flesh and, more often than not, they are simply thrown away as the fish are cleaned. Roe for which there is a regular market demand, such as the eggs of salmon, sturgeon, cod, burbot (almost the entire production of burbot roe goes to Japan), and shad, are often available in specialty seafood markets and gourmet shops (see Appendix), but the gourmet has to collect many of the less common—though sometimes exceptionally delicious—roe himself, as opportunity permits. This is especially true of the tasty spawn of our saltwater invertebrates.

Sea urchins are sold during the spawning season, from about August to April (sometimes as late as early summer), by some northwest fishmongers, but these echinoderms' gonads and roe (the two are hard to separate) are more flavorful when the animals are collected fresh. The urchins can be cracked like eggs and eaten whole in the Mediterranean fashion, or only the mustard-colored roe may be eaten in the Japanese fashion. It is the latter morsel which is most popular in the Pacific Northwest.

The taste of sea urchin roe can vary widely, from a bland saltiness to a rich, mangolike fruitiness. No one quite seems to know why these taste variations occur—they appear to be unrelated to seasonal or environmental conditions—unless it is true, as John Steinbeck once stated, that male sea urchins taste sweet and females sour. But how do you tell a male sea urchin from a female? Only the females contain eggs, of course. Perhaps the variation in taste signals a difference between fertilized and unfertilized eggs? The roe (mixed with the gonads) is delicious when spread on sushi or canapés, and it adds a nice flavor to sauces and omelets. It is an acquired taste; but keep trying, it is bound to grow on you!

Black Katy chitons, segmented molluscs found grazing on algae-covered intertidal rocks, also contain edible eggs. These two-and-a-half-inch shellfish show color variations ranging from pitchy black to dark brown tones. For some reason, the lighter colored Katys have the best taste. The gonads and egg masses are very dense and look somewhat like little red or orange tongues. These commonly ooze from the animals' bodies when about half the shell plates have been pulled off. They may be eaten raw or cooked, like sea urchin roe and gonads.

Abalone roe is also edible and quite delectable. It is a light orange color and very dense, looking more like a liver than aggregates of eggs. Another molluscan roe shaped like a tongue is that from scallops. The pinkish gonads and spawn of this delicious bivalve may be eaten straight from the shell, small though the tidbits are, or they may be used to garnish the scallops' adductor muscles when these are served as sautéed nuggets.

The roe of a number of crustaceans are also quite tasty. Larger than other invertebrate ova, the eggs of crabs, shrimps, and crawfish look somewhat like small-egged caviar. Capturing female Dungeness crabs and their roe is illegal, but the eggs of other crab species, especially those of the large red rock crab, may be collected. Shrimp and crawfish, if not trapped by the gourmet himself, must always be bought fresh and whole to make sure one has the chance of getting crustaceans' delectable eggs. Crabs carry their bittersweet roe under their belly flap (this gapes widely as the eggs bulge, sometimes making walking difficult for the female); shrimp and crawfish transport their ova attached to the underside of their tails. These roe may be eaten like fresh fish eggs and are particularly good in sauces or garnishes designed to accompany their parent dish.

As far as I know, gourmets eat only the roe from female invertebrates (with the possible exception of "milky" sea urchins), though we eat the gonads of both sexes. But the roe of male fish, also known as soft roe or milt, is consumed quite regularly by those gourmets who are not too squeamish to eat tasty sperm. Milt can be quite delectable, and it may be used in a number of different ways. The most simple of these is a soft roe butter which is prepared by grinding the poached and cooled milt of various fishes (after removing the large center vein) in a mortar with an equal amount of fresh butter and then rubbing this mixture through a sieve. Herring and carp milt are especially good for this preparation. Milt butter may be added to seafood sauces; it can be spread over steaks or fillets of lean fish, such as sole or cod, before they are broiled; or the milt butter may be spread on toast and crackers and garnished with some chopped parsley, chives, or with a dab of caviar.

A positively sybaritic dish can be made from very fresh herrings swollen with milt: sprinkle the ungutted fish with salt and pepper on both sides. Let them sit in a flat clay, glass, or china dish for about six minutes. Pour a marinade made from nine-tenths wine (a rich, sweet dessert wine such as a muscat or late-harvest riesling) and one-tenth vinegar (preferably a heavy balsamico) over the fish. Remove the herrings from the marinade after about six hours, pat the fish dry, and smoke them over alder or applewood chips for a couple of hours. Carefully remove the milt, gut and fillet the herrings, and bone them as completely as possible (use tweezers if necessary). Rub the smoked soft roe through a sieve, add one teaspoon of mustard (Dijon or Düsseldorf), a half cup of apricot seed oil (a little at a time), and a teaspoon of a good white wine vinegar to the milt. Cut the herring fillets slantwise into strips, place them individually on slices of dark rye bread, and pour the milt sauce over them. Sprinkle with chopped parsley or shallots. They may be served cold, as appetizers.

Milt may also be baked in pastry shells, sautéed in butter, blended into mayonnaises or sauces, mixed into salad dressings, used as a delectable stuffing for baked potatoes, or served as a garnish for braised or poached fish.

The "hard" roe or spawn of several fish are made up of eggs so small that they seem more like milt than caviar. Cod roe, for example, is almost pastelike, with a pleasantly delicate fishy taste. It may be substituted for anchovy paste, and it is good as a flavoring agent in sauces or salad dressings. Cod roe is also delicious spread on sushi. The small-egged roe of other fish, such as shad, may be treated in a similar fashion.

The fish roe of the Pacific Northwest have been explored only incompletely by gourmets—there is lots of room for individual discoveries. Only one of our fish appears to have a toxic roe, the cabezon, a large sculpin. This fact was not established by taste tests, however, but by a marine biologist's observation that the egg masses of the cabezon were not eaten by gulls and other predators, even when they were exposed to full view at low tide (the pikes, who are also said to have poisonous roe, do not occur in our area). But the native tribes of the Pacific Northwest once treated just about all of our fish roe as special delicacies, and there are many different fish roe in our region that are perfectly good to eat and often exceptionally delicious.

I follow a simple rule of thumb when I first taste a fresh fish roe hitherto unknown to me: I cut a small hole into the membrane enclosing the eggs and extract a few of the shiny globules with the tip of a wooden spatula (all fish eggs should have as little contact with metal as possible, for metal spoils their taste). I slowly savor them to check on their consistency, aroma, and taste. If they taste good as they come from the sac, I will serve them, lightly salted, on crackers, toast, or sushi. If the taste leaves something to be desired, I gently sauté or poach the roe. Cooking can really improve the flavor of some fish eggs, and the cooked roe may be used in sauces, pâtés, or stuffings.

Sometimes, though not often, I find a roe whose taste really fails to excite me. In that case I rescue the eggs for the table and make them palatable by spicing them quite heavily, usually with a Mexican chili salsa (anything becomes "tasty" if only enough salsa is applied). All fish eggs are highly nutritious and, as long as they are fresh and unspoiled, it would be a shame to throw them out, even if their taste does not match that of the finest salmon or sturgeon caviars. But a certain amount of caution should be used. I always taste the roe from several different individuals of a species before making up my mind about them: roe with a less than desirable taste may be at an awkward stage in their development, or they may not be as fresh as they should be.

Fish eggs should always be absolutely fresh, unless they have been converted into caviar by judicious salting, or cooked, in which case they must always be chilled, especially when they are removed from the cooler and exposed to the warmth of the dining room table. Roe may spoil quickly if they are kept too warm: this is one reason why caviar should always be served on a bed of crushed ice. The roe of different fish vary widely in flavor, but, when they are fresh, each has a unique taste. It is always exciting to find an as yet untasted fish roe and, from time to time, I make pleasant discoveries where I least expect them.

Last spring, Sinclair Philip (of Sooke Harbour House fame) and I decided to indulge in a thorough exploration of the grocery stores and fish markets of Vancouver's Chinatown. This city within a city is now North America's second largest Chinese community (after San Francisco) and, its population swelled by recent immigrants, it seems to become more Chinese and less occidental almost from one day to the next. This culture change is progressing so rapidly that even Chinese-American visitors encounter difficulties in dealing with all of the new and exciting foodstuffs offered for sale in the numerous retail stores. We were not to be disappointed in our search for exotic foods. Aside from the diverse offerings of strange dried or frozen or pickled foods, such as Asian fish, *trepang* (whole dried sea cucumber), blanched sea horses (for tea or soup), mushrooms of scurrilous shapes, and unfamiliar, locally grown vegetables, we found quantities and varieties of fresh northwest clams, scallops, and fish from live carp and greenlings to cleaned and iced deepwater fish.

Toward the end of the day, we inspected several freshly delivered rockfish in a tiny seafood shop on Pender Street. They had just been gutted, and I discovered two elongated, yellowish pouches lying on the ice next to a large orange rockfish. I asked what the sausage-shaped, four-inch-long objects were, and the fishmonger told me in his broken English (between his accent and mine, we had quite a communication problem) that they were the fresh roe of the orange rockfish and, yes, they were perfectly edible and delicious. He suggested I poach them in hot water. Sinclair asked if they could be eaten raw and received an affirmative reply. These roe were ridiculously inexpensive, a dollar and a half per pound, which came to about fifty cents for the two of them.

It seemed strange to us, but neither Sinclair nor I had ever heard of anyone eating the roe of rockfish. Later that evening, in my kitchen, I took a good look at my culinary acquisition. The roe were very firm, their enclosing membrane seemed a bit tough, like sausage skins, and they were held together at their tips by a short piece of membrane, again like sausages. Unable to judge the size of the ova through the opaque sheathing, I made a small incision into one of the membranes and a multitude of tiny yellow-orange eggs burst forth. I spread a few of them onto a cracker. They were quite delicious, with a taste that reminded me of shad roe. Though these eggs were perfectly edible raw, I next decided to follow the Chinese fishmonger's advice and gently poached the roe in hot water. Since they looked so much like seafood sausages, I decided to treat them like sausages, pricking their skins with the top of a sharp bamboo skewer to make sure they would not burst. One of them burst anyway, but the roe had firmed up from the heat and the individual eggs continued to cling together.

Cooking altered the color and flavor of the rockfish roe. They turned quite pale and began to emit a delicious aroma which resembled freshly cooked crab and their taste became correspondingly crablike, but their texture retained a delicate crunch. I bound a part of these fish eggs with a delicate mayonnaise and spread the mixture onto pieces of toast. Then I carefully broke up the remaining egg clusters, pulling out all of the connecting tissues and membranes, and salted them lightly. They tasted superb, folded into an omelet. The roe-spread toast and a bottle of 1981 semillon from Associated Vintners were a perfect accompaniment. I had inadvertently discovered a new gourmet treat—and all because of my curiosity about the odd, sausagelike objects lying on ice in a Chinatown fish market.

Fresh rockfish roe is also delicious on sushi, as are the eggs of a number of different fish, from the golden roe of trout to the orange ova of smelt. Herring eggs are sometimes marinated, but other fish eggs, especially large- and medium-sized ones, are eaten either fresh or salted on sushi. All edible roe may be sautéed or gently fried or poached. The liver and roe of the burbot (also called ling or loche), a freshwater member of the cod family, are delicious fried together. This dish is very popular in western Canada, where the fish itself is often discarded or fed to the dogs (this is a shame, since a properly prepared burbot is very good to eat). Burbot are commonly caught through the ice (Banks Lake in eastern

Washington is a good spot), and they spawn in midwinter. This allows the lucky fishermen to get the fish home in prime condition. The burbot's liver is very high in vitamins (it is said to equal that of the saltwater cod) and contains a nutritious oil.

The roe of carp are commonly cooked and served as a garnish with the fish, but they are also good on crackers, toast, or sushi. So are the eggs of goldfish (either the pond or aquarium variety), minnows, daces, chubs, and suckers. I have never heard of anyone eating the large yellow eggs of the channel catfish (a common catch in the rivers bordering the Palouse), but the small, oval, sticky eggs of lampreys (perhaps our most misunderstood "fish") have long been a gourmet's delight.

The roe of lumpfish, whitefish, salmon, and sturgeon are commonly processed into caviar before they are eaten. Much of the lumpfish caviar consumed in the Pacific Northwest is imported from Iceland (where these weird fish grow to a length of almost two feet), and a large share of our whitefish caviar comes from the Great Lakes. Yet representatives of these fish are fairly common in our waters, and the gourmet willing to undergo the trouble of searching for them will be well rewarded—at least in the case of the whitefish.

Two things speak against eating the commercially processed eggs of lumpfish and whitefish: they are commonly dyed black with sticky, greasy coal-tar derivatives to make them look like sturgeon caviar and they are pasteurized. Fresh whitefish caviar, known also as golden caviar, is sometimes available in gourmet shops, a treat not to be missed. But to obtain local lumpfish caviar, you must first catch a Pacific spiny lumpsucker, our most conspicuous representative of the lumpfishes. This fish prefers the deeper waters of the open coast and of Juan de Fuca Strait to the shelter of the inland waters. It is a very odd creature, an erratic fish which is not easily caught by angling since it attaches itself to rocks (and sometimes to crab pots) with a ventral suction disk. It is hardly worth the bother, however, since it grows to a length of only five inches and contains few eggs.

Whitefish, on the other hand, are quite common in the rivers and in some lakes of the Pacific Northwest, and their roe should always be eaten when they are found in a captured female. These fish obligingly spawn in winter, like the burbot, when the cold helps keep their eggs fresh. Whitefish roe may be prepared like other fish roe, but the small eggs have a delicate crunch (they release little bursts of flavor onto your taste buds as you pop them with your teeth), and they are at their best when they are prepared as caviar.

Here's how: gently separate the individual eggs, making sure not to break them with clumsy fingers (or long nails), and carefully remove as much of the membrane and connecting tissue as possible (commercial processors use special brass screens). The eggs must be salted—a very tricky operation—to thin the fat, separate the "berries" (as the individual eggs are known in the trade) from each other, and give a tender bite to their taste. Here knowledge and experience separate the experts from the amateurs.

The eggs may be salted directly (this is strictly for the experts) or they may be suspended in a brine (¼ cup of well-dissolved salt and 1 cup of cold water for each cup of eggs). The latter method is the only one amateurs should attempt; it gives the novice at least a fighting chance to avoid breaking the berries. Carefully drop the eggs into the brine and stir them very gently. Allow them to stand for about half an hour. The berries will soak up some of the salt and firm up. Pick out the remaining particles of membrane and tissue; these will have turned white in the water and should now be easy to see. Rinse the eggs (again with the utmost gentle caution) in a large dish of cold water and strain them again. Pick them over once more, to remove the last bits of membrane. Immediately chill the "caviar" and keep it chilled. Let the eggs cure for at least a few days before eating them. At first, just after the eggs have been salted, you may taste nothing but salt; but as they mellow, the delicate fish flavors will reassert themselves and blend the berries' taste into little nuggets of complexity. They should keep for a week or two if handled properly. Caviars can be kept fresh for longer periods of time if they are stored at a temperature of about twenty-six degrees Fahrenheit (the salt will keep them from freezing).

I prefer to leave the complex operations involved in making caviars to the experts, since several other critical factors such as the quality of the ova, the state of development of the spawn, a sure touch in salting, et al., must be taken into account before an acceptable caviar can be produced.

True caviar, prepared from the eggs of specially handled sturgeon, is rather an expensive delicacy. But this was not always so. Until a combination of overharvesting and pollution drastically reduced the world's sturgeon population (after all, the eggs you eat as caviar were meant to produce new little sturgeons), caviar was quite an affordable treat, and it was fairly common in the Pacific Northwest. Of the two species of sturgeon occurring in our rivers, only one, the white sturgeon, has roe that is treasured for conversion into caviar.

The white sturgeon is a noble fish of truly epic proportions. The largest white on record was a twenty-foot monster taken in the Fraser River. It weighed an incredible eighteen hundred pounds. Sturgeons take a long time to reach such a size, and the Russians, the world's traditional purveyors of caviar, have developed a method of removing the roe from pregnant female sturgeons through a caesarean section, which does not harm the fish much. West Coast marine biologists are currently trying to discover how this is done, because the rewards are quite amazing, and not just for the fish who is returned to the water to breed again at a future time. An eight-hundred-pound female produces about fifty pounds of roe which, after it has been processed into caviar, will bring a price of about fifteen to twenty dollars an ounce.

The best sturgeon caviars of the Pacific Northwest compare favorably with the best Russia can produce, but our roe production is even more limited. The commercial sturgeon fishery in the Northwest is very restricted to protect the shriveling stocks of nubile females and, though there appears to be a flourishing illegal trade in sturgeon roe from sport-fished and poached fish, our processors have problems acquiring sufficient amounts of eggs to ensure a regular supply of fresh sturgeon caviar for the gourmet trade. Even when northwest sturgeon caviar is available, it may be shipped out of the region, to New York, Paris, and Los Angeles (I once had to order Columbia sturgeon caviar from a California supplier, because none was to be had in either Seattle or Portland). There is only one way to assure yourself of a periodic supply, spotty as it may be: establish a good relationship with a seafood market or gourmet shop which sells the stuff, try to convince them to call you when the caviar comes in, and buy as much as you can afford before it sells out. Like whitefish caviar, it will keep at twenty-six to thirty degrees for several months. This will allow you to parcel out your stash to your best friends at leisure.

Sturgeon caviar is traditionally served with iced vodka, but it goes even better with the first-rate moonshine made by the Skagit County Tarheels. The connoisseur's problem is that it is easier nowadays to get a good supply of local sturgeon caviar than it is to lay down an ample quantity of Lyman, Washington's best. But, once you've tried the combination, you will never again want to do without it. The best of our sturgeon caviar has glistening gray-black berries with a subtle, nutty flavor and a hint of delicate fruitiness (if you didn't know you were eating fish eggs, you might be hard pressed to find clues of taste about the origin of these luscious pearls). The best of Skagit mountain dew has a rich, mouth-filling fruitiness that perfectly complements the caviar. Czar Nicholas never knew what he missed when he drank mere vodka with his sterlet and beluga.

Salmon eggs, in particular the roe from the large-egged chinook, silver, and chum salmon, make different, though in their own unique ways equally excellent, caviars. I must admit somewhat shamefacedly that, until quite recently, I had not thought of local salmon caviar as a gourmet food. Oh, I often carried a jar of the berries about me during fishing season, using them to garnish sharpened barbed hooks, perhaps accompanying this delicacy with a small, milky kernel of corn or a tiny, flavored marshmallow or a piece of Cheddar cheese. Rainbow trout just love the stuff and sometimes swallow it hook, line, and sinker. I just didn't know that people did, too.

In the spring of 1983, during an Olympia oyster tasting held at Ray's Boathouse in Seattle, manager Bob Viggers lured me backstage to the kitchen with the promise of a special taste treat. Bob took a five-gallon plastic container from the cooler, opened it, and exposed a mass of tightly packed, lustrous, light-orange chum salmon eggs. He handed me a spoonful, and I reluctantly took a bite. What flavor! This salmon caviar was simply delicious (fortunately I got to eat my fill right there and then), totally unlike anything I had expected. My previous experience with salmon roe had come to a somewhat precipitate end: I had tried to salt down a few skeins of fresh Samish Island king salmon roe, but the taste was something else, and I gladly used my misguided experiment as chum and fish bait. Yet these chum salmon eggs were in a different league. Chum salmon eggs have the lowest fat and oil content of any salmon roe, and this caviar was very light, nutty, and fruity, with a fine, underlying taste of the sea.

A week later I talked to Garry Shaw, the owner of Cossack Caviar in south Seattle, the company which produced those delectable golden berries. He was justifiably proud of his caviars, pointing out that only the best and freshest fish eggs qualify. His company turns out three different salmon caviars—light-orange king and chum and reddish silver—during the salmon seasons, when fresh eggs can be got. Only the best and most perfect skeins of roe are made into caviar; the less satisfactory eggs are turned into fish bait.

Cossack also makes sturgeon caviar from time to time, when a supply of eggs can be got. But, as Shaw pointed out, even then there are problems. There is a great variety in the quality of local sturgeon eggs and about half the catch may not be usable. The roe may be too immature, there may be too much fat in the membranes, or the eggs may be green or brown (this is an indication of an undesirable taste) instead of gray-black. Salmon roe present similar problems, but these are overcome more easily because the selection is so much greater; there are simply more salmon than sturgeon eggs to be had.

Despite my lingering affection for sturgeon caviar, it seems to me that salmon caviar most represents the tastes of the Pacific Northwest. Salmon caviar has never before been as popular as it is now, perhaps because no one has ever before made a salmon caviar of such a high quality. Good salmon caviar is a seasonal product: fresh king salmon eggs are processed first, because the kings are the first salmon to come in from the ocean, and is available from June through August. The silver salmon run in August and September and the chum from September through November. Pink and sockeye salmon eggs have not the proper flavor to warrant their conversion into caviar.

The fresh salmon eggs are rushed to the processor and generally are cleaned and salted within twenty-four hours. Cossack Caviar adds nothing but salt to the berries—no hidden chemicals or preservatives—and these caviars are not pasteurized. Salmon caviar may be eaten the day after the eggs were salted, but it is usually left to ripen for at least a month, because this will improve its taste. Proper storage in a cooler at twenty-six degrees allows a small supply of salmon caviar to be held over, and you may sometimes find it out of season; but most of the salmon caviar sold between seasons comes from Japanese sources and is pasteurized.

Jars of unpasteurized salmon caviar last for about a month in the home refrigerator (two weeks if they have been opened) and can be frozen, though this may cause some breakage among the berries and a loss in quality. Salmon caviar is good to eat by itself, on sushi, in salads, and as a garnish for just about anything short of dessert and ice cream. Best of all, this delicacy is quite inexpensive, about a dollar to a dollar and a half per ounce. Cossack makes the bulk of the Northwest's salmon caviar. It is sold under the company's own label (identified rather garishly by two crossed sabers), and under a multitude of both domestic and foreign labels and brand names.

Salmon, whitefish, and sturgeon roe may also be fried, sautéed, or poached—like other, more mundane, fish eggs—as long as you use only fresh eggs and avoid very ripe eggs, which tend to explode like popcorn (this gets to be messiest with large salmon eggs). The roe and the milt from male fish can also be eaten fresh in fish or vegetable salads.

In the past, salmon eggs were fermented into a cheeselike substance by the native tribes of the northwest coast. This is still done from time to time and is quite simple: dig a pit (about three feet deep and two feet in diameter) in soft, loamy ground. Line the cavity with the large destemmed leaves of a big-leaf maple. Puncture small holes in the bottom layer of leaves to let the oil drain off. Fill the pit with skeins of salmon roe. Cover the roe with a thick layer of maple leaves and shovel a heavy layer of soil onto this cover. Leave the eggs in the ground for about two months. They will have achieved the consistency of cheese and may be eaten raw, boiled for soup, or pressed into cakes (a cheese press works well) and stored.

This method of fermenting salmon eggs is surprisingly close to a method long used by the Chinese for making a kind of egg cheese which helps to preserve poultry eggs and improves their flavor. I am talking about the renowned hundred-year-old eggs.

These egg cheeses are quite easy to make: cover fresh, raw duck eggs with a paste made of wood ash (alder works well), slaked lime, and kosher salt; bury them in the ground for about three to four months. The quality of the ground is the critical part, and you have several choices which will affect the flavor of your product. You may wish to bury the eggs in loam (it should be moist, but not wet, and free of rocks) for a mild, cold-fermented cheese, or you may wish to warm-ferment them in a compost pile or in horse manure. The latter process will give you cheese with a riper taste. A connoisseur of hundred-year-old eggs will generally be able to tell you by which method an egg was fermented, just like a connoisseur of fine cheeses can tell a Camembert from a Brie.

During the fermentation period, the yolks of these eggs will become curdy (somewhat like cottage cheese) and turn dark green (the particular shade is an indication of quality and method). The egg white will firm up, like gelatin. These eggs are watched carefully during fermentation: dig one up from time to time to check on the progress of the batch and to tell when they are ripe enough for you. They are peeled, sliced thin, and eaten with soy sauce, vinegar, and chopped gingerroot. Duck eggs should be used wherever possible, because they have a sturdier flavor and are oilier than chicken eggs, but fresh goose eggs may be substituted, and as a last resort, when the eggs of these waterfowl are unobtainable, chicken eggs. Large duck eggs can also be ripened by being suspended in brine for thirty to sixty days. The eggs are then hard-cooked (the exact reverse of the pickling process for chicken eggs) and served with rice dishes. These eggs are a great favorite with the Vancouver Chinese.

Duck eggs are surprisingly popular in the Pacific Northwest. In northwestern Washington and southwestern British Columbia, duck eggs are not only the favorite eggs of the area's Chinese population, but they are also preferred by Dutch dairy farmers. Many farmers raise special breeds of laying ducks, such as Indian runners. I like county fairs very much, and I first learned about laying ducks at the Skagit County Fair, when I tried to figure out why a scraggly looking, lean drake—which looked more like a cormorant than a duck—had won a blue ribbon.

Later, at the Lynden Fair, I encountered a surprisingly large number of laying duck breeds: black runners, white runners (these look like malnourished Peking ducks), gray and long-tailed, penciled runners. These are tough and stringy birds, much like laying chickens in consistency, and their coarse meat is not suited for dainty dishes. But they lay a lot of excellent eggs. Duck eggs are larger than chicken eggs, have a stronger, eggier taste, the whites tend to be thicker, and the dark yolks are slightly oily. They are excellent for making mayonnaise, giving it a better texture and superior flavor, hollandaise sauce, quiche, and, especially, cheesecake. The best cheesecakes in the Northwest are made with fresh cream cheese and fresh duck eggs.

Several meat breeds, especially the white Peking duck and the related mallard, are also good layers. I once had a pet mallard named Quack-Quack who would not quit laying eggs. She laid at least one a day—a considerable achievement, since she never came close to a drake—and promptly abandoned it. She acted just like a chicken when her light-green creation appeared but, instead of cackling, she QUACK-QUACk-QUAck-QUack-Quack-quacked each time she laid a new egg. Though she was an indefatigable producer, her one egg a day didn't get us very far, and we often mixed it with chicken eggs.

We had no problems using duck eggs in recipes calling for chicken eggs. Most cookbooks standardize the egg at two ounces when they list quantities of ingredients. We always weighed our eggs and adjusted the recipes accordingly, by adding or subtracting as required. This rule also applies to goose eggs and other eggs—whatever you can get your hands on, from pigeon eggs to peacock eggs and even ostrich eggs. Small eggs, like quail or pigeon eggs, are quite expensive, however, and since it takes several to make up the bulk of one chicken egg, you're better off using them in special dishes. If you raise your own quail or pigeons and have plentiful supplies of these dainties, you can use them in all recipes that call for eggs.

Quail should never be underestimated as layers. A quail hen begins to lay when she is only five or six weeks old (compared to five or six months for a chicken) and she may lay as many as two hundred fifty to three hundred eggs a year. Quail take up less space than chickens, are cleaner birds, and eat less. Quail eggs have a mild flavor, and they make beautifully dainty garnishes when hard-cooked and sliced. They may be eaten whole, half a mouthful each, or their raw yolks may be used to garnish sushi or beef or seafood tartare.

I have often eaten quail eggs in restaurants, but I was quite surprised when I saw my first quail eggs in the shell (they were for sale at Seattle's Pike Place Market). Quail are very small and have buff shells, heavily spotted with brown and even blue or green splotches. They look like, but aren't, wild bird eggs. Once they are cracked, they take on a more familiar appearance—white egg white and yellow yolk—looking just like tiny chicken eggs.

But how do you cook a quail egg? I failed to find any detailed instructions anywhere. So, for the purpose of this book, I went out and bought a dozen (at Seattle's Uwajimaya Market), took them to the Pacific Search Press offices, and handed them to Marlene Blessing, my editor. We decided to hard-cook them to establish a standard of comparative cooking times. Marlene looked at the eggs' size and, after some quick calculation, decided they should be treated like chicken eggs, but cooked for a shorter period of time. She carried the eggs to the small office kitchen, placed them in a pot of cold water, and brought the water to a boil. When the water began to seethe, she removed the pot from the heat and let the eggs sit, covered, for about three minutes, instead of the twenty minutes recommended for hard-cooked chicken eggs. The quail eggs came out cooked to perfection and were very tender. I have used Marlene's three-minute method ever since.

We have become so accustomed to buying chicken eggs graded by size and packed into convenient cartons, that we may be surprised to find ungraded eggs in a market. Quail eggs are sometimes graded by size and packed into tiny plastic egg boxes but, more often than not, they are sold assorted in packages in which eggs of different sizes, from half-inch midgets to one-and-a-half-inch "giants" are jumbled together. There is less variation in the size of duck eggs, but here again no grading standards exist. But I have never had any problems with the quality of either the duck eggs or quail eggs I have bought in the Pacific Northwest. Chicken eggs, on the other hand, are almost always graded, for both size and quality.

United States Department of Agriculture standards apply to eggs sold in Oregon, Washington, and Idaho; in British Columbia, eggs are graded according to the somewhat different regulations established by Agriculture Canada. Most egg cartons on U.S. supermarket shelves display the letters AA, A, or B. These egg grades tell the consumer about the appearance of the yolk (the higher the grade, the firmer and more well-rounded it is), about the condition of the white (the higher the grade, the less the white will spread when the egg is broken out—low-grade whites are very watery and runny). Most eggs sold in the U.S. fall into the grade-A category, or even into grade B, except for the eggs produced in the Pacific Northwest.

The quality of the chicken eggs produced in our region is so high, that I had problems finding grade-A or -B eggs when I wanted to hold a comparison egg "cracking" and tasting. In contrast to the rest of the country, almost all eggs marketed in our area are grade AA. The difference between grade-A and -AA eggs is best exemplified by the fact that the quality of grade-AA eggs will decline to grade A after one week of refrigerator storage. Whatcom and Skagit counties in northwestern Washington regularly produce the best eggs in the Northwest, perhaps even the best eggs in the country.

Egg sizes indicated on the cartons tell you the average weight of a dozen eggs, not the physical size of an individual egg. For example, a dozen extralarge eggs must weigh at least twenty-seven ounces; one dozen large eggs—large eggs are the standard size called for in most recipes—must have a minimum weight of twenty-four ounces, or two ounces per egg (this, as I have pointed out, is important to consider when you substitute another bird's eggs for chicken eggs in a given recipe); medium eggs must weigh at least twenty-one ounces a dozen.

Neither egg grades nor sizes will tell you anything about the freshness of the eggs you buy. I always make sure to find out on which day fresh eggs are delivered to my market, unless I buy directly from a chicken farmer. The freshest eggs are the healthiest and tastiest, and you can tell how fresh your eggs are by a simple test: plunge an egg into a 12-percent solution of salted water. A fresh egg will fall to the bottom; a two-day-old egg floats mid-way; if the egg is four days old, it will rise to the surface; a two-week-old egg will float on top. This is the French way of checking on an egg's freshness; the American method calls for dropping the egg into a plain glass of water: if it floats, it's bad. I prefer to test the egg in salt water because I have found that an egg needs to be very old and to have generated a good supply of gas before it floats in freshwater. But even this method is an improvement over the procedure recommended in a mid-1940ish cookbook: "If the contents of an egg rattle when it is shaken, it is not fresh." I would say so! In Canada, egg grades run from A (roughly equivalent to our A) to C. There is no category equal to our AA, but most of the eggs marketed in British Columbia fall into this category, because of the high quality of the local product.

The best and most tasty chicken eggs come from free-running hens who are fed on grain and who are also able to eat natural foods, such as plants, worms, and insects. The color of an egg is no indication of its flavor or nutritive quality (nor does it matter if an egg is fertilized or not). In the Pacific Northwest, brown eggs come primarily from New Hampshire and Rhode Island Red chickens; Plymouth Rock hens lay eggs that are light brown to quite reddish brown. Most of our white eggs come from White Leghorns. The excitement for a gourmet buying eggs in our region lies with the small eggs, however. Our farmers raise a large number of different breeds, of often very small chickens: the blue or green eggs from Araucanas are the most conspicuous, but many other breeds also produce excellent, though not always plentiful, eggs. Bantams, Cornish, Orpingtons, Polish, Sebrights, Dorkings, rose combs, and Chanteclers are all well represented in local flocks and, on a more exotic level, so are pheasants of various breeds, guinea fowl, and even peacocks.

The Pacific Northwest egg fancier has an amazingly varied offering of delicious eggs at his disposal. Many different kinds are sold at farmers' markets and at the public markets in Vancouver, Seattle, Portland, and Eugene, but it is a good practice to read the farmers' advertisements in local newspapers and to scan bulletin boards in rural communities to find sources for the more exotic offerings (many eggs are available for short periods of time, or seasonally, only). A pleasant drive into the country may often bring surprisingly delicious culinary rewards.

Rockfish Roe on Toast

This has become one of our favorites ever since we learned (in Vancouver's Chinatown) that rockfish roe are not only edible, but also exceptionally tasty. Serve with a crisp sauvignon blanc.

Butter   2 tablespoons
Fresh lemon juice   2 tablespoons
Rockfish roe   2 sacs, cleaned
Butter   1 tablespoon
Bread   1 slice, cut in half lengthwise
Bread crumbs   2 teaspoons
Parsley   1 teaspoon finely chopped
Fresh lemon juice   2 squeezes
Parsley   garnish

1. Melt 2 tablespoons butter in cast-iron skillet over medium heat. Add lemon juice and blend.
2. When mixture bubbles, add roe. Poach until they have changed from gold to whitish opaque.
3. In a separate pan, melt 1 tablespoon butter and fry rectangles of bread until crisp. Remove from pan.
4. Fry bread crumbs in butter residue.
5. Place roe on toast rectangles, sprinkle with bread crumbs, and squeeze lemon juice over each.
6. Sprinkle with parsley.

Serves 2

Caviar Cucumber Rounds

This is a tasty appetizer—perfect finger food—that goes well with a nice dry northwest sparkling wine like the bubblies made by Hinzerling Vineyards in Prosser, Washington, or Château Benoit in Carlton, Oregon.

Cream Cheese (see Index)   3 ounces, softened
Milk   2 teaspoons
Small cucumbers (preferably Japanese *kyūri*)*   2, sliced ⅛-inch thick
Salmon caviar   4 teaspoons
Fresh lemon juice   from 1 lemon
Tiny cocktail onions   24

1. Blend Cream Cheese and milk.
2. Spread mixture on cucumbers.
3. Spoon a little caviar into the center of each cucumber round (use ¼ teaspoon measuring

spoon or small melon baller).
4. Sprinkle with lemon juice.
5. Drain onions on paper towels. Place 1 on each round, in the center of the caviar.

* If you use American cucumbers, peel them first.

Serves 6 to 8

Nooksack River Omelet

This is a very tasty variation on the standard omelet fillings available today. If you like salmon caviar as much as I do, you'll probably want to increase the amount of salmon caviar called for in the recipe. Serve with well-chilled northwest champagne.

Chicken or duck eggs 2
Cold water 1 tablespoon
Salt pinch
Unsalted butter 2 tablespoons
Crème Fraîche (see Index) 2 tablespoons
Salmon caviar 2 tablespoons

1. Beat eggs with water and salt, using a wire whisk, until blended, but not frothy.
2. Heat a heavy 8- or 9-inch skillet until a drop of water sizzles.
3. Film with butter.
4. Add beaten egg mixture.
5. With spatula, carefully lift and pull cooked portions around edges to center; tilt pan to distribute uncooked egg.
6. When omelet is nearly done on top and golden underneath, loosen and fold in thirds, tilting out onto plate.
7. Garnish with Crème Fraîche and caviar.

Serves 1

Salmon Caviar Dip

If you have guests who are afraid to try salmon caviar straight, try breaking them in slowly with this dish. You get the great taste of salmon caviar combined with the familiarity of that great American classic, dip. Serve with toast and a dry, austere chardonnay, semillon, or sauvignon blanc.

Sour Cream or Crème Fraîche (see Index)   1 cup
Green onions   2 tablespoons chopped
Salmon caviar   2 ounces, plus 2 tablespoons, drained

1. Combine Sour Cream with chopped green onions. Chill for at least 1 hour to develop flavor.
2. In the meantime, drain salmon caviar by laying on its side open (with lip of jar above bowl) in refrigerator.
3. Fold 2 ounces caviar into dip with a spatula.
4. Garnish with 2 tablespoons of caviar.

Variation: You may also use chopped parsley or lemon wedges as garnish.

Serves 8 to 12

Quail Eggs with Salmon Caviar

This dish has become one of our favorite party appetizers—ever since a local farmer began raising laying quail, assuring us of a regular supply of these dainty little eggs (the Uwajimaya supermarkets in the Seattle area are the most reliable commercial outlet for quail eggs). Serve with a tart young chardonnay or with a Hinzerling or Château Benoit sparkling wine.

Quail eggs   12, hard-cooked and peeled
Chinese cabbage   2 leaves, center vein removed
Sour Cream (see Index)   ¼ cup, chilled
Green onion   1 teaspoon finely chopped (green part)
Salmon caviar   3 teaspoons (approximately)
Fresh lemon juice   to taste

1. Cut eggs in half lengthwise and arrange open-faced on a platter on a bed of finely shredded Chinese cabbage. Chill.
2. Combine Sour Cream and minced green onion. Chill for at least 1 hour to develop flavor.
3. Dab ½ heaped teaspoon of mixture on each quail egg yolk. Flatten slightly with spatula.
4. Place 4 salmon eggs in center of each dab (stack them like cannonballs: 3 in a triangle at bottom, 1 on top, in center of triangle).
5. Squeeze a drop of lemon juice onto each cluster of salmon eggs.

Serves 4 to 8

Salmon Caviar Pie

This really is not a "pie" in the true sense, since it is not baked, but it looks gorgeous, tastes delicious, and goes very well with black homebaked bread. Serve with a well-chilled dry northwest chardonnay, sauvignon blanc, pinot noir blanc, or sparkling white.

Large Walla Walla sweet onion   1, finely chopped
Unsalted butter   1 tablespoon
Chicken or duck eggs   6, hard-cooked and chopped
Mayonnaise   3 tablespoons
Fresh Cream Cheese (see Index)   8 ounces
Firm Crème Fraîche (see Index)   ⅔ cup
Salmon caviar   3½ ounces (or more, if needed)
Parsley   several sprigs
Lemon wedges   12
Edible blue borage flowers   12
Quail eggs   12, hard-cooked, peeled, and halved

1. Drain chopped onion on paper towels for 30 minutes.
2. Generously butter bottom and sides of an 8-inch springform pan.
3. In a bowl, combine chopped chicken eggs and mayonnaise. Spread mixture in bottom of pan in an even layer. Sprinkle with onion, also in an even layer.
4. In bowl, combine Cream Cheese and Crème Fraîche, beating until smooth.
5. Carefully drop mixture onto onion layer, 1 spoonful at a time. Spread gently to smoothen with wet table knife. Cover. Chill for at least 3 hours, but preferably overnight.
6. Thirty minutes before serving, drain salmon caviar by opening jar and laying it on its side in refrigerator (over bowl) to allow juices to run out. Then distribute salmon caviar on top of the cream cheese layer.
7. Run thin knife around sides of pan; loosen and lift off the sides.
8. Garnish "pie" with lemon wedges, parsley sprigs, flowers, and quail eggs.

Serves 8 to 16

Beer and Spirits

W e are flying just above the treetops, close to the valley floor, to get a better look at the fields. Apple orchards and vineyards flash by beneath us, separated by stretches of green and ochre pasture and grayish-brown fallow land. Here a dairy herd chews its cud in unison, there a small abandoned farm—windmill askew, bullet holes in the water tank, roof tiles missing—recedes slowly into the ground. New farms to the right: metal barns and equipment sheds reflecting the morning sun, suburban homes with satellite disks amongst the fields, feedlots with fatty cattle waiting to be killed.

High up on the dry slope to our left lies the architect of all this profusion, a sinuous irrigation canal snaking its way along the arid edge of the encircling hills. Without this water—brought all the way from the higher reaches of the river, miles away, where it flows from the glaciers of the Cascade peaks—much of the valley would be seasonally green, semiarid grazing land. The rainfall here (eight inches per year) is sufficient to grow only one crop of pasture grass a season; but with the help of artificial rain (sprinkler, ditch, or drip irrigation), you can extend the growing season to last from spring thaw to fall frost and take full advantage of the long northern growing days and the warmth of the summers to put flavor and substance into corn, tomatoes, grapes, and hops.

Along with a gaggle of Seattle wine writers, I was flown to the Yakima Valley by Mike Hogue, a hop farmer, to observe the hop harvest. We did not need to fly low to spot the hop fields—their junglelike wire enclosures are so distinctive they can be spotted from afar. Hop plantations are common along the Yakima River and in the Willamette Valley. But it's the quality of the hops grown near Prosser that has made the United States the world's second largest hop producer (after Bavaria).

Hops, the bitter herb most people have only vaguely heard of (usually in conjunction with beer), have quite a pedigree. Seventeenth-century herbalist Nicholas Culpeper placed hops under the dominion of Mars, the god of war (and the red planet), and attributed to it all sorts of cleansing properties, even the power to expel poison. Other herbalists consider hops a tonic, a febrifuge, and a sedative (hops stuffed into a pillow are said to ensure sound sleep and sweet dreams).

The average beer-drinking American has never seen hops, though he consumes large quantities of its extract in his favorite brew. Nor do many people know that hops are one of Washington State's most important cash crops. Hops are perennial trailing vines with large, coarse leaves. They reach a length of twenty feet and are customarily grown on tall wire trellises. These enclosures also serve to confine the hops, for the plants are very aggressive climbers (their Roman name *Lupus salictarius* attests to this: hops were thought to run wild among the willows the way wolves run wild amid a herd of sheep). A modern hop field gives the appearance of rows of closely spaced telephone poles overgrown by rank climbing weeds. Only the papery cones (or strobiles) produced by the female flowers are commonly used. But to get at them, the whole plant is harvested. The cones are used for medicine and in the brewing of beer and ale.

In years past, all hops were gathered by migrant pickers who descended upon the hop fields in large numbers during harvest season and who gathered each strobile by hand. Today the process has become highly mechanized. After harvest, the hops are dried with hot air, baled, and put in cold storage. If not stored properly, they will deteriorate rapidly, losing up to 50 percent of their brewing value in six months. (It seems that the freshest hops go to the commercial breweries—where different varieties are carefully blended to achieve a "house" flavor—and that home brewers must do with rejects and sweepings. No wonder so much home brew has a peculiar taste.)

The papery scales of the hop strobiles contain a yellow, grainy powder called lupulin. These tiny grains are the most valuable part of the hops, the constituent most important for brewing. Lupulite, the bitter essence of hops, is extracted from lupulin during the brewing process. Hop strobiles are very fragile and, unless handled with care, the lupulin will drop out, making the hops just about worthless for brewing.

The Yakima Valley hop farmers grow a number of different hop varieties, primarily mild Cascades (with about 6 percent brewing value), and stronger Galenas, Eroicas, and Yakima Clusters (with 12 to 14 percent brewing value). Some breweries, like Coors or Redhook, use mostly Cascade hops. Others prefer a stronger extract. But all brewmasters maintain a secret blend of hop varieties for their beers—we can thus never be quite sure of their exact composition.

Hops are good for all kinds of things besides beer. The vines can be turned into acceptable rope (hops are related to hemp); the leaves make good cattle fodder and stimulate milk production. Young hop shoots make a tasty vegetable—they can be treated like asparagus spears—and they are particularly good when sautéed in butter or simmered in fresh cream. Hop cones make a tasty, though very bitter, tea that is recommended by naturopaths for nervous diarrhea, insomnia, and restlessness. (Ever wondered why beer calms you down?) It will help dispel flatulence and relieve intestinal cramps. But hops are at their best in beer.

Beer made from grain alone tastes cloying and, if it is a heavy brew, sticky. Drinking nothing but the standard domestic brews for several years, I had slowly adapted to their peculiar flavor (the good domestics and imports were either out of my price range or had deteriorated in the bottle by the time they reached our markets). During the last couple of years, however, I have taken advantage of the wider range of imported beers and ales now available at more reasonable prices and, especially, of the excellent new brews produced by our region's new microbreweries. Now, whenever I drink a standard beer (usually under duress), I am irritated by its underlying sweetness. Many American consumers have forgotten how important the addition of good hops is for a beer's taste and aroma. I made the experiment: I bought a standard, inexpensive domestic beer and steeped a handful of fresh Yakima hops in the brew. The transformation was magic. Suddenly here appeared the elements I had missed: a good aroma, a fruity taste, and a pleasant bitterness.

Not all of these elements were provided by the hops, of course; the hops merely brought out some of the flavors already in the beer. A number of tart and bitter aromatic herbs have been used for several millenia to balance the malty sweetness of barley beers, but hops alone have been preferred since the late Middle Ages. Despite their importance, however, hops are not a major constituent, rather a sort of catalyst and a flavoring agent. They also contain tannins, which help clarify the beer, and resins which serve as antiseptics and preservatives.

Beer, in its most simple and best form, is a natural beverage made by fermenting an extract of germinated barley (a malt wort), flavored with hops, with the help of a special yeast (the type of yeast used is another brewmaster's secret, since it can affect the taste of the beer). Its final quality depends largely on the initial quality of the two main ingredients, barley malt and water. Six-rowed barley, the best variety for malting, does exceptionally well in the Pacific Northwest. It is widely grown on the grainlands of the Columbia Basin and is considered to be among the best in the world. The quality of our water is, of course, impeccable, whether it is springwater, rainwater, or meltwater from the Cascade glaciers. Little wonder that, for the last century, the Northwest has made some of the best beer in the country.

But in the Northwest, as elsewhere on the continent, regional breweries were swallowed up by huge national conglomerates during the last decade. Though here, unlike elsewhere in the country, the breweries have been allowed to continue making their distinctive beer styles—such as, for example, the highly individualistic Rainier Ale—for which they had become famous. One brewery, Blitz-Weinhard in Portland, was even permitted to develop a new quality beer, Henry Weinhard's Private Reserve. Yet even more important things are in store for the lovers of good beer in the Northwest.

In recent years the trend toward the elimination of small breweries and control of the market by a few large conglomerates has been reversed. "Microbreweries," dedicated to the limited production of handmade beers, have sprung up in different parts of the country. Nowhere have they proliferated more than in the Pacific Northwest. It is of more than passing significance that in 1982, just before Washington's venerable Olympia Brewery was slain in the corporate wars, three microbreweries opened in our region: the Troller Pub Brewery in Horseshoe Bay, British Columbia, the Yakima Brewing and Malting Company in Yakima, and the Independent Ale Brewery in Seattle. Now, a couple of years later, these tiny breweries are still doing well and are even expanding their output—despite the fact that the Troller Pub makes its Bay Ale for sale in the pub's tap room only and that Independent Ale sells its Redhook and Blackhook ales and Yakima Brewing its Grant's ales to a limited number of pubs. So far, these rich, full-flavored brews are only available in kegs (though some may be bottled soon).

The new attitude in beer making is most noticeable in Seattle (after all it was a Seattleite, Charlie Finkel, and his import company, Merchand du Vin, who were responsible for the current boom in both domestic and imported quality beers). Seattle now has two breweries. As late as the spring of 1982, it had only one. The huge Rainier Brewery rises like a technocrat castle above the south Seattle industrial flats; the tiny Independent Ale Brewery (with a production of only some six thousand barrels annually, less than 1 percent of a large brewery's capacity) is tucked into a former transmission shop in Ballard, a few blocks north of the Lake Washington Ship Canal. It is quite inconspicuous; only a small, painted sign sets it apart from the ship chandlers and other maritime enterprises of this industrial enclave.

Once you are inside the brewery, it seems even smaller; but I found it a great place to visit. President Paul Shipman and brewmaster Charles McElevey like to talk beer, ale, and porter. And they just love making the stuff. The brewery has only one kettle—a smallish, German-built copper contraption—and a few fermentation vats, but it makes up in quality what it lacks in quantity of output. After touring the brewing and storage rooms, I sat down to talk and sample ale in the brewery's small unofficial pub.

We started by tasting different malts and roasted barley grains. The quality of a malt is determined by the type of barley used (the best northwest barley malts are used for both Redhook and Blackhook), by the length of the germination period (barley is sprouted only until a mere tiplet of the germ shows outside the grain), and by the intensity and duration of roasting the grain in a malt kiln. Tasting the different grains gave me a better idea of how they affect the taste of a finished beer or ale: a lightly toasted malt which is still golden in color after roasting has a delicate toasted grain flavor (a bit like a good, natural breakfast cereal) and will give a light amber wort; a medium-toasted malt has a pleasantly nutty taste, giving a darker beer; a really dark malt, roasted until it is almost scorched, tastes more like coffee beans than grain and will dye the wort dark, almost black.

As we tasted the different malts and the beers, it was inevitable that we would also discuss the different styles of beer made today. Both Paul Shipman and Chuck McElevey strongly believe in making completely natural ales by methods that had been all but forgotten.

An ale is a beer, often (but not necessarily) based on a heavy, concentrated, malt wort that has been fermented with a highly active yeast strain at a relatively high temperature of fifty-nine to sixty-eight degrees Fahrenheit for two to four days. These ales are called "top-fermented" beers because the yeast floats to the top of the vat when the fermentation stops. It takes a real artist to make a proper ale: due to the violent nature of the fermentation almost anything can go wrong. Ales are heavily spiked with hops to help in stabilizing the beer, they mature quickly, and are ready to drink within a week or two after fermentation stops. Brewmaster McElevey prefers making natural ales, because it is a more exciting and natural process; but he was trained in the making of lighter beers during a long apprenticeship in Germany, and he once made a totally different style of beer—a few years ago, when he brewed for Rainier.

This beer, the kind most commonly drunk in the country is called *lager* (the German word for storage), because of the long period of aging necessary before the beer is ready to drink. It was invented back in the nineteenth century when some German brewmasters invented a novel process, using a different type of yeast.

Lager beer is fermented slowly, at low temperatures (about fifty degrees), for about five to seven days. At the end of fermentation, the yeast sinks to the bottom where it is drained off. Undesirable substances are precipitated from the brew as it ages in storage. Lagers don't need as high a hopping as ales, because they are naturally stable, clean-tasting beers. They are so stable that they are easily transported from one place to another, unlike ales which have to be handled with kid gloves, particularly if they are refrigerated and pasteurized. It has been precisely this toughness of lager and its clean taste that have made the rise of huge supraregional breweries possible. On the other hand, modern transportation and refrigeration methods have also made the safe transport of ales possible and these hand-made beers are once again competing successfully.

But to get away from these technical digressions and back to our beers: Redhook Ale is a distinctive reddish-brown brew, a true top-fermented ale that is very fruity for a beer. Its nose and taste have the flowery cereal fruitiness I have found previously only in the best, full malt Skagit County moonshine whiskey, and it has an underlying dry hop taste that balances its malty body and yeasty fruitiness. Blackhook Porter, a heavy beer that is much hoppier and more austere than Redhook, is closer in taste to the heavily hopped ales produced by the Yakima Brewing and Malting Company.

Yakima's Bert Grant worked for a Canadian brewery conglomerate and later spent a dozen years with a Yakima hop company (perfecting pelleted hops) before he started his own brewery. Yakima Valley hops play a major role in his beers. The first of these, Grant's Scottish Ale (Bert Grant was born in Scotland), is an austere, aromatic, bitter, and very dry ale. It is, in other words, quite delicious. Its intensity is more than surpassed, however, by Grant's Russian Imperial Stout, a heavy, black, almost syrupy ale that seems at first to have an underlying sweetness, but that on further tasting reveals a flavor very much dominated by the bitterness of Cascade hops.

Unlike the Seattle and Yakima ales, the handmade beer of the Troller Pub Brewery was not created to meet the rising consumer demand for fine local beers (though it does so anyway). John Mitchell, the pub's owner, became angry when British Columbia's last beer strike left his pub dry. He simply decided to brew his own so he wouldn't run out again. Bay Ale is more English in taste and body than other northwest ales, has a sharper flavor, a slightly lower alcohol level, a lighter body, a mellower infusion of bitter hops, and a delicate nutty finish. And all because John Mitchell hired himself an English brewmaster.

This brewmaster is now in Victoria, where he is about to open a brewery of his own. Vancouver Island already has one pub brewery, the Prairie Inn Pub Brewery in Saanichton; another new brewery has just opened in Surrey, on the lower British Columbia mainland, making a slightly sweet light brown ale. It is planning to expand its production and to begin exporting its beer to northwestern Washington; a new ale brewery in Colville, north of Spokane, is also thinking about taking its beer all the way to Seattle.

All of these Pacific Northwest ales have met with an instant, open-armed acceptance by northwest beer drinkers. At this time, they remain a uniquely regional phenomenon. As Michael Jackson, the world's foremost authority on beers, stated so enthusiastically:

> In the context of American beer drinking, it is a remarkable sight to see, in a Seattle bistro, every table being served with pints of a copper-colored beverage that is unmistakably ale, and then to realize that the customers are busily comparing the merits of two quite different brews, Grant's and Redhook. Most American cities have no local ale (many, including Chicago, don't even have a brewery); in Seattle, you get a choice.

Two ales? What about four? six? eight? The rush is on. Even in stodgy, dry-as-dust Bellingham a new brewery has just incorporated and plans to release its first commercial brew late in 1984. It looks like the Northwest, with its abundance of first-rate barley, hops, and water, will soon have a proliferation of small, distinct breweries. And may we once again be blessed with as many different ales, porters, stouts, and lagers as there are brewmasters!

A good beer, heavy with extracts—dextrins, unfermented remainders of maltose, soluble nitrogenous matter, protides, minerals, vitamins (especially B, B_2, B_{12}, and PP)—is not merely a healthful drink, but a food: the higher the malt content, the more nutritious the beer (*Larousse gastronomique* recommends malt beer be used as a tonic). Ales and well-made lagers are high in calories and taste; light beers are neither.

Beer may be a food in itself, but its greater virtue rests in its ability to go well with foods that are difficult to match with a proper wine. Take smoked salmon for example, the rich, sweet alder-smoked salmon of the Pacific Northwest: I haven't found a wine yet to drink with it, but it goes beautifully with Redhook Ale. The flavor of smoked oysters or smoked ham is nicely complemented by Grant's; Rainier Ale seems just right with barbecued goat (though a heavy red wine will do the job as well), and if you think oysters should always be enjoyed with a crisp white wine, try them with Blackhook Porter. It's hard to discover a reason why delicate gray oysters go so well with a heavy, dark beer, but it works. This combination was recognized in Europe a long time ago, but our strongly flavored Pacific oysters from, say, Gig Harbor or Samish Bay match much better.

You'll have to buy your Blackhook in a jug from your friendly neighborhood pub, but it is worth taking along on your next oystering trip (don't waste it on the more delicate oysters from Quilcene, Willapa Bay, or Tillamook—these need a delicate white wine). And don't forget a loaf of crusty bread (preferably bought that day from a small-town bakery en route).

Or drink any of our regional ales while you're barbecuing steaks, lamb chops, or hamburgers. And don't be shy about using them to baste the meat. It works and adds a great flavor. Unless you prefer stronger drink with your food. In that case you'll have to look much harder for a supply of locally produced products and, most importantly, make sure no one catches you.

On first glance, it seems strange that no large quantities of distilled spirits are produced in the Northwest. With our superabundance of grain for mash, wine for brandy, and cull fruit for fruit spirits, we should enjoy a vigorous distilling industry in our region. Unfortunately, this has proved to be economically unfeasible.

Alcoholic grain spirits can be produced much more cheaply in the Midwest, where the surplus of grain, especially corn, is so much greater than it is elsewhere on the continent. A few handmade whiskies are still made commercially in Tennessee, Kentucky, and in other parts of the Southeast, but these are luxury whiskies. They survive in a market dominated by fiercely competitive multinational corporations only because they have firmly established reputations for excellence and adhere to old-fashioned methods of production based on years of experience and an impeccable tradition of quality. These aged whiskies are fruity, complex, and very mellow (from long aging in oak). But the bulk of modern grain distillates is not fit to be served to discriminating drinkers. Only a few chemicals and artificial flavoring agents separate these alcohols and serve to dress them up as vodka, blended whiskey, or gin.

The picture is even more dismal with brandies made from wine. While a good, aged Bourbon whiskey can hold its own against a French cognac, North America produces no brandy worthy of the world's attention. The Christian Brothers in California make quite a passable brandy (though this lacks the complexity of cognac), but the brandies turned out by other West Coast distillers should never be served in polite company. The small Hood River Distillery tried to produce a series of brandies made from the superb fruits of the region, but there is an insufficient market for these exquisite essences of tree-ripened fruit, so the distillery has stopped making spirits of its own. The company now limits itself to buying spirits (vodkas, whiskies, et al.) elsewhere (i.e., the American and Canadian Midwest) and blends and markets these under its own label.

There is only one way in which the Northwesterners have succeeded in competing in both quality and price against the international conglomerates: by making whiskey illegally. Producers who avoid paying the exorbitant federal and state taxes levied on distilled liquor may survive in a cutthroat market. It is unfortunate that there is not a lower tax for the small producer to allow him a competitive margin and a higher tax for large distilleries who can better afford to pay it.

The selling price of liquor is as important as the selling price of beer for many consumers: there is little doubt that many consumers are willing to sacrifice quality in order to obtain cheap alcoholic beverages. This may be blamed in part on the proliferation of an objectional national habit, the cocktail.

The main justification for this concoction seems to be the need for a vehicle which allows the imbiber to ingest as much potent alcohol as possible within the shortest period of time and with the least amount of pain. Exotic ingredients added to cocktails serve primarily to smoothen the drinks and to mask the raw flavors of cheap vodkas, gins, and whiskies. It seems significant that the cocktail habit is least pronounced among those Northwesterners who have developed a taste for the uncamouflaged delights of good ale, wine, and brandy, and among those who make or have access to home-distilled whiskey.

Much illicit alcohol has been produced in the Northwest and with gusto. The output peaked during Prohibition, but even today quite a few stills operate clandestinely in the western foothills of the Cascades from Oregon north into the Skagit Valley of northwestern Washington.

The cottage still—legal or not—had a centuries-old tradition in Scotland and Ireland and, when North America was settled by immigrants from the British Isles, the newcomers brought their distilling skills along. Hard liquor arrived in the Pacific Northwest with the early white explorers, fur traders, and homesteaders. As early as 1837 Methodist missionaries and Willamette Valley farmers felt the need to buy out Ewing Young's still at Champoeg (they appear to have had little faith in the strength of their willpower in the presence of homemade whiskey); later many a miller in the Northwest would become wealthy from converting surplus grain into liquid refreshments. And the distilling continued despite the crusades of the prohibitionists and the legal objections of the U.S. government.

One of the more hilarious exposures of illicit distilleries during Prohibition occurred in Bandon, Oregon: the lids began to blow off milk cans destined for the local cheese factory. The story goes that testers analyzing the milk found a high percentage of yeast in the milk, which had created gases that caused the blowouts. Upon checking the water supplies of the Coquille valley dairy herds, the testers discovered numerous stills belonging to the area's leading citizens hidden along the banks of the watercourses. Word went out that the milk would be less explosive once the stills were removed. I question the accuracy of this story, for I suspect that the frugal Bandonites fed the spent cornmeal mash, left after distillation, to their dairy cows (cattle just love the taste of the stuff, or so a Skagit Valley farmer tells me).

One of the biggest efforts at producing illegal whiskey in the Northwest took place in the Skagit Valley a few years ago. Several interesting tales are told in the valley about this operation, but here is what really happened (as closely as we can reconstruct it—we can't mention names, since no one was ever convicted): one of the big problems with making whiskey illegally lies with the smoke and the fume. One is highly visible, the other has a rather distinctive odor. Distillers have tried all kinds of ruses, from working at night when the smoke is less visible (thus the name of "moonshine"), to directing it into trees, rock faces, and even creeks. But they are still stuck with the savory aroma of the distilling process: the strong, pungent smell travels far in the pristine mountain air of the Pacific Northwest.

Well, a couple of Skagitonians had a great idea. They hypothesized that no Federal agent would suspect a still right in the middle of town. So they rented some commercial space in an old dairy condensery in Burlington and opened a "candy" factory. The rented rooms were adjacent to the condensery's tall smokestack. It was quite simple to punch a hole into the base of the stack and let all of the smoke and fumes escape by this elevated route. Being able to work at their leisure, and during regular eight-to-five days, the illicit distillers came up with an excellent product which was soon served in bars from Everett to Bellingham under a variety of assumed labels.

Here the stories begin to differ. One version claims that the Feds finally became suspicious about the operation when they noticed that a lot of sugar went into the candy plant, but no candy ever came out; another, more accurate one, maintains that a Bellingham barkeeper, disgruntled over a price hike, blew the whistle. In any case, the Feds became so overstimulated when they finally learned about what had conspired right under their very noses that they rushed right down to the plant and stormed into the building, forgetting to pick up a search warrant in their eagerness to see justice done. The case was thrown out of court.

While many Skagitonians talk about moonshine, few can or will procure any mountain dew when pressed by an outsider. All agree on one point, however: that the homemade mountain dew from the Skagit and Snohomish foothills is far superior in taste to the blended commercial whiskies sold in the liquor stores. Some maintain they regularly buy the illegal whiskey not as much to save money, but because they consider the commercial distillates to be unacceptably inferior.

All of this talk aroused my curiosity and, though I do not regularly drink hard liquor (with the exception of a glass of good, well-aged brandy now and then), I decided I must try some real, authentic Skagit Mountain Dew. Announcing to Skagit Valley friends that I was in the market for some moonshine, I hoped to quickly satisfy my odd desire. But, to my surprise, none of the friends who had assured me of a ready supply, grandly promising moonshine by the gallon, could obtain even a drop. Nor were they able to put me in touch with anyone who could. The stills remained inaccessible, so I had to try a different approach.

Much of the moonshine in the northwestern counties is made by Tarheels, the hardy descendants of depression-era migrants from the Blue Ridge country of North Carolina. My first break came when a Tarheel friend, Possum Burweed (most Tarheels go by their nicknames instead of their given names), agreed to take me around and help me in my search for some good local whiskey. We began our quest in a small Tarheel barbershop in Mount Vernon. Possum talked to the barber and to several other old-timers, chatting about family happenings, the decline of local steelhead fishing, and the slump in the logging industry. In the course of gossip, he got a few leads to several small stills in the upper Skagit Valley and was told about one large operation near Darrington. But we also got a firm warning to proceed with utmost care. Some of the boys were nervous, and we might be shot on sight if we arrived too precipitously. Better contact the moonshiners through friends first, and set up a few appointments.

We decided to pay a visit to Possum's parents and discuss a proper approach to the problem with them. We had a good chat about Tarheel food and drink. Finally the talk got around to whiskey, and Possum asked his dad if he knew of anyone who made or had made moonshine. At this point his mother burst out laughing: "You know Burweed, here's one I don't think your dad ever told you about!" She dissolved in mirth: "That's what you get for not drinkin'." Possum's dad cleared his throat and said, somewhat sheepishly: "Well, son, this is funny, 'cause none of us have touched likker for years. Parson won't have it. But I guess you never learned how we put you through college." Possum seemed annoyed; he had obviously not planned on parading this skeleton from his family's rummage closet.

Old Burweed, ignoring his son's protestations, asked me: "I can still remember how to make the stuff. Do you care to have the recipe?"

I indicated my willingness and reached for my notebook. "Here goes!" he said. "Now this is going to be made in a copper still. Copper gives it the sweetest taste. You've got to have a kettle you can close off tightly and you've got to have a worm—that's a cooling coil. You can improvise the rest. I never made my own kettle; that's hard work. But it's easy to make a coil: you take a three-quarter-inch copper pipe and you fill it with sand, packed real tight, and you wrap the pipe around an old stump, coil it close together, and then lift it off the tree and drain off the sand.

"Why, for your kettle, you can use a thirty-five gallon pot; but then you've got to do two runs and you're much better off with a seventy-gallon still that'll let you go for a single run. You'll have to build yourself a furnace and work the kettle into it and make the flue go around it so's to heat it evenly on all sides. Then you've got to put a cap on your still. That can be made from copper, too, or you can use an old cider barrel. You'll put your worm into a small keg, so's you can run water past the worm and cool the stream, and you run a pipe or a horn from the cap to a thump barrel and another one from the thump barrel to the worm. I'll tell you about the thump barrel later.

"Now, you'll need to make yourself some beer. Go fetch yourself a sixty-gallon barrel and make some sweet mash: you'll take fifty-five pounds of cornmeal and twenty-five pounds of sugar and put 'em into the barrel and finish it off with good, clean water till it's almost full to the top.

"Or you can sprout your corn. Just fetch one of those sacks of feed corn and lay it into a crick until the corn's good and soaked, and then you'll lay that out on a rack in the sun so's to sprout it. It's got to have warmth, or it'll just rot. When it's really cold out, you'll take the sack to your horse stable to keep it warm, or you'll maybe have to bury it in horse manure to get your heat. When the sprouts are about an inch long, you dry your corn, and grind it real fine in a feed mill.

"But even when you'd rather use cornmeal, you've got to have some malt: you'll sprout yourself about a gallon of shelled corn, then you'll dry it out real well, and you'll grind it in an old coffee mill. You'll mix that ground malt into your barrel, with your cornmeal and sugar, and you'll put a smother of rye on top of the open keg, and then you'll just sit back and let it go to work.

"Now you've got to add sugar to the mash, 'cause if you don't and run it on corn and malt alone, you'll get only about a gallon of whiskey out of your barrel, 'cause the alcohol will be low, but with sugar it'll give you about four and a half. If you'll want more whiskey, you'll just add more sugar—but your likker won't be as good.

"It'll take about four days, maybe more, in good warm weather, say somewhere from sixty-five to eighty degrees to make your beer. If it's cold out, you'll have to bury your barrel to keep it warm, or maybe bring it into your stable or your garage. But watch out your animals don't get into your barrel! Hogs just love the stuff.

"Then, when your beer comes up to blubber, when it has cleared off all but about a third of your rye meal smother, then you're ready to ladle it into the still and run it. You've got to heat your still now. We used to use wood, but you can use propane, 'cause it won't give off any smoke, though it won't heat the kettle as nicely. When your beer gets good and hot, you'll cap the still and seal it real tight with rye paste, and you'll run the horn to the thump keg. Now you'll have to fill your thump keg with about ten gallons of beer. Leave a good space between the beer and the top of the keg and run a pipe from the top of the keg to the worm. When the beer heats up, the alcohol and flavorings evaporate and the steam'll push through the horn into the thump keg. When the hot steam bubbles through the beer in the thump keg, it'll pick up extra alcohol and flavorings, doubling the strength of your whiskey. Then it'll go to the worm to cool down.

"The thump keg gets its name from the thump, thump, thump it makes when the steam bubbles up through the beer. Now, you've got to make sure the steam cools properly as it condenses, or your whiskey'll taste hot. You've got to let it come down real slow like, so it doesn't get to tasting bad. And then, when it comes out of the end of the pipe, you've got to catch it and filter it proper, to get out the bad stuff, and all that. Then you've got yourself some of the finest drinking whiskey you'll ever find anywhere. None of that potato junk in it. And it'll be better yet if you'll lay it by in an oak barrel for a while."

"That's real medicine, that is," Possum's mother chimed in. "Why, my dad, he'd take some of that there whiskey and he'd mix it with ginger 'n' black pepper 'n' boil it in water 'n' he'd take a drink of that before he went to bed at night and it sweated the cold right out of him.

"And my dad, he'd take a drink of that homemade whiskey every morning and he never had himself any stomach trouble all his life. . . . Nor much of any other trouble. . . Was his blood pressure finally got him."

I tried to learn more about the actual running of the still and about the filtering of the raw whiskey, but I didn't have much luck.

"Well, I can't right tell you, 'cause it depends on the kind of beer you've got, and on the kind of still, and the heat of your fire and all that. Experience'll teach you. You'll just have to do it often enough and you'll learn. You'll just throw out the bad stuff and keep the good. But you've got to use your nose and taste buds. Experience'll tell you. It'll teach ya!

"Now, when that first shot of whiskey comes out of the worm, it'll be about two hundred proof or so, and you'll run it until it breaks, till it stops running alcohol. Then you'll take the backings that'll come through the worm and you'll run an equal amount of those, and you'll mix them with the alcohol down to about eighty proof. That'll be the cleanest, the sweetest tasting whiskey you've ever had. Better than anything you can buy!

"It'll take you about two hours to do a run, and you'll only get four and a half, maybe five, gallons of whiskey out of it. So it doesn't pay to sell it. But it's sure good. Best medicine you can get!"

Making whiskey is still illegal, even for home consumption, so I asked about the law.

"Let me tell you! You've got to be careful, of course. You'll never go into a still the same way twice. But it's much easier here than it is in the South. Woods are denser and the country's more rugged and less settled. With any luck you can keep your still at home. Most guys get caught when they get careless, or drunk, or they'll sell it to kids. Some people sell it from their garage, but you can't do it too close to a school or church, or you're just asking for trouble. If a man doesn't bother the churches he's left alone.

"You can hide it all right. You can put it into fruit jars and set it into a crick, and nobody can see a thing, 'cause the jars are clear. One fella stored it right above the rafters in his ceiling. Had a pipe run to a dummy light fixture. Just unscrewed the light bulb when he needed to drain it. There's another guy they never caught. Why, he had a fake bottom in his wheelchair, and that's how he carried the stuff to customers. I had this old '37 Ford, and I loaded the trunk full of fruit jars when I delivered.

"You don't have to use corn to make likker. Don't even have to use grain. Some crooks'll use everything: apples, potatoes, molasses, blackberries. But that'll split your head wide open. Some fellas now make it legally from surplus wheat and barley. You can get a permit to make gasohol. And some of that stuff even gets mixed in with gasoline. A lot of it goes...why, you can make some real good stuff that way...."

So much for the history of Possum's family enterprises. The crazy thing was that the more I talked to people in the Tarheel country, the more I heard about moonshine, yet I just couldn't get a taste of the real thing. Beer and jug wine were much more a regular day's drink, even back in the hills. I did, finally, acquire a small sample of the real mountain dew, but it came to me by ways so devious and indirect that my futile attempts at tracing it were doomed to failure from the outset. The only still I got to see is the one in the Skagit Historical Museum in La Conner.

But at least I got to try the real stuff. The quality of this homemade whiskey was every drop as good as the Tarheels claimed. I got only half a baby jar's full, and I doled it out to friends with a spoon. Just about every one liked it. It had a rich, fruity nose (one friend thought he was sampling a fruit brandy) and it was very mellow. But then it had been aging in oak for a few years. There was a suspicion that it may have come from the (un-) confiscated batch made in the Burlington "candy" factory.

Ever since the fine art of making home-distilled whiskey arrived in the Pacific Northwest with the first white settlers, the tasty distillate served as a means of quenching a particular kind of thirst. It never became a means of taking hard-to-transport grain to market in a more easily carried form, as it did in the rugged vales of the Appalachian Mountains. Moonshining in the Pacific Northwest was, and still is, simply a way of creating flavorful, refined, handcrafted whiskies of a superior quality. The only exception to this was the unfortunate teetotalitarianism of the Prohibition, when everything connected with alcohol sold like crazy, and nobody cared much for quality. But once commercial distilling became legal again, moonshining in the Northwest returned to its former status as a fine, though arcane, art, crafted by knowledgeable artisans with utmost skill, and fully appreciated by true lovers of noble drink and low prices. Thanks to the invention of gasohol, legal stills are popping up throughout our region—especially in the grainlands of Transcascadia—and, as Possum's dad said, some of that alcohol may even find its way into gas tanks.

If my experience with northwest mountain dew represented a true example of the state of the art, it may well be worth one's while to find a good, regular supply of homemade whiskey—if only for "medicinal" purposes.

Skagit River Dip

Here's a somewhat different dip that goes very well with our northwest ales, with Black-hook Porter, and, of course, Skagit moonshine. Serve with crackers or black bread.

Cream Cheese (see Index) 6 tablespoons, softened
Thick Crème Fraîche (see Index) 1 cup
Skagit moonshine* **2 tablespoons**
Salmon or sturgeon caviar ¼ cup

1. Beat softened Cream Cheese until smooth.
2. Fold in Crème Fraîche, moonshine, and caviar.
3. Refrigerate for at least 3 hours before serving.

* If you cannot find moonshine, substitute vodka or a good sour mash corn liquor.

Makes about 1¾ cups

Shrimp in Beer

This is a very nice recipe for freshly caught shrimp. It is very easy to make, so you can quickly prepare your shrimp at the source, whether you're at a campsite on the shores of Washington's Hood Canal or in a seaside motel on the Oregon coast. Serve hot with toasted french bread and chilled beer.

Fresh uncooked shrimp in the shell 3 pounds
Medium garlic cloves 4, peeled
Allspice 6
Tabasco sauce dash
Salt and freshly ground pepper to taste
Bay leaf (Oregon Myrtle) 1
Fresh parsley sprigs 6
Fresh dill sprigs 2
Good lager beer (preferably Henry Weinhard's Private Reserve) 12-ounce can

1. Combine all ingredients in heavy skillet. Cover closely and bring to boil.
2. Let shrimp simmer for 2 minutes and remove from heat. Serve in the shell, letting each guest peel his or her own.

Serves 6 to 8

Crawfish in Skagit River Moonshine

Serve with chilled moonshine, beer, or dry wine—and chunks of fresh country bread to mop up the sauce.

Medium crawfish tails, unshelled   20
Fresh lemon juice   ¼ cup
Salt and freshly ground pepper   to taste
Unsalted butter   2 tablespoons
Shallots   1 tablespoon finely chopped
Moonshine*   ¼ cup
Heavy cream   ¾ cup
Chervil   1 tablespoon finely chopped

1. Marinate crawfish tails in lemon juice, salt, and pepper for 5 to 10 minutes.
2. Heat butter in a skillet and when it is quite hot, but not smoking, add crawfish tails, stirring rapidly. Cook for about 2 minutes. Sprinkle with shallots and stir for about 10 seconds. Add moonshine. (Take care the whiskey does not catch on fire—it can be pretty potent.)
3. Remove tails from pan; shell and return. (Lower heat while shelling.)
4. Add cream and cook over high heat about 1 minute.
5. Salt and pepper to taste.
6. Remove tails with slotted spoon. Keep warm.
7. Bring sauce to a full rolling boil for about 30 seconds and add chopped chervil. Spoon sauce over crawfish tails.

* This dish will be tastiest when you use some of the intensely fruity moonshine distilled in the woods bordering the Skagit River. But if you lack access to this delectable tipple, you may substitute a good sour mash corn "likker."

Serves 4

Wines

I t's the end of September, and fall comes early to the Yakima Valley—quite unlike the wine country of California, where even now temperatures may regularly rise above eighty degrees. A chill breeze wafts through the cottonwoods and sumacs and rustles the weeds which crowd the empty lot separating the winery from the river road. The river itself, tamed by dams and placid in its bed of reeds, hides behind the trees and brush of a fall-colored bank.

The small, cylindrical, stainless steel wine press has been pulled from the storage shed where it lives for most of the year and now stands just outside the fence enclosing the utility yard of the Hinzerling winery. Donna Wallace bends over the open press as a steady stream of purple gewürztraminer pulp and skins plop from an overhead feeder pipe. Donna's arms are immersed in the fragrant pomace; she pushes the slippery mass about, pressing it into every nook and cranny of the press cylinder. This pomace is the residue, the dissipated semifirm matter remaining after most of the grape juice has run off on its own. This particular pomace stems from last night's crush. The juice, skin, and pulp have rested in a cooled tank overnight, just long enough for the must to leach the varietal flavor from the macerated skins, but not so long as to pull the color from the pale hulls and dye the wine.

The bulk of the free-run juice is strained off before the pomace reaches the press; more juice runs freely through the slats of the press into the collection trough below the drum, as Donna packs down the skins. Mike Wallace, the wine maker, scurries back and forth, regulating the flow of the pomace from the tank to the strainer and on to the press, making sure the juice reaches the fermentation vat without exposure to air or contaminants.

Filling the press is a slow and tedious process, but finally the drum is loaded to capacity, the top closed, and gentle hydraulic pressure applied. Inside the press cylinder, a long horizontal steel screw pulls two plates together, from the ends into the center, trapping the pomace in between. As the press slowly rotates, several metal hoops attached to loose chains inside the drum break up the caking grape skins.

Mike Wallace keeps the pressure low, to avoid breaking the pips, which can release evil-tasting oils and other undesirable substances into the juice; even so, the pressing will extract harsh flavor elements from the skins, and thus most of the press juice will be kept apart from the free-run juice and fermented separately. It may be sold as cheap wine, or small quantities may be blended into the free-run wine to increase its complexity, acidity, or to give more balance to a flat or dull wine. When all of the juice has been squeezed from the pomace, the spent residue is loaded into a trailer to be taken back to the vineyard, where it will be plowed under as organic fertilizer.

The Hinzerling vineyard is not idle while the grapes are being pressed. Long before the last of the juice has been extracted from the current batch, Mike has returned to the vineyard to check on the pickers and to measure the grapes' sugar and acid levels to determine which rows will be picked next. Shortly after the day's pressing is finished—after the press and the plastic pipes have been cleaned thoroughly—a new load of ripe grapes arrives at the winery, ready to be crushed.

Crushing differs from pressing in several important ways, primarily because in crushing no excess force is applied to extract the juice from the berry. The newly picked gewürztraminer grapes are trucked the few miles between the Hinzerling vineyard and the winery in open plastic half-barrels. Mike Wallace and an assistant slide the barrels down a slanted conveyor to the stemmer/crusher. Here the containers are tilted carefully and the grapes slid into a large hopper. Fast-moving, rotating paddles knock the grape berries off the stems, forcing them through a perforated drum onto an Archimedian screw which further breaks up the skins and, as a lovely fruity fragrance rises above the machine, pushes the slurry of juice, skins, and pulp into clear plastic pipes connected with the holding tank. The denuded stems are flipped out of the rear of the stemmer and collected, because they, like the spent pomace, will be returned to the vineyard as fertilizer.

This initial process is similar for all grape varieties, but from here on each variety will be treated somewhat differently. Mike adds sodium dioxide powder in tiny amounts to the crushed gewürztraminer berries to sterilize the juice. He also drops in small quantities of a peptic enzyme which will help break down the gewürztraminer skin, extracting more free-run juice, as well as a larger share of precious flavor-bearing elements. The pulp is held in the storage tank that has been primed with carbon dioxide gas to minimize the juice's exposure to air, since oxidation may turn the clear juice of fresh grapes brown and create all kinds of off-flavors (once fermentation starts, the carbon dioxide released naturally will protect the new wine).

Riesling and chardonnay grapes are crushed and the juice is filtered off the skins immediately and sent to the fermentation vats; the pomace is then pressed just like the gewürztraminer residue. Merlot, cabernet sauvignon, and other red wine grapes are also sent directly to the fermentation tanks, but they are not removed from the skins or pulp until the fermentation is complete and all the sugar in the juice has been converted to alcohol. When fermentation stops, the vat's tap is opened, and the "free-run" wine is drained off; the remaining pomace is pumped into the wine press. Some wineries take their red wine must off the skins after a few days now to make lighter, quicker-maturing reds; but Mike Wallace commonly lets his wines stay the full course to get rich, full-flavored reds, which may take a decade or more to mature.

As Mike moves the barrels to the hopper, his father shows me the variations among individual gewürztraminer grapes. There are big, plump, purplish berries—high in sugar and fruit and a bit flat in taste—and smaller yellow berries—with excellent fruit, high acid, and a lingering aftertaste. It takes both to make a good gewürztraminer wine. Many of the bunches are studded with wholly or partially shriveled berries. These grapes have been affected by a beneficial fungus, *Botrytis cinerea*, which breaks the berries' skins and allows excess water to evaporate; acids, sugars, and fruit extracts stay behind. We can taste the difference between berries that are just slightly wrinkled and just a tad more intense in flavor and sweetness than the unaffected grapes, and the heavily dehydrated, almost raisinlike berries which each give up only a drop or two of a dense, honeyed, fruity nectar.

Mike Wallace hopes that conditions this fall will continue to favor the development of Botrytis in the vineyard, for he is an expert at making aromatic, balanced dessert wines that can be created only in those years when the ripe grapes are properly affected by Botrytis. Riesling grapes, when fully ripe and with good levels of acid, make an even better dessert wine under optimum Botrytis conditions than the gewürztraminer.

But, back to the more prosaic (and useful) world of table wines: once the must has been pumped into the fermentation vats, it undergoes a series of steps that convert it from mere fruit juice to wine. Yeasts are added to ferment the sugars. All of the sugars may be fermented into alcohol to make a totally dry wine, or the fermentation may be arrested to make a sweet or semisweet wine, and so on, depending on the wine maker's skill and on the style of wine he is planning to make. It is at this stage that the public is excluded from observing the wine making process, for each wine maker has his own secrets, ranging from the amount of time the wine is left on the skins, to the special yeasts used during fermentation, to the temperature at which the wine has been fermented. (Some labels will state this information after the wine is finished.) It is here that the wine maker's special talent, his understanding of the special requirements of his wines, comes into play, the special something that distinguishes an artist from a dilettante.

The northwest wine maker is, to a certain extent, very fortunate, because the juice extracted from his grapes needs no (or few) additives to make excellent wine. Unlike German or French wine makers, the northwest vintner need add no sugar (or sweet grape extract) to his must to raise the alcohol levels of his finished wines. Unlike the Spanish, Italian, or Californian wine makers, he need not worry about low acid levels in his grapes (nor need he add artificial tartaric acid to balance his wines).

The hot summer days of the Yakima Valley in eastern Washington—and of the Willamette, Umpqua, and Rogue River valleys in western Oregon—help raise the grapes' sugar levels. The long northern days (up to seventeen daylight hours in June) increase the growing period and help produce excellent fruit; the cool summer nights and the cool daytime weather in early fall keep the beneficial acids, necessary for the creation of a balanced wine, in the berries.

My own introduction to the mysteries of wine began in the vineyards of Franconia. Wine was a part of our meals from early childhood on. And the making of wine was part of the annual cycle of life (the grapes were tended, picked, and pressed even during the ferocious strife of World War II), starting with the spring's pruning and cultivation of the vines and ending with the harvest of the grapes and the crush in fall. We children were everywhere. No one minded our presence very much. It seemed natural that we were about, investigating the wine making, and getting our share of the freshly fermented grape juice.

At an early age, I learned to recognize the different tastes of wine—dry riesling, sylvaner, and gewürztraminer, the luscious Botrytis sweetness of the late-harvest wines, and the thin redness of the locally produced pinot noir. I learned to distinguish between the soils on which the wines were grown, to discuss the effect of our distinct miniclimates, and to evaluate the elusive nuances of each local varietal. I was taught to prefer the wines from the hillside vineyards, because they showed depth and complexity and aged well. But mostly we drank the less expensive wines from bottomland vineyards, because they were pleasant, mildly fruity quaffing wines which had to be drunk young, for they had only a short period of liveliness before they faded or turned sour. Perhaps because of a similarity in growing conditions, the same holds true for the wines produced in the Pacific Northwest.

A wine's ability to age properly is a good indicator of how well it is made. A clumsily made wine will either sour in a short time, lose all of its flavor, or perhaps even fall apart into its inadequately bonded chemical components as it ages in barrel or bottle. Here is the one area where the wine maker from a small winery, who has time to treat his limited production of handmade wines with special care, triumphs over the harried technician of the bulk wineries. It is often difficult to predict what will happen within the arcane confines of a sealed wine bottle over a period of time—northwest wines really have not been around long enough to provide a solid framework of past experiences. But there seems to be little doubt that some of the wines produced by a handful of our most excellent small wineries will last for a long time, improving as they age. More than anything else, this demonstrates that vinifera grapes have found ideal growing conditions in the valleys of the Pacific Northwest.

Wine grapes have been grown in the Pacific Northwest for a very long time, ever since Peter Britt planted a vineyard near Jacksonville in southern Oregon in 1854 and produced his first commercial wine ten years later. Wineries proliferated in the Northwest until Prohibition dealt them a severe blow from which they were slow to recover. Oregon's vineyards were replanted first, in the early 1960s, but Washington followed suit by the early 1970s. As late as 1978, there were only some seven wineries in Washington State, as compared to some twenty for Oregon; by 1980, the number of Washington wineries had doubled; in 1983, it had increased to thirty-seven wineries which were either producing or about to have their first crush.

In some ways, Northwesterners today are confronted by an almost unmanageable number of both wineries and wines. Connoisseurs of fine wines in our region now face the same kind of dilemma that confronted Californians just a few years ago: there are so many new wineries, even the experts have problems keeping track of them all—much less of the different number of wines produced each year. But who would complain of the task when it is such a pleasant chore?

The best thing about the wines of the Pacific Northwest is that, pleasant though many are for drinking by themselves, most go very well with food. More than any wines made outside the vineyards of France, the wines of our region—whether crisp, intensely fruity whites or rich, full-bodied reds—are made to go with the foodstuffs produced by our own farmers, fishermen, ranchers, and gardeners.

My first experience with a northwest wine was through a chenin blanc. Victoria and I had been driven off a small lake on the Olympic Peninsula by a sudden, fierce squall. Our canoe rested safely in a bed of reeds as we prepared a picnic luncheon under cover of a dense cedar tree—two fat, freshly caught trout, cleaned, spitted, and propped up by our small fire, a mess of crawfish roasting over the coals, and handfuls of just-picked juicy huckleberries. The bread we brought was soggy from the unexpected rain, but the Tillamook Cheddar was fine. The wine, both drunk in small sips straight from the bottle and gently sprinkled over trout and crawfish, fixed taste and place in our minds forever.

But we have memories of many noteworthy northwest wines—like the surprisingly delicious late-harvest gewürztraminer served with a splendid peach tart at Rick O'Reilly's

La Petite Maison in Olympia. The gewürztraminer is a difficult grape to grow and properly vinify; it gives its best only when conditions are entirely to its liking. The austere, bone-dry traminers made in Europe in the Alsatian tradition go well with a surprising variety of foods. It is, however, quite difficult to find a good sweet late-harvest gewürztraminer in Europe.

The story is different in the Pacific Northwest. I was pleased to learn that the late-harvest gewürztraminer served at La Petite Maison—the best I had ever tasted—was a local product. Looking over my euphoric tasting notes, I can still remember this wine's powerful, flowery nose, its lovely underlying traminer varietal taste, its beautiful Botrytis tone, and its excellent sugar-acid balance. I was surprised to find that such a magnificent wine could have been produced in the still very young wine-growing district of the Yakima Valley. There was only one thing to do: I headed east of the mountains to take a good look at the winery which had created this liquid art, Hinzerling Vineyards in Prosser.

It was during this trip that I first talked to Mike Wallace about the wines in his cellar. The winery itself seemed unimpressive and not exactly designed to inspire confidence—an old cinder-block garage filled with barrels and gadgets—but the contents of those barrels were something else! Mike demonstrated his different styles of making red and white wines by giving me an impromptu barrel tasting. Using a "thief" (a specially designed large pipette), he took samples of the aging wines through the barrel bungholes. Here were merlots, cabernet sauvignons, chardonnays, gewürztraminers, and rieslings, some young and crisp, others affected by varying degrees of Botrytis. Finally, tucked away in two small kegs, was another batch of nectar—only this one was made from riesling grapes, not from gewürztraminer.

The riesling, a grape that makes a honeyed, delicately wild-flower-scented wine at its best, is the grape which is most responsible for the Northwest's renown as a major wine-growing region. In its area of origin, the vineyards of southern Germany, the riesling is made primarily into sweet wine, to be enjoyed after dinner on its own, not with food. Yet this varietal is capable of making excellent dry and sweet wines. In the Alsace, in Franconia, and in western Oregon, it is vinified into austere dry wines with good fruit—firm, full, strong enough to accompany not only fish and fowl but some red meats as well, though it can be light and delicate.

In Washington, it is made either into light sipping wines or, when the heat of summer ripens the grapes to perfection and when a succession of fall fogs and sunshine create ideal growing conditions for *Botrytis cinerea*, it may be crafted into rich dessert wines. This may result in flowery wines that are sweet but contain sufficient acids to balance the sugars, wines with bouquets that hint of tree-ripened apricots and peaches, with aromas that can fill a room with their delicate yet powerful fragrances. Such wines do not need any foods to accompany them, though they go well with aged Oregon blue cheese, fresh, tree-ripened fruits, sweet bombes and other desserts, and even with fish in sweet fruit sauces. But the versatility of a big, dry riesling is almost unsurpassed. It enhances an array of foods, from tangy European flat oysters (the kind grown at Westcott Bay and Shelton) and Olympia oysters to limpets, crab, and crawfish; from white-fleshed fish in gentle sauces to lusty barbecued salmon; from delicate rainbow trout *au bleu* to poached carp and roast pork with sauerkraut. I have enjoyed it with sole and with steak in mustard sauce. If you travel and can bring only one good wine with you, let it be a northwest riesling—you're bound to encounter harmonizing fare.

Our rieslings are well worth experimenting with. Try the austere Washington wines made by Mike Wallace at Hinzerling with fresh, steamed mussels; or John Rauner's softer Yakima River Winery rieslings with ripe strawberries or Comice pears; or taste one of the lighter rieslings made by Max Zellweger at Langguth as a party or summer afternoon sipping wine; or have one of the dry, almost severe rieslings from the Salishan vineyard (located west of the mountains in La Center) with sea cucumbers, crabs, or smelt.

The Oregon wine makers believe in making dry rieslings almost exclusively—although they have shown themselves capable of making superb late-harvest wines as well (in particular, Pat Campbell at Elk Cove). Western Oregon is especially well suited to making good fish and oyster wines from this cool climate varietal: after all, it was Richard Sommer of Hillcrest Vineyards in Roseburg who reestablished the riesling in western Oregon. Some very lovely dry rieslings, comparable to the best produced in the Alsace, now come out of the valleys of the Umpqua and Willamette, well-suited to accompany the Northwest's best fish, crab, clams, mussels, oysters, and fowl.

Other European white wine grapes also do well in the Pacific Northwest. The sauvignon blanc and the semillon blanc, two southerly French varietals, make good food wines in eastern Washington; the semillon may make a better wine in the Columbia Valley than it does in its native France. Both of these varietals hold up nicely with oysters, crab, and fish (though I prefer a riesling or chardonnay with mussels). I prefer the semillon with the more gently flavored freshwater fish and crustaceans and the sauvignon blanc with more robust fare like carp, sturgeon, rockfish, poached or grilled salmon, beach crabs, barnacles, and marine snails. An intensely varietal sauvignon blanc can also enhance herbed smoked pork or ham and is superb with stuffed goose, sausages, sea cucumbers, geoduck, Marblemount goat Cheddar, and ripe Oregon blue cheese.

The world's greatest white dinner wine, a wine which vies with the riesling, the chardonnay of Burgundy, shows great promise in the Pacific Northwest. It is made into big, dry "blockbuster" wines, powerful enough to accompany red meats, in the warm vineyards of eastern Washington and into crisp, dry fish and oyster wines in the cooler climes of western Oregon (one of the great pleasures of northwestern seafood lovers lies in the wide varieties of wines available to them to match to their favorite food: eating fish or shellfish need never be dull). Our two major growing regions thus produce chardonnays with distinctive characters.

The quality of our chardonnays has continually improved over the last several years and the best—the complex chardonnays made by Scott Henry in Roseburg on the Umpqua, by Dave Lett at Eyrie in McMinnville, and Pat and Joe Campbell at Elk Cove—are very exciting, complex, and drinkable. The chardonnay is more austere than the average riesling (though the two may approach each other at times) and, though it gets along well with many of the foods that are enhanced by a riesling, it prefers these foods to be cooked in different ways and with different herbs and spices. Rieslings are best with fish and shellfish in light sauces (or with just a delicate beurre blanc); the chardonnay stands up well to heavy cream concoctions. The riesling goes along with parsley, chervil, dill, and lovage; the chardonnay harmonizes with mustard, rosemary, and tarragon. I have, in fact, often wondered if the chardonnay's affinity for tarragon has led the French to place special emphasis on this fragrant herb, using it in a variety of dishes designed to complement and enhance their favorite dinner wine.

Chardonnay, unlike riesling, may also accompany spicy young goat cheeses and old Cheddar but, for some not completely understood reason, it does not agree with salmon (unless the fish is impeccably fresh), for it tends to make the salmon seem "fishier" in taste than it actually is.

The chardonnay's relative, the pinot gris, is perhaps our best wine for accompanying salmon, whether this delectable fish is steamed, poached, fried, baked, barbecued, or smoked (though I prefer a sweet riesling or a heavy native ale with my smoked salmon), but it is currently produced by only two of our wineries: Eyrie in Oregon and Gray Monk in British Columbia. Of these, the Eyrie pinot gris is the more robust wine, the Gray Monk has more finesse.

It was Dave Lett at Eyrie who first made me aware of the affinity between pinot gris and salmon, when he sold me this wine only after I promised to consume it with freshly caught salmon. Salmon has never been easy to match with wine because it is such a rich, oily fish. One might think a red wine would go well with the red-meated flesh, but most red wines bring out an annoying "metallic" taste in the salmon; sweet rieslings sometimes work, especially if the salmon is prepared in a sweet fruit sauce; chardonnay may not only bring out a fishy taste, but it may clash with any lemon juice that has been used to cut the salmon's oiliness.

Yet the pinot gris, which is often considered a minor varietal, far inferior to the chardonnay, works very well, even when the salmon's flavor has been enhanced by barbecuing. This pungent wine is sometimes slightly flat in its native south-central Europe, but ours have a very good acid balance and are big enough to match the salmon's distinctive flavor. This applies as well to the lighter, more ethereal Gray Monk pinot gris, which is able to hold its own and enhance the taste of a fresh poached salmon.

Another wine that goes surprisingly well with poached salmon is made from a truly minor grape, the Aligoté. This Burgundian quaffing wine grape is currently raised by only one of our wineries, Quail Run, but it is well worth searching out because it makes better wine in the Yakima Valley than it does in its native Burgundy and because it is somehow just right for fresh poached silver salmon.

Good as our white table wines are, we also have excellent reds to go with our meals, and there have been some pleasant surprises for fanciers of fine dinner wines since red wine grapes were first planted in the Northwest. The lemberger, a red wine grape that makes an inconsequential wine in its native Germany, may just turn out to be one of those unexpected boons wine makers always hope for. I have tasted the light-bodied, faintly flavored quaffing wines made from this grape in the hills of southern Germany and thus was not very excited when John Williams and James Holmes of Kiona Vineyards insisted I try their lemberger. The setting was as apt and lovely as it could be: a cool day in early June amongst the vines of Hinzerling Vineyards. I had just filled my wineglass and raised it to my nose, sniffing its fruity aroma, when a sudden wild skirl of pipes burst from the vines. Sure enough, a piper stepped from the serried green rows, dressed in filibeg and sporran, plaid and bonnet, blowing away to his heart's delight on a well-tuned set of pipes. The piper, as it turned out, had nothing to do with the wine; he was just a neighbor who liked to play his pipes on solemn occasions.

As I listened to the rousing performance, I took my first sip of the deep red wine—and promptly forgot the blaring piper. This was not the thin, acetic lemberger I remembered from Germany, but a surprisingly rich wine. This must be the red wine eastern Washington winegrowers have been waiting for: a good, easily cultivated red wine grape, high in color and extract, rich in flavor, and aromatic—the perfect wine for accompanying the Northwest's superb lamb and beef. In some respects it occupies a place similar to that of California's zinfandel which, as the *primitivo di puglia*, makes an indifferent wine in its native Italy, but a superb wine in the Sierran foothills of California.

The lemberger is by no means a great wine grape; it cannot match a pinot noir, cabernet sauvignon, or merlot, for example. But because it grows well in eastern Washingon and is prolific, it has the potential of making a very good, affordable dinner wine. And it lends itself to quite a variable treatment by the wine maker. The second lemberger I tried from Quail Run was not as rich and full as the Kiona lemberger, but light and fruity, much like a California quaffing wine.

Yet the lemberger is more than just a quaffing wine. It has sufficient body and fruit to go well with meats and cheeses. While it may be a bit rough around the edges for the best prime rib, it readily harmonizes with the varied flavors of wild meats. Drink it with barbecued wild rabbit, sharp-tailed grouse, chukar, roast mallard, goose, or porcupine and beaver stew. Put it into a stew, especially when there's some bear or squirrel in it too (or marmot). Lemberger also goes with elk and buffalo, but black-tailed deer demands an even bigger wine: a rich merlot or cabernet sauvignon, huge in taste, almost black in color, like the fat red wines made in the Yakima and Columbia valleys.

Of these, the merlot is the softer wine; the cabernet can be quite harsh when young. Both do well in eastern Washington, making flavorful, well-balanced wines that age with grace. The best of our claret-style reds may be a blend of these two wines, designed carefully to meld their various complexities. These wines are our meat wines par excellence. Delicate enough to accompany feathered game such as quail, pigeon, grouse, partridge, duck, and goose (this applies especially to the lighter cabernets made by Preston and the Associated Vintners), they also enhance such diverse foods as fresh cheeses, sausages, hamburgers, tenderloin steaks, venison, lamb, and aged Cheddars. Cabernet sauvignon goes well with chocolate, too! This is a boon if you want to serve a multicourse dinner, but dislike sweet dessert wines: you can serve a big northwest cabernet with a decadent chocolate torte, a scrumptious mousse, or an assortment of hand-dipped chocolates. (I didn't believe this would work, until it was sprung on me after a luncheon at Seattle's Alexis Hotel. Try it! You'll be surprised how nicely it works.)

The climate in the Oregon wine-growing regions is too cold for merlot to ripen properly and even the cabernet grows vigorously only in the Rogue and Umpqua River valleys. But the pinot noir, the world's most fickle red wine grape and the one that makes the best red wine—when conditions are just right—prospers in western Oregon. Well, relatively speaking.

The pinot noir is the grape every wine maker hates—and loves—and hates. It makes great wine in the Burgundian vineyards of France, but then only sometimes, and only when the weather is right. And it only makes really good wine in a few vineyards where it likes the soil and the miniclimate, while it makes bad wine in the neighboring vineyard, just on the other side of the stone wall. And it has a number of confusing clones, some of which make great wines, and some of which produce wine that is barely fit to drink. No wonder wine makers get frustrated.

But in a good year, pinot noir can make a red wine so complex and intense that all production woes are forgiven and forgotten. It makes just such an excellent wine in the valleys of western Oregon...when and if conditions are right. Eyrie Vineyard's David Lett, the pioneer who planted the first pinot noir vines in the Red Hills of Dundee, has won honors in France—that country fiercely jealous of the superior quality of its Burgundian pinot noirs—for one of his Oregon pinots. So has Myron Redford of Amity. Most Oregon pinot noirs are still on the level of pleasant dinner reds, however, without too many pretensions, good for accompanying dark-fleshed fowl or red meat. In a good year, they will be firm and fruity; in a less perfect year they may be a bit thin and acetic (but then they agree with salmon, as does a blushingly pink wine made from red pinot grapes).

Nothing can match a good pinot noir when it is served with perfectly roasted pheasant or grouse, stewed, braised, or grilled venison, barbecued lamb chops, or tenderloin of kid. It is enhanced by the delicate flavors of soft, newly made cheeses, whether made from goat's or cow's milk; it heightens the flavors of grilled white meats—chicken, turkey, veal, and pork; and it is a big enough wine to stand up to the pungency of aged Cheddar and Oregon blue. You may even drink it with such delectable peasant fare as the excellent Swiss brat-wurst and landjäger made by Fred Bucheli at the Matterhorn in Yakima or the garlicky kielbasa and pepperoni from John Carek's butcher shop in Roslyn, or with such snobby dishes as the exquisite trout pâté from R & R Aquaculture in Quilcene, or tangy Marble-mount Cheddar or Cascadian goat cheese.

Who can tell how many "perfect" combinations of wine and food there are? This is a field without unassailable experts: you may come up with a favorite food and wine com-bination that goes against the grain of the established "rules." Well? Enjoy it! Nobody can tell you that you shouldn't do it, when it works for you. Experiment! Try different com-binations, and try experimenting continually! What, for example, is the best wine to drink with sea urchin roe? Or chiton? Or muskrat? You'll have to find out yourself, but you'll have fun doing so!

There is a great future for northwest wines in our dining rooms. As time progresses, our wines should continue to improve, both in quality (as our vintners become more familiar with the specific quirks of grape varieties, soils, and miniclimates), and with age (as select bottles mature slowly in our cellars). Nothing goes better with our sumptuous twelve-month harvest feast than a bottle of good northwest wine: a crisp, young chardonnay with fresh sturgeon caviar, a big Yakima Valley cabernet sauvignon with prime roast of Charo-lais, or a lemberger with muskrat stew; an Oregon pinot noir with island lamb chops, or an austere, almost herbaceous sauvignon blanc with limpets, salmon roe, and pink scallops; a gewürztraminer with sea urchin roe, and a rich late-harvest riesling with soft-ripened Comice pears and lightly smoked trout. It would be a sin not to take advantage of this proffered bounty and enjoy it to the fullest!

Donna Wallace's Hinzerling Vineyards Cabernet Chocolate Cake

Donna Wallace, wife of Hinzerling Vineyards wine maker Mike Wallace, gave me this recipe after a simple wine country harvest dinner I enjoyed with the Wallace family during the 1983 crush in Prosser, in the heart of the Yakima Valley wine country.

Butter   ¾ cup
Sugar   1¾ cups
Large eggs   2
Vanilla extract   1 teaspoon
All-purpose flour   2 cups unsifted
Cocoa   ¾ cup
Baking soda   1¼ teaspoons
Salt   ½ teaspoon
Cabernet sauvignon   1⅓ cups
Sifted confectioner's sugar   ½ to 1 cup

1. Cream butter and sugar until light and fluffy.
2. Add eggs and vanilla, and beat 1 minute at medium speed.
3. Combine flour, cocoa, baking soda, and salt; fold in dry ingredients alternately with wine to creamed mixture.
4. Pour batter into 2 greased and floured round cake pans. Bake at 350° 35 to 40 minutes for 8-inch pans; 30 to 35 minutes for 9-inch pans. (Test for doneness by inserting toothpick in center. It should be clean when cake is done.)
5. When baked, remove pans and cool for 10 minutes; remove cake from pans and place on cooling racks until cooled completely. Dust with sifted confectioner's sugar.

Serves 12 to 16

Riesling Custard Foam Sokol Blosser

Try this dish with a nice late-harvest riesling and with fresh northwest raspberries or straw-berries.

Egg yolks   3
Sugar   ½ cup
Riesling   ½ cup

1. In medium saucepan or bowl, beat egg yolks with sugar until thick, about 10 minutes.
2. Fill a large skillet with water and heat until simmering.
3. Place bowl of egg yolk mixture in skillet and beat, slowly adding riesling until mixture is

light yellow and tripled in volume.

4. Remove custard from hot water and place that bowl in large bowl filled with ice cubes.
5. Beat until well chilled. Serve.

Serves 4 to 6

Captain Whidbey Inn Hot Mulled Wine

This is great stuff for a cold winter evening, when the solstice winds whip Penn Cove into a froth. There's usually a big pot of this mulled wine steaming in the bar's fireplace. A couple of cups will take the winter chill from your bones.

Water   2 cups
Sugar   4 cups
Cinnamon   1 tablespoon
Ground cloves   1 teaspoon
Dry red wine   1 gallon
Oranges   3, thinly sliced
Lemon   1, thinly sliced

1. Combine water and sugar and boil until sugar has been absorbed into liquid.
2. Add cinnamon and cloves. Stir to blend.
3. Add wine; reheat mixture to just below boiling.
4. Add orange and lemon slices.
5. Place kettle with wine in fireplace (on coals) or set onto stove on low heat. Make sure it does not boil.

Serves 8 to 12

Chefs of the Northwest

Martin Hahn stands in his tiny kitchen, deftly boning fresh trout (delivered from a nearby trout farm only an hour ago). A basket of wild huckleberries sits on the counter, next to the cutting board. The berries will be reduced later in sweet butter, blended with a fumet (a light stock made from fish heads, bones, and fresh herbs), and used to glaze fresh halibut steaks that were poached in the fumet.

Martin removes the last fine bones from the trout with tweezers, walks to his cooler, and removes a bin of fresh Oregon scallops. "Here, try one!" They're quite small, crisp, and very sweet. "Have you tried the European flat oysters grown at Crescent Beach on Orcas Island yet?...No?...Here, this is a nice one.... Where's my oyster knife?...Here you go; don't spill the juice!" The oyster is tasty—not as flavorful, perhaps, as the flat oysters grown by Bill Webb at Westcott Bay or by Peter Becker at Little Skookum—but tasty nevertheless.

The chef spreads the scallops on his cutting board, quickly cuts them in half, and tosses them with freshly chopped tarragon, chives, parsley, some sweet butter, a touch of lemon juice, and a few sprinkles of salt and pepper. He stuffs the trout with the aromatic mixture, wraps the fish in parchment, and poaches it for a few minutes—until the trout is just done—and presents it, dabbed with a tarragon hollandaise sauce, to a delighted customer.

Other dinner guests at Martin Hahn's small but renowned restaurant, The Black Swan in LaConner, Washington, order the red huckleberry-glazed halibut, the fresh squid cooked in a flavorful sauce made from its own ink, or Oregon scallops in cream sauce. Most of them finish their meal with a delightful wild huckleberry tart—tangy wild huckleberries served on a ricotta base, glazed with crème de cassis.

The Black Swan is a tiny restaurant, huddled beneath the tall bluff that separates LaConner's upper town from the waterfront business district. The view from the open kitchen door goes down a maple-lined walkway, across the village's busy main street, to a waterfront parking lot. You can almost see the water. Beyond the water—on the other bank of the Swinomish Slough (which separates Fidalgo Island from the mainland)—sprawls the Swinomish Indian Village, a community that (despite its modern appearance) predates LaConner by several centuries.

Up the street from The Black Swan, within easy walking distance, the piers and wood-frame processing sheds of fish buyers rise from the channel. The processors handle not only salmon—forever the staple of the Northwest—and the rockfish and bottom fish for which the Puget Sound waters are renowned, but also some occasional oddities (at least as far as the wholesale trade is concerned) like sea urchins or sea cucumbers. And whenever a strange fish makes its appearance, Martin will be right there, ready to determine its culinary qualities.

The Skagit River lowlands surrounding LaConner grow some of the tastiest produce in the world, and the sloughs, dry, rocky hillocks, and the shady, moist forests provide a bounty of wild edibles. Martin Hahn makes full use of the local plenty, and he avoids using foods produced out of the area, relying on local farmers, fishermen, and gatherers to supply his restaurant. He often prepares these foods in true northwest style—with as little ado as possible—yet he also maintains a secondary approach to cooking these fresh local foods. In contrast to the ways of other chefs of the northwest cuisine, Martin Hahn's cookery shows a strong, though very much transformed, Mediterranean influence.

Martin thus works in the great culinary tradition of the southern European immigrants who came to the Puget Sound region in the nineteenth century: of the Greek and Yugoslav fishermen who caught the salmon that made the canneries wealthy and who raised their families on the incidental catch of greenlings, rockfish, and sculpins (and odd little crabs and molluscs); of the Sephardic Jews from Rhodes and the Sea of Marama, who sold the fresh fish caught by the fishermen and who shared in the incidental catch to feed their own families and who sold the fruits and vegetables (with proper advice on how to prepare them) produced by skilled Japanese gardeners in the hinterland of the Green River Valley; of the Italian farmers who grew superb produce in the Rainier Valley and hawked it in the budding Pike Place Market.

Martin Hahn can look back upon a long family tradition of preparing fresh northwest foods in the Mediterranean fashion. His grandfather, Victor Manca, who came to the Sound from Sicily, opened a Seattle restaurant, Manca's Café, in 1898. This café, later operated by Martin's father and then by his uncle, remained a favorite eating house of Seattle gourmets until it was torn down in the late 1950s to make room for the Norton Building.

When Martin and his wife Amy were ready to open their own restaurant, they decided to locate in the country, in proximity to food producers, to assure themselves of a reliable supply of impeccably fresh raw materials for their cooking. In this they were not alone.

It appears that one of the major characteristics of the new northwest cuisine is that its chefs, who have raised our cookery from a tasty form of home cooking to a refined (though still simple) culinary art, have deliberately chosen not to open their restaurants in our metropolitan areas (in contrast to much of the New American Cookery, which is primarily an urban art form). They have settled in the smaller towns of the Coast, the interior farm villages, and in the metropolitan fringe instead, in places like Yakima, Olympia, Edmonds, or Bellingham. Some have settled in rural retirement or tourist centers like Port Townsend, Sooke, LaConner, Lincoln City, or Coupeville; others have really gone out into the remotest country, to tiny, isolated villages like Nahcotta, Cathlamet, Waldport, or Yachats.

None of the chefs proudly establishing themselves amid the fresh food supplies of the countryside cooks exclusively for the loggers, fishermen, petty businessmen, or other rural folk who inhabit the small communities of the Pacific Northwest. They have gambled instead on their ability to provide meals so fresh and of such superior taste that they would be able to lure the urban connoisseurs of fine foods into the countryside, to feast upon the best river and sound, field and forest could produce. This gamble has paid off handsomely, and today most of these small restaurants are doing very well indeed, catering to both the educated upper crust of the rural population and to throngs of eager urban connoisseurs.

Some of our cooks, as for example, Janice Willinger and Janice Hoffmaster at The Experience in the small Oregon coastal village of Waldport, Jimmy Harper and Neil Koch at the Country Inn near Eugene, Pierre Pype at Pierre's in Cathlamet, Geoff Stone at the Captain Whidbey Inn in Coupeville, or Larry and Willie Lewin at The Windmill in Wenatchee, merely continue doing what they have done all along: they produce tasty, hearty meals using the best of locally available ingredients, whether these be eastern Washington steaks or racks of lamb, freshly caught sole, sand dab, or sturgeon, local oysters, raft-grown mussels, off-shore shrimp, or halibut cheeks.

Others have gone beyond the simplest approach to cooking the local bounty and have tried to create a more sophisticated northwest cuisine (in which catsup, steak sauce, et al., are banned from both dining room and kitchen) with the fresh raw materials available seasonably—with varying success and reliability.

In most of these restaurants, the seafood dishes (make sure to order only what's available locally) and the vegetable dishes are generally the most reliable entrées. These restaurants are still undergoing a few transformation pains—their chefs were trained in French country cooking, in the spurious "Northern Italian" cuisine, in East Coast-style fish and chowder houses, or in the ambiguous international hotel-restaurant tradition. But all of them are beginning to understand and appreciate the special quality of the foods of the Pacific Northwest. La Serre in Yachats, The Bay House in Lincoln City, The Shelburne Inn in Long Beach, The Oyster Creek Inn in Bow, and the Mountain Song restaurant in Marblemount, all fall into this category. All are characterized by a sincere effort on the part of the chefs; but the little special, undefinable something, the thing that sets them apart as something of commendable quality, is still missing. Yet time alone should bring an improvement as the chefs become more familiar with the special handling requirements of the freshest and best of northwest foods. One important thing that distinguishes all of these restaurants from their run-of-the-mill fish house and steak house brethren is the lack of freezer space for prepared meals and the absence of that bane of good eating, the microwave oven.

We can only expect (and hope) that other chefs will follow in the footsteps of these pioneers and open their own restaurants specializing in northwest cuisine; that is, in obtaining the best and freshest of locally available foods and preparing them in such a fashion that the method of cookery, the sauces, herbs, spices, and condiments, will enhance the superb flavor of our fresh, natural ingredients and not detract from it. Fortunately for the connoisseurs of fine foods in the Pacific Northwest, several adventuresome chefs have already carried this approach to cooking to the level of a fine art. At their best, the results can be spectacular.

Oregon still trails Washington and British Columbia in the development of a native northwest cuisine. This appears largely due to an "inferiority" felt by many Oregonians, a fear of seeming rustic in the eyes of the world (a fear nurtured, unfortunately, by Oregon's most famous culinary native son, James Beard), a nagging suspicion that when judged against French cuisine, an indulgence in local foods may seem provincial. Even Seattleites have been known to defend the budding signs of northwest cuisine in their fair city as a sign of diversification; that is, it's fine to have northwest restaurants, if you also have a sufficient number of eateries catering to the pleasures of nouvelle cuisine, Northern Italian cooking, Thai, Chinese, Japanese, or other exotic ways of preparing and spicing foods.

Yet throughout our region, as people travel abroad and begin to understand the true natures of ethnic and regional cuisines, they are increasingly willing to do what they did abroad: to live on the best foods the land can produce instead of subsisting on exotic imitations of somebody else's approach to cookery.

Take Rick O'Reilly at La Petite Maison in Olympia, for example. Rick is a bit of a French traditionalist (though his wine list emphasizes the best bottlings of northwest wineries over French offerings). This shows not only in the name of his restaurant, but especially in the types of dishes he serves regularly, from the time-honored appetizer pâté with cornichons to his tournedos bearnaise and the renowned tarte Tatin. Rick loosened up at lunch (back in the old days, when he still served lunch), when he prepared pastas accompanied by scads of garlic, or Greek dishes making copious use of the delectable goat cheeses produced by the Briar Hills Dairy in nearby Shelton.

But Rick has also been a pioneer in the northwest style of cooking. Even when he prepares the most classic of French dishes, a different touch can be felt. His sauces are lighter and less deliberately complex than their classic models, allowing the pure, exquisite taste of the foods, rather than the superimposed harmonies of stocks, herbs, and spices, to determine the flavors of his dishes. Rick uses less cream and flour—though perhaps more butter—than his traditional recipes call for, and his nouvelle cuisine dishes are less artificially exotic, less confrontational, designed more to highlight the special taste of a particular food—whether this be steak, clams, or oysters—than to create titillating contrasts for the sake of contrasts.

Yet despite Rick O'Reilly's mastery of traditional cooking styles, his true skills show when he prepares fresh local foods with a light hand and with a sure touch. He has the rare ability to transform plain roasted potatoes, a simple roast, and freshly dug asparagus spears into an exquisite feast. He can present oysters—the locally grown Olympias, Pacifics, and European flat oysters (or tasty mussels and clams)—in an inimitable fashion, creating new, tasty dishes with a seeming flick of the wrist. And he has an almost intuitive feeling for determining which cooking method best agrees with the specific textures and flavors of a given food.

One Northwesterner who stays closely in touch with the best foods available to her is Jerilyn Brusseau of brusseau's in Edmonds. Jerilyn indulges in contrasts: she uses flour stone-ground locally to her specifications to make rustic breads and fancy pastries; she uses fresh country butter and keeps well-aged local and imported cheeses in stock; she sells both local wines and fancy imported vintages.

Jerilyn serves simple country breakfasts and lunches at her small, cheery café, and she caters fancy, multicourse dinners—all made from the best raw materials she can find. And, to make sure the ingredients are impeccable, she drives out into the countryside every week to buy directly from suppliers. Her specially equipped food van takes her to the Hansen Creamery in Snohomish for butter, to the Barn in Granite Falls for pickles, to the Natural Foods Warehouse in Mountlake Terrace for stone-ground flours (white, whole wheat, cracked wheat, rye, barley, oat, and bran). She buys farmhouse Gouda at the Pleasant Valley Dairy in Ferndale and goat Cheddar from Michael and Carmen Estes in Marblemount. Her fresh produce comes from the Snohomish Valley and her cream from the Smith

Brothers Dairy in Auburn. Her jams and jellies are made by her father, Bun Cheney (a transplanted Montana cowboy and brand inspector), from fresh northwest fruits. Yet hers is not a parochial attitude for, besides using the best our region can provide, she also makes use of the best of the imported foods available to her, from perfectly ripened Brie to well-aged proscuitto.

Jerilyn's menu varies with the seasons, ranging from simple northwest seafood dishes to Provençal pissaladieres and Burgundian country dishes. Her breads and pastries are superb and baked fresh every day (the bakers arrive at midnight to prepare and bake the day's assortment before the first customers arrive for breakfast): big flavorful cinnamon rolls, chock-full of sweet butter, walnuts, and freshly ground cinnamon; a raw vegetable "nutrient" bread that doesn't taste the way it sounds; almond sour cream pretzels, blackberry cobblers, fruit-filled whole grain muffins, and a chewy, tangy, sourdough rye made with her own wild sourdough starter.

But Jerilyn's greatest attributes are her curiosity and her willingness to constantly explore. She is ever on the lookout for the best of local foods, for new ways of cooking the foods produced in our region, and she is more than willing to guide and advise those who are new to the exciting world of northwest foods.

Many of the prominent regional chefs in the Pacific Northwest are self-taught. Unlike professional chefs trained in the complicated preparation and intricate cooking methods of the traditional cuisines of France, Japan, Vietnam, or China, the cooks of the Pacific Northwest practice a method of cookery that is simple enough to allow for easy mastery—once a thorough understanding of the nature of the raw materials has been achieved. This most important precondition, the feeling for the true freshness of food and a knowledge of its textures, is easily taught. But these are skills that must be taught at the source, where food is truly at its best; no second-rate comestibles can take its place.

Deft knife-handling skills and a feeling for the proper length of cooking—whether the food is sautéed, stir-fried, steamed, or baked—can also be readily learned. Yet our best chefs have an almost uncanny sense of what makes a dish right; they are in tune with its structures and requirements and they have a knack for displaying food, for artistically arranging it on a platter to best show its quality and to appeal to the senses of the diner fortunate enough to be served such a dish.

It is a constant, almost fierce dedication to quality, to absolute freshness of the raw materials, that sets the rural chefs of the Northwest apart from many of their urban brethren. This is not to say that our metropolitan restaurants serve no fresh food. Some do. But they are not always able to procure an abundant—and regular—supply of locally produced victuals.

Take Ray's Boathouse, for example, Seattle's foremost fish house. Owners Bob Viggers and Russ Wohlers proved their dedication a few months ago when they completely rebuilt the restaurant's kitchens to ease the handling of fresh fish; they even constructed a special holding room designed expressly for the proper cold storage of fresh (and proper thawing of frozen) fish. Yet even though Chef Wayne Ludvigsen is thus able to cook with the freshest of raw materials, few of the foods he serves are produced locally. Ray's, like other large restaurants, finds it easier to buy its foods abroad (because of the large quantities needed at a given time) and to have them flown in as fresh as possible. Much of the salmon and other ocean fish handled by Ray's Boathouse, for instance, is flown in regularly from Alaska.

The owner/chef of a small rural restaurant, on the other hand, does not cater to large urban crowds of diners and has the freedom to work with even small suppliers. His volume is often small enough to allow him to shop for the ingredients he needs for the day's lunch or dinner in person, buying only enough for one or two meals at a time. Or he may contract with fishermen, truck farmers, and shellfish growers to have a specified quantity of fresh foods delivered daily.

Michael Anter, the owner/chef of Michael's Place in Coupeville, Washington, does just that. Michael arrived in Coupeville in the early 1970s, knowing nothing about the foods of the Pacific Northwest. He arrived more or less by accident: he was hitchhiking north from California to a summer job in Banff National Park, when he stopped at the Captain Whidbey Inn, fell in love with the place, and talked manager John Stone into giving him a job.

Michael started out as gardener, handyman, and oddsbody, but soon worked his way up to bartender and occasional cook. After quitting at the Captain Whidbey, he rented a small hole-in-the-wall store in Coupeville's Front Street mall with the determination of turning it into the best breakfast, (health-food) sandwich, and hamburger place on the island. He succeeded—almost too quickly. Michael soon tired of the monotonous daily routine demanded by his fast-food restaurant, and he began to contemplate changes. But he appreciated the loyalty of his customers and went out of his way to prepare special meals for them.

Today, after a number of transformations in which the restaurant has spread, amoebalike, first across one part of the mall, then across another, Michael's restaurant has lost all vestiges of its fast-food days. This is partly due to an informal apprenticeship Michael Anter served with John Rios, formerly of the Captain Whidbey and Le Provençal and now of Château Rios on Lopez Island. John adheres almost exclusively to a Provençal style of cooking—and he does not rely on the best and freshest of local ingredients. Yet it was through the practical and intellectual interchange with John Rios that Michael Anter was able to work out his personal style of cooking and develop his uniquely northwest approach to cooking with only the best of fresh local ingredients.

Because of the quality of his cooking, and thus the success of his restaurant, Michael can enjoy the luxury of buying only the best raw materials—locally grown vegetables and fruits, raft-grown Penn Cove mussels and oysters, et al.—for his kitchen, preparing them in as simple a fashion as possible to enhance their exquisite natural flavors. As Michael's tastes have changed and matured, so has the appreciation of his customers. Michael has been known to serve toothsome raw oysters to finicky eaters who never thought they'd have the nerve to down such an "exotic" dish.

Dan and Kathe Ripley's M'sieurs restaurant in Bellingham also started out as a fast-food place (M'sieur Munchy), dedicated to the serving of quickly prepared French "gourmet" fare. The Ripleys readily admit that they learned cooking on the job. As their skills improved, and as they became more familiar with the fresh foods available locally, they began serving formal dinners as well. Several years and transformations later (the restaurant began its life as a gas station), M'sieurs has emerged as the most elegant restaurant in Bellingham and as perhaps the best restaurant in northwest Washington. Despite the place's "French" name, the Ripleys have stopped serving "French" food and now concentrate on northwest dishes instead. In the process, Dan, the chef, has abandoned his formerly rigid menu and now serves only whatever is fresh in season.

Every afternoon, local farmers bring in fresh produce from the countryside and, just before dinner, Dan walks to a local fish market and looks over the day's catch, selecting only the freshest fish and shellfish. If he is dissatisfied with the quality of the catch, he will serve no seafood that night. Dan also has contracts with local truck gardeners who grow berries, vegetables, and culinary herbs for him and buys wild greens—lamb's-quarters, chickweed, sheep sorrel, et al.—and mushrooms (especially chanterelles) from a number of knowledgeable gatherers.

I learned one day just how flexible Dan can be. I had just bought several huge, succulent, French sorrel plants at an herb farm. The plants needed to be pruned before I could transplant them into my herb garden, yet I was faced by an unwieldy harvest. You can't just prune a sorrel plant and throw away the leaves (this is tantamount to a culinary sacrilege), but there were many more sorrel leaves than I could possibly use. I solved the problem by dropping in on Dan at the restaurant and offering the leaves to him. Dan eagerly accepted; it was quite a sight as he stood out in the street, chopping back the plants with his large chef's knife. And it was worth all the effort: the next day I had lunch at the restaurant and enjoyed a bowl of exquisite, delicately perfumed sorrel soup, the special of the day.

Dan constantly experiments with unusual vegetables, from wild lamb's-quarters to cultivated purslane, from salsify to yellow zucchini. In August of 1983, when Dan and Kathe's first child was born, Dan (who had been in the delivery room) worked off the tensions of new fatherhood by going back to his restaurant and cooking up a batch of delectable yellow zucchini soup—the best he ever made. In fact, Dan may become so enamored by the freshness and tastiness of a particular seasonal vegetable that he may, at times, serve only this one vegetable for weeks on end, say, asparagus or green beans, prepared, of course, in a number of different ways.

Kathe generally keeps well away from the kitchen, but she contributes a number of superb desserts, decadent cakes, fresh fruit pies and, especially, luscious berry sorbets. Dan and Kathe buy their berries from local specialty growers and take great delight in the fact that these selfsame berries from the northwesternmost growers are regularly flown to the San Francisco Bay region where they play an important part in the new "California" cuisine.

A chef's true quality lies not only in how well he can satisfy the tastes of his customers, but also in how much he can guide them toward the discovery of new, and perhaps unusual, foods. Dan Ripley first introduced Bellinghamsters to such unfamiliar dishes as poached greenling, steamed mussels, sautéed chanterelles, tangy soups made with wild greens, purslane salads or, more recently, Lopez Island lamb cooked with fresh local (mild) rosemary. At first, Dan met with quite a bit of resistance from timid diners accustomed only to eating hamburgers with catsup or crab with steak sauce (he and Kathe ate what the customers didn't order); but he has finally succeeded in educating his clientele and may just have transformed Bellingham eating habits forever.

The future of regional cooking seems assured in the Puget Sound region, and things are improving on the east side of the Cascades as well. Here Wil and Sandy Masset have succeeded with a most difficult task: changing the stodgy eating habits of Yakima Valley businessmen and farmers.

Wil is a chef trained in classic French cuisine. Before "retiring" to Yakima, he worked as a chef in Switzerland and at the old Olympic Hotel in Seattle, where he taught classical cuisine at several Seattle community colleges (several of our region's renowned chefs took classes from him) for a number of years.

Wil and Sandy have turned an old, antique-filled farmhouse east of town, the Birchfield Manor, into an intimate rural restaurant. The Massets serve their well-planned, prix-fixe dinners only on weekends: two seatings on Friday and Saturday nights, one on Sundays. Wil uses only the best and freshest of ingredients in his cooking. In the fall of '83, I tagged along to watch him do his food shopping.

It's early on a Friday morning, and Wil is shopping for the night's dinner. The large warehouse is surprisingly empty. I expected a bustling produce market, but I merely encounter a few widely spaced stacks of cardboard boxes: celery here, prechopped greens (for the salad bar trade) near the loading dock, boxes of lettuces, cabbages, cauliflowers, and eggs clustered here and there against the walls of the enormous hall. The walk-in cooler, on the other hand, is quite filled with boxes. This is where they keep much of the fresh regional produce: apples from nearby Selah, mushrooms from Olympia, rutabagas from Umatilla, red potatoes from Ellensburg, Yakima Valley greens, and Skagit broccoli.

So far Wil has only a vague notion of what he will serve his guests tonight. He inspects the lettuces, pokes at the rotting cores, and frowns: "Well, I'm not serving any lettuce tonight! Just look at this!" He crosses to a stack of broccoli boxes, breaks open the tops, removes some of the green stalks, probes, smells. "Ah! Cold broccoli with a light vinaigrette for salad!" He sets aside the best box.

Wil rejects the mushrooms as too old and spongy, but the rutabagas look fine. A forklift whines in through the insulating plastic curtain. The driver yells over his shoulder: "Four lettuce and two mushrooms?" "Yep!" He lifts off the top three boxes of lettuce, piles on two flats of mushrooms, and the forklift purrs from the cooler. "You see how they shop?" asks Wil. "They just call in and order so much of this and so much of that and have it delivered to their back doors—and they'll serve their customers whatever they get, no matter what shape it's in."

Wil searches through a crate of celery, selecting only the best stalks. He ignores several stacks of California bell peppers. "I buy my peppers down the valley at Krueger's. They have forty different varieties. And the best eggplant I've seen. They're U-pick only, but it's worth the extra labor." A bag of Walla Walla-grown Spanish onions and a box of fresh eggs complete the purchase. Wil pays cash.

On the way back to the Birchfield Manor, we stop at Fred Bucheli's sausage shop, a gray, unprepossessing concrete brick structure set in a flourishing cherry orchard (Fred planted all of the trees himself and he tends them during the summer when the sausage business is slow). We enter the shop through the back door, walking right into a large cooler. Fred beams when he recognizes Wil. "I think it worked this time! Just a minute." He disappears into another cooler and returns with two sausage molds. He carefully opens the metal contraptions and removes a large, square-sectioned veal sausage from each. Fred carefully cuts a slice from each sausage. "You see—it worked!" In the center of the slices is a large B, for Birchfield Manor. Wil turns to me: "I can't serve just any old sausage to our dinner guests. I like to make them feel they are getting something really special, something made to order just for them."

Fred Bucheli learned sausage making in his native Switzerland. Before settling in Yakima, he worked in some of North America's most famous restaurants and hotel kitchens, including the old Olympic Hotel in Seattle (he left just before Wil began to work for the Olympic). But why Yakima? "Only place where I could afford to build a sausage shop to my specifications."

Fred has adapted well to local conditions. He points at several racks of freshly smoked bratwurst. "The top ones are antelope. The bottom row's bear. Pretty soon, after the season opens, I'll be making deer and elk sausages. I've even made some pheasant sausage before." He pushes the half-carcass of a farm-butchered hog out of the way and wipes the counter clean. We're going to have a sausage tasting. Fred slices moist sausages and dry sausages, tangy sausages and mild sausages, the best Canadian bacon I have ever tasted, and excellent jerky. Finally, he plunks down a big, smooth-textured sausage and cuts us a slice. "Here, try that." "What is it?" we both ask. "It's delicious!" "That's bologna—that's what bologna is supposed to taste like."

Wil buys some bologna for his young sons' school lunch sandwiches (the children of chefs are often teased in school when they bring fancy foods for lunch—pâté foie de gras sandwich just won't do) and an assortment of other sausages and some bacon for the restaurant. "This is why I'm reluctant to plan a menu ahead of time. I never know what I want to serve until the last moment."

We have one more stop: the old (1869) water-powered gristmill in Union Gap, east of Yakima. Wil bakes all of the restaurant's breads, and he planned to buy some tasty stone-ground flour at the mill. But Larry Burmaster, the miller, has recently opened a small bakery of his own in the mill, and he has problems grinding enough flour to meet the demand. He has only bread but no flour for sale this day.

Wil has his meat and fish delivered to the restaurant. The salmon comes all the way from Seattle and other Puget Sound ports. "They tried to pawn off old or frozen fish on me," he protests, "but the fishmongers quickly learned that I refuse to take rejects. They're very reluctant to carry spoiled fish all the way back to the Coast, so now they bring me only the freshest salmon."

The meals at the Birchfield Manor are a delight. They are quite elaborate—too elaborate sometimes for the puritanical tastes of the Yakimans—but each of the successive courses is really very simple. Since the food is based primarily on the freshest of local and regional ingredients, most of the complexity resides in the exquisite sauces, which are handled with great finesse (as is only to be expected from a great chef trained in the classical tradition). Dinner is always finished with a fresh fruit dessert and with an assortment of absolutely luscious handmade chocolates. Wil protests that these are also extremely simple, since he received no formal training as a chocolatier, but they are among the best produced in our region.

Yet Wil Masset, like Rick O'Reilly, Jerilyn Brusseau, and other northwest chefs who enjoy the luxury of working with the exceptional meats, fish, fowl, and vegetables and fruits of our region, has modified his formerly traditional approach, placing less emphasis on the complexities and flavors of the sauces and other condiments themselves (no more sauce for sauce's sake), and letting the natural flavors of the superb northwest foods dominate the dishes instead.

This transformation affects every chef in the Northwest sooner or later. Confronted with the delicacy, flavor, and other outstanding qualities of northwest raw materials, every serious chef, that is, every chef who is truly concerned with the quality of his comestibles and who tries to show them off in their best light, will cease to impose the exotic flavorings of foreign cuisines and will begin to work with the foods, cooperating with their natural textures and flavors instead of trying to subdue them.

Rick O'Reilly, Michael Anter, Jerilyn Brusseau, Dan and Kathe Ripley, and Wil and Sandy Masset have all achieved the seemingly impossible: they have not only changed their personal attitudes toward the foods of the Northwest, but they have helped others appreciate the unique quality of our locally produced foodstuffs. Starting with a clientele whose palates were jaded by an incessant exposure to "new" foods, whether these be "junk" foods or the exotic sweepings of other cuisines, these chefs have competently guided their customers onto the path of true food and wine appreciation.

This process is, of course, a continuing one (and it has its ups and downs), but much good has already been done. A few years ago, for instance, I met with astonished stares when I asked the cheesemongers in Seattle's Pike Place Market for local cheeses. Except for the giants in the field (Darigold, Olympia, Mazza, Tillamook, et al.), the merchants felt they couldn't afford to stock local cheeses. Today, Rick O'Reilly and Jerilyn Brusseau proudly serve local cheeses, Pleasant Valley farm cheese from Ferndale and goat cheeses from Marblemount and Chehalis, to their customers—not because these cheeses have finally achieved regional fame, but because Rick and Jerilyn know good cheeses when they taste them, and because they have no fear of being thought provincial when they prefer a superior local product. This is not to say that all imported cheeses are inferior—far from it (and the best are very popular throughout the Northwest)—but it shows that foreignness alone is no longer sufficient to constitute superiority.

The Pacific Northwest, perhaps more than any other region, has shown that chefs working far from metropolitan centers are capable of creating a sophisticated cuisine and of exerting a profound influence over regional eating habits. Their importance is, admittedly, magnified far beyond a merely local significance by the constant presence of peripatetic urban gourmets who like to frequent these outstanding restaurants. This is particularly true of our two best-known regional restaurants, The Ark in Nahcotta, Washington, and the Sooke Harbour House in Sooke, British Columbia, places which are really far out in the country. Both have attracted favorable national attention, The Ark in the United States, and the Sooke Harbour House in Canada.

The Ark's owners and co-chefs, Nanci Main and Jimella Lucas, had the good fortune of being noticed by a vacationing James Beard at a time when they were still struggling to establish themselves at the Shelburne Inn in nearby Long Beach. They left the Shelburne several years ago, and their new restaurant is in a much more picturesque spot—wedged in between heaps of old oyster shells and two (active) oyster sheds on the old Nahcotta wharf—and has a much larger kitchen.

The Ark's chefs believe in using the freshest produce—berries from the nearby woods, fish delivered by rubber-booted fishermen, crawfish from local sloughs and rivers, oysters from the adjacent tideflats, tiny coastal strawberries in season. Yet there is a question if theirs is a truly regional northwest restaurant or if the food they serve is more akin to the somewhat generalized "New American Cuisine" or perhaps even to French "nouvelle cuisine." The dishes served at The Ark often lack the finesse that is becoming the trademark of other northwest restaurants. The Ark's chefs like to use copious amounts of Dijon mustard in their sauces and impregnate just about every dish with scads of garlic—garlic for the sake of garlic—an amusing experiment perhaps, but certainly not refined cookery. Or they may slather the fresh, locally caught salmon with barbecue or teriyaki sauce. The chefs also overdo their fruit sauces a bit—which can be great when handled in moderation, but which too often clash with the natural, exquisite taste of the foods (and with the accompanying wines). Experimentation is, of course, necessary in any cuisine, but sometimes there can be too much experimentation, meaningless play at the expense of the taste buds.

There can be an occasional dearth of exciting, fresh local products at Nahcotta, but the

Sooke Harbour House is able to flow with the seasons, adjusting the menu to whatever the Strait of Juan de Fuca, nearby farms, and the inn's twelve-month garden provide.

The inn is a simple place, a white clapboard farmhouse tucked into a grassy glen at the break of the land, where Whiffen Spit divides the calm waters of Sooke Harbour from the turbulent currents of Juan de Fuca Strait. The innkeepers, Sinclair and Frédérique Philip, have not only created a superb restaurant, but also one of the most satisfying hideaways on the Coast. Frédérique is French; Sinclair was born in West Vancouver and grew up with local foods, but lived in France for a dozen years.

When they moved to Sooke in 1980, they brought along a respect for fresh, locally produced foods. Since their arrival, they have put together a most amazing supply system for their restaurant kitchen. Local fishermen harvest fish, including oddities no one else will keep, from local and offshore waters (they call the inn over marine radio to discuss each day's catch with the chefs), then rush it from the boats to the kitchen, where it is prepared and served immediately. Just before dinner, Sinclair Philip (or his brother-in-law) often scuba dives in search of free-swimming scallops, rock scallops, sea urchins, and different species of crab, all served to the guests a short time later.

The menu also offers tender chunks of sea cucumber, dainty pink morsels of goose barnacles, rich sea urchin roe, sautéed rockfish, and several kinds of smoked salmon. Oysters, farm-raised abalone, and clams are obtained from local growers. No other restaurant serves a greater variety (and quality) of seafood than the Sooke Harbour House.

Yet the exceptional quality of the cooking is not limited to seafood: fresh local rabbit, duckling, beef, and lamb are also on the menu. (The exquisite lamb comes from nearby Metchosin, where the tender weanlings feed on the flavorful bromegrass, salt grass, wild rye, and herbs exposed to salt-laden shore breezes.) Oyster mushrooms, chanterelles, morels, and other wild mushrooms are served in season. Vegetables and herbs are either procured from local growers or raised in the Philips' garden: French tarragon, sorrel, purslane, rocket, watercress, nasturtium, Belgian endive, and even artichokes (which do very well in the mild Sooke climate). Lettuce grows throughout the year on the temperate bluffs of the inn.

The wine list is short, but carefully chosen. Forced to rely primarily on Canadian wines by medieval protectionist customs regulations, Sinclair selects the best varietals produced by the new cottage wineries in the Okanagan Valley—some of the rarer bottlings are only available through the Sooke Harbour House. Because Sinclair has gone out of his way to help the new wineries get off to a good start, he has gained access to wines which the wineries do not sell on the open market.

Sinclair and Frédérique are very excited about the food they serve and are always looking for little-known local products or novel methods of preparation. They constantly search for new, better suppliers, working closely with the diverse local ethnic groups to include their specialties on the menu. Sinclair also serves fruit sauces—in moderation. One of his favorite dishes is fresh local kid (three-month-old goatling) served with tart cranberries, sweet Japanese plums, and fresh chanterelle mushrooms.

I have searched through the fish markets and produce stands of southwestern British Columbia with Sinclair, looking, probing, asking questions, discovering foods we had not previously known about. We learned about the amazing variety of oriental vegetables grown in the province on one such excursion, about rare fruits on another, about rockfish roe and local shrimp, and we discovered numerous new ways of cooking fish, squid, and vegetables. Sinclair possesses the true explorer's energy and, since he rarely has to cook himself, he can take the time to explore, to experiment, and to search to perhaps a greater extent than the other chefs of our region; but his approach differs in intensity and in scope only, not in principle.

A search for the best of local foods, an ongoing experimentation with the various edibles of the Pacific Northwest, from vegetables to meats, from grapes to cheeses, from cider apples to shellfish, from grains to fish, marks the culinary excitement that is sweeping the region. Our chefs are, for the first time, becoming fully aware of the almost limitless bounty of the Northwest, and they are beginning to take full advantage of this delectable plenty. We are at the edge of a new frontier in regional cooking, a frontier where the best of the old, simple cuisine will be combined with the new refinement, with the most exciting aspects of the new approach to cooking, where the highest quality—peak freshness, taste, aroma, texture—will become increasingly important (and recognized), where we, in Jerilyn Brusseau's words, will enjoy our meals in a stimulating environment of "food, art, music, and beauty."

Appendix

The sources listed in this appendix are not a complete guide to the superb meats, shellfish, fowl, fruits, vegetables, eggs, cheese, and so on, produced in the Pacific Northwest. Far from it. A complete list of the purveyors of excellent foods in British Columbia, Oregon, and Washington would demand a very hefty book of its own. The listings in the present volume were selected largely on the basis of my personal experience and preference—though I have also taken the recommendations of friends and other knowledgeable gourmets into account.

If, after reading this list, you feel that I have omitted some of your favorite butchers, bakers, cheesemongers, or greengrocers, please feel free to write to me. I'll go and check out the places you recommend and, who knows, they might show up in the next edition of this book.

I have been particularly strict in my selection of wineries. Wine marketing is full of hype these days; thus I have included only those wineries which have consistently made good wine or those new ones which show promise.

But go out and experiment on your own and establish your own taste, your own lists of what you consider to be our region's best food shops and wineries. You're bound to make a lot of very pleasant discoveries and have great fun in the process.

Mail-Order Foodstuffs

Here are a few places that mail northwest gifts. Send away for free catalogs.

Oregon

Blue Heron French Cheese Co.
2001 Blue Heron Drive
Tillamook, OR 97141
(503) 842-8281

Brie

Butte Creek Mill
Box 561
Eagle Point, OR 97524
(503) 826-3531

Stone-ground flour, natural cereals, seeds, nuts

Coquille Valley Dairy Co-op
P.O. Box 515
Bandon, OR 97411
(503) 347-2461

Bandon cheeses, huckleberry jam, canned salmon, smoked shad, smoked beef sausage, Cranberry Sweets, sour mustard, smoked Cheddar, candied roasted hazelnuts, et al.

Harry & David
2518 South Pacific Highway
Medford, OR 97501
(503) 776-2400

Fruits and nuts—you name it; Fruit-of-the-Month Club; Comice pears that masquerade as "Royal Riviera" pears, Washington State apples

Josephson's Smokehouse & Dock
P.O. Box 412
Astoria, OR 97103
(503) 325-2190

Smoked salmon, sturgeon, black cod, et al., specialty canned seafood, lox

Made in Oregon
P.O. Box 3458
Portland, OR 97208

Assorted Oregon gifts

Pinnacle Orchards
441 South Fir
Medford, OR 97501
(503) 772-6271

The world's best Comice pears

Rogue River Valley Creamery
P.O. Box 3606
Central Point, OR 97502
(503) 664-2233

Oregon blue, Cheddar, Jack, Colby cheeses

Norm Thompson
Department 02-106
P.O. Box 3999
Portland, OR 97208
For free catalog, call 1-800-547-1160

Cougar Gold cheese, smoked salmon, hazelnuts, Trappist fruitcake from Our Lady of Guadeloupe in Lafayette, Oregon, beer cookies, et al.

Tillamook County Creamery Association
P.O. Box 313
Tillamook, OR 97141
(503) 842-4481

Tillamook Cheddar

Washington

Briar Hills Dairies Inc.
279 Southwest Ninth
Chehalis, WA 98532
(206) 748-4224

Goat cheeses

Cascade Harvest
Brewster, WA 98812
(509) 689-3201

Gift-boxed apples and pears

The Cascade Sampler
1000 Northwest 167th
Seattle, WA 98177
(206) 546-1605

Washington food gifts

Cougar Gold
Washington State University Creamery
Pullman, WA 99164

Cougar Gold cheese

The Country Store and Farm
Route 2, Box 304
Vashon, WA 98070
(206) 463-3655

Culinary herbs, food gift boxes

Guilford's Fine Seafoods
P.O. Box 1219
Port Townsend, WA 98368

Northwest gourmet seafood gift packs

The Maury Island Farming Co.
Route 3, Box 238
Vashon, WA 98070
(206) 463-9659

*Preserves, jams, Stretch Island fruit leathers,
Wax Orchard fruit spreads, canned fish*

Northwest Forage Co.
1741 Cedardale Road
Mount Vernon, WA 98273
(206) 428-0191

Northwest food gifts

Northwest Pantry
1000 Northwest 167th
Seattle, WA 98177
(206) 546-1605

Northwest food gifts

Old Town Mill
4315 Main Street
Union Gap, WA 98903
(509) 452-5959

Stone-ground flours, cereals, coffee blends

Walla Walla Gardeners' Association
210 North Eleventh Street
Walla Walla, WA 99362
(509) 525-7070
(509) 525-7071

Walla Walla sweet onions, asparagus

Vegetables

**Many of the vegetable markets listed also sell
fruits in season.**

British Columbia

Davidson's Fresh Fruit and Produce
R.R. 4
(junction of Transcanada Highway and 97B)
Salmon Arm, B.C. V0E 2T0
(604) 832-8868

Fresh Shuswap and Spallumcheen asparagus

Gardiner's Farm
16975 64th Avenue
Surrey, B.C.
(604) 574-5980

Yellow Finn potatoes, red or white potatoes, parsnips, carrots, beets, other vegetables in season

Granville Island Public Market
Granville Island
(under the Granville Street bridge)
Vancouver, B.C. V6H 3R9

Fresh vegetables (and fruits) in season

Krause Brothers Farm
6179 248th Street
Aldergrove, B.C.
(604) 856-7912
(604) 856-5725

Cauliflower, dill weed, pickling cucumbers; other vegetables in season

Mitchell's Family Farm Market & Hay Ranch
Keremeos, B.C.
(on the bypass road north of Keremeos)
(604) 499-2494

Fresh vegetables, fruits, canning tomatoes (vine-ripened)

Murphy's U-Pick
6909 248th Street
Aldergrove, B.C.
(604) 856-0241

Pickling cucumbers, broccoli, cauliflower, dill, beans, beets, carrots, peas, corn

Oregon

Joe Casale & Son
Route 2, Box 60
Aurora, OR 97002

Beans, cabbage, cauliflower, corn, peas, tomatoes, carrots, beets, cucumbers, peppers, squash, dill, garlic, broccoli

Hansen's Coast Fork Berries
Sears Road
Creswell, OR 97426

Beans, broccoli, cabbage, carrots, cucumbers, peas, pumpkins, squash, tomatoes

Honey Wind Herb Farm
(Highway 101 north of Seaside)
Seaside, OR 97138

Organically grown herbs

Pocket Creek Farm
Route 1, Box 290
Cornelius, OR 97113

Superb culinary herbs

Sauvie Island Produce Farms
Take Highway 30 west from Portland to the Sauvie Island turnoff; cross the bridge, turn left at foot of bridge and follow road to farms and produce stands.

Great vegetables, berries, et al., in season

Toney's Farm Marketing
42340 Southeast Highway 26
Sandy, OR 97055

Peas, corn, Brussels sprouts, beans, cabbage, cauliflower, broccoli

West Mushroom Farm
225 50th Northeast
Salem, OR 97305
(503) 581-2471

Cultivated mushrooms

Wilhelm Family Farms
6001 Southwest Meridian Way
Tualatin, OR 97062

Beans, cabbage, corn, cucumber, peppers, squash, tomatoes

Yamhill Market
110 Southwest Yamhill
Portland, OR 97204

Vegetables and fruits in season

Washington

Arbordown Farms
Route 1, Box 1354
Lopez, WA 98261

Nationally renowned garlic

Julio Arreola's Produce
Route 3, Box 3332
Wapato, WA 98951

Corn, tomatoes, melons, squash, white sweet corn, et al.

Dick Bedlington Potato Warehouse
8497 Guide Meridian
Lynden, WA 98264
(206) 354-5264

Superb Whatcom County potatoes: Nooksacks, Norgolds, Red LaSoda, Red Pontiacs, et al.

Cascadian Farms
Star Route
Rockport, WA 98283
(206) 873-2481
(206) 873-2781

Organic produce, including potatoes

Cedarbrook Herb Farm
986 Sequim Avenue South
Sequim, WA 98382
(206) 683-4541

Vast range of herbs, scented geraniums, tea herbs, et al.

Cedarville Farm
3122 Goshen Road
Bellingham, WA 98226
(206) 592-5908

Organically grown produce; yellow Finn potatoes

Conway Farmers' Market
(Conway exit off I-5)
Conway, WA 98238
(206) 445-2851

Not a true farmers' market, but an outlet for the area's superb produce; some hard-to-find fruits and vegetables

The Country Store and Farm
Route 2, Box 304
Vashon, WA 98070
(206) 463-3655

Herbs, et al.

Davis Farms
Route 3, Box 3202
Toppenish, WA 98948
(509) 877-4394

Asparagus, potatoes, sweet Spanish onions, dry beans, tomatoes, squash, melons

Diversified Farms
Route 1, Box 143
Outlook, WA 98938
(509) 837-4884

Asparagus picked fresh daily, April to June

Duris Cucumber Farm
6012 44th Street
Puyallup, WA 98373

Pickling cucumbers

Russell Elliot Organic Gardens
P.O. Box 183
Wapato, WA 98951
(509) 877-3159

*Excellent selection of vegetables: kohlrabi,
snow peas, tomatoes, et al., plus several
kinds of melons*

Hackney Farms
5920 State Route 92
Lake Stevens, WA 98270
(206) 691-7641

*Cucumbers, dill, garlic, Blue Lake and Ken-
tucky Wonder beans*

The Hand That Feeds You
Darlyn Del Boca
7208 Lankhaar Road
Lynden, WA 98264
(206) 354-5782

*Outstanding, organically raised produce, plus
wild vegetables*

Householder's Farms
Route 8, Box 447
(Kershaw Road, just off Highway 12; four
    miles west of Yakima)
Yakima, WA 98908
(509) 965-3320

Fresh and dried herbs; fruit

Krueger's Pepper Gardens
Route 1, Box 1086 C
Wapato, WA 98951

*Forty-five varieties of peppers, mild to hot,
and a few hard-to-find exotic ones from
Europe and Mexico; superb eggplant, other
vegetables; fruits*

Lane Morgan
834 Victoria
Sumas, WA 98295
(206) 988-5264

Winter produce: leeks, chicory, chard, et al.

Morgans
Box 5114
Oso, WA 98223

Carrots, potatoes, "sunchokes," et al.

Mark Musick
Pragtree Farms
Arlington, WA 98223
(206) 435-4648

Wild greens

Mount Baker Mushroom Farm
7334 Goodwin Road
Everson, WA 98247
(206) 966-5309

Cultivated mushrooms

Madame Mushroom
3420 West Malaga Road
Malaga, WA 98828
(509) 663-5594
(206) 482-2722

Wild mushrooms

Mr. Mushroom
Steve Czarnecki
1338 Ellis Street
Bellingham, WA 98225
(206) 671-4042

Seasonal wild mushrooms.
Spring: morels, meadow mushrooms
*Summer: chanterelles, matsutake, blewits,
    gypsy mushrooms*
*Fall: chanterelles, hedgehog mushroom,
    chicken of the woods*

Oak Hills Vegetable Farm
8208 288th Street South
Roy, WA 98580
(206) 843-2225

Broccoli, cauliflower, beets, et al.

Pike Place Market
Pike Place
Seattle, WA 98101

Our region's best showcase of locally raised fruits and vegetables

Rainbow Nursery
617 East Laurel Road
Bellingham, WA 98226
(206) 398-2701

Organically grown herb plants and dried herbs

Remlinger Farms
Northeast 32nd Street
(one mile south of Carnation)
Carnation, WA 98014
(206) 333-4135

Beans, cukes, you name it—this is the U-pick place for Seattleites.

Serres Happy Valley Vegetable Farm
20306 Northeast 50th
Redmond, WA 98052

Beans, beets, corn, dill, broccoli, cabbage, lettuce, squash

Snow Goose Produce
2100 Fir Island Road
Conway, WA 98238
(also listed under Mount Vernon, WA 98273)
(206) 445-2611

Superb assortment of Skagit delta vegetables

Tillinghast Seed Co.
623 East Morris
La Conner, WA 98257
(206) 466-3329

The best place to buy vegetable seeds on the west side: the company's been around since the nineteenth century and has some seeds that were specially developed for our area.

Troops Gardens
1303 North Pearl Street
Centralia, WA 98531

Garlic, dill, beans, beets, carrots, corn, squash, cucumbers

Victoria Village
503 316th Southwest
Stanwood, WA 98292
(206) 629-2172

Organic vegetables, garlic

Walla Walla Gardeners' Association
210 North Eleventh Street
Walla Walla, WA 99362
(509) 525-7070/71

Walla Walla sweet onions, asparagus

Fruit

Keep in mind that many fruit stands sell vegetables, and vice versa.

British Columbia

Begg's Fruit Stand
8709 Highway 97
Box 1277
Summerland, B.C. V0H 1Z0
(604) 494-6321

Fresh Okanagan fruit in season

Blossom Fruit Stand
R.R. 2, Highway 97
Summerland, B.C. V0H 1Z0
(604) 494-5141
(604) 494-1229

Fresh fruit beneath Giant's Head Mountain

Davidson's Fresh Fruit and Produce
R.R. 4
(Junction Transcanada Highway and
    Highway 97B)
Salmon Arm, B.C. V0E 2T0

*Shuswap fruit and vegetables, including
northern strawberries, raspberries, peaches,
pears, apples, and blueberries*

Annell Long's Cherry Orchard
Lakeshore Road (four miles east of Salmon
    Arm, Shuswap Lake—just follow the
    road along the lake)
Salmon Arm, B.C. V0E 2T0

Superb Shuswap cherries in season

Penticton Edible Goods Ltd.
Box 843
667 Eckhardt Avenue West
Penticton, B.C. V2A 6X7
(604) 493-4093

Dried fruits, fruit leathers

Robert's Fruit Market and Orchard
Highway 97
Summerland, B.C. V0H 1Z0
(604) 494-5541

Fruits picked fresh every day

Summerland Sweets
R.R. 2 Canyonview Road
Summerland, B.C. V0H 1Z0

*Natural fruit syrups, fruit jams, fruit
candies, et al.*

Ta'lana Fruit Stand
Sorrento Plaza
Sorrento, B.C.
(604) 675-2537

Shuswap Lake fruits and honey

Tamri Orchards
2019 East Lakeshore Drive
R.R. 1
Osoyoos, B.C. V0H 1V0
(604) 495-2084

*Five thousand apple trees—seven different
varieties—beside Osoyoos Lake*

Vernon Fruit Union
2601 Third Street
Vernon, B.C.
(604) 545-2115

Fresh north Okanagan fruits

Oregon

Boyd's Garden Fresh Produce
P.O. Box 86
(on Highway 99 West)
Amity, OR 97101
(503) 835-4322

*Excellent fruit (including quince in season),
superb pear jam; local raw honey*

Joe Casale & Son
Route 2, Box 60
Aurora, OR 97002

Strawberries

Comella & Son Produce Center
6959 Southwest Garden Home Road
Portland, OR 97223
(604) 245-5033

Seasonal fruits

The Dalles Natural Foods & Fruits
314 Court Street
The Dalles, OR 97338
(503) 298-1906

Local fruits

Fenton's Farmers' Market
Highway 101 just north of Seaside
Seaside, OR 97138

Fruit, honey, vegetables

The Fruit Tree
Hood River Village
(Exit 64 from I-84)
Hood River, OR 97031
(503) 387-4122

*Diamond Growers' outlet for Hood River
Valley fruit: apples, pears, cherries, et al.*

Hansen's Coast Fork Berries
Sears Road
Creswell, OR 97426

Raspberries, strawberries

Harry & David
2518 South Pacific Highway
(Old Highway 99)
Medford, OR 97501
(503) 776-2400

*This mail-order company's outlet is a good
place for buying inexpensive seconds, as well
as prime fruit. Comice pears, apples, et al.*

Johnny's House of Wild Blackberry
(George and Deborah Teeter)
Box 959
Port Orford, OR 97465
(503) 332-0015

*Wild blackberry jelly; will ship cases of
twelve by UPS.*

Little Pine
3560 Hayden Bridge Road
Springfield, OR 97477

*Blackberries, boysenberries, blueberries,
grapes, plums, quince, raspberries, cherries,
walnuts*

Nut World
Highway 99 West
Dundee, OR 97115
(503) 528-2156

Nuts and fruits

Pinnacle Orchards
441 South Fir
Medford, OR 97501
(503) 772-6271

The best Comice pears in the country

The Prune Tree
12393 Smithfield Road
The Dalles, OR 97338

*One of the last outlets for the delectable
Oregon prune (Parson sweet prunes), plus
dried fruits and nuts*

Rasmussen's Fruit Stand
(Highway 35, five miles south of Hood River)
Hood River, OR 97031
(503) 386-4622

*A whole range of local fruits from straw-
berries to cherries, pears, and apples*

Toney's Farm Marketing
42340 Southeast Highway 26
Sandy, OR 97055

*Strawberries, raspberries, marionberries,
boysenberries*

Wilhelm Family Farms
6001 Southwest Meridian Way
Tualatin, OR 97062

Strawberries, marionberries

Woodsman's Own
Oregon Coast Wild Berries
Woodsman's Native Wild Nursery
Route 1, Box 280
Florence, OR 97439

Wild berry jams such as wild huckleberry, wild salal jelly (which goes rather well with king salmon)

Yamhill Market
110 Southwest Yamhill
Portland, OR 97204

Regional and local produce in season

Washington

Alta Vista Farms
Route 1, Box 1615
Zillah, WA 98953
(509) 829-5169

Ten varieties of peaches, Criterion apples, other fruit

Anne's Berry Farm
Route 2, Box 361
La Center, WA 98629

Strawberries, boysenberries, blueberries, black and red raspberries

Aplets & Cotlets
117 Mission Avenue
Cashmere, WA 98815
(509) 782-2191

Sweetish fruit and walnut confections made from an old Armenian family recipe (produced here for decades)

Applewood Farm
3711 Cabrant Road
Everson, WA 98247
(206) 966-5183

Large number of different west-side apple varieties

Aunt Thelma's
Box 88
Manson, WA 98831
(509) 687-3715

Excellent hill apples

Babe's Berries
1125 Central Road
Everson, WA 98247
(206) 398-8891

Excellent strawberries; several varieties

Beckwood Farms
3736 Cape Horn Road
Concrete, WA 98237
(206) 853-3655

Raspberries, mountain apples

Bering Sea
Route 1, Box 182
Okanogan, WA 98840
(509) 422-2127

Superb Okanogan apples

Susan Bill
Arbordown Farms
Route 1, Box 1354
Lopez, WA 98261
(206) 468-2175

Many rare apple varieties, including Cox's Orange Pippin

Bob's Apple Barrel
Cashmere, WA 98815

Apples, honey, et al.

Boitanos
7602 Valley Avenue East
Puyallup, WA 98371

Gooseberries, grapes

Brunsbrae
7607 Naches Heights Road
Yakima, WA 98908
(509) 965-0873

*Bing, Lambert, Royal Anne, Van, Rainier
cherries; Red Haven, Elberta peaches*

Bushel & A Peck
1350 East Badger Road
Lynden, WA 98264
(206) 354-3540

*Strawberries, raspberries; superb fruit jams
and syrups*

The Cameron Farm
8301 Riverview Road
Snohomish, WA 98290
(206) 568-5948

*Rhubarb; west-side Gravenstein, King,
Northern Spy apples; Italian prunes*

Carsten's Apple Berry Farm
1342 Pulver Road
Mount Vernon, WA 98273
(206) 424-4157

Luscious strawberries; produce

Cascade Harvest
Brewster, WA 98812
(509) 689-3201

Boxed apples and pears

Cascadian Farms
Star Route
Rockport, WA 98283
(206) 873-2481
(206) 873-2781

Organically grown Skagit Valley fruits

The Cider Shed
17902 Interurban Boulevard
Clearview, WA 98290

Freshly squeezed apple cider

Cloudy Mountain Farms
6906 Goodwin Road
Everson, WA 98247
(206) 966-5859

Several varieties of excellent west-side apples

Day's Raspberries
15725 Broadway
Snohomish, WA 98290

Meeker raspberries

Deer Mountain Berry Farms
Granite Falls, WA 98252

Very nice natural fruit jams

The Granger Berry Patch
Route 1, Box 1150
Granger, WA 98932
(509) 854-1413

*Strawberries, raspberries (till October!),
grapes, rhubarb, boysenberries, blackcaps,
raspberry preserves, and syrups*

Green's Acres Blueberry Farm
32326 132nd Northeast
Sultan, WA 98284
(206) 793-1714

Excellent berries

Hauff Orchards
Highway 2/Blewett Pass Junction
Peshastin, WA 98847
(509) 548-7370

*Fresh fruit, honey, juice; outstanding
apricots!*

The Homesteader Farm
Route 1, Taber Road
Cashmere, WA 98815
(509) 782-1630

Mountain cherries

Hurricane Canyon Ranch & Canvas Top
    Fruit Stand
Box 87
(a few miles up the Methow River
    from Pateros)
Pateros, WA 98846
(509) 923-2750

Superb nectarines, peaches, apples

Hush Ranch
Route 2, Box 2356-A
Wapato, WA 98951
(509) 877-4737

*Beauty, Climax, Duarte, Santa Rosa plums;
Criterion, Ryan Red apples*

Hyder's Raspberry Farm
Highway 2 (east of the city limits)
Sultan, WA 98284
(206) 793-0076

Organically grown raspberries

Lone Fir Orchard
Box 204
Mallot, WA 98829
(509) 422-5607

Excellent pears and apples

The Maury Island Farming Co.
Route 3, Box 238
Vashon, WA 98070
(206) 463-9659

Fruits, jams, et al.

McGlade's Dwarf Orchard
Dunn Road—Green Bluff
Mead, WA 99021

*Cherries, peaches, pears, apples, straw-
berries, raspberries, blackberries*

McLean Berry Ranch
Box 174
Lynden, WA 98264
(206) 354-5895

*Superb fruit jams; sold through such
national outlets as Williams-Sonoma in San
Francisco*

Merritt Apple Farm
898 Bayview-Edison Road
Mount Vernon, WA 98273
(206) 766-6264

*Superb Gravensteins grown in an orchard
above Padilla Bay*

Mielke Orchards
East 4502 Buckeye
Spokane, WA 99207

Strawberries, raspberries, cherries, melons

Mountain View Berry Farms
7617 East Lowell Larimer Road
(131st Southeast)
Snohomish, WA 98290
(206) 668-3390

Blueberries, loganberries, boysenberries

Pippin Farm
3081 Goshen Road
Bellingham, WA 98226
(206) 592-5594

West-side apples, raspberries, blueberries

Ram Orchards
Route 2, Box 2358
Wapato, WA 98951
(509) 877-2407
(509) 877-4546

*Cherries to apples, including Tydeman Red,
Jonathan, Criterion*

Remlinger Farms
Northeast 32nd Street
(one mile south of Carnation)
Carnation, WA 98014
(206) 333-4135

*This is the Seattle area's great U-pick
emporium: it has almost everything, from
berries to pickling cucumbers.*

Rest Awhile Fruit Stand
Highway 153
(½ mile west of Pateros)
Pateros, WA 98846
(509) 923-2256

*Elberta peaches, Bartlett pears, nectarines,
McIntosh, Jonathan, and Ozark Gold apples*

Richter's Farm
4512 70th Avenue
Puyallup, WA 98371

*Strawberries, raspberries, marionberries, pie
and sweet cherries*

Roche Berry Farm
6828 State Route 92
Lake Stevens, WA 98258
(206) 691-7015

Rainier, Shuksan, Hood strawberries

Schwecke Ranch
Fish Creek Uplake
Chelan, WA 98816

Excellent Chelan apples

Serendipity Orchards
Route 1
Manson, WA 98831
(509) 687-3941

Superb Chelan apples

Smith's Hilltop Orchard
Route 1, Box 141A
Colbert, WA 99005

Strawberries, cherries, peaches, pears

Sunrise Farm Blueberries
5022 44th Street East
Tacoma, WA 98443

Outstanding blueberries

Suyematsu Berry Farm
12589 Southeast Green Valley Road
Auburn, WA 98002

Excellent strawberries

Tiedeman's Raspberries
8015 Vernon Road
Everett, WA 98205
(206) 334-3243

Rhubarb, raspberries, gooseberries, currants

Turcott Orchard
Route 2, Box 2146
Wapato, WA 98951
(509) 877-4359

*Different varieties of peaches, nectarines and
other fruit; Prime Gold apples*

Van Doren Ranch
(Highway 97, seven miles north of Brewster)
Brewster, WA 98812
(509) 689-2701

Excellent Red Globe peaches

Wax Orchards
Route 2, Box 95
Burton, WA 98013
(206) 682-8551
(206) 463-9735

Excellent apple cider, fruit jams

Honey

Oregon

Boyd's Garden Fresh Produce
P.O. Box 86
(Highway 99 West)
Amity, OR 97101
(503) 835-4322

Washington

The Cameron Farm
8301 Riverview Road
Snohomish, WA 98290
(206) 568-5948

The Honey Farm
41021 State Route 2
(½ mile east of Gold Bar on Highway 2)
Sultan, WA 98294
(206) 793-0064

Many flavors of bottled mountain honey

Kuhlman Farms
3728 Machias Road
Snohomish, WA 98290
(206) 568-5948

Lange's Farm Honey
1875 Cedardale Road
Mount Vernon, WA 98273
(206) 428-2884

Silver Bow Honey Co.
1220 Thirteenth
Snohomish, WA 98290
(206) 568-2191

Sires Honey Co.
3916 Main Street
Union Gap, WA 98903
(509) 453-9539

Orchard and wild flower honeys

Twin Maples Apiary
7346 Delta Line Road
Ferndale, WA 98248
(206) 366-3665

Fish

British Columbia

Bella Coola Smoker Plant
Box 390
Bella Coola, B.C. V0T 1C0
(604) 799-5334
(604) 799-5939

Indian smoked salmon (natural)

Granville Island Public Market
Granville Island
(under the Granville Street bridge)
Vancouver, B.C. V6H 3R9

*Several fish shops have fresh fish available.
Shop around to find the day's freshest.*

Imperial Salmon House Ltd.
1632 Franklin Street
Vancouver, B.C. V5L 1P4
(604) 251-1114

Smoked British Columbia salmon

Steveston Dock
Steveston, B.C.
(Take exit after Fraser River tunnel off
    Highway 99.)

*Fresh fish sold directly from boats on
Thursday, Friday, and Saturday mornings*

Win Fung Seafood Ltd.
Columbia and Pender
Vancouver, B.C. V6A 2Z6
(604) 669-8588

*A very fine Chinese fish market; offerings
vary; check on other Chinese fish markets to
compare and see what's available.*

Oregon

Barnacle Bill's Seafood Store
2174 North Highway 101
Lincoln City, OR 97367
(503) 994-3022

Fresh fish plus smoked salmon, sturgeon, albacore, sablefish

Chuck's Seafoods
P.O. Box 5502
Charleston, OR 97420
(503) 888-5525

Smoked shad, salmon, et al. (canned)

Jake's Famous Fish Market
2200 Baseline Road
Cornelius, OR 97113
(503) 351-5211

Fresh fish

Jake's Fish Market
7700 Southwest Beaverton-Hillsdale Highway
Beaverton, OR 97005
(503) 292-1388

Fresh fish

Josephson's Smokehouse
106 Marine Drive
P.O. Box 412
Astoria, OR 97103
(503) 325-2190

Pickled and smoked sturgeon, tuna, and black cod (sablefish). Nationally renowned cold-smoked salmon; sweet and sour pickled salmon; kippered fish; fresh seasonal seafood; frozen, canned fish

McCormick's Fish Market
9945 Southwest Beaverton Highway
Beaverton, OR 97005
(503) 643-1322

Fresh fish

Troy's Seafood Market
816 Northeast Grand
Portland, OR 97232
(503) 231-1477

Fresh fish

Troy's Seafood Market
11130 Southeast Powell
Portland, OR 97236
(503) 760-2566

Washington

East Point Seafoods
(Bendiksen's)
NP Terminal Grounds
South Bend, WA 98586
(206) 875-5507

Crabapple-smoked fish, oysters

Ferndale Fish Market
1985 Main
Ferndale, WA 98248
(206) 384-6200

Fresh fish

Guilford's Fine Seafoods
P.O. Box 1219
Port Boat Haven
Port Townsend, WA 98368

Northwest gourmet seafoods and gift packs

Island Seafoods
9920 Southwest 176th
P.O. Box 911
Vashon, WA 98070

Fresh seafood, smoked salmon

Jack's Fish Spot
1514 Pike Place
Seattle, WA 98101
(206) 622-3727

Fresh fish

King Arthur's Seafood Market
Highway 101 East
Sequim, WA 98382
(206) 683-6010

Fresh fish

Mutual Fish
2335 Rainier Avenue South
Seattle, WA 98144
(206) 322-4368

Fresh fish

Port Chatham Fish Co.
632 Northwest 46th Street
Seattle, WA 98107
(206) 783-8200
(206) 783-8240

Smoked salmon, sablefish, sturgeon, et al.

Quilcene Aquaculture
Quilcene, WA 98376

Smoked trout, et al.

Jon Rowley
Seafood and Quality Consultant
P.O. Box 71069
Seattle, WA 98107
(206) 283-1623

If you need it, here's the man to find it for you and show you how to use it.

Scan Fish
5416½ 20th Avenue Northwest
Seattle, WA 98107
(206) 782-0888

Superb lox, smoked salmon

Sea-K-Fish Co.
Fisherman's Wharf
Blaine, WA 98230
(206) 332-5121

Fresh fish

Slathar's Smoke House
Highway 101 (just north of Forks)
Forks, WA 98331
(206) 374-6258

Canned and smoked salmon

Specialty Seafoods
1719 Thirteenth Street
Anacortes, WA 98221
(206) 293-4661

Alder-smoked salmon

Swinomish Indian Fish Company
955 Moorage
La Conner, WA 98257
(206) 466-4949

Year-round fish, smoked salmon, other seafood

Totem Smokehouse
1906 Pike Place
Seattle, WA 98101
(206) 223-1710

Smoked salmon

Uncle Bob's Pacific Harvest Gourmet
    Seafoods
(Uncle Bob's Custom Cannery)
P.O. Box E
2002 North Pacific Highway
Long Beach, WA 98631
(206) 642-2508

Custom canned tuna (including salt-free), smoked oysters, alder-smoked salmon, white sturgeon, et al.

University Seafood & Poultry
University Way and Northeast 47th
Seattle, WA 98105
(206) 632-3700
(206) 632-3900

Fresh fish

Uwajimaya
Sixth South and South King
Seattle, WA 98104
(206) 624-6248

Fresh fish, including oddities

Uwajimaya
15555 Northeast 24th
Bellevue, WA 98007
(206) 747-9012

Fresh fish

Uwajimaya
South Center Mall
Tukwila, WA 98188
(206) 246-7077

Fresh fish

Crab

Oregon

The Crab Broiler
Highway 101 (four miles south of Seaside)
Seaside, OR 97138
(503) 738-6170

Fresh Dungeness

Hoy Brothers Fish & Crab Co.
604 South Commercial
Garibaldi Boat Basin
Garibaldi, OR 97118
(503) 322-3500

Fresh Dungeness

Karla's Krabs
2010 Highway 101 North
Rockaway, OR 97136
(503) 355-2362

Very fresh Dungeness

Phil and Joe's Crab Company
1009 Garibaldi Avenue
(Highway 101 North)
Garibaldi, OR 97118
(503) 322-3410

Fresh Dungeness, shrimp, prawns

The Pier
Mooring Basin Road
Garibaldi Mooring Basin
Garibaldi, OR 97118
(503) 322-3362

Very fresh Dungeness

Washington

C Fresh Seafoods
300 Admiral Way
Edmonds, WA 98020
(206) 771-4148

Very fresh Dungeness

Cornell's Crab Pot
Long Beach, WA 98631

Very fresh Dungeness, or you may rent your own crab pot and try catching them yourself.

Ferndale Fish Market
1985 Main Street
Ferndale, WA 98248
(206) 384-6200

Fresh Dungeness

Jack's Fish Spot
Pike Place Market
Seattle, WA 98101
(206) 622-3727

Fresh Dungeness from live tanks, cooked on the spot

La Conner Fish & Crab
115 North First
La Conner, WA 98257
(206) 466-4166

Fresh Dungeness

Shrimp

Try the Hood Canal in season (watch your local newspaper for opening and closing times); there'll be lots of places selling freshly caught shrimp on the canal. Or try the more regular supplies at the following commercial outlets.

Oregon

Phil and Joe's Crab Co.
1009 Garibaldi Avenue
(Highway 101 North)
Garibaldi, OR 97118
(503) 322-3410

Shrimp and prawns

Smith Pacific Shrimp Co.
608 Commercial Street
Garibaldi, OR 97118
(503) 322-3316

Shrimp

Washington

Little Skookum Shellfish Growers
Southeast 2262 Lynch Road
Shelton, WA 98584
(206) 426-9759

Crawfish

Strom's Shrimp
Highway 20 and Dewey Beach
Anacortes, WA 98221
(206) 293-2531

Shrimp. The store is located on Highway 20, north of Deception Pass State Park.

Oysters

Oregon

Barnacle Bill's Seafood Store
2174 North Highway 101
Lincoln City, OR 97367
(503) 994-3022

Local Pacific oysters

Hayes Oyster Company
Highway 101 (waterside)
Bay City, OR 97107
(503) 377-2210

Excellent, mild Pacifics and Kumamotos

Tillamook Oyster Company
1985 Bay Ocean Road Northwest
Tillamook, OR 97141
(503) 842-6921

Local Pacifics

Washington

Blau Oyster Company
919 Blue Heron Road
(Samish Island)
Bow, WA 98232
(206) 766-6171

Pacifics

Calm Cove Oyster Company
Southeast Fagergren Road
Shelton, WA 98584
(206) 426-3523

Olympia oysters, Pacifics, European flat oysters (belons)

Canterbury Quilcene Oysters
Linger Longer Road (end of road at marina)
Quilcene, WA 98376
(206) 765-3959

These are the only "true" and original Quilcene oysters.

Coast Oyster Company
Highway 101
South Bend, WA 98586

*This is the retail place for Pacific oysters; the wholesale outlet for "Willapoint" oysters is:
Hilton Seafoods, Inc.
P.O. Box 9307
Seattle, WA 98109*

Ekone Oyster Company
Star Route, Box 465
South Bend, WA 98586
(206) 875-5752
(206) 875-5494

Superb smoked oysters (plus smoked green and white sturgeon)

Hama Hama Oyster Company
P.O. Box 60
Lilliwaup, WA 98555
(206) 877-5811

Pacifics, shucked, in the shell, and smoked; the plant and retail store are at the mouth of the Hamma Hamma River just south of Eldon on Hood Canal.

Little Skookum Shellfish Growers
Southeast 2262 Lynch Road
Shelton, WA 98584
(206) 426-9759

Pacifics, European flat (belon), and Olympia oysters

Minterbrook Oyster Company
South Elgin Road
Gig Harbor, WA 98335
(206) 857-4351

Pacifics

Rockpoint Oyster Company
239 Chuckanut Drive
Blanchard, WA 98231
(206) 766-6002

Pacifics

Shoalwater Bay Oysters
Randy Shuman
7525 44th Northeast
Seattle, WA 98115
(206) 523-2702

Pacifics

Skookum Bay Oyster Company
Route 3, Box 696
Shelton, WA 98584
(206) 426-6076
(206) 426-8996

Olympia oysters, Pacifics. This company has been the most steady and reliable supplier of Olympias for the last several years.

Webb Camp Sea Farms, Inc.
4071 Westcott Drive
Friday Harbor, WA 98250
(206) 378-2489

*Pacifics, Pacific/Kumamoto hybrids,
European flat oysters (belons, whitstables)*

Shellfish

Oregon

Phil and Joe's Crab Co.
1009 Garibaldi Avenue
(Highway 101 North)
Garibaldi, OR 97118
(503) 322-3410

Assorted clams

Washington

Calm Cove Oyster Company
Southeast Fagergren Road
Shelton, WA 98584
(206) 426-3523

Manila clams

Hama Hama Oyster Company
P.O. Box 60
Lilliwaup, WA 98555
(206) 877-5811

*Manila clams, geoduck; the store is located
at the mouth of the Hamma Hamma River,
just south of Eldon on the Hood Canal.*

Kamilche Sea Farms
Southeast 2741 Bloomfield Road
Shelton, WA 98584
(206) 426-5276

Cultured mussels

Little Skookum Shellfish Growers
Southeast 2262 Lynch Road
Shelton, WA 98584
(206) 426-9759

Manila clams

Penn Cove Mussels
Pete Jefferds
Coupeville, WA 98239
(206) 678-4803

Cultured mussels (wholesale only)

Webb Camp Sea Farms
4071 Westcott Drive
Friday Harbor, WA 98250
(206) 378-2489

*Cultured mussels, Manila clams (wholesale
only)*

Odd Marine Creatures

Washington

La Conner Fish & Crab
115 North First
La Conner, WA 98257
(206) 466-4166

Mutual Fish
2335 Rainier Avenue South
Seattle, WA 98144
(206) 322-4368

University Seafood & Poultry
University Way and Northeast 47th
Seattle, WA 98105
(206) 632-3900
(206) 632-3700

Ursin Seafoods Inc.
150 Nickerson
Seattle, WA 98109
(206) 283-2722

Uwajimaya
Sixth South and South King
Seattle, WA 98104
(206) 624-6248

Meats

British Columbia

Heritage Farms
8438 200th Street
Langley, B.C. V3A 4P7
(604) 888-2755

Odd fowl and gamebirds; purebred fowl.

Holland Aviaries
14891 72nd Avenue
Surrey, B.C. V3S 2E0

Strange and interesting edible fowl

Jan's Dutch Meat Market
7325 Kingsway
Burnaby, B.C. V5E 1G4
(604) 526-5122

Sausages and custom meats, et al.

Oregon

Alexander's
938 Circle Boulevard
(Circle Nine Shopping Center)
Corvallis, OR 97330
(503) 753-0144

Meats and sausages

Chicken Market
960 Aspen Court
Canby, OR 97013
Portland phone (503) 223-3184

Grain-fed Oregon chickens

Custom Meat Company
577 Pearl Street
Eugene, OR 94701
(503) 345-4213

Edelweiss Sausage & Deli
3119 Southeast Twelfth
Portland, OR 97202
(503) 238-4411

Sausages

German Smoked Meats
2805 Oak Street
Eugene, OR 97405
(503) 686-9201

Excellent meats, hand-tied sausages

Tillamook Country Smoker
8250 Warren Street
Garibaldi, OR 97118
(503) 377-2252

Superb smoked meats, jerky

White Poultry and Meat Company
2704 Southeast Steele
Portland, OR 97202
(503) 233-7721

Willamette Poultry Co.
855 Northwest Eighth
Corvallis, OR 97330
(503) 754-6210

Oregon grain-fed poultry

Washington

A & J Meats
2401 Queen Anne Avenue North
Seattle, WA 98109
(206) 284-3885

Cut-to-order fresh meats, sausages

BB Meats
1401 F Street
Bellingham, WA 98225
(206) 734-5330

Renowned jerky, hams, sausages

Bar-LB Meats
Route 2, Box 160
(Thrall Road)
Ellensburg, WA 98926
(509) 925-9864

Country-smoked sausages, bacon, ham, beef stick, pepperoni, beef jerky, and cut-to-order fresh meats

Bob's Quality Meats
4719 California Avenue Southwest
Seattle, WA 98116
(206) 937-5640

Fresh grass-fed beef, nitrite-free sausages

Carek's Market
P.O. Box 185
4 South Shaft Street
Roslyn, WA 98941
(509) 649-2930

Excellent jerky, pepperoni, Polish sausage

Carl's Market
403 South Tower
Centralia, WA 98531
(206) 736-8952

Cut-to-order fresh meats

China Poultry Co.
715 South King Street
Seattle, WA 98104
(206) 623-4433

Fowl

Clearview Caprine Dairy
17806 Snohomish Avenue
Snohomish, WA 98290
(206) 668-2581

Kids, lambs, Toulouse geese, muscovy ducks, rabbits, Araucana chickens

Cudahy Bar-S Meats
East 2500 Sprague
Spokane, WA 99202
(509) 535-7741

Beef

Don & Joe's Meats
85 Pike Place
Seattle, WA 98101
(206) 682-7670

Variety meats, veal, whole lambs and suckling pigs

Draper Valley Farms
100 Jason Lane
Mount Vernon, WA 98273
(206) 424-7947

Western Washington fryers (superbly tender chickens)

Isernio's Sausage
1225 South Angelo
Seattle, WA 98108
(206) 762-6207

Italian sausage

Lemolo Custom Meats
17166 Lemolo Shore Drive Northwest
Poulsbo, WA 98370
(206) 779-2447

Curing and smoking of hams, bacon, jerky, salmon, and full range of locally raised meat

Loback Meat Co.
1529 Pike Place
Seattle, WA 98101
(206) 622-7450

Pork products, poultry, deli meats

Mark Almond Squab Farm
Mesa, WA 99343
(509) 265-4599

Squabs (young pigeons for the table)

Matterhorn
Fred Bucheli
1313 North Sixteenth Avenue and Freeway
Yakima, WA 98902
(509) 248-1600

*Superb custom sausages, smoked hams,
Yakima Valley beef*

Middle Farm
Marti Clark
Route 1, Box 1406
Lopez, WA 98261
(206) 468-2406

*Lopez Island grass-fed lamb (and kid by
special order)*

PD & J Meats
25020 Frager Road South
Kent, WA 98031
Seattle (206) 624-4211
Tacoma (206) 924-0668

*This, according to several butchers, is the
best meat available, because the company
raises the best cattle there is on its eastern
Washington feedlots.*

Pederson Fryer Farms
East 1414½ Cleveland
Spokane, WA 99207
(509) 498-8410

Eastern Washington grain-fed fryers

John Peth & Sons Inc.
Ranch Meats
1137 D Arcy Road
Bow, WA 98232
(206) 766-6113

*Western Washington grass-fed beef: some
like it, others don't.*

Service Meats
1514 Northeast 177th
Seattle, WA 98155
(206) 364-4394

Extensive selection of beef, lamb, pork, veal

Swiss Family Sausage
21812 Meridian East
Graham, WA 98338
(206) 847-1441

Sausage

Tualco Valley Bunny and Egg Farm
17910 State Route 203
Monroe, WA 98272
(206) 794-6326

*Chickens, standard and exotic breeds; ducks,
geese, turkeys, pigeons, doves, pharaoh
quail, guinea fowl; meat rabbits, kid, lamb,
beef, pork; hides and pelts; blackberries in
season*

University Seafood & Poultry
University Way and Northeast 47th
Seattle, WA 98105
(206) 632-3700
(206) 632-3900

*From fryer chickens to quail, pheasant,
chukar, squab, guinea fowl, fresh duckling,
goose*

Wallace Poultry
1319 Railroad Avenue
Bellingham, WA 98225
(206) 734-1350

Chickens, pheasants, rabbits, et al.

Warren's Country Meat Market
412 Fairhaven
Burlington, WA 98233
(206) 755-0088

*An excellent little market with some of the
best beef available anywhere. Excellent pork
and potato sausages*

Lynn Weidenbach
1101 McLean Road
Mount Vernon, WA 98273
(206) 466-3383

*The best west-side beef we tasted. It's
custom grain-fed.*

The Wilson's Rabbit Tree
"The one-stop rabbit shop"
6630 60th Southeast
Everett, WA 98205
(206) 334-4147

*Meat, show, and pet rabbits; rabbit fur
products*

Dairy Products

British Columbia

Alamar Farms Ltd.
Delta, B.C. V4K 3N1
(604) 946-9811

*Jersey Farm yogurt: whole Jersey milk
yogurt; natural, no additives*

Dutchman Dairy
(Dewitt's Holsteins LTD)
Route 1
Sicamous, B.C. V0E 2V0

Natural Cheddar, cream, ice cream

Scardillo Cheese Ltd.
6319 Beresford
Burnaby, B.C. V5E 1B3
(604) 430-1348

Mozzarella, several kinds of ricotta

Oregon

Blue Heron French Cheese Company
2001 Blue Heron Drive
(½ mile north of town)
Tillamook, OR 97141
(503) 842-8281

Brie, Camembert

Coquille Valley Dairy Co-op
P.O. Box 515
(Highway 101)
Bandon, OR 97411
(503) 347-2461

Bandon Cheddar

Rogue River Valley Creamery
311 North Front Street
P.O. Box 3606
Central Point, OR 97502
(503) 664-2233

Oregon blue, Cheddar, Jack, and Colby cheeses

Tillamook County Creamery Association
4175 Highway 101 North
P.O. Box 313
Tillamook, OR 97141
(503) 842-4481

Tillamook Cheddar

Washington

Briar Hills Dairies Inc.
279 Southwest Ninth
Chehalis, WA 98532
(206) 748-4224

Raw milk goat cheeses, whey cheese

brusseau's
Fifth and Dayton
Edmonds, WA 98020
(206) 774-4166

*Excellent selection of hard-to-find northwest
cheeses*

Cougar Gold
Washington State University Creamery
Pullman, WA 99164

Washington State University firm, Cheddar-like cheese

Green River Cheese
19029 84th Street
Kent, WA 98031
(206) 852-7600

Cheese and dairy products

Hansen Creamery
P. O. Box 397
Monroe, WA 98172
(206) 794-4424

AA sweet cream butter

Marblemount Cheese
5715 Highway 20
Rockport, WA 98283
(206) 873-4011

Goat's milk Cheddar and feta

Mazza Cheese Company
Orting, WA 98360
(206) 893-2151

Mozzarella, Romano, and feta

Okanogan Highland Cheese
Roger and Sally Jackson
Star Route 1, Box 106
Oroville, WA 98844

Goat's milk cheeses, cow's milk cheeses, and a blend of both

Olympia Cheese Company
1515 Hogum Bay Road
Olympia, WA 98501
(206) 491-5330

Cheddar, mozzarella, and Jack cheeses

The Pike Place Market Creamery
Stall #3
1514 Pike Place
Seattle, WA 98101
(206) 622-5029

Cow's milk, goat's milk, raw cream, et al.

Pleasant Valley Cheese
6804 Kickerville Road
Ferndale, WA 98248
(206) 366-5398

Farmhouse Gouda

Washington Cheese
900 East College Way
Mount Vernon, WA 98273
(206) 424-3510

Cheddar, Jack cheese, et al.

The Wedge
4760 University Village Place Northeast
Seattle, WA 98105
(206) 523-2560

A superb cheese shop with an excellent selection of northwest cheeses

Eggs

Oregon

The Egg Lady
500 North 58th
Springfield, OR 97477
(503) 746-5874

Chicken eggs

Portland Fish Co.
301 Northwest Third Avenue
P. O. Box 2706
Portland, OR 97208
(503) 224-1611

Columbia River caviar (at times)

Willamette Egg Farms
31348 South Highway 170
Canby, OR 97013
(503) 651-2152

Chicken eggs

Wyne's Poultry Farm
34970 Ranch Drive
Brownsville, OR 97327
(503) 466-5124

Chicken eggs

Washington

Melody Blevins
6121 Mission Road
Bellingham, WA 98226
(206) 966-4949

Araucana, Cochin, Rhode Island Red eggs

Sally Brown
P.O. Box 849
Mercer Island, WA 98040
(206) 232-2973
(800) 222-8427

Sturgeon, whitefish, salmon caviars

Clearview Caprine Dairy
17806 Snohomish Avenue
Snohomish, WA 98290
(206) 668-2581

Fertile Araucana eggs (call before coming)

Cossack Caviar
101 South Dakota Street
Seattle, WA 98134
(206) 624-2995

Salmon caviars, some sturgeon caviar; the chum salmon caviar is renowned

Jonlyn Hansen
1125 Central Road
Everson, WA 98247
(206) 398-8891

Quail eggs

Hanson's Poultry Farms
2310 Jess Road
Custer, WA 98240
(206) 366-5384

Chicken eggs

The Pike Place Market Creamery
Stall #3
1514 Pike Place
Seattle, WA 98101

Fresh farm eggs in the city

Velma Rose's Farm Fresh Eggs
Route 6, Box 278A
Yakima, WA 98908
(509) 966-6169

Large brown eggs

Tualco Valley Egg Farm
17910 State Route 203
Monroe, WA 98272
(206) 794-6326 (evenings best)

Organic, fertile blue and brown hen's eggs; duck and goose eggs

Uwajimaya
Sixth Avenue South and South King
Seattle, WA 98104
(206) 624-6248

Our most reliable outlet for quail eggs

Beer

British Columbia

Prairie Inn Neighbourhood Pub
7806 East Saanich Road
Saanichton, B.C.
(604) 652-1575

Only outlet for the pub brewery's beer

The Troller
6422 Bay Street
Horseshoe Bay, B.C.
(604) 921-7616

This is the pub owned by the Troller Pub Brewery and the only outlet for its Bay Ale.

Washington

Redhook Ale Brewery
(Independent Ale Brewery, Inc.)
4620 Leary Way Northwest
Seattle, WA 98107
(206) 784-0800

Makers of Redhook ale and Blackhook porter

Mark Tobey Pub
90 Madison Street at Post Alley
Seattle, WA 98104
(206) 682-1333

The best selection of northwest beers and ales in the region and also a very good selection of northwest wines. Other mini-brewery beers from California, et al., served (good for comparison of styles).

Yakima Brewing & Malting Co.
25 North Front Street
Yakima, WA 98901
(509) 575-1900

Makers of Grant's Scottish Ale, Russian Imperial Stout, Light American Ale, et al. The Brewery Pub next door serves only Grant's ales.

Wine

British Columbia

Gray Monk Cellars
Box 63
Okanagan Centre, B.C. V0H 1P0
(604) 766-3168

Sumac Ridge Estate Winery
P. O. Box 307
Summerland, B.C. V0H 1Z0
(604) 494-0451

Uniacke Estate Wines
R.R. 4, Lakeshore Road
Kelowna, B.C. V1Y 7R3
(604) 764-8866
(604) 764-4848

Oregon

Adelsheim Vineyard
Route 1, Box 129D
Newberg, OR 97132
(503) 538-3652

Amity Vineyards
Route 1, Box 348-B
Amity, OR 97101
(503) 835-2362

Anderson's
9525 Beaverton-Hillsdale Highway
Beaverton, OR 97005
(503) 643-5415

Good selection of Oregon wines

Ashland Wine Cellar
38 C Street
Ashland, OR 97520
(503) 488-2111

Good selection of wines, including northwest wines

Beverage Bin
Highway 101
Nehalem, OR 97131

A great place for buying a northwest wine for that special beach picnic

Cellar 100
100 Garden Valley Shopping Center
Roseburg, OR 97470
(503) 673-1670

Good vintage selection of regional wines

Château Benoit
Route 1, Box 29B-1
Carlton, OR 97111
(503) 864-2991
(503) 864-3666

Crane & Company
8610 Southwest Terwilliger Boulevard
Portland, OR 97219
(503) 246-4323

Good northwest wine selection

Elk Cove Vineyards
Route 3, Box 23
Gaston, OR 97119
(503) 985-7760

The Eyrie Vineyards
935 East Tenth Avenue
McMinville, OR 97128
(503) 472-6315
(503) 864-2410

Glen Creek Winery
6057 Orchard Heights Road Northwest
Salem, OR 97304
(503) 371-9463

Of Grapes & Grains
260 Valley River Center
Eugene, OR 97401
(503) 345-9463

Good bread and good wine

Harris Wine Cellars
2300 Northwest Thurman
Portland, OR 97210
(503) 223-2222

A very good wine shop with a nice selection of northwest wines

Henry Winery
P.O. Box 26
Umpqua, OR 97468
(503) 459-3614
(503) 459-5120

Hidden Springs
Route 3, Box 252B
Amity, OR 97101
(503) 835-2782

Hillcrest Vineyard
240 Vineyard Lane
Roseburg, OR 97470
(503) 673-3709

Hinman Vineyards
27012 Briggs Hill Road
Eugene, OR 97405
(503) 345-1945

Jacksonville Inn Wine & Gift Shop
175 East California
Jacksonville, OR 97530
(503) 899-1900

Has some of the rarer local wines

Lawrence Gallery
Bellevue, OR
(503) 843-3787

*An art gallery that's also a showcase for
local wines (the gallery is on Highway 18,
nine miles southwest of McMinnville).*

Northwest Wine and Cheese
296 Fifth
Eugene, OR 97401
(503) 343-0536

Good selection of both

Oregon Sampler
160 East Broadway
Eugene, OR 97401
(503) 342-1111

Wine and other Oregon gifts

Ponzi Vineyards
Route 1, Box 842
Beaverton, OR 97007
(503) 628-1227

Sneed's Cheese and Wine Co.
104 Southwest Madison
Corvallis, OR 97330
(503) 753-4042

*A good place for stocking up on cheese, wine,
and other fare for formal dinner or picnic*

Sokol Blosser Winery
Blanchard Lane
Dundee, OR 97115
(503) 864-3342

Tualatin Vineyards
Route 1, Box 339
Forest Grove, OR 97116
(503) 357-5005

Valley View Vineyard
1000 Applegate Road
Jacksonville (Ruch), OR 97530
(503) 899-8468

Wheyside Cheese Company
701 East Third Street
McMinnville, OR 97128
(503) 472-8819

*Excellent assortment of cheeses and nice
selection of regional wines*

The Wine Depot
126 Ferry Street Southwest
Albany, OR 97321
(503) 967-9499

Very good inventory of northwest wines

The Wine Shack
236 North Hemlock
Cannon Beach, OR 97110
(503) 436-1494

*Another great place for selecting a good
northwest wine for a beach feast*

Washington

Arbor Crest
East 4506 Buckeye
Spokane, WA 99207
(509) 489-0588

Bacchus Wine Shop
2930 Colby
Everett, WA 98201
(206) 259-1730

*Best place to stock up on wine after you've
left Seattle to go north*

The Cellar
1215 Mill Street
Bellingham, WA 98225
(206) 734-2630

*Your last chance to stock up, if you haven't
done so at Bacchus*

Champion Cellars
108 Denny Way
Seattle, WA 98109
(206) 284-8306

One of Seattle's best wine shops

Haviland Vintners
Colony Park Complex
19029 36th West
Lynnwood, WA 98036
(206) 771-6933

Hinzerling Vineyards
1520 Sheridan Avenue
Prosser, WA 99350
(509) 786-2163

Kiona Vineyards
Sunset Road
Route 2, Box 2169E
Benton City, WA 99320
(509) 588-6716

Franz Wilhelm Langguth Winery
2340 Southwest Road F-5
Mattawa, WA 99344
(509) 932-4943

Latah Creek
13030 Indiana Road
Spokane, WA 99216
(509) 448-0102

Leonetti Cellars
1321 School Avenue
Walla Walla, WA 99362
(509) 525-1428

Mont Elise Vineyards
315 West Steuben
Box 28
Bingen, WA 98605
(509) 493-3001

Mount Stuart Wine Gallery
103 East Fourth, Davidson Building
Suite 206
P.O. Box 1269
Ellensburg, WA 98926
(509) 925-2444

Very good selection of Yakima Valley wines

Pike & Western Wine Merchants
Pike Place Market
Seattle, WA 98101
(206) 623-1307

One of the best selections of northwest wines around—if you're looking for it, they probably have it.

Preston Wine Cellars
McGregor Road
Star Route 1, Box 1234
Pasco, WA 99301
(509) 545-1990

Quail Run Vintners
Morris Road
Route 2, Box 2287
Zillah, WA 98953
(509) 829-6235

Quilceda Creek Vintners
5226 Machias Road
Snohomish, WA 98290
(206) 568-2389

Safeway
University Village
3020 Northeast 45th
Seattle, WA 98105
(206) 522-8350

This is one of our region's most complete wine shops, thanks to the presence of Richard Kinssies, wine columnist for the Seattle Post-Intelligencer, *as wine steward.*

Salishan Vineyards
La Center North Fork Road
Route 2, Box 8
La Center, WA 98629
(206) 263-2713

Tucker Cellars
Highway 12 at Roy Road
Route 1, Box 1696
Sunnyside, WA 98944
(509) 837-8201

The Wine Cellar
5 North Front Street
Yakima, WA 98901
(509) 248-3590

Good selection of Yakima Valley wines

Woodward Canyon
State Highway 12
Route 1, Box 387
Lowden, WA 99360
(509) 525-4129

Worden's Washington Winery
7217 West 45th
Spokane, WA 99204
(509) 455-7835

Yakima River Winery
North River Road
Route 1, Box 1657
Prosser, WA 99350
(509) 786-2805

Restaurants

British Columbia

Sooke Harbour House
R.R. 4
1528 Whiffen Spit Road
Sooke, B.C. V0S 1N0
(604) 642-3421

Oregon

Bay House
5911 Southwest Highway 101
Lincoln City, OR 97367
(503) 996-3222

The Country Inn
4100 Country Farm Road
(five miles north of Eugene)
Eugene, OR 97401
(503) 345-7344

The Experience
Highway 34
(three miles east of Waldport)
Waldport, OR 97394
(503) 563-4555

La Serre
Second and Beach streets
Yachats, OR 97498
(503) 547-3420

Washington

The Ark
Peninsula Road
Nahcotta, WA 98637
(206) 665-4133

Birchfield Manor
Birchfield Road
Yakima, WA 98901
(509) 452-1960

Black Swan Café
First and Washington
La Conner, WA 98257
(206) 466-3040

brusseau's
Fifth and Dayton
Edmonds, WA 98020
(206) 774-4166

Captain Whidbey Inn
Whidbey Inn Road
(three miles north of Coupeville)
Coupeville, WA 98239
(206) 678-4097

La Petite Maison
2005 Ascension Avenue Northwest
    at Division
Olympia, WA 98502
(206) 943-8812

Michael's (Your Place) Café
Mariner's Court—Front Street
Coupeville, WA 98239
(206) 678-5480

Mountain Song Restaurant
Highway 20
Marblemount, WA 98267
(206) 873-2461

M'sieurs
130 East Champion
Bellingham, WA 98225
(206) 671-7955

Oyster Creek Inn
302 Chuckanut Drive
Bow, WA 98232
(206) 766-6191

Ray's Boathouse
6049 Seaview Avenue Northwest
Seattle, WA 98107
(206) 789-3770

The Shelburne Inn & Restaurant
Pacific Highway 103 and J Street
Seaview, WA 98644
(206) 642-4142

The Windmill
1501 North Wenatchee Avenue
Wenatchee, WA 98801
(509) 663-3478

Related Reading

Here are a few books that provide useful and interesting background reading:

Amerine, Maynard A., and Edward B. Roessler. *Wines: Their Sensory Evaluation.* San Francisco: W. H. Freeman & Co. Publishers, 1976.

Beard, James. *James Beard's American Cookery.* Boston: Little, Brown & Co., 1972.

Bollen, Constance, and Marlene Blessing. *One Potato, Two Potato: A Cookbook.* Seattle: Pacific Search Press, 1983.

Brame, Louise. *Seattle's Gastronomic Shopper.* Seattle: Reynard House, 1981.

Carroll, Ricki, and Robert Carroll. *Cheesemaking Made Easy.* Charlotte, Vt.: Garden Way Publishing, 1982.

Cox, Beverly, with Joan Whitman. *Cooking Techniques: How to Do Anything a Recipe Tells You To.* Boston: Little, Brown & Co., 1981.

Ellis, David W., and Luke Swan. *Teachings of the Tides: Uses of Marine Invertebrates by the Manhousat People.* Nanaimo, B.C.: Theytus Books, 1981.

Ellis, Eleanor A., ed. *Northern Cookbook.* Edmonton, Alberta: Hurtig Publishers, in cooperation with Indian and Northern Affairs Canada and the Canadian Government Publishing Centre, Supply and Services Canada, 1979.

Ellis, Merle. *Cutting-up in the Kitchen: The Butcher's Guide to Saving Money on Meat and Poultry.* San Francisco: Chronicle Books, 1975.

Fessler, Stella Lau. *Chinese Seafood Cooking.* New York: New American Library, 1981.

Fisher, M. F. K. *The Art of Eating.* New York: Vintage Books, 1976.

Franey, Pierre. *The New York Times 60-Minute Gourmet.* New York: Times Books, 1979.

———. *The New York Times More 60-Minute Gourmet.* New York: Times Books, 1981.

Franz, Carl, and Lorena Havens. *The On & Off the Road Cookbook.* Santa Fe: John Muir Publications, 1982.

Furlong, Marjorie, and Virginia Pill. *Edible? Incredible!* Tacoma, Wa.: Erco, Inc., 1973.

Gault, Lila. *The Northwest Cookbook.* New York: The Putnam Publishing Group, 1978.

Gault, Lila, and Betsy Sestrap. *The Cider Book.* Seattle: Madrona Publishers, Inc., 1980.

Geise, Judie. *The Northwest Kitchen: A Seasonal Cookbook*. Seattle: B. Wright & Co., 1978.

Haydock, Yukiko, and Bob Haydock. *Japanese Garnishes: The Ancient Art of Mukimono*. New York: Holt, Rinehart & Winston, 1980.

———. *More Japanese Garnishes*. New York: Holt, Rinehart & Winston, 1983.

Holden, Ronald, and Glenda Holden. *Touring the Wine Country of Oregon*. Seattle: Holden Travel Research, 1982.

———. *Touring the Wine Country of Washington*. Seattle: Holden Pacific, 1983.

Holm, Don. *The Old-Fashioned Dutch Oven Cookbook*. Caldwell, Ida.: The Caxton Printers, Ltd., 1980.

Hom, Ken, with Harvey Steiman. *Chinese Technique: An Illustrated Guide to the Fundamental Techniques of Chinese Cooking*. New York: Simon & Schuster, Inc., 1981.

Hunter, Beatrice Trum. *How Safe Is Food in Your Kitchen?* New York: Charles Scribner's Sons, 1981.

Jones, Evan. *American Food: The Gastronomic Story*. 2d ed. New York: Vintage Books, 1981.

Mabbutt, Bill, and Anita Mabbutt. *North American Wild Game Cookbook*. Moscow, Ida.: Solstice Press, 1982.

McClane, A. J. *The Encyclopedia of Fish Cookery*. New York: Holt, Rinehart & Winston, 1977.

McKenny, Margaret. *The Savory Wild Mushroom*. rev. and enl. by Daniel E. Stuntz. Seattle: University of Washington Press, 1980.

Meredith, Ted. *Northwest Wine: The Premium Grape Wines of Oregon, Washington, and Idaho*. 2d ed. rev. Kirkland, Wa.: Nexus Press, 1983.

Mohney, Russ. *The Dogfish Cookbook*. Seattle: Pacific Search Press, 1976.

Nathan, Joan. *The Jewish Holiday Kitchen*. New York: Schocken Books, Inc., 1979.

Pellegrini, Angelo M. *Lean Years, Happy Years*. Seattle: Madrona Publishers, Inc., 1983.

Puget Sound Mycological Society. *Wild Mushroom Recipes*. Seattle: Pacific Search Press, 1969.

Root, Waverly. *Food: An Authoritative and Visual History and Dictionary of the Foods of the World*. New York: Simon & Schuster, Inc., 1980.

Root, Waverly, and Richard de Rochemont. *Eating in America: A History*. New York: The Ecco Press, 1981.

Shorett, Alice, and Murray Morgan. *The Pike Place Market: People, Politics, and Produce*. Seattle: Pacific Search Press, 1982.

Somerton, David, and Craig Murray. *Field Guide to the Fish of Puget Sound and the Northwest Coast*. Seattle: Washington Sea Grant, 1976.

Sovold, Pamela, Margaret Wherrette, and Eilisha Dermont. *The Market Notebook*. Seattle: Madrona Publishers, Inc., 1980.

Tsuji, Shizuo, with Mary Sutherland. *Japanese Cooking: A Simple Art*. Tokyo, New York, and San Francisco: Kodansha, Ltd., 1980.

Waaland, J. Robert. *Common Seaweeds of the Pacific Coast*. Seattle: Pacific Search Press, 1977.

Wydoski, Richard S., and Richard R. Whitney. *Inland Fishes of Washington*. Seattle: University of Washington Press, 1979.

Index

Selected Books from Pacific Search Press